Blood of the Earth

D1665941

Blood of the Earth

Resource Nationalism, Revolution, and Empire in Bolivia

KEVIN A. YOUNG

University of Texas Press Austin

Portions of this book appeared previously, in different form, in the
following publications: K. Young, "Restoring Discipline in the Ranks:
The United States and the Restructuring of the Bolivian Mining Industry,
1960–1970," *Latin American Perspectives* 38, no. 6 (2011): 6–24,
doi:10.1177/0094582X11412926; and K. Young, "Purging the Forces of
Darkness: The United States, Monetary Stabilization, and the Containment of
the Bolivian Revolution," *Diplomatic History* 37, no. 3 (2013): 509–537, used
by permission of Oxford University Press.

Library of Congress Cataloging-in-Publication Data
Names: Young, Kevin A., author.
Title: Blood of the earth : resource nationalism, revolution, and empire in
    Bolivia / Kevin A. Young.
Description: First edition. | Austin : University of Texas Press, 2017. | Includes
    bibliographical references and index.
Identifiers: LCCN 2016023299| ISBN 978-1-4773-1152-3 (cloth : alk. paper) |
    ISBN 978-1-4773-1165-3 (pbk. : alk. paper) | ISBN 978-1-4773-1153-0
    (library e-book) | ISBN 978-1-4773-1154-7 (nonlibrary e-book)
Subjects: LCSH: Natural resources—Bolivia—Management—20th century. |
    Social conflict—Bolivia—History. | Bolivia—Economic conditions—20th
    century. | Bolivia—Economic policy—20th century. | Bolivia—Politics and
    government—20th century. | Bolivia—Military relations—United States. |
    United States—Military relations—Bolivia.
Classification: LCC HC182.5 .Y68 2017 | DDC 333.70984—dc23
LC record available at https://lccn.loc.gov/2016023299

doi:10.7560/311523

Contents

Acknowledgments   vii

List of Abbreviations   ix

Introduction: Natural Resources, Economic Visions, and
US Intervention in Twentieth-Century Bolivia   1

1. The Road to Resource Nationalism: Economic Ideas and Popular
   Coalitions in La Paz, 1927–1952   16

2. A New Type of Bolivian Economy: Competing Visions,
   1952–1956   35

3. The Political Economy of Containment: Privatization, Austerity,
   and the MNR's Shift to the Right, 1955–1964   59

4. The Battle for Men's Minds: Economic Paradigms, Propaganda,
   and the Iconography of Revolution   90

5. The Limits of Containment: Anti-Austerity and Resource
   Nationalism in La Paz Factories   114

6. Oil and Nation: The Crusade to Save Bolivia's Hydrocarbons   149

Epilogue: Resource Nationalism and Popular Struggle in the
Twenty-First Century   176

Appendix: Professional Backgrounds of Key Middle-Class
Participants in Economic Debates, 1940s–1960s   187

Notes   191

Bibliography   239

Index   265

Map of Bolivia. Source: United Nations, Cartographic Section.

Acknowledgments

During the research for this project I encountered what seemed like constant roadblocks, unrelated to the literal roadblocks that have been a hallmark of popular protest in Bolivia in the past half century. Anyone who has attempted archival research in Bolivia will know what I mean. Although it is not customary to begin an acknowledgments section by bemoaning one's research travails, I do so in order to underscore how much I appreciate the individuals and institutions who did assist me with this project.

Many individuals in Bolivia facilitated my access to archives and sources. Wendy Limachi, René Mérida, Luis Oporto, Silvia Rivera, Cecilia Salazar, Carmen Soliz, and Ludmila Zeballos were especially helpful. The Tinker Foundation and faculty research funding from the University of Massachusetts Amherst helped underwrite two of my trips to Bolivia.

Many people read the full manuscript or key chunks of it. Brooke Larson provided invaluable feedback and was a constant source of help throughout the entire process. Paul Gootenberg and Ian Roxborough each encouraged my interest in economic ideas and helped me think about the project in more sociological terms. Sinclair Thomson encouraged my focus on Bolivian resource nationalism and gave detailed comments on all six chapters. A number of others also provided constructive critiques and suggestions, either informally or as formal reviewers: Steve Cote, Matt Gildner, the late Ben Kohl, Erick Langer, Hernán Pruden, James Siekmeier, Diana Sierra Becerra, Jeffery Webber, Laurence Whitehead, Steve Volk, and anonymous reviewers at *Diplomatic History* and the *Hispanic American Historical Review*. I have taken most of the recommendations that these people offered and stubbornly rejected others, but all were thought provoking and profoundly appreciated.

Countless other people have contributed to this project through conversations and advice. Recent years have seen a resurgence of interest in the Bolivian Revolution, and as a result I have benefited from the assistance and friendship of many people whose research overlaps with mine. Beyond those mentioned above, James Dunkerley, Thomas Field, José Gordillo, Sarah Hines, Fernando Ríos, Olivia Saunders, and Elizabeth Shesko all contributed important insights, questions, or criticisms. Bolivianists who focus on other periods but who likewise proved helpful to me include Emily Achtenberg, Estela Alarcón, Jorge Derpic, Linda Farthing, Carwil James, Gabrielle Kuenzli, Pablo Rivero, and Robert Smale. Non-Bolivianists who gave advice on one or more aspects of the project include Juan Pablo Artinian, Tarun Banerjee, Froylán Enciso, Andrés Estefane, Seth Fein, Sung Yup Kim, Gary Marker, Michael Schwartz, Anna Revette, Mark Rice, Joel Wolfe, and Eric Zolov. My new colleagues at the University of Massachusetts—too many to list by name—provided an exceedingly collegial and welcoming environment where I finished writing the book.

Lastly I thank my family. My parents and brother, all in their own ways, are the three people most responsible for shaping my values. Though not directly engaged in this project, they all deserve indirect credit for whatever contribution it might make. My partner, Diana, has been an incomparable source of feedback and wisdom on this project and so many other things.

Abbreviations

CEPAL	Comisión Económica para América Latina (UN Economic Commission for Latin America [UN ECLA])
CGTFB	Confederación General de Trabajadores Fabriles de Bolivia (Bolivian General Confederation of Factory Workers)
CNI	Cámara Nacional de Industrias (National Chamber of Industries)
COB	Central Obrera Boliviana (Bolivian Workers Central)
COD	Central Obrera Departamental (Departmental Workers Central [one in each department])
COMIBOL	Corporación Minera de Bolivia (Bolivian Mining Corporation)
CSTB	Confederación Sindical de Trabajadores de Bolivia (Bolivian Workers Union Confederation)
CUB	Confederación Universitaria Boliviana (Bolivian University Confederation)
FAD	Federación Agraria Departamental (Departmental Agrarian Federation), La Paz
FOF	Federación Obrera Femenina (Women Workers Federation), La Paz
FOL	Federación Obrera Local (Local Workers Federation), La Paz
FOT	Federación Obrera del Trabajo (Workers Labor Federation)

FSB	Falange Socialista Boliviana (Bolivian Socialist Phalange)
FSTMB	Federación Sindical de Trabajadores Mineros de Bolivia (Bolivian Mine Workers Union Federation)
FSTPB	Federación Sindical de Trabajadores Petroleros de Bolivia (Bolivian Oil Workers Union Federation)
FUL	Federación Universitaria Local (Local University Federation)
IMF	International Monetary Fund
LEC	Legión de Ex-Combatientes (Legion of Ex-Combatants)
MAS	Movimiento al Socialismo (Movement toward Socialism)
MIR	Movimiento de la Izquierda Revolucionaria (Movement of the Revolutionary Left)
MNR	Movimiento Nacionalista Revolucionario (Nationalist Revolutionary Movement)
OIAA	Office of the Coordinator of Inter-American Affairs
PCB	Partido Comunista de Bolivia (Communist Party of Bolivia)
PDC	Partido Democrático Cristiano (Christian Democratic Party)
PIR	Partido de la Izquierda Revolucionaria (Party of the Revolutionary Left)
POR	Partido Obrero Revolucionario (Revolutionary Workers Party)
USAID	US Agency for International Development
USIA	US Information Agency
USIE	US International Informational and Educational Exchange
USIS	US Information Service
USTFN	Unión Sindical de Trabajadores Fabriles Nacionales (National Union of Factory Workers)
YPFB	Yacimientos Petrolíferos Fiscales Bolivianos (Bolivian State Oil Fields Company)

Blood of the Earth

Natural Resources, Economic Visions, and US Intervention in Twentieth-Century Bolivia

Bolivian social movements captured the world's attention in the first years of this century. From 2000 to 2005 they defeated a plan to privatize water, toppled two governments, and catapulted an indigenous union leader, Evo Morales, into the presidency. While a host of demands fueled this cycle of revolt, anger over the private appropriation of Bolivia's natural resources was the single most important unifying issue. The catalyst for the popular coalition that ousted President Gonzalo Sánchez de Lozada in October 2003 was the government's plan to export unrefined natural gas to the United States at cheap prices rather than refining the gas domestically and producing hydrocarbon derivatives or at least demanding a bigger share of the proceeds. More than a decade later, debates over natural resource wealth continue to dominate the Bolivian political scene.[1]

Recent struggles over extractive resources have their roots in the mid-twentieth century. Natural resource wealth—particularly tin and oil—occupied the central position in the popular nationalist imaginary that developed starting in the 1920s and crystallized with the 1952 revolution. At multiple political junctures from the 1930s through the 1960s, resource nationalism—the idea that resource wealth should be used for the benefit of the nation—would be the key factor uniting mine workers, urban workers, students, war veterans, middle-class professionals, and other urban sectors. Natural resources do not always spark only conflict and division, as some of the scholarly literature suggests; they can also generate powerful political coalitions.[2] The popular coalitions that emerged between the 1930s and 1960s left enduring legacies that are still being felt today.

Resource nationalism is especially important for understanding the tumultuous rule of the Nationalist Revolutionary Movement (MNR, Movimiento Nacionalista Revolucionario), which took power when the revolution triumphed in 1952. While most of the MNR leadership favored a relatively conservative version of revolution, urban popular sectors like factory workers, students, and war veterans articulated more radical visions. Subterranean resources—tin, oil, and eventually natural gas—were at the center of their visions, with proposals revolving around how to use these nonrenewable resources as a lever to diversify and industrialize Bolivia's mono-export economy while promoting a progressive redistribution of wealth. Although the MNR was nominally at the helm, the party's control over urban popular sectors remained superficial and tenuous. By the late 1950s diverse voices began accusing the MNR of betraying its pledge to use Bolivia's resources for economic development and social welfare. The alienation of the MNR's support base in the cities and mines compelled the MNR and its major foreign ally, the US government, to resort to military repression after 1956 and facilitated the party's ouster by the army in 1964. Yet the decade of the 1960s also witnessed the emergence of a new popular coalition independent of the MNR that focused on the effort to protect Bolivia's state oil company.

Appearances of coalitional unity were also deceptive, however, for resource nationalists were a very diverse crowd. Some sought to replace capitalism with socialism, some just wanted to ameliorate capitalism's worst excesses, and some favored economic modernization but not redistribution. Conservatives used resource nationalism as a way to defuse class conflict and avoid confronting inequality. Some were driven by a chauvinistic nationalism more akin to fascism than socialism. The failure of popular nationalist coalitions to confront ethnic, gender, and regional hierarchies also hindered unity. The economic and political visions of urban Bolivians, even most of those on the socialist left, excluded or marginalized the rural indigenous population. Women experienced a parallel subordination.

Resource nationalism, even more so than other nationalisms, may be particularly prone to this mix of progressive and exclusionary potentials. On one hand, it constitutes a powerful challenge to capitalist markets, private property rights, and the prerogatives of both imperial and regional elites.[3] On the other hand, resource-nationalist coalitions tend to conceal drastically different visions for the future, and resource nationalism itself is often used to silence the demands of subordinate groups. Bolivian resource nationalism, with both its tremendous power and its internal tensions and contradictions, is the primary subject of this book.

Extractive Economies and Resource Nationalism

Economic dependence on extractive industry is an enduring predicament throughout much of Latin America, Africa, and Asia. A large body of economic literature has linked extractivism to high poverty and inequality, low growth, and structural tendencies toward rent-led development. Paradoxically, resource-poor countries may be better off in some respects than those that are rich in natural resources, as "resource curse" theories argue.[4] Scholars in this school highlight the ways that dependence on a single primary export commodity can deform a country's economy, leaving it especially vulnerable to fluctuating world market prices. Part of this alleged curse is the so-called Dutch disease, referring to how a primary export boom can lead to appreciation of a country's currency; appreciation makes imports cheaper and exports less competitive, thus hindering the development of other export sectors and domestic industries. Extractivism can also have far-reaching consequences for the rest of a society. Many political scientists argue that resource wealth can distort a country's political institutions, giving rise to a rentier state uninterested in responding to the long-term needs of the population through diversification, progressive tax reform, and other policies. Historical studies of Latin America have often focused on Venezuela's oil wealth and its implications for state formation, culture, and popular consciousness.[5]

Dependence on primary exports is usually accompanied by subordination to foreign capitalists or at least domestic elites far removed from their fellow citizens. Resource nationalism has thus remained a crucial element in the political cultures of many resource-abundant countries. Resource nationalists are united by their demand that the home nation be the main beneficiary of natural resource extraction. Beyond that goal their specific policy proposals vary significantly, from advocating the total exclusion of private enterprise to merely favoring higher taxes on private companies, higher market prices, technology transfer, the training of national technicians, or other benefits.[6] Most go further and advocate specific uses for the proceeds, for instance to fund diversification programs, the development of manufacturing, or increased social spending. Many resource nationalists also condemn their countries' economic elites—who are symbolically excluded from the "imagined community" of the nation—and demand a more equitable distribution of wealth.[7] Some, as in Bolivia in the twentieth and twenty-first centuries, insist that the natural resource sector in question should itself be industrialized, meaning that exports like natural gas would be further processed in the country prior to export.

Resource extraction and the nationalist sentiment that so often accompanies it have become increasingly central to world events in the early twenty-first century. The explosive economic growth of the BRICS (Brazil, Russia, India, China, South Africa), declining supplies of many natural resources, and the wasteful and fossil-fuel-based structures of production and consumption in the global North have accelerated a race for resources with profound implications.[8] This context, in conjunction with rising global inequality since the 1970s, has made subterranean resources a focus of popular mobilizations across the world. In Latin America, the Middle East, and northern Africa, resource nationalism has animated recent debates over wealth distribution, democracy, indigenous rights, and ecological crisis. Protesters have demanded a reorientation of economic policy to increase the flow of rents to "the people," and some have also put forth proposals for diversification and industrialization.[9] These mobilizations, in turn, have confronted the perennial problems of co-optation, repression, foreign imperialism, divergent agendas among the protesters themselves, and the perils inherent in resource-based development. They have also been forced to deal with questions that were marginal to policy debates until recently, particularly involving indigenous territorial rights and environmental destruction.[10]

Recent resource struggles and debates have not emerged out of thin air. In the decades that followed the famous 1917 Mexican Constitution, which declared natural resources the property of the nation, Latin American nationalists engaged in heated debates over resource wealth, economic development, and socioeconomic rights.[11] These debates were by no means restricted to economists and policy makers, as the Bolivian case makes clear. Given the continued centrality of resource conflicts around the world, now is an opportune time to reexamine the long cycle of Bolivian mobilization that began in the 1920s. This period can help illuminate developments across the global South in both the twentieth and twenty-first centuries.

Legacies of Revolutionary Struggle

Much research of the past several decades has stressed the role of popular actors in the formation of modern Latin America. Historians have shown how political institutions, economic history, and social relations have been shaped in part by popular initiatives.[12] Twentieth-century Bolivia, with its highly organized civil society and array of powerful social movements, offers remarkable examples of how ordinary people can influence history.

The enduring impact of Bolivia's mid-century social movements has remained underappreciated until recently, however. Most contemporary accounts of the MNR period argued that the revolution resulted in major changes to the country's political, economic, and social structure. They highlighted especially the agrarian reform initiated in 1953, the establishment of universal suffrage, the nationalization of the country's large mines, and the downsizing of the old army. Yet most of these accounts insisted on the MNR's role as a vanguard force in the revolution, downplaying the initiative of popular groups.[13]

Starting in the late 1950s, a second wave of studies presented a much more critical view of the MNR. Disillusioned nationalists and Marxists described a party that had betrayed the revolution by welcoming foreign capitalists back into the country and repressing popular demands for redistribution. Some of these critics also downplayed the MNR's importance to the revolution. Trotskyist writer Guillermo Lora, for instance, portrayed party leaders as cynical opportunists who manipulated popular radicalism, while nationalists like Sergio Almaraz Paz and Amado Canelas criticized the MNR's alleged betrayal of resource nationalism.[14] By the 1970s and early 1980s a spate of studies expanded on this analysis, painting the MNR as a relatively conservative force in the country.[15] Following the emergence of a new indigenous movement in the 1970s, revisionist critiques appeared from a different angle. Silvia Rivera Cusicanqui and others published historical studies highlighting the paternalism and ethnic assimilationism of the MNR. They especially criticized how the MNR cultivated clientelistic ties with campesino (peasant) leaders and how its agrarian policy prioritized individual over communal landownership.[16] While these studies were much more attuned to popular mobilization, their main emphasis was on the co-optation and defeat of popular forces.

Recently a third, postrevisionist school has begun to temper this critique. New research has stressed the complicated dialectic between popular forces, particularly the peasantry, and the MNR government, revealing the limits to MNR power. Some researchers have emphasized the enduring structural changes brought by the revolution, such as the agrarian reform that had benefited about half of the Bolivian population by 1970.[17] From the perspective of diplomatic history, recent research has also pointed out how MNR officials after 1952 were able to exercise significant power vis-à-vis foreign forces like the US government, for instance by playing up the threat of a radical turn in the revolution in order to obtain more US aid. Indeed, the very fact that Washington chose to aid the MNR rather than try to overthrow it seems to reflect the constraints on US imperial power.[18]

Building upon this recent scholarship, I argue that popular mobilization before, during, and after the MNR period had enduring legacies that are essential to understanding present-day Bolivia. The revolution was not simply a story of popular defeats. Despite the revolution's rightward shift and the MNR's overthrow in 1964, some significant changes persisted long after that. In the realm of economic and fiscal policy, the MNR and subsequent governments were unable to initiate a full-scale reversal of progressive nationalist reforms. The country retained a large public sector into the 1980s, including state control over most of the oil and mining industries and educational expenditures that were high by Latin American standards.[19] In the realm of political culture, resource nationalism has survived as a defining aspect of the country's mainstream discourse until the present, to the point that even neoliberal measures like the privatization of mining in the 1980s and of oil in the 1990s have been publicly justified using resource-nationalist language.[20] Although the revolution's legacies in popular political culture are impossible to quantify, they are perhaps even more significant than the policy legacies. In the early twenty-first century a series of mass mobilizations reminded the world that the resource nationalism, anti-imperialism, and egalitarian values that animated past struggles had not faded away. These ideas have remained core elements of urban Bolivia's enduring, if ever-evolving, "political cultures of opposition."[21]

My emphasis is not on MNR diplomats or government leaders. While the skillful diplomacy of Bolivian officials played some role in allaying US suspicions about the revolution, the demands and mobilization of ordinary Bolivians were more important.[22] Specifically, it was the threat of more radical forces displacing the MNR that ultimately lent the Bolivian diplomats their power when negotiating US aid packages and export contracts. Though MNR leaders used that threat to their advantage, they were also unable to fully control it. Popular forces constrained both the US and MNR governments, and it was those forces that were primarily responsible for the revolution's long-term imprint on society.

At the same time, I do not wish to overstate the impact of popular resistance. Radical dreams were indeed crushed, and one need only visit Bolivia today to see that the legacies of colonialism (formal and informal, foreign and internal) and other forms of exploitation continue to be felt. I also want to avoid fetishizing popular resistance as inherently heroic. As noted above, such resistance takes many forms and often incorporates oppressive elements within it.[23] Even Marxists and anarchists were not immune to the influence of patriarchy, racism, and authoritarianism. The contest among currents and tendencies within Bolivia's political cultures of opposition, and the implications for the course of history, form an important subplot in the chapters that follow.

Resources and Revolution

Bolivian sociologist René Zavaleta argues that a popular nationalist consciousness emerged in Bolivia in the aftermath of the Chaco War with Paraguay (1932–1935). For Zavaleta the war was a "constituent moment" that helped give rise to a "national-popular" collective identity.[24] At the heart of this emergent revolutionary nationalism was resource nationalism, which prioritized the protection of Bolivian resources and usually carried a vague orientation in favor of a more egalitarian distribution of wealth and power.[25] Resource nationalism became the centerpiece of popular economic thought starting in the 1920s and after the war served as a consistent unifying force for popular coalitions.[26]

Although the MNR eventually triumphed over competing opposition parties, it did so by riding the crest of a popular wave. Its recipe for success lay in selectively appropriating ideas already in circulation yet keeping its program sufficiently vague to avoid alienating the disparate groups affiliated with it. Its leaders attacked the anticapitalist left, with its imagery of global and domestic class conflict, and instead promoted a development vision based on mutual benefits. The only losers in this vision would be a small cabal of oligarchs and nebulously defined "imperialists." Bolivian capitalists were explicitly included in MNR conceptions of the national community, and most foreign capitalists and Western governments were spared the imperialist label. In this sense the MNR was a classic populist regime and decidedly less radical than many other leftist and nationalist groups of the pre-1952 era.[27]

The vision of the mainstream MNR leadership was never fully embraced by the population, however. Even after 1952, the party's political hegemony would remain fleeting and superficial, with its legitimacy persisting only to the extent that it was perceived as fulfilling revolutionary values. Workers, students, and others articulated radical conceptions of revolutionary nationalism that went well beyond the MNR's vague and relatively conservative program, even as they continued to offer formal allegiance to the government. In the late 1950s and 1960s, as policy shifted rightward, a range of popular forces united around a resource-nationalist and anti-austerity agenda that challenged government policy from the left. These forces included not just the country's famous mine workers, whose radicalism has been the focus of many studies, but also a host of urban groups such as factory and construction workers, teachers, students, and war veterans.[28] The increasing alienation of these groups from the MNR contributed to the regime's downfall in 1964. This political trajectory contrasts with that of other postrevolutionary situations (Mexico, Cuba, and China, to name three) in which the new regimes were able to consolidate strong and durable states based in large part on mass consent.[29]

Popular interventions in economic policy debates were remarkably constant and visible in mid-century Bolivia, in part due to the virtual absence of formally trained economists. These interventions offer insight into the contours of popular economic thought. In addition to newspaper accounts of events, I make use of two broad categories of sources. First, statements and resolutions from unions and other grassroots organizations provide a sense of their members' beliefs and demands. While usually authored by organizational leaders, such sources offer valuable clues about rank-and-file sentiment. In organizations that are at least moderately democratic, leaders' rhetoric—if not their actions—will normally give an approximate reflection of their constituents' views. My second and less conventional source for gauging popular sentiment is the declassified records of the US government. US agents in Bolivia were unlikely to exaggerate the unpopularity of foreign capital, the US government, or their own activities.

Their candid observations about ordinary Bolivians' resource nationalism and egalitarianism thus provide reasonably reliable measures of public attitudes.[30]

My argument about resource nationalism is more controversial than it might appear. Some Marxists have downplayed the importance of popular nationalism in twentieth-century Bolivia. A Bolivian Trotskyist historian once told me that such sentiment had "existed only in Zavaleta's mind." Students of Bolivian labor history have gravitated toward the mine workers in part because they view that sector as having had a proper, internationalist sense of class consciousness; other working-class sectors and the peasantry, meanwhile, are often dismissed as politically backward and easily duped victims of elite manipulation. Such portrayals are empirically dubious on several levels. They exaggerate the quiescence of the latter groups, they wrongly imply class consciousness and nationalism to have been mutually exclusive, and they dismiss popular nationalism as simply a sign of false consciousness. While I sympathize with those who are suspicious of nationalism in all its guises, I see no sense in denying its historical importance in the country's political culture. We can acknowledge that nation-states are artificial constructions while still striving to understand the consequences of nationalist sentiment.

In Bolivia those consequences were very real, including for the Marxist left. The inability of Marxists to garner the allegiance of the majority of workers owes much to the resonance of resource nationalism and the MNR's success in delivering at least modest benefits, both perceived and real, to its supporters. Marxists and anarchists did still exercise influence on political and economic debates, and one argument of this study is that nationalism and anticapitalism often reinforced rather than contradicted each other. But the existence of a nationalist reform party deprived competitors to the MNR's left of formal support.[31]

My analysis of Bolivian resource nationalism and anti-imperialism will also be controversial among those who, from the opposite end of the political spectrum, dismiss such sentiments as conspiracy theories motivated by xenophobia and irrationality.[32] Even some recent academic literature has pathologized popular sentiment in this way, bemoaning the "deep-seated loss aversion" of the Bolivian masses with regard to the country's resources.[33] I present a more nuanced picture of Bolivians' thinking about natural resources. Popular visions were more diverse and sophisticated than many commentators have suggested. Anti-imperialism was not so much a product of visceral anti-Americanism as it was a targeted rejection of the economic vision of the US government and its Bolivian allies. Moreover, most Bolivian anti-imperialists were not opposed to all elements of US or Western influence, for they selectively appropriated certain ideas and discourses promoted by Western intellectuals, social movements, and institutions.[34]

Nor were popular demands as unrealistic as critics often allege. While these demands did sometimes reflect overly grand expectations for rapid economic development, their basic analysis of Bolivia's underdevelopment was quite reasonable. The blame they directed at foreign enterprise was usually grounded in fact. And they were right to focus attention on how the Bolivian government might increase its share of natural resource rent and utilize it to foster redistribution, export diversification, national food production, and perhaps limited industrialization, either by processing raw materials domestically or fomenting consumer goods industries.

The barriers to these goals in a small, landlocked country like Bolivia were formidable; extensive industrialization, in particular, was much less realistic than in larger countries like Brazil or Mexico.[35] But there was no objective economic or geographic reason preventing Bolivia from achieving, within the span of a generation or two, an economy that was considerably more diversified, stable, and equitable than the one inherited in 1952. Small, resource-abundant countries are not simply doomed to perpetual poverty and underdevelopment. Historically, resource-rich countries have varied significantly in terms of their developmental advances, from relative successes like Norway to notoriously corrupt and exclusionary cases like Nigeria, and a broad spectrum of examples in between those two poles.[36] Bolivia's natural resource wealth could have been reinvested in productive ways while also allowing for substantial increases in immediate consumption. Even if Bolivian activists have sometimes harbored overly optimistic expectations, neither their critiques nor their prescriptions for alternative policy can be dismissed as irrational fantasy.[37]

While I am largely concerned with ideas, ideas do not exist in a vacuum. Economic ideas are never implemented based merely on their technical merits. Although economists, advisers, and other individuals may play significant roles in shaping policy trajectories, their power to do so is mostly a reflection of the balance of forces in the broader society.[38] This pattern was true of those interests that sought to contain the Bolivian Revolution and of those workers, students, peasants, and others who sought to deepen it. Any study of ideas must therefore trace the political conflicts among the key players.

Bolivia, the United States, and the Cold War

The US government was one of the key players in Bolivia's political conflicts. While it has often responded to revolutionary change with violence, in Bolivia it sought to influence events in more subtle ways. Starting in 1953 it used foreign aid and tin purchase agreements as means of restraining resource nationalism, progressive fiscal policy, and the power of labor. US policy makers forged an alliance with so-called moderates in the MNR who shared the US interest in suppressing more radical forces in Bolivia. Accompanying these levers of influence were extensive cultural and educational efforts. The US Information Agency (USIA) was deployed to Bolivia with the goals of "promoting popular acceptance of private capital investment" and convincing Bolivians "to think and act in ways that will further American purposes." The US Information Service (USIS, as foreign branches of the USIA were known) showed films in schools, factories, and neighborhoods and organized public photo exhibits, distributed educational leaflets, and ran a "news placement" program in which papers published unattributed articles written by USIS agents. These efforts were all part of what US officials called "the Campaign of Truth" and "the battle for men's minds."[39]

In addition to highlighting US strategies, USIS records reveal what was really at stake in Cold War Bolivia. The battle was not between totalitarianism and democracy, nor was it primarily motivated by superpower conflict or US fears of Soviet-style communism implanting itself in Bolivia. Rather, the main threat was Bolivian revolutionary nationalism, which conjured fears of resource nationalism, material redistribution, and an independent foreign policy. USIS agents sought to replace Bolivians' resource nationalism, demands for redistribution, and suspicion of imperialism and private enterprise with faith in the mutually beneficial nature of capitalism. For the most part, this mission aligned with that of MNR officials. The real battle during these years was among competing visions of economic and social development and among more expansive and more limited conceptions of democracy—conflicts not adequately captured by standard characterizations of the Cold War.

My analysis of the contest among these competing visions adds to a growing body of literature on the Cold War in Latin America that has redirected attention from the motives behind US policy making to the question of "what was being fought over in Latin America itself."[40] In Bolivia and elsewhere, US intervention did not encounter empty terrain but rather added to an existing cauldron of conflicts. Integrating the toolkits of social and diplomatic historians allows for a fuller understanding of Cold War–era Latin America and of the transnational negotiation of power in the region. At the same time, I am still interested in the motives behind US policy, since this question is closely related to the issue of what was being fought over. More often than not, US officials' perceptions of what was at stake were reasonably accurate, and those perceptions helped shape policy. Moreover, I would argue that neither the motives behind US policy nor the issues at stake have been adequately understood. Traditional accounts, like official rhetoric, have typically argued that superpower rivalry and anticommunism were the central determinants of US policy. I argue instead that the main threats to US state and corporate interests were economic nationalism, redistributive demands, and independent foreign policies. I further maintain that many US government officials understood those threats and that their policies consciously aimed to counter them.

Overview

The chapters that follow focus special attention on the city of La Paz, the Bolivian capital situated nearly twelve thousand feet above sea level on the arid altiplano, the sprawling high plateau region east of Lake Titicaca. For over a century La Paz has been the political capital of the country, making it the most important site of popular mobilization, protest, and debate. What happened in La Paz had major implications for the rest of the country, and its political centrality made it a hub for communication with other regions. If certain features like its ethnic landscape—heavily infused with Aymara indigenous people and culture—made it somewhat distinct from other cities and regions, it was also increasingly connected to the rest of the country in the middle decades of the twentieth century. Thus, while not a comprehensive study of Bolivia, this book is more than just a study of La Paz.

Chapter 1 traces economic visions and debates in La Paz during the quarter century before 1952. In it I examine the rise of resource nationalism in the years just before and after the Chaco War, describing the 1937 nationalization of Standard Oil's properties—the first such nationalization in Latin America—and a 1939 measure to increase state control over mining revenue. During these years resource demands became increasingly central to popular political culture, a shift that was most apparent in the rise of the MNR party in the 1940s. Resource nationalism was not the only motivation behind popular mobilization; a variety of political projects in and near La Paz confronted a host of other problems as well, from capitalist workplace relations to ethnic and gender hierarchies. But the rise of the MNR entailed the partial suppression of these other agendas. The chapter presents an explanation for why the MNR was able to triumph over other opposition forces prior to 1952, highlighting the party's vague populist program and ability to appropriate others' ideas.

In chapter 2 I examine economic policy debates in Bolivia in the early postrevolution period, analyzing proposals for resource-based development, diversification, and redistribution. I highlight a fundamental conflict between advocates of social revolution and more moderate voices who sought mainly capitalist modernization and diversification, or economic revolution. This conflict did not correspond neatly with party affiliations, for the MNR itself was also deeply split. I situate this tension in the context of broader Latin American debates about economic development, external dependency, and social justice taking place in the postwar years. Structuralism and dependency theory both found deep resonance in Bolivia, though the popular beliefs on which they were based—above all, progressive resource nationalism—predated these doctrines' formal introduction around Latin America in the 1950s and 1960s. This second chapter also introduces the question of US intervention and how the US government sought to contain the Bolivian Revolution by bolstering the power of the MNR's more conservative voices. The aims of MNR moderates did not align precisely with the US agenda, but the moderates shared the US interest in limiting the scope of the revolution and were willing to compromise even their own modest plans for change when faced with threats from below and pressure from the North.

In chapters 3 and 4 I explore this theme of revolutionary containment in more depth. The first of these two chapters concerns three major economic policy reforms undertaken by the MNR with strong US support: a 1955 oil privatization law, a monetary stabilization and austerity program begun in 1956, and the 1960s Triangular Plan to restructure the mining industry. These plans were not simply imposed by the imperial power; they were favored by most top leaders in the MNR as well. It was not out of concern for economic efficiency and growth that US and MNR leaders supported these reforms, and indeed, none of them was particularly successful in those regards. Rather, the reforms gained official favor because of their political implications. They were designed to undermine resource-nationalist policies, reduce the power of labor, and favor the Bolivian middle and upper classes along with US companies and creditors. Alternative proposals made by unions and others in Bolivia were disregarded.

In chapter 4 I approach containment from a different angle, using the records of the USIS and the MNR's own statements and propaganda. Although USIS records offer insights about US thinking and strategy, they also reveal the failures of the US-MNR project. USIS agents are remarkably candid about the "uphill struggle" facing them. Although most Bolivians were not formally Marxists or even anticapitalists, a "leftist thought pattern" was widespread and posed constant problems for capitalists and Western governments in the country.[41] The MNR had nationalist credentials that US agents did not, but it too faced a growing crisis of legitimacy in the late 1950s and early 1960s as its economic policy shifted to the right. If revolutionary resource nationalism had become the hegemonic political framework in Bolivia, the MNR's conservative conception of it had not. The increasing resort to violence by the US and Bolivian governments after 1956 ultimately reflected the failure of nonviolent persuasion to reshape Bolivian political culture.

In chapters 5 and 6 I expand upon this argument. The case study in chapter 5 of the La Paz working class, focused on factory workers, shows the extent to which labor militancy constrained the ability of both the US and MNR governments to contain the revolution. By the late 1950s, as the full implications of the 1956 stabilization plan became clear, factory workers were consistently challenging MNR economic policy from the left. This history challenges the notion that mine workers were the singular driving force behind working-class militancy. Especially noteworthy is the extent to which factory workers and other working-class sectors concerned themselves with economic issues that did not directly affect them. For example, they were leading participants in the debates over tin, oil, and gas, demonstrating the way in which resource nationalism inspired mobilization across diverse popular sectors. This concern for broad social questions by unions—sometimes called "social-movement unionism"—has been common in Bolivian history and is crucial to understanding popular politics in the country.

Chapter 6 presents debates about hydrocarbons. By the early 1960s the MNR's reopening of the oil sector to private companies had become a focus of controversy, especially as the 1956 austerity plan drained the Bolivian State Oil Fields Company (YPFB, Yacimientos Petrolíferos Fiscales Bolivianos) of much-needed resources. The US-based company Gulf Oil became the prime target. At a time when Bolivians increasingly pinned their hopes for national development on the promise of oil, and soon natural gas as well, Gulf came to signify the betrayal of revolutionary values by the government. The 1960s saw a reprise of earlier coalitions as diverse sectors joined calls for defense of YPFB and for the nationalization of Gulf's concessions. In 1969 a short-lived military government sympathetic to economic nationalism finally expelled Gulf from the country.

Popular power notwithstanding, however, the movements I analyze in chapters 5 and 6 also embodied some of the conservative elements within popular political culture. While these chapters highlight popular accomplishments, I also call attention to a recurrent set of contradictions within *lo popular* in general and within resource nationalism in particular. These contradictions helped preclude the cross-sector popular coalitions, especially urban-rural coalitions, that might have prevented the conservative turn in the revolution.

In the epilogue I reflect upon continuities and changes since the 1960s, focusing on the cycle of mobilization in 2000–2005 and the presidency of Evo Morales that began in 2006. Despite important changes, key currents in Bolivian political culture—especially resource nationalism—have endured over time. Those currents testify to persisting social and economic problems as well as the inability of successive Bolivian governments and their foreign allies to extinguish deep-seated beliefs about natural resources, socioeconomic rights, and democracy.

CHAPTER 1

The Road to Resource Nationalism: Economic Ideas and Popular Coalitions in La Paz, 1927–1952

The specter of revolutionary nationalism began to spread across Latin America in the 1920s. In economic terms, revolutionary nationalism centered especially around resource nationalism, the quest to assert national control over natural resource wealth and overcome dependence on foreign enterprise. In most cases it also targeted domestic elites and advocated a progressive redistribution of wealth and power among the national population. The Mexican Revolution of 1910 was a landmark event in the growth of Latin American revolutionary nationalism. In 1917 it produced a constitution that declared state ownership of the land and subsoil. Emboldened by this example, populations elsewhere began demanding major changes to the liberal capitalist order that had reigned since the late nineteenth century. In the decades that followed, revolutionary and resource nationalism became major currents in urban political cultures across the region and were reflected to varying degrees in economic policy.[1]

In Bolivia several factors gave these sentiments special intensity. Bolivia had many features of an enclave economy, dependent on mineral extraction for export and with little other industrial development to show for four centuries of silver and tin mining.[2] Ownership of the mines was also highly concentrated, with three "tin barons"—Patiño, Aramayo, and Hochschild—dominating the industry in the first half of the twentieth century. The history of these mines was peppered with company and state massacres of mine workers and their families—at Uncía in 1923, at Catavi in 1942, at Potosí in 1947, and a number of other examples. The biggest massacre of all, however, was the notorious Chaco War with Paraguay from 1932 to 1935, in which more than 56,000 Bolivians and 36,000 Paraguayans died.[3] By the war's end, Bolivians of diverse social groups were already blaming its instigation on two factors—the meddling of Standard Oil and Royal Dutch Shell in Bolivia and Paraguay, respectively, and the moral bankruptcy of a Bolivian political elite beholden to economic oligarchs. The war galvanized Bolivian revolutionary nationalism more than any other factor.

The notion that Bolivia needed to reassert control over its natural resources in the interest of national development found resonance among a diverse cross-section of the urban population, including factory workers, artisans, students, middle-class professionals, and war veterans. Resource nationalism increasingly resembled a "structure of feeling"—a set of understandings, values, and aspirations loosely rooted in material experiences—that pervaded popular thought and discussion, particularly in the cities and mines.[4] Whatever their differences, the new anti-oligarchic political parties that emerged after the war were broadly united by this sentiment. Even internationalist groups like anarchists and Trotskyists, though officially hostile to nationalism, agreed on the desirability of national control over natural resources. "What benefit have Bolivia and Bolivians received from the enormous wealth extracted from this exuberant land?" asked a socialist newspaper in 1927, answering that Bolivian resources had only gone toward "increasing the economic power of Wall Street and other financial institutions in Europe."[5] Early Marxist party platforms linked Bolivia's dependence on mineral exports and "lack of industries" to the "deforming" role of "imperialism in countries reduced to exploiting raw materials." True development required stopping elites from "systematically handing over wealth" to companies that made "monstrous profits," instead redirecting the economic surplus "in benefit of the country."[6]

The coalescence of what René Zavaleta calls "national-popular" forces was especially apparent in the years 1936–1939, when two nationalist military rulers, David Toro and Germán Busch, moved to increase state control over the country's resources. Toro's government (May 1936–July 1937) nationalized the holdings of Standard Oil—the first major nationalization in Latin American history—and created YPFB to administer the country's oil industry. In 1939 the Busch government (July 1937–August 1939) issued a decree requiring mining companies to turn over all of their foreign exchange earnings to the Central Bank, thus limiting the companies' ability to transfer profits abroad without reinvesting in the Bolivian economy. Each move was both a response to popular demands and a trigger for popular mobilization. The widespread expressions of support for these government measures highlight the importance of resource nationalism in uniting a wide range of popular and middle-class groups.

Resource nationalism was only one of the currents in La Paz's pre-1952 popular political culture. In the quarter century prior to the revolution, leftist and nationalist forces confronted economic poverty, inequality, and underdevelopment, but many also challenged other forms of hierarchy. Anarchists and Marxists demanded a fundamental reorientation of workplace and community relations. Working-class women in La Paz formed their own anarchist labor federation, the Women Workers Federation (FOF, Federación Obrera Femenina). Student activists envisioned an educational system free of government and church intervention that would serve the needs of the working and middle classes. Outside the cities, indigenous communities and hacienda workers formed cross-regional networks that fought for land, autonomy, labor rights, and an end to ethnic subordination. These diverse groups sometimes worked together. The period featured impressive moments of collaboration between mestizo leftists and Indians, male and female workers, and urbanites and campesinos who defied traditional boundaries and prejudices.

The rise of the MNR and its particular version of revolutionary nationalism entailed the suppression of these other agendas. The MNR's paternalistic views of the Indian, for instance, contrasted with the more respectful approach of urban anarchists and some Marxist currents in the pre-1952 era. The party's nebulous populism was also much less coherent than the policy agendas of other leftist and nationalist groups. Rarely were these other visions entirely erased, however. There were significant changes in the MNR's politics between its founding in 1941 and the mid-1950s, mainly in the direction of a more assertive economic nationalism and more progressive social policy. These changes occurred mainly because the party was forced to evolve in order to attract popular support.

The rise of the MNR reflected the growth of resource nationalism among La Paz workers, students, war veterans, and other nonelite sectors. Yet the party also had to compete with the diverse alternatives to liberal oligarchy then operating in urban Bolivia. It triumphed by riding the crest of the resource-nationalist wave while selectively appropriating the platforms, rhetoric, and organizing practices of its competitors. The end result was a contradictory set of recipes for economic and social policy, in some ways radical and in other ways quite conservative. This ambiguity was central to the party's ascendance in the 1940s but would also contribute to its downfall.

Alternatives to Liberal Capitalism

Though the end of the Chaco War would help accelerate popular protest, workers and students had already been mobilizing around radical ideas in the 1920s.[7] This decade witnessed the growth of new political organizations, new union federations in La Paz and other cities, and the first serious attempts at national-level confederations of unions and student organizations. As part of their organizing efforts, these groups held national conferences and published newspapers, manifestos, and pamphlets to disseminate their ideas. These sources suggest a deep engagement with economic and social policy questions on the part of worker activists and progressive intellectuals.

The more radical of these groups were typically led by anarchists and Marxists who competed for influence among urban workers in the 1920s and 1930s. Both groups denounced not just poverty and inequality but also capitalism itself, advocating varying forms of worker and state ownership in its place. They went well beyond sloganeering, often proposing specific policy alternatives. In arguing for the eight-hour day in 1926, the socialist paper *Bandera Roja* pointed out that a shorter workday would reduce unemployment "and therefore the miseries and degeneration" of the working class. The same article challenged the mystique of technological efficiency under capitalism, arguing that technology "has been monopolized by capitalists in order to accumulate greater wealth at minimal expense, and not to facilitate the labor of the worker as its objective should be."[8]

Though most of the writers and formal leaders of these groups were male, urban, and mestizo, some also concerned themselves with the exploitation of women, peasants, and Indians. One 1926 *Bandera Roja* article by anarchist Jacinto Centellas decried "the situation of subordination and slavery" of Bolivian women and, directing himself to women, proclaimed that "the hour of your emancipation has arrived" and "is in your hands." The newspaper regularly exhorted non-indigenous working-class readers to defend the Indian "because he is your brother!"[9] Around the same time, various anarchist and Marxist voices were beginning to call for land redistribution, with the famous cry of "land to the Indian." In contrast to most of their Leninist successors, some even declared that the "liberation of the Indian will be the work of the Indian himself," thus adapting the familiar Marxist dictum about the agency of the working class.[10] Working-class women and indigenous Bolivians also had independent organizations of their own, including the anarchist Women Workers Federation in La Paz and a parallel federation in Oruro, and a growing network of indigenous community leaders in the countryside. Some women in La Paz wrote for the anarchist newspaper *Humanidad* in the late 1920s.[11] Through their participation in the larger organizations of the urban left and their work in autonomous organizations, women and Indians played important roles in expanding the meaning of liberation on the left.

Resource nationalism, however—not anticapitalism and certainly not indigenous or women's liberation—was the key thread that would unite popular organizations in the city. Most of the working-class population in La Paz was probably not anticapitalist, at least not in a formal or self-conscious sense. At the same time, anarchist and Marxist arguments enjoyed broad resonance, and popular conceptions of resource nationalism tended to have a strong egalitarian thrust. For most, the purpose of increasing national control over natural resources was specifically to increase the well-being of the popular sectors. Furthermore, by advancing the notion that the collective social good took priority over the individual right to accrue wealth, resource nationalism almost inherently challenged key tenets of liberal capitalism such as the sanctity of private property and free enterprise. Socialism and resource nationalism thus coexisted as overlapping currents in urban political culture.

The popular demand for nationalization of the country's mines first emerged in the 1920s and came to constitute the central plank in the resource-nationalist agenda. Formal calls for mine nationalization began at least as early as 1920, from the La Paz–based Socialist Workers Party (Partido Obrero Socialista).[12] In 1926 the socialist intellectual Tristán Marof published his classic book *La justicia del inca*, in which he advocated the formula "land to the people, mines to the state" to help overcome the country's underdevelopment. The national workers' congress in Oruro the following year echoed the nationalization demand, though newspaper reports are unclear on whether the delegates intended full state ownership or just "mandatory state control of tin revenue," in the words of the La Paz Workers Labor Federation (FOT, Federación Obrera del Trabajo). This demand was accompanied by a call for state-promoted industrialization starting with "industries of basic necessity."[13] The first national university students' convention in 1928 also advocated the nationalization of the mines and called for oil nationalization as well. In its call for limiting the "monstrous personal and economic privileges established in favor of foreign capitalists," the student convention evoked "the healthy values of nationalist defense practiced in Mexico since 1917."[14]

The popular political effervescence of these years was temporarily stifled by the Chaco War. President Daniel Salamanca likely started the war with Paraguay partly for this very reason, and once it had begun he used it as a pretext to justify repression of labor, indigenous organizations, and the left. Not only was a new "social defense" law imposed to prohibit leftist agitation, but most leftists themselves were either conscripted and sent to the front lines or forced to flee the country.[15] Equally important was the government's ability to garner public support by promoting a chauvinistic nationalism among large portions of the population. The war was cast as a test of Bolivian masculinity, with the government appealing to "the legendary virility of our people" in its quest to "step firmly in the Chaco."[16] Many popular organizations simply ceased to exist between 1932 and 1935.

In the long term, however, the disastrous course of the war proved to be a powerful mobilizing force for groups opposed to the political, economic, and social order in Bolivia. It ended up strengthening the popular resource nationalism that had arisen in the 1920s, particularly in relation to oil. In the wake of Bolivia's devastating defeat and even prior to the war's end, public suspicions began to develop about the role of international oil companies in instigating the war. Standard Oil on the Bolivian side and Royal Dutch Shell on the Paraguayan were widely blamed for provoking hostilities due to their interests in the potential oil fields of the Chaco region and, in Standard's case, its interest in gaining access to waterways to facilitate export.[17] Starting around 1934 public intellectuals like Tristán Marof and Carlos Montenegro helped popularize this argument, and various popular organizations adopted the same narrative.[18] It was a significant oversimplification that downplayed President Salamanca's own role in provoking Paraguay, perhaps as a way to increase his own popularity at home amid an economic crisis, and neglected the fact that almost none of the fighting occurred close to known oil fields.[19] Yet the Chaco War entered the popular consciousness as a "war for oil," as a 1954 MNR newspaper article labeled it.[20] Few moments in the country's history have produced such unity of interpretation among Bolivians. In the decades that followed, this narrative of the war would serve as a reminder of Bolivia's subordination to imperialist economic forces.

The war also came to symbolize the failure or even treason of Bolivian elites. The long duration of the war, the devastating human toll, and Bolivia's loss of territory to Paraguay were widely interpreted as signs that a cavalier and morally bankrupt oligarchy ruled the country.[21] Among its gravest sins, the oligarchy had failed to utilize the country's resource wealth—oil but also minerals—in the interest of national development. In light of these popular interpretations of the war, a final aspect of the war's legacy was a bit paradoxical: it would simultaneously enter popular memory as a heroic campaign to defend the country's oil, given the location of oil-rich territories in the southeast near where the fighting took place. All of these perceptions led to the same conclusion, though, insofar as they all underscored the need to safeguard Bolivia's resources in the interest of national development.

The aftermath of the war witnessed the remobilization of many prewar organizations and the emergence of new ones. In La Paz the anarchist Local Workers Federation (FOL, Federación Obrera Local), the anarchist women's FOF, and the Marxist FOT all reemerged, as did many of the affiliated local unions that had been dormant during the war. Efforts at national-level coordination among print workers, railroad workers, teachers, and others followed within the next several years. The power of these groups was most evident in May 1936 when La Paz print workers went on strike and were followed a few days later by all three of the city's labor federations.[22] The general strike paralyzed the city and helped lead to the military's ouster of President José Luis Tejada Sórzano, who had succeeded Salamanca in late 1934.[23]

The war's end also marked the rise of a new organized political element, the war veterans grouped in the Legion of Ex-Combatants (LEC). Although the organization was formally apolitical, its abstention from party alliances did not preclude political intervention in a broader sense. This veterans group would remain a significant political force for decades to come, frequently intervening in policy debates and expressing solidarity with other popular struggles. Its early statements stressed that its "apolitical program" did not mean "avoiding national problems" but rather "evaluating them carefully" and acting. Abstention from politics meant only that the organization refrained from party politics and "unconditional adhesion to any current or future government."[24]

Its political inclinations would vary over time and by locale, but in

the several years following the war many LEC branches had a decidedly leftist orientation. They issued a statement of sympathy for the
May 1936 general strike, for example, and would form alliances with
the FOT and other workers' groups around the country.[25] The LEC
branches in La Paz and Sucre and perhaps others formally identified
as socialist and leftist as of early 1936—significantly, before Toro and
Busch rose to power and declared themselves "military socialists." In
public statements veterans denounced "capitalist exploitation" and
even identified the Legion of Ex-Combatants itself as "a great union
institution with a socialist ideology." An unmistakable class resentment pervaded the league's early postwar publications, which attacked
"the capitalist *rosca*," a common pejorative for the country's oligarchy, and "the comfortable ones" who had not fought in the war. The
war, argued the Sucre veterans, had been "started by foreign capitalists and sustained by national enterprises."[26]

Resource nationalism was a recurring element in LEC statements
and speeches. In early 1936 the Sucre branch's newspaper, *El Ex-
Combatiente*, decried "the private appropriation of the richest sources
of State wealth" and "the unequal distribution of collective wealth,"
pointing to "a bloody paradox" at the heart of Bolivia's suffering,
"that of a pauperized people arguing in a land whose insides contain
incalculable riches." The paper proposed limiting the duration of private mining concessions "as a preparatory step before the Nationalization of the mines." The national veterans' convention in Oruro in June
of that year called for "nationalization of the country's major sources
of wealth."[27]

The veterans' experience in fighting a war widely associated with
oil gave their political interventions particular symbolic weight. LEC
statements often noted veterans' "maximum sacrifice in the Chaco
war" to legitimize their demands, even while criticizing the war itself.[28] With the possible exception of the mine workers, no sector or
organization could claim such a close association with the struggle for
national control over Bolivia's resources. For the remainder of the century, surviving Chaco veterans would play prominent roles in resource
debates, particularly regarding oil and natural gas.

Resource Nationalism and Urban Coalitions, 1936–1939

In the postwar climate of urban Bolivia, the term *socialism* pervaded
mainstream political debate. A proliferation of political groups claimed

the socialist label, from the reformist Republican Socialist Party and Socialist Party to the more radical Marxist parties, the Trotskyist Revolutionary Workers Party (POR) and the Stalinist Party of the Revolutionary Left (PIR).[29] A host of unions and grassroots organizations like the LEC also identified with socialism, though with varying understandings of what the term meant in relation to capitalism and the state. For Marxists and anarchists, socialism meant the overthrow of capitalist ownership, while for reformers it implied only the mitigation of capitalism's worst excesses through social legislation, limited state intervention in the economy, and worker-management collaboration. In line with worldwide developments at the time, the quasifascist Bolivian Socialist Phalange (FSB) established in 1937 also appropriated the term. Despite wildly divergent conceptions of socialism, the popularization of the term itself reflects the widespread repudiation of liberal capitalism in 1930s Bolivia.

The self-labeled military socialist governments of David Toro and Germán Busch capitalized on this sentiment. Military socialism combined resource nationalism and mildly progressive labor policies with an authoritarian corporatist vision intended to bring society's conflicting interest groups under state direction. On one hand, the regimes made substantial changes in economic and labor policies that partially fulfilled key popular demands. On the other hand, they outlawed the radical left, sought to prohibit debate over economic policy, and, in the eyes of many leftists, co-opted mass discontent in a way that forestalled further radicalization.[30] Ultimately the policies of the military socialists garnered them broad popular approval and deprived more radical groups of potential support, a pattern that would be repeated several times in the decades that followed.

The two most significant economic policy measures of these regimes were Toro's March 1937 nationalization of Standard Oil's holdings and Busch's June 1939 decree requiring mining companies to sell their export earnings to the Central Bank.[31] Broad urban coalitions formed in support of both measures, with popular voices hailing government actions as bold assertions of national sovereignty and steps toward economic development.

The oil nationalization elicited demonstrations of support from workers, veterans, and other popular sectors in La Paz and around the country, including in some provincial towns.[32] In the years that followed, the adjudication of the nationalization by presidential administrations, the Bolivian Supreme Court, Standard Oil, and the US government and an eventual compensation agreement in 1942 continued to hold public attention. When the Supreme Court ruled against Standard in early 1939, popular organizations in La Paz, Cochabamba, and elsewhere held demonstrations in support of the ruling. The Bolivian Workers Union Confederation (CSTB), formed in late 1936, mobilized members in La Paz to oppose accommodation.[33] Following the mysterious 1939 death of Germán Busch, a Marxist newspaper warned that the "big oil companies are again scheming to take over our resources" with the collaboration of the government.[34]

Public intellectuals and the popular press helped reinforce oil-nationalist sentiment among urban middle-class and working-class sectors. In the late 1930s writer Carlos Montenegro, who would later co-found the MNR, published a series of articles in the newspaper *La Calle* indicting Standard Oil's actions.[35] Montenegro's more detailed 1938 pamphlet, *Frente al derecho del estado*, summarized the charges against the company. He accused it of violating its contract with the government by delaying production for several years and then evading taxes from 1924 to 1932 by secretly exporting oil. Whether or not Standard directly instigated the war, he said, it had certainly sabotaged the war effort by refusing to provide aviation fuel to the Bolivian military.[36] Montenegro lauded the Toro regime and its popular supporters for their "virile position in defense of the nation's oil patrimony." The nationalization of this "blood of the homeland" was no less than "the most important act ever in American history, except for the republican emancipation of the New World." Rhetorical flourishes aside, much of the population undoubtedly shared Montenegro's feeling that the struggle against Standard was indeed "a war for the second emancipation of Bolivia."[37]

Although Germán Busch's June 1939 decree on mining revenue left private ownership intact, it was no less monumental a political event. Its objective was to establish, in Busch's words, state "control over exports, in order to prevent capital flight and the impoverishment of the country."[38] He spoke of the measure as part of a grand plan for economic development. The state was to play a central role in directing capital investment, promoting national industry, and generally coordinating "the production, circulation, and consumption of wealth." The goal was "the economic independence of the Republic," with a particular focus on "reducing the cost of living and protecting the well-being of the dispossessed classes." This rhetoric was a sharp repudiation of orthodox liberal capitalism. For one thing, it qualified the sanctity of private property by saying that it must serve a "social function." Busch invoked Article 17 of Bolivia's 1938 Constitution, which had established this guideline. He also asserted the need for a strong developmentalist state given an unjust world division of labor in which countries including Bolivia "play the subaltern role of simple providers of raw materials, and of agricultural countries [países-campo] to the industrial countries [países-máquina]."[39]

An even greater outpouring of popular support followed this decree than the oil nationalization two years before. Labor leaders in the CSTB confederation and veterans in the Legion of Ex-Combatants issued a joint manifesto celebrating "the start of liberation of this humiliated and suffering people" and that mining revenue "from now on will stay in the country, fomenting agriculture, transportation, education, [and] the well-being of all Bolivians."[40] A week after the decree the two organizations cosponsored a march in La Paz that reportedly drew sixty thousand people.[41] Although attendance figures—even when accurate—are not always reliable measures of mass support, there is no doubt that the Busch decree elicited genuine enthusiasm among the public. One Marxist critic of the Toro-Busch version of socialism even admits that "the mobilization in support of the June 7 Decree was essentially popular and had the contours of spontaneity, at least in its first moments."[42]

Newspaper reports on the CSTB-LEC march offer a snapshot of the forces that mobilized in support of the decree. Marchers' signs carried pointed messages. One veteran's sign read, "For Bolivia's exploiters, lead and gunpowder," and another said, "Veteran, your machine gun will defend the wealth of your homeland." One presented the country's redemption as a responsibility to the dead: "For those fallen in the Chaco, liberate Bolivia economically." For another marcher, protecting the vulnerable Bolivian nation was an explicitly masculine duty: "A traitor and bad son is he who does not defend the wealth of the Mother Land." An interesting aspect of the event, according to a La Paz reporter, was that many marchers saluted the president "in the communist way," with a closed fist in the air, while others used the fascist open-hand salute.[43]

With the oil nationalization and the decree on mining revenue, the government was enacting policy changes that various labor and political groups had long proposed. Standard Oil had been the subject of heated controversy virtually since its arrival in Bolivia in the early 1920s. Even at the very start of the Chaco War some were already demanding its expulsion.[44] The national labor congress in late 1936 called for the "expropriation of the oil concessions illegally held by Standard Oil and their exploitation by the State."[45] Similarly, urban sectors had long urged greater state control over the mining industry. Delegates to the 1927 workers' congress adopted a proposal from the La Paz FOT for "compulsory state control" of tin revenue. The 1936 congress called for state royalties of 40 percent on mineral exports as well as worker profit sharing. The second CSTB congress, in January 1939, six months before the decree, resolved in favor of a "state monopoly over foreign trade."[46] Often these proposals were part of larger calls for industrialization. Increased state control over revenue was considered a key to creating "those large industries of which there is not even a trace in our homeland" and developing "agriculture, transportation, education," and other sectors.[47]

Government measures were often less radical than popular proposals. Demands for full nationalization of the mines went back to the 1920s, and they only accelerated as a result of the war. At the June 1939 march in La Paz, many demonstrators supported the Busch decree but repeated the more far-reaching call for "mines to the State"; one sign read, "We ask for and will support the nationalization of the mines."[48] Many also called for the nationalization of additional sectors like agriculture and transportation and other bold actions like the dismissal of Bolivia's foreign debts.[49] In contrast, Busch stressed that his government was not hostile to the presence of large private capital and that "the State leaves the exploitation of the mines to private companies and only intervenes in the control of exports." He made a further distinction between "finance capital," which he characterized as parasitic, and "industrial capital that allows [the country] to mobilize its natural wealth based on just compensation."[50] This rhetorical distinction appealed to a current in popular economic thought that reserved particular scorn for finance capital.[51] Similar contrasts between industrial and finance capital, or between the "industrial" and purely "extractive," would be common in the popular economic discourse of later decades.

As the proposals for nationalization suggest, debates over policy retained a degree of independence despite the military socialists' efforts to subordinate mass organizations to corporatist control and despite many of those organizations' formal professions of support for the government. The force of popular pressure also contributed, if indirectly, to the economic nationalist and pro-labor policy changes enacted during these years. In addition to the oil nationalization and decree on mining revenue, a new set of labor laws instituted under Busch, known as the Código Busch, was in part a result of the increasing working-class mobilization that had made possible the May 1936 general strike.[52] All of these policies fell short of widespread popular demands and in the case of the labor code included obligatory unionization and other corporatist aspects that sought to bring workers under state control. But they also show that relations between the urban masses and the military socialist regimes were somewhat more contentious than scholars have sometimes implied.[53]

One clue that popular politics did not always stay neatly within corporatist parameters is the record of cross-sector urban coalitions. Formal pacts of solidarity among unions, federations, and other civil society groups became increasingly common in the late 1930s. Some, such as the late 1936 alliance between the La Paz FOL and FOT branches, were rather short-lived.[54] Others were more enduring. The CSTB and school teachers maintained a formal alliance with the university students of the FUB for several years. Veterans in the LEC signed pacts with the CSTB and other labor organizations at various points in the late 1930s.[55]

Urban organizations were generally much less focused on the situation outside the cities. Nevertheless, since the 1920s there had been some noteworthy instances of collaboration between urban leftists and rural indigenous networks. These alliances were typically based not on resource nationalism but on rural struggles for land, education, and better labor conditions on the haciendas. Prior to the 1927 Chayanta revolt, indigenous community leaders in the Bolivian south had been in close contact with urban socialists, with rural education a particular point of focus.[56] In the 1930s the indigenous school at Warisata in the department of La Paz likewise became a site of interethnic collaboration between rural indigenous communities and urban radicals.[57] A number of urban labor organizations also supported rural struggles between the late 1930s and late 1940s, including unionization drives, sit-down strikes, and indigenous conferences.[58] Particularly impressive was the alliance in La Paz department between the urban anarchists of the FOL and the Departmental Agrarian Federation (FAD) formed in 1946. By mid-1947 the latter federation included about twenty rural unions, some of which participated in the wave of hacienda uprisings that spread across the altiplano that year.[59] Such alliances produced great consternation among landlords and government officials, and various pre-1952 governments would attempt to outlaw urban-rural coalitions.

Still, these budding coalitions were more the exception than the rule, and not just due to government repression. Even urban leftists often viewed the rural Indian with a mix of paternalism and suspicion.[60] Such attitudes crystallized with the MNR's ascendance and the more general consolidation of resource nationalism as the leading animator of urban struggle.

Resource Nationalism and the MNR

The rise of the MNR in the 1940s paralleled resource nationalism's emergence as the most pervasive ideological force in Bolivian politics. The party's program was both more focused and more ambiguous than that of other opposition groups. On one hand, the need to reclaim Bolivia's natural resources for Bolivians was the central theme in early party statements. Other issues and debates, such as indigenous rights or agrarian policy, received far less attention. On the other hand, party leaders typically kept their policy prescriptions vague and, instead of attacking the privileges of wealthy and middle-class Bolivians, implied that all classes would benefit from their program. This mix of resource nationalism and populist vagueness defined the MNR's revolutionary nationalism. It attracted radically different groups and individuals, including Marxists and fascists alike. By the end of the decade the party had become the dominant voice channeling popular nationalism. At the same time, the expansion of the party's base in the late 1940s would necessitate its endorsement of policies that were more concrete and more progressive, somewhat reducing the vagueness of earlier platforms and marginalizing the openly profascist elements.

The twelve men who founded the MNR in 1941 were all under forty, white or mestizo, and members of the urban middle class. Eleven of the twelve were either lawyers or journalists. Most had served in the Chaco War, primarily as officers, and had graduated from the University of San Andrés in La Paz.[61] (The appendix lists some MNR founders, among other influential middle-class participants in economic debates.) The group included some with overt fascist sympathies, some who were mildly sympathetic to Marxism, and a number with no strong ideological inclinations. They were united mainly by a shared sense of indignation at the country's economic and political order and, like so many middle-class revolutionaries, their own exclusion from power. Their early discourse appealed particularly to the "impoverished middle class" and conceived of revolution not as class war but as the struggle of the nation against the antination.[62]

Though party leaders thought of the MNR as a vanguard force in society, its success derived from its ability to channel and co-opt popular grievances.[63] MNR leaders' skillful appeals to resource nationalism and anti-oligarchic sentiment were the main reason for its improving fortunes in the early 1940s. In 1941 a group that included the party's founders and scores of others issued a fiery manifesto attacking Standard Oil. The authors blamed Standard for the Chaco War and accused the company of "systematic sabotage against YPFB" to deny it resources. They also declared that the oil industry should be "under the complete control of the Bolivian State." In the gendered nationalist rhetoric increasingly common after the war, the pamphlet appealed to "all the real men of Bolivia" to honor "the soldiers of the Chaco" by defending the country's oil.[64]

Perhaps most important in the MNR's early rise was its forceful response to the December 1942 massacre of tin miners by the military at the Catavi mine owned by Simón Patiño. Víctor Paz Estenssoro of the MNR, then a congressional deputy, aggressively denounced the government, and his critiques were widely publicized.[65] The massacre quickly became a symbol of the exploitation of Bolivia—its natural resources and workers alike—by foreign or foreign-oriented capitalists and of the state's subordination to powerful economic interests. Soon after the massacre government leaders felt compelled to invite an international team to investigate. The resulting 1943 study, commonly known as the Magruder report, helped cast a spotlight on the atrocious conditions in Bolivian mines and became an outside source to which mine workers could appeal when demanding better wages and conditions. The MNR's public response helped identify the party with the workers' interests as well as the defense of Bolivian resources.[66]

Throughout the 1940s MNR statements and writings would continue to emphasize resource nationalism. The party's program said that the state must act to secure for the nation "the wealth deriving from extractive industry."[67] In 1946–1947 Luis Peñaloza Cordero, an economist who would later serve in the MNR government, published one of the first detailed economic histories of the country. His account indicted "the Patiños, Aramayos, and other nationals and foreigners who enriched themselves off Bolivian minerals, and, paying truly starvation wages to the Bolivian mineworkers, transferred massive profits abroad." Peñaloza charged the companies with opposing reinvestment and paying low taxes, abetted by negligent government administrations.[68] Implicit was the need for a stronger and more patriotic state that would enforce fair taxation and ensure that Bolivian resource wealth was channeled into diversification, industrialization, and economic development.

This militant language notwithstanding, the MNR was much less radical than many of the other anti-oligarchic voices in Bolivia, as revisionist scholars have noted.[69] For the most part, the MNR's central leaders and intellectuals emphasized the need for economic modernization rather than any dramatic overhaul of the existing order. They sought capitalist development and a state strong enough to help the process along. In this regard the party leaders favored an agenda only slightly more ambitious than contemporary government administrations that had already taken important modernizing steps in creating a central bank in 1928, a mining bank in 1936, an agricultural bank in 1942, and the Bolivian Development Corporation (CBF) in 1942.[70] MNR leaders hoped that these institutions would form part of a "strengthened State" that could "diversify the national economy, overcoming the current stage of monoproduction."[71] They harangued against monopolies in industry and the system of "anachronistic feudalism" in the countryside, but in the 1940s they did not endorse large-scale land redistribution or nationalization of the mines. They explicitly denounced calls for socialist revolution. After the mine workers federation adopted the Trotskyist "Thesis of Pulacayo" in 1946, forswearing any compromise with the national bourgeoisie, the MNR published a counterthesis rebuking it and advocating cross-class collaboration in the interest of capitalist development.[72]

In other ways, too, the MNR vision—to the extent that one existed—represented a rather traditional and conservative view of society. Compared to the Marxist parties and the urban anarchists, the MNR was even less focused on the countryside, and it was the most reticent about encouraging peasant political mobilization. Not until the late 1940s did the MNR even try to mobilize rural support, and even then the extent of its connections to organizing is unclear.[73] Its view of Indians and indigenous political agency also lacked the humility of the FOL or some of the earlier urban Marxists. Party leaders typically only discussed Bolivia's indigenous cultures and identities in the interest of assimilation or "redemption" or to assert their own rights as part of an "indigenous" nation vis-à-vis outside conquerors. Carlos Montenegro in 1938 wrote that Bolivia's "ownership right" over the country's wealth derived from its history because Bolivia "is the descendant of the children of the Sun and the Earth of America."[74] While the party's celebration of "the Indo-mestizo race" marked a departure from the overt white supremacy of the traditional oligarchy, it also reinscribed a set of ethnic, cultural, and political hierarchies.[75]

Many MNR leaders were also anti-Semitic, even if their Nazi sympathies were overstated at the time by their critics. The party program denounced "the maneuvers of Judaism" and demanded "the complete prohibition of Jewish immigration."[76] In the early 1940s MNR congressional deputies—including the future president Hernán Siles Zuazo—and the MNR's unofficial newspaper, *La Calle*, railed against "the Jewish invasion." The party's resource nationalism sometimes singled out one of the tin barons, Mauricio Hochschild, for particular criticism because of his Jewish background. Meanwhile, Marxists and anarchists who denounced anti-Semitism were often tarnished as "Jews" and "traitor[s] to the workers' cause."[77]

The internal contradictions and ambiguities of MNR thought ultimately helped more than they hurt, for they allowed diverse supporters to project their own goals onto the party. Beyond their emphatic statements of resource nationalism, MNR leaders kept their program vague and sought to accommodate a range of different, often competing interests within the party. No other oppositional force in 1940s Bolivia was as flexible and capacious.

The leadership's promises to disparate groups were not merely demagogic opportunism. The party's posture of revolutionary nationalism was matched by its deeds just enough to win it substantial credibility among the population in the decade prior to 1952. In particular, the party reaped long-term benefits from its participation in the coalition government of General Gualberto Villarroel (1943–1946). Praise for Villarroel after 1946 was especially common in the countryside due to his government's decrees against forced servitude. Though in reality the government had been pushed into that action by indigenous pressure, Villarroel's name became identified with the cause of rural justice.[78] The regime also sought to resurrect Busch's policy of requiring the mining industry to channel all export proceeds through the Central Bank, lending it a resource-nationalist reputation that greatly concerned capitalists at home and abroad.[79] The Villarroel government was toppled, but it lived on in popular memory as a progressive reformist regime tragically cut short by reactionary forces. Villarroel himself, who was hanged from a lamp post in La Paz's Plaza Murillo, became a martyr for many future revolutionaries in a way similar to Busch before him. There is no doubt that the MNR later benefited politically from having participated in his administration. The party's close association with Villarroel and other military officers also enhanced the MNR's credibility among veterans.[80]

Similarly, the regime had garnered substantial support in the labor movement. In 1944 the MNR supported the foundation of the Bolivian mine workers federation, the FSTMB, whose leader Juan Lechín had become a party member in 1943.[81] The MNR's turn to labor was more a reflection of political exigency than of ideology. Party founders initially paid little attention to the working class—denunciations of the Catavi massacre notwithstanding—and at the start of the Villarroel regime were more closely aligned with corporatist and neofascist elements in the secretive military lodge Cause of the Homeland.[82] Only during the Villarroel period and especially during the *sexenio* period that followed Villarroel's overthrow (1946–1952) did the party engage in sustained outreach to workers out of a need for broader mass support.[83]

In turn, new connections to organized labor helped transform the party. Herbert Klein observes that "the increasing importance of the worker base brought with it an increasing radicalism in the party ideology." The presence of the mine workers, in particular, "changed the 'nationalism' of the MNR into concrete and dynamic programmes."[84] The MNR's leftward shift involved the adoption of demands previously espoused only by the radical left. In 1951 it finally endorsed calls for agrarian reform and mine nationalization under workers' control.[85] Its first years in power would feature a more expansionary fiscal and monetary approach than that earlier pursued by Víctor Paz Estenssoro in his role as finance minister under Villarroel.[86] Party discourse also changed somewhat as the 1940s progressed. Speeches and manifestos of the late 1940s sometimes implied critiques of capitalism. In 1948 Paz Estenssoro denounced the "supercapitalism" that "oppresses national life," warning against "private companies that are only concerned with profit."[87] Anticapitalism never became a consistent theme in MNR rhetoric, and especially after 1952 party leaders would emphasize their procapitalist orientation. But the subtle rhetorical shifts of the late 1940s and early 1950s reflected the expansion of the MNR base and an increased effort to appeal to workers.

Other opposition forces, meanwhile, made crucial errors in the mid-1940s. The Stalinist PIR, which initially enjoyed major support among urban labor, helped oust Villarroel and collaborated with the right-wing regimes that followed.[88] The PIR's strongest base in the labor movement, the CSTB, boycotted the 1944 congress at which the FSTMB was founded.[89] The anarchist FOL's firm abstention from all party politics probably increased support for the Marxist and nationalist opposition parties.

Its competitors' mistakes were not the main reason for the MNR's triumph, though. More important was the party's loose but powerful vision of resource nationalism and its capacity to absorb diverse ideas and interests within it, adapting itself to popular sentiment in the process. Some scholars have theorized that reform-oriented nationalists who succeed in delivering real reforms will usually win out over radical challengers to their left, and this insight seems applicable to the Bolivian opposition of the 1930s and 1940s.[90] After 1952 liberals in the United States made a similar argument when advocating US support for the MNR.[91] At the same time, however, socialist organizing was by no means a lost cause; the MNR's leftist competitors and the need to garner mass support helped change the party's trajectory, pushing it to develop a more assertive, progressive resource nationalism in the years before 1952. This pattern of contention would continue after the MNR's rise to power, when the time came to define the precise content of revolutionary policy.

CHAPTER 2

A New Type of Bolivian Economy: Competing Visions, 1952–1956

Among revolutions, the April 1952 Bolivian uprising is notable for its rapid triumph: in less than three days popular militias vanquished the regime's forces. The revolution was far from bloodless—about six hundred people were killed—but there was no protracted warfare.[1] By 1952 the regime and the order it represented were so lacking in support and repressive capacity that one quick blow was enough to knock them out.

Yet as in other revolutions, the apparent unanimity of the revolutionary movement was deceptive, for its constituent elements entertained very different visions of the future society they wished to build. The key conflict in the years that followed was between the so-called moderate and left camps within the MNR. This tension was already subtly apparent in April. While popular forces led by La Paz factory workers and miners had done the fighting, it was the party's exiled middle-class leadership that returned to assume the reins of government on April 12. At the end of the month, newly installed President Víctor Paz Estenssoro wrote privately of "the need to make the bases ... discipline themselves" and accept the "authority and the hierarchical structure of the government apparatus."[2]

Division was clearly evident in the economic policies advocated by the different camps. Most agreed, at least nominally, on the need to transform the "structure of development"—to diversify the nation's exports, expand production of agricultural staples, and promote industrialization. This last goal usually encompassed two concrete aims—increasing the value added to raw materials prior to export through mineral smelting, oil refining, and the more extensive processing involved in producing goods like petrochemicals and fertilizers; and fomenting light industries to supply consumer goods such as textiles and foodstuffs for the Bolivian market. But the left sought much more than just growth and diversification. It also advocated major changes in the model of development—meaning the form of administering the economy—and a social revolution that would bring equity and justice as well as growth.[3] Although the urban left was itself diverse and not entirely anticapitalist, it was united around a set of basic demands that distinguished it from the moderate MNR leaders: public control over major natural resources, greater workplace democracy, and a progressive reorientation of fiscal and monetary policy to favor redistribution.

This conflict paralleled debates that emerged all over Latin America in the 1950s and 1960s, when a range of new ideas began to challenge economic liberalism and even capitalism itself. The two key emergent doctrines were structuralism and dependency theory.[4] Structuralists advocated government intervention in the economy to transform domestic structures and international trade relations that inhibited growth and caused high inflation. They argued that through a combination of foreign investment and subsidies to domestic industry, states could foment industrialization and thereby allow countries like Bolivia to prosper in the global economy. Dependency theorists (*dependentistas*) likewise asserted the need for strong state action but had a far less sanguine view of foreign capital and the domestic bourgeoisie. Most MNR leaders espoused a cautious version of structuralism, while more radical currents below and to the left advocated more aggressive policies reflecting a mix of structuralism, dependency theory, resource nationalism, and socialism.

Popular economic thought in Bolivia derived far more from endogenous traditions than formal academic doctrines, however. Antipathy toward foreign extractive enterprise and demands for public control over natural resources reflected the accumulation of historic grievances in a country that exemplified the ills that structuralism and dependency theory were meant to remedy. By the early 1950s these grievances and proposals for how to resolve them had already been gestating in La Paz and other cities for several decades, fueled by resource nationalism, Marxism, anarchism, and other traditions.

Managing popular demands proved enormously difficult for MNR leaders given their own aversion to social revolution. They developed a populist strategy in an effort to maintain their ideologically heterogeneous and multiclass coalition. The party's leadership structure incorporated representatives of the left, right, and center who would serve as liaisons with different groups in society. Rhetorically, MNR leaders specifically defined the *pueblo* to include the country's bourgeoisie, which had been "blind" and "idiotic" but "opened its eyes" later, according to President Víctor Paz Estenssoro, who first held office from 1952–1956. The only groups excluded from the new national community were "the servants of imperialism and feudalism" represented by the mining *rosca* and the landed aristocracy and, on the other side of the spectrum, the "communists" who slavishly followed foreign ideologies.[5] Otherwise, MNR leaders allowed the discourse of revolutionary nationalism to remain sufficiently vague to encourage different audiences to ascribe to it their own meanings.

The MNR's fiscal and monetary policies up to 1956 aimed to placate the disparate elements in its multiclass coalition. Wage increases, consumer subsidies, the expansion of the civil bureaucracy, and other forms of government spending were deemed necessary to satisfy popular demands. These measures were possible in the short term only because of the government's resort to high inflation and the delivery of US aid starting in 1953. However, high spending was ultimately unsustainable given the country's weak economic base and the MNR's own commitment to appeasing wealthy stakeholders as well as the population at large. A more sustainable development policy would have entailed profound transformations in the structure and model of the economy to foster balanced growth and reduce inequality, but MNR leaders were both unwilling and unable to pursue that path given their commitments to retaining US favor and generally respecting capitalist private property.

The US government played an important role in the revolution's development. In opting to aid the MNR, it was in fact driven by the same motivations that led it to attack revolutionary experiments elsewhere. In the early Cold War era, Latin America and the "Third World" more generally were quickly becoming battlegrounds—not between the forces of communist totalitarianism and capitalist democracy, as government rhetoric claimed, but between competing visions of economic and social development. In Bolivia the US government perceived the key danger to be independent nationalism, which in the economic realm took the form of ideas like resource nationalism, left-wing Keynesianism, structuralism, and socialism. The major US aim in Bolivia was to promote private control of natural resources while limiting state intervention in the economy to that which would assist private capital or guarantee the minimal social stability needed for capitalist prosperity. The goal and effect of US intervention were to amplify the existing conservative tendency within the MNR government. In so doing, however, the United States further constrained the MNR's ability to appease the urban labor and left segments of its coalition, increasing the tensions that eventually led to the government's overthrow in 1964. Thus, even as US aid temporarily propped up the MNR, the policies of the US-MNR team, coupled with the revolutionary expectations of ordinary Bolivians and an underdeveloped economy, contributed to the government's eventual downfall.

That outcome was not preordained, however. Looking back from today, it is easy to forget the fluidity and contingency of the revolution's first four years. The MNR moderates dominated the new government but effectively shared power with popular sectors through a new structure of "cogovernment" (*cogobierno*) and by the de facto veto power of the mobilized masses. Landmark policies like the nationalization of the mines in October 1952 and the land reform decree in August 1953 were hybrid reflections of the MNR leaders' modernization objectives and the insurgent demands of forces to their left; the MNR's belated embrace of mine nationalization (1951) and land expropriations (1953) were directly traceable to the influence of labor, the left, and peasant agitation in the countryside.[6] The Bolivian Workers Central (COB, Central Obrera Boliviana) established after the April revolution was a powerful voice for revolutionary demands, even after the MNR succeeded in purging Trotskyists from its leadership in late 1952.

Nor was the triumph of conservative forces complete. Even after 1956, as policy shifted rightward and leftists lost power within the government, the MNR moderates' hegemony remained more superficial than real. Revolutionary nationalism and resource nationalism had become hegemonic, but the MNR mainstream's interpretation of those concepts had not.[7] In many ways the discourse and policy of the government continued to reflect pressures emanating from below and from the left.

Latin American Economic Thought in the 1950s

The economic policy debates of the early MNR period revolved around questions then being addressed all across Latin America: how to promote industrialization in raw-material-exporting economies, how to diversify production and trade, and how to achieve a more equitable distribution of wealth. Despite Bolivia's shortage of formally trained economists, the basic ideas circulating in workplaces, neighborhoods, universities, and the halls of congress closely paralleled the arguments that structuralists and dependency theorists in other countries were starting to articulate more formally.

During the half century prior to the 1930s, the dominant economic doctrine in Latin America had been liberalism, which prescribed an international division of labor based on the concept of comparative advantage. David Ricardo and his disciples had argued that some countries would specialize in manufactured goods while others exported primary goods but that the economic benefits of technological progress would naturally diffuse from the former to the latter in the form of lower prices for industrial goods. In response to the world crisis of the 1930s, however, economists like Argentina's Raúl Prebisch argued that technological innovations and increases in productivity in the "center" countries had not in fact diffused to the "periphery" but had simply translated into higher profits and wages in the center. By contrast, increased primary production in the periphery had led to reductions in world prices for primary goods rather than price and wage increases. According to Prebisch, the terms of trade for primary-exporting countries—the world prices of primary goods relative to manufactured goods—had been steadily declining since the 1870s.[8] This pattern formed the basis for Prebisch's concept of "unequal exchange" between central and peripheral countries.

Prebisch's work was the intellectual foundation for the UN Economic Commission on Latin America (ECLA, known as CEPAL in Spanish, Comisión Económica para América Latina), established in 1948, and the structuralist school associated with it, often called *cepalismo* or *desarrollismo* in Spanish.[9] The structures that impeded development included the drastic inequality of landownership, inefficient and quasi-feudal agricultural systems, the lack of infrastructure, the shortage of skilled labor and abundance of unskilled labor, the small size of domestic markets, and the separation of mono-export enclaves from the rest of the economy.[10] All these problems were present in acute form in Bolivia, as CEPAL reports noted in the 1950s.[11]

The structuralists' main solution was state-promoted industrialization. Government tariffs on imports and subsidies to domestic industry would aid new enterprises, which would supply a growing domestic consumer market. The decline in unemployment would increase wages across all economic sectors, thereby also increasing the world prices for primary products. This basic policy proposal was widely implemented by regional governments in the 1950s and 1960s.[12] Although it was not the unmitigated failure that many later critics implied,[13] the model as implemented clearly failed to resolve some key problems. Prioritizing domestic industry over exports exacerbated balance-of-payments problems and led to a new dependence on capital imports. Small domestic markets were an insufficient outlet for the new industrial goods, an especially grave impediment to industrialization in Bolivia. The model did not significantly reduce inequality and may have actually increased it.[14]

The rise of dependency theory reflected these shortcomings. While most of dependency theory's central tenets coincided with those of structuralism, the *dependentistas* took issue with what they considered a naïve faith in foreign capital and the national bourgeoisie.[15] Most structuralists had accepted the "mutual-benefit" premise of global capitalism—the idea that rich and poor countries could derive simultaneous and roughly symmetrical benefit from economic interaction—and therefore encouraged underdeveloped countries to seek the assistance of foreign capital in order to develop. The *dependentistas*, by contrast, saw exploitation and imperialism as fundamental to the center-periphery relationship. They located the sources of unequal exchange not only in unequal terms of trade but also in the direct extraction of Third World wealth by foreign capital and the domestic distortions exacerbated by foreign control.[16] They explicitly accused the center nations of profiting at the periphery's expense and limiting peripheral nations to, at best, a form of "dependent development." They also challenged the assumption that the native bourgeoisie in peripheral countries could be a progressive force for development.[17] Dependency arguments were often compatible with Marxism, though they initially derived more from structuralism.[18]

Bolivian intellectuals and MNR policy makers followed these debates, and many of them would draw upon CEPAL's studies during the 1950s and 1960s. There was also direct communication between foreign *cepalistas* and Bolivians. In May 1957 CEPAL held its international conference in La Paz, where it was hosted by the government of Hernán Siles Zuazo (1956–1960).[19] During the conference Bolivian delegate Manuel Gisbert Nogué, an economic official in the government, gave a lengthy presentation that sheds light on how the mainstream MNR leadership understood the country's underdevelopment.

Gisbert Nogué invoked CEPAL recommendations when describing the MNR's agrarian reform and argued for continued state intervention to increase agricultural production.[20]

Most notable in Gisbert Nogué's presentation, though, was the assertion of Bolivia's uniqueness in relation to other countries. Bolivia, he argued, faced a particularly harsh predicament resulting from its geography, demography, and history. Unlike many other Latin American countries and even "certain colonies in Africa" where foreign investments had proven "the great levers of their development," Bolivia's landlocked position had kept it uniquely isolated. The result was a deformed "autochthonous capitalism" that continued to reflect "the mark of our feudal backwardness" in its primitive technology and organization.[21] Industry and services constituted a much lower proportion of total economic output than in many other less-developed countries, and Bolivia had "barely start[ed] a timid substitution of essential imports" since the 1930s.[22] Progress was further hindered by the country's racial stock, with the Spanish conquest having failed to generate "that intimate mixture of peoples which, in other Latin American countries, has bestowed *mestizaje* with the conditions of political possibility." The result was that "modern Bolivia" remained tiny and confined to urban centers, surrounded by "the other Bolivia, that which represented the past" and constituted "a sort of social museum."[23] Gisbert Nogué's speech was a mixture of moderate *cepalista* structuralism, with its advocacy of state intervention to propel capitalist development, and the Eurocentric racial and cultural assumptions that characterized most MNR leaders' thinking.

The MNR's later "Plan de desarrollo económico y social" (1961), formulated with the aid of CEPAL and other UN advisers, lacked the racist undertones but otherwise expanded on this analysis. It cited a host of structural contributors to inflation, such as agricultural inefficiency and mineral monoculture.[24] Like Gisbert Nogué, the authors also stressed Bolivia's qualitative differences from other "backward" economies. While the liberal export era had brought growth in some countries, Bolivia's export economy had contributed little to development. The country's small domestic market was only partly to blame; other reasons included the particularly extreme concentration of mine ownership and the high rate of profit transfer abroad, plus "a very liberal import policy."[25]

Despite MNR leaders' substantial contact with CEPAL, though, Bolivian economic debates were informed more by domestic circumstances than by foreign economists. The popular embrace of state intervention in the economy—through resource nationalization, land reform, progressive fiscal and monetary policies, and so on—long predated CEPAL. In 1952 no one needed to convince most Bolivian miners, urban workers, and students that state intervention was necessary to promote economic diversification, growth, and equity. Historical events had already done so, notably the devastating Chaco War, the memory of the 1937 oil nationalization and the Busch regime's assertion of control over mining revenue, and the massacres of mine workers that filled the country's recent history. The interpretations that Marxists, anarchists, and nationalists gave to these events contributed to a nebulous but powerful culture of resource nationalism that united urban popular sectors. Moreover, Bolivian debates in the early 1950s were already going well beyond CEPAL's cautious prescriptions, prefiguring the dependency school. Local debates were shaped more by the particularities of Bolivian history and political culture than by ideas filtering in from outside.[26]

The limited influence of formal doctrines makes sense given the virtual nonexistence in Bolivia of a technocratic class of professional economists. While larger Latin American countries witnessed the growth of a substantial economics profession in the 1930s and 1940s, in Bolivia the discipline remained much smaller. Few of those who did have formal economics training had received it abroad, and they usually opposed structuralism, Marxism, and dependency thought.[27] This vacuum may have allowed the urban and rural working classes, alongside middle-class professionals like lawyers, journalists, and engineers, to play a more central role in public debates.[28]

A New Type of Bolivian Economy?

Racist explanations aside, Bolivia in 1952 was in many ways distinct from the more developed economies of Latin America. Its population was much smaller, it was dependent on a single mineral export that was in decline, and the extent of prior industrialization was much lower. For all these reasons Bolivia lacked the development potential of larger economies. At least for the foreseeable future it was not going to develop, for example, an automobile manufacturing industry, as Brazil and Mexico did after World War II. Furthermore, the history of global capitalism shows that relatively few peripheral countries have successfully risen to the ranks of the center or even the semiperiphery and that doing so may be even more difficult in small economies dependent on natural resource extraction. A 1955 MNR statement said simply that the underdeveloped state of national industry "is not going to change in the near future."[29]

One of the most obvious problems with the Bolivian economy was its almost total dependence on mining. Mineral exports constituted about 95 percent of the total in the 1940s, with 70–80 percent of foreign exchange coming from tin alone. All of that tin went to two countries, the United States and Britain.[30] The mining industry also had an even lower multiplier effect than other primary-commodity industries, meaning that it generated relatively little in the way of secondary and tertiary activity.[31] Industrialization in Bolivia was very limited prior to 1952 and mostly confined to light industries like textiles, food, beer, and cement.[32] In 1952 the COB stated the obvious: "We are a country exclusively dependent on minerals with grave effects on the rest of the economy."[33] Some commentators described a sort of mining complex akin to the "plantation complex" of tropical slave societies, arguing that "mining exerts a total and absorbing domination, not only over the economy but over every activity: political, cultural, and even psychological."[34] The declining quality of Bolivian ores and falling world tin prices after 1952 only underscored the perils of dependence on mineral exports. Most resource nationalists of the 1950s realized that there was no long-term future in minerals; if Bolivia was to prosper, it had to use its remaining minerals to develop other productive sectors.

In the countryside, the extreme concentration of land ownership in the feudalistic *latifundia* system greatly limited food production. Fewer than 2 percent of landowners controlled 39 percent of the land.[35] Many large landowners cultivated only very small portions of their property, holding the land for speculative reasons or in order to force peasants to work for them. They had little incentive to improve efficiency or invest in new technologies.[36] The result was that agricultural goods comprised 45 percent of Bolivian imports in the early 1950s. As of 1950 Bolivia was importing 90 percent of its sugar, 76 percent of its wheat, 75 percent of its meat, and all of its cotton.[37]

A range of other problems further impeded development. As a CEPAL report later noted, "The extreme concentration in income distribution and the virtual exclusion of a large part of the population from economic life," in addition to the country's small population overall, impeded the growth of the national consumer market.[38] The lack of infrastructure for transporting goods and providing electricity and the shortage of skilled labor also hampered new investment.[39] Foreign indebtedness limited the Bolivian state's potential capacity to overcome these problems. Debt service payments consumed about half of annual government revenue in the years just before the revolution, with owed interest constituting 58 percent of all debt in 1949.[40] The pre-1952 regimes' own spending policies also made clear that they were unwilling to use what fiscal freedom they did have to spur development; debt service was the biggest expenditure in the 1950 budget, but the military came in second place.[41]

Notwithstanding these formidable obstacles, however, foreign assessments of the early and mid-1950s often stressed the country's economic potential. Agriculture and oil were singled out. CEPAL noted that "Bolivian agriculture is capable of supplying nearly all the items required by the domestic market." According to a US Embassy report issued one week prior to the revolution, "On its land resources alone Bolivia could establish a stable and viable economy." The same report argued that "potentialities for development of substantial petroleum production are excellent," echoing the conclusions of a 1942 US study directed by foreign service officer Merwin Bohan. "Few countries in the world have been endowed by nature with a greater diversity of raw materials," argued the 1951 report of a UN technical team, adding that "there would seem to be no material reasons to prevent the people of Bolivia from living a life of reasonable comfort."[42] Given its small size and underdevelopment, Bolivia was not going to become the next Brazil or Mexico in the near term. But with the right policies it might at least achieve a diversification of its primary exports, food sovereignty, and consumer and intermediate industries to service domestic needs.

Almost all Bolivians agreed, at least superficially, on the desirability and potential for economic diversification and the state's basic responsibility for helping to promote it. Diversification was a key popular demand and a central promise of the MNR leadership.[43] Senator Ciro Humboldt would argue in 1958 that "the April Revolution was not made with the goal of simply altering the export commodity" but rather "to build a new type of national economy for the benefit of Bolivians."[44] In 1953 President Paz Estenssoro promised "the end of mono-production" and pledged increased state investment in oil, agriculture, ranching, and manufacturing in order "to produce, even in part, what we consume."[45] Oil, in particular, was also considered a promising export commodity.

The most detailed early outlines of MNR economic objectives appeared in the 1953 "Plan de diversificación de la producción" and the 1955 *Plan inmediato de política económica*. These documents, authored by Foreign Minister Wálter Guevara Arze and based largely on the 1942 Bohan and 1950 UN missions to Bolivia, represented a moderate structuralist view in their diagnosis of Bolivian underdevelopment and their policy prescriptions.[46] They acknowledged the long-term crisis of the mining industry, which they attributed to a variety of structural factors beyond the direct control of Bolivians, and focused on the development of alternative sectors as a remedy.[47] Agriculture received particular emphasis, with the sparsely populated Santa Cruz region considered especially promising. Guevara noted that the agricultural goods that accounted for nearly half of import expenditures "can be produced in the country under favorable economic conditions." To complement the agrarian reform then under way, the 1955 plan called for new investments in sugar mills and storage and processing facilities for rice, corn, and meat. State credits to industry were to "give priority to industries that use national raw materials," thus linking agricultural production with urban industry. The plan envisioned new factories that would make glass, tires, cement, and chemicals. It touted $15 million in Central Bank loans extended to industry the previous year and noted specific projects like a $3.6 million sugar mill to be constructed through the Bolivian Development Corporation (CBF).[48]

Some later critics have accused the revolutionary nationalists of the 1950s of viewing nationalization and agrarian redistribution as panaceas, arguing that they neglected to pursue long-term solutions to low production.[49] While this characterization may be valid for some MNR officials, it ignores the detailed development outlines found in certain government proposals like the *Plan inmediato*, which made clear that nationalization and land redistribution were insufficient in themselves. Top MNR leaders called for the construction of smelters to process tin and other minerals.[50] Many of the MNR's left-leaning officials were especially adamant about the need for economic planning, which they considered a revolutionary imperative. Soon after a January 1953 right-wing coup attempt, Minister of Mines and Petroleum Mario Torres told an MNR party convention that "only the industrialization of our natural resources and economic diversification can give us the freedom sought. And this can only be accomplished by beginning planning, which is the sign of the times." Torres warned that by letting "nonrevolutionary classes direct the path of the MNR," top officials were "running the risk of facilitating the counterrevolution."

He called for immediate elevation of more worker and peasant voices into top positions to avoid a replay of the recent coup attempt.[51]

The charge that 1950s revolutionaries were simplistic and short-sighted is even more misleading when directed at grassroots sectors and intellectuals outside government, who often proved more thoughtful, comprehensive, and radical than MNR ideologues in their approaches to changing both the structure and model of the economy. Countless union statements advocated using mining exports not merely as a source of rent-based income but as a lever for diversifying and industrializing the economy. In place of the "brutal and systematic theft of our raw materials" by foreign interests, the Cochabamba branch of the COB envisioned a reorientation of production and spending to prioritize human needs:

> We could create new manufacturing industries, exploit our [own] natural resources, promote agriculture through state aid, build roads and railroads, create thousands of schools and teaching institutes, establish hospitals, [and] provide sanitary housing for the population. We Bolivians have fought for the nationalization of the mines with this goal in mind. We want the mines to serve the interest of Bolivians and not that of foreign monopolists.[52]

The theme of mining as a lever for development was also apparent in the statement of the construction workers' national congress in April 1953. Delegates demanded "the free sale of tin" on the world market at "appropriate prices"—a condemnation of the US-British monopoly on Bolivian tin exports and perhaps also the below-market prices that Bolivia had accepted during World War II and which had not ceased to be a source of popular anguish. Fairer prices for the country's tin would "make way for the country's industrialization, breaking in that way the siege of Yankee imperialism."[53] With the same intent, the COB advocated formal cooperation among primary-commodity economies in the interest of price stabilization.[54]

As part of its economic development vision the COB advocated nationalization in additional sectors, including "basic industry," transportation, and public services. Its 1954 program called for state intervention in industry "to create, parallel to private industry, cooperative industry in the hands of the unions." Complete state control over railroads and other transport was deemed particularly important for achieving "economic Independence, the planning of industrial development, and economic diversification."[55] When the COB issued these proposals in 1954, its most radical leaders had already been purged by MNR intervention, and it now explicitly avoided calls for "proletarian revolution."[56] Nonetheless, its demands continued to go beyond those of MNR officialdom.

University students were important participants in these early debates as well. By 1952 most major cities had a Local University Federation (FUL) as part of the national-level Bolivian University Confederation (CUB).[57] The local federations and the universities more generally were key sites of leftist influence prior to 1952 and would be vocal proponents of radical change throughout the MNR period. The CUB's 1952 program asserted the place of students alongside the "working classes of the country" in the struggle for "liberation from the capitalist yoke."[58] The program prefigured later *dependentista* characterizations of the center-periphery relationship: "Bolivia is a semicolonial country with a backward economy due to the actions of Yankee imperialism, [and has] therefore been converted into a simple source of raw and strategic materials for the benefit of the militarist ends of finance capital and into a secure market for its products."[59] In addition to mobilizing in support of workers many times during the 1950s and 1960s, students organized public conferences on economic issues that sometimes had an important influence on policy debates.[60]

The La Paz federation explicitly rejected the notion that nationalization was sufficient in itself. Its June 1952 resolution supporting mine nationalization warned, "We do not think this to be the definitive step." Its program two months later advocated the construction of mineral smelters.[61] Additional proposals included nationalization of the banks and railroads under workers' control, state control over exports, and—in a rebuke to US pressures and MNR anticommunism— "commercial relations with all countries of the world that respect our sovereignty."[62]

Even in the area of agrarian policy, which urban labor and the left in the 1950s tended to underemphasize, FUL–La Paz and CUB proposals did not view land redistribution as a panacea. In 1952 these organizations were already calling for technical assistance, training, and state investment in the mechanization of agriculture as well as redistribution. They displayed somewhat more sensitivity toward peasant wishes than most government officials and urban leftists did. While their goal was "agrarian revolution," they called for the transfer of the old estates "to communities for their collective exploitation or under other forms, taking into account the labor customs and social life of the peasantry."[63]

In many ways the economic development proposals of urban workers and university students were thus more farsighted and comprehensive than those of MNR leaders. The gulf between these sectors and the MNR leadership was even more pronounced on the question of redistribution of wealth and income.

Economic Revolution and Social Revolution

MNR officials repeatedly emphasized that their goal was an "economic revolution, not social revolution."[64] Economic revolution meant state intervention to promote capital accumulation, reinvestment, and diversification—basically, a moderate version of structuralism. MNR leaders counterposed these goals to the social objectives of redistributing wealth and attacking capitalist private property. Their explicit model was the postrevolutionary Mexican state, which had taken a sharp turn away from redistribution starting in the late 1930s.[65] The left, meanwhile, agreed that economic revolution was necessary but insisted that it could not be separated from social revolution, for the sake of justice and because each was doomed to fail without the other. The unfolding dialectic between these two visions is central to understanding the MNR period.

Starting with their earliest statements in the 1940s, MNR leaders envisioned the capitalist class continuing to play a central role in Bolivian economic development. Their enemy was not capitalism itself, they emphasized, but that small group of monopolists and imperialists who circumvented the free market and were often associated with "the maneuvers of Judaism" in party documents of the 1940s.[66] Much of Guevara's 1946 "Thesis of Ayopaya" was an explicit rebuke to the miners' radical Thesis of Pulacayo, which called for socialist revolution. Once they took power in 1952, party leaders emphasized their preference for private investment in oil, mining, agriculture, and other industries.[67]

They meanwhile strove to limit reform to that which did not involve redistributing existing wealth or infringing on private property rights. Prior to 1953 MNR leaders were reticent to endorse any program of far-reaching land expropriations, instead promoting labor reforms or sharecropping arrangements and stressing plans for "colonization" of the eastern lowlands.[68] Even after peasant land occupations in the countryside compelled the government to embrace expropriations in August 1953, the MNR framed the expropriations as an attack on feudal lords who were impeding modernization and an imperative of nation-building that would bring indigenous peasants into the national community and market. Víctor Paz Estenssoro claimed that "agrarian reform will benefit the bourgeoisie as much as the peasants."[69] MNR agrarian policies promoted private landownership over communal, fostering the growth of a new smallholding class and, in the eastern lowlands, a new elite of large landowners.[70]

The nationalization of the country's large mines and establishment of the state-run Bolivian Mining Corporation (COMIBOL) resulted from a similar dynamic. While the demands of labor and the left compelled the MNR to embrace the cause of nationalization, the shape of the October 1952 expropriation decree and ensuing policies also reflected MNR leaders' preference for a developmentalist path rather than a socialist one. The Paz government established a shallow and bureaucratized form of workers' control in which individual workers were tasked with monitoring conditions and the workforce as a whole was largely excluded from the process.[71] It also dutifully promised compensation to the deposed Patiño, Aramayo, and Hochschild mining companies, partly in order to retain the goodwill of the US government. And as with the agrarian reform, MNR leaders emphasized that the nationalization was an exceptional measure against parasitic monopolists rather than a reflection of general hostility toward private property. "Nationalization of private property is not the policy of Bolivia," ambassador to the United States Víctor Andrade reassured his audience.[72]

The bourgeoisie was explicitly included within the MNR vision of the national community, with even the official leader of the MNR left, Juan Lechín, emphasizing the "neither bourgeois nor proletarian" nature of the revolution.[73] Such statements implied that all classes would benefit from the MNR's economic policy and that the solution to underdevelopment lay in economic growth rather than redistribution of property, wealth, and power. Capitalist modernization under the guidance of a wise and pragmatic elite would uplift all Bolivians. The only losers would be a handful of monopolists and imperialists—labels not applied to foreign capital, Western governments, or most of the Bolivian bourgeoisie. The MNR's mutual-benefit discourse thus concealed the economy's continued privileging of capitalist and middle-class sectors at the expense of the working-class and peasant majority.

This populist economic rhetoric went hand in hand with the MNR's vision of ethnic and cultural *mestizaje*. To a far greater extent than oligarchic regimes of the past, the MNR embraced Bolivia's nonwhite, non-European identity. A party program of 1946 proclaimed "our faith in the power of the Indo-mestizo race."[74] But as many historians have noted, official visions of *mestizaje* in Bolivia and most other Latin American states in the mid-twentieth century continued to denigrate indigenous peoples and cultures even as they rejected the unabashed Eurocentrism of the past. State visions of *mestizaje* valued the mestizo over the Indian and the "white" and European aspects of the mestizo over the "indigenous" aspects. A 1954 editorial in the MNR's official newspaper argued that "the Indian is still like a child." Minister of Peasant Affairs Ñuflo Chávez Ortiz agreed, stating simply in early 1953 that the Indian "is ignorant, [and] does not yet have a revolutionary consciousness." As in most of Latin America, *indio* remained a derogatory term and was replaced by *campesino* whenever MNR leaders sought to speak favorably about rural residents.[75] The MNR's cult of *mestizaje* was intimately tied to its vision for agrarian development; party leaders viewed indigenous communal landholdings, culture, and subsistence agriculture as impediments to modernization and the unification of the Bolivian nation. These views—a capitalist bias mixed with racism—were used to justify first the MNR's hesitancy about land expropriations and later the individualist thrust of the land reform.[76]

At no point did MNR leaders enjoy unilateral policy-making power, however. Their economic vision clashed constantly with more radical visions at the grassroots level. Although most workers, peasants, and students formally supported the government during this period, their rhetoric defied the government's vague populism, and their policy proposals went well beyond those of MNR leaders. In the countryside, peasant and indigenous visions of justice clearly conflicted with MNR leaders' conservatism and distrust of Indians. In the cities and mines, the most visible early difference between the Paz administration and popular sectors concerned the specifics of the mine nationalization. While government officials emphatically promised to compensate the tin oligarchs, the COB demanded "nationalization of the mines without compensation."[77] The COB, and the miners specifically, also demanded meaningful worker participation in the management of the mines. The national university student organization echoed the demand for nationalization without compensation and under the "control and administration" of workers.[78] Many of the revolution's supporters in the cities and mines demanded the nationalization of transportation, public services, and sometimes even urban factories. The COB's 1952 draft program, denounced as "contrary to all nationalist sentiment" by leaders of the MNR right, included such demands and called for genuine control by workers in the nationalized industries.[79]

Popular pressures had crucial impacts on agrarian and mining policy. The peasant land occupations of 1952–1953—preceded by many decades of rural activism—helped to radicalize the MNR leadership's decidedly modest plans for reform. The August 1953 land reform decree and ensuing expropriations were a major concession to a militant peasantry that pushed MNR leaders much further than most of them wished to go.[80] The mine nationalization policy announced in October 1952 was a compromise between the MNR and COB positions, incorporating a limited form of workers' control but also maintaining the promise of compensation. Nationalization, however limited and flawed from the perspective of the left, might never have happened had it not been for the mobilization of workers and leftists in the mines and cities. The MNR, after all, had only publicly advocated nationalization in 1951, and many MNR core leaders remained ambivalent or even opposed it after taking power.[81] The nationalization decree was a compromise, but compromises by definition imply power on both sides.

In this same way, even the MNR's co-optation of more radical forces to its left reflects the weight of popular power. By October 1952 the party leadership had wrested control of the COB from the Trotskyists and subsequently used the COB and the semblance of cogovernment to suppress radical energies at the base level.[82] Through ideological appeals, material rewards, and repression of the Marxist left, the MNR succeeded in maintaining the allegiance of the majority of rank-and-file urban workers. Even after 1956, when MNR policy turned decisively to the right, most workers would remain electorally loyal to the MNR despite their growing disenchantment with government policies. Yet critical observers have often exaggerated the MNR's power. Guillermo Lora, for one, accuses the regime of co-opting the POR's political program.[83] But the co-optation process itself is a dialectical one, and the need for co-optation reveals the strength of the left as well as the government.

Moreover, even after the MNR's expulsion of Trotskyists from the COB, the COB retained more independence than Lora admits. Its 1954 program advanced a series of demands for nationalization and redistribution that went beyond government policy and rhetoric. It criticized the positions of Stalinists and Trotskyists alike but reaffirmed "the traditional strategic line of revolutionary Marxism." The document pledged to defend the MNR government but declared the COB "the motor force behind the National Revolution" that would "keep it from becoming corrupted, spoiled, or stopped; therefore, its support is critical or conditional."[84] Lora goes a bit too far when he asserts that the COB was "transformed into a docile instrument" and a mere "appendage of the petit-bourgeois government."[85]

The lasting impact of popular pressures on fiscal policy is often overlooked. Urban labor and the left advocated increased social spending in the form of consumer subsidies, social security, and higher expenditures on education and health care. Popular demands forced the MNR to maintain a relatively high level of social spending until 1956. Even after that momentous year and under the military dictatorships of the 1960s and 1970s, social spending levels would remain well above the level of the early 1940s.

There is usually assumed to be a trade-off between immediate consumption and reinvestment, since surplus wealth that is consumed cannot be plowed back into production.[86] But implicit in many worker statements is the argument that the two need not always be at odds, that redistribution could enhance growth and help build a more stable economy. Consumption was not the main factor depriving Bolivia of funds for reinvestment; much of the country's potential surplus was being sent abroad through the compensation agreement and debt service, and large amounts of land and other resources were being employed inefficiently or not at all. Moreover, the country's fledgling industries needed a consumer market. In the words of a statement by factory workers in 1963, only when workers are well paid "can they become the main consumers of the country's industrial production."[87] Consumption—one part of social revolution—was not inherently incompatible with reinvestment, or economic revolution, and in fact the two processes could be mutually reinforcing if pursued in the right way.[88]

Throughout the MNR period the party leadership's agenda would continue to clash with the more comprehensive visions of Bolivian workers and the left, who articulated more far-reaching proposals for both economic and social revolution. While MNR moderates after 1952 would have preferred to limit Bolivia's resource nationalism to the initial nationalization of the mines, Bolivians to their left insisted on a more robust conception of resource nationalism that entailed not just nationalizations in other sectors but additional policy measures to redistribute wealth and power and lay a basis for more stable long-term development.

In this contest of ideas and forces, the MNR moderates soon obtained the support of a powerful outside ally. Although their vision did not fully align with that of US officials, US intervention starting in 1953 would bolster the strength of the moderates vis-à-vis their leftist competitors.

The Bolivian Tinderbox and the US-MNR Pact

Prior to 1952, US leaders had been concerned with two related objectives in Bolivia: promoting private economic investment, preferably from US companies, and maintaining the flow of Bolivian resources, especially minerals but also oil, to the United States. Even before the revolution US officials and private business representatives worried that Bolivia might nationalize its tin industry.[89] Such actions would not only endanger US access to Bolivian tin but could provide a dangerous example for other countries. In 1951 a State Department official wrote that the US government "is engaged in trying to protect the interests of American investors in underdeveloped countries against the strong desire of those countries to expropriate and nationalize." Allowing nationalization in Bolivia, he contended, would make it "very difficult for us to protect the American owners of low cost mining properties in other countries."[90] With regard to Bolivia's state oil industry, the goal was denationalization. In 1950 US Ambassador Irving Florman wrote, "Since my arrival here, I have worked diligently on the project of throwing Bolivia's petroleum industry wide open to American private enterprise."[91]

US officials in Bolivia kept a close eye on opposition political movements in the 1940s. The initial presence of MNR figures in the Villarroel government triggered fierce protests from the State Department, which demanded their removal.[92] The increasing militancy of mine workers worried them, especially after 1946, the year of the Pulacayo Thesis and the last year of relative US tolerance for reformist democratic regimes across Latin America.[93] Post–World War II US officials were much less concerned with the threat of Soviet-style communism coming to Bolivia than with the resource nationalism and demands for redistribution that were gaining popularity among Bolivians. In this respect Bolivia reflected a continental trend. "Economic nationalism" and the demands for greater equality that often accompanied it were "the common denominator" all across Latin America, wrote State Department adviser Laurence Duggan in 1948. "Latin Americans are convinced that the first beneficiaries of the development of a country's resources should be the people of that country."[94] The rise of revolutionary nationalism in its economic, political, and social manifestations posed a profound threat to US objectives in the region.[95]

Given these concerns, the US response to the April 1952 revolution may seem paradoxical. Rather than seeking to undermine the MNR, the US government recognized it in June 1952 and the following year launched a large economic aid package for Bolivia. By June 1956 the United States had given the MNR roughly $60 million in economic aid, and by 1964 total aid would top $300 million, the highest per capita average in the world.[96] Since the US government has led or supported military intervention to overthrow left-leaning nationalist regimes in Guatemala, Cuba, Chile, Nicaragua, and elsewhere, its response to Bolivia at first glance seems to have been remarkably tolerant. Why did the Truman administration and its successors respond to the Bolivian Revolution with aid rather than force? One reason was that US officials correctly perceived the internal conflict within the MNR. They recognized that Paz, Siles Zuazo, Guevara, and the party's other core leaders shared their interest in limiting the revolution to economic modernization and suppressing demands for social revolution. The MNR moderates, for their part, were acutely aware of US perceptions and skillfully presented themselves as bulwarks against radicalism, denouncing and even jailing leftists.[97] The MNR's rhetorical posture stood in marked contrast to those of revolutionary regimes in Guatemala and Cuba, which were more openly defiant of US domination and made less effort to distance themselves from anticapitalist thought.[98]

On the economic policy front, MNR leaders appealed to elements in US government circles that recognized the need for limited reforms along the lines of CEPAL recommendations. By promoting economic development, they argued, the MNR state would silence radical demands and bring political stability to Bolivia.[99] They made clear that their interpretation of structuralism maintained a central place for US capital, issuing repeated promises "that the Bolivian government will welcome foreign capital to exploit its natural resources" and that it would give foreign companies "full guarantees against expropriation and discriminatory taxes." Bolivian Ambassador Víctor Andrade promised in August 1952 that Bolivia's strategic mineral resources "will always be available for continental defense and for US industry and civilization."[100] President Eisenhower's brother Milton traveled to Bolivia in 1953 and confirmed the picture offered by MNR officials, arguing that the United States should try to promote what he called a "peaceful revolution."[101] By early 1953 most State Department officials were convinced. One recommended aid in part "to keep this tinder box, which might set off a chain reaction in Latin America, from striking fire."[102] US aid began a few months later.

A second reason for the US decision was the lack of any alternative political force that Washington would have preferred over the MNR. Once in power the MNR greatly reduced the size of the army and tacitly permitted the growth of popular militias, eliminating one option that was available to the United States when it helped overthrow Jacobo Arbenz in Guatemala. There is no evidence that US diplomats ever seriously considered toppling the MNR. President Paz, in fact, openly emphasized the lack of alternatives to the MNR in conversations with US diplomats in late 1953, contrasting Bolivia with Iran, where the United States had just helped to overthrow the government of Mohammad Mossadegh.[103]

The US government thus decided that it could use economic aid to exert leverage on the MNR, strengthening the moderate elements within it. The written terms of the aid agreement stipulated that aid "may be terminated" at any time "if it is determined that because of changed conditions the continuation of the assistance is unnecessary or undesirable."[104] The first US condition was that the MNR compensate the Patiño, Aramayo, and Hochschild mining companies and their investors. In 1953 US officials publicly stated that a preliminary compensation agreement with Patiño would help "set the stage for US action" in the form of a long-term tin purchasing contract and potentially in direct US aid. MNR leaders followed suit with an agreement giving Patiño the rights to process a share of Bolivian tin exports at his smelter in the United Kingdom, and the tin contract and aid followed a few months later.[105] For the next five years US officials continuously insisted that the MNR take further steps toward compensating the former mine owners.[106] They were willing to countenance the nationalization itself but only if the mine oligarchs received compensation.

US officials demanded that this nationalization not lead to more attacks on private property. The prevention of further nationalizations and the promotion of foreign private investment remained central goals of US policy, as they had been before 1952. Assistant Secretary of State Henry Holland wrote in 1955 that the United States should push the MNR "to take actions and follow policies which we consider desirable," most importantly measures to develop an "economy based on private enterprise and improve the atmosphere for private foreign capital." Among the steps he recommended the MNR take to attract foreign investors was a new "Investment Guaranty Agreement" to protect future investors against nationalization. He noted that Bolivia's oil industry offered promising "prospects" for investors. The MNR's "obligations," according to Holland, included "an oil law which will afford [a] sound and attractive basis for the U.S. companies to come into the country."[107] Holland and his colleagues did more than just encourage the MNR; they forbade the use of aid to assist nationalized industries, namely tin and oil, for the duration of the decade and in 1955 worked alongside allies in the MNR government to initiate the reprivatization of the oil industry.[108]

US policies usually did not derive from a strong commitment to particular corporations. North American investments in Bolivia as of 1950 were miniscule compared to those in other Latin American countries. US stockholders did hold substantial shares in Patiño, but their economic interests were much less important than two broader aims: preventing the rise of state enterprises that could compete with US companies and preventing the example of Bolivian nationalization from inspiring similar actions in other countries.[109] One 1953 memo warned that a successful nationalized tin industry might "tempt other countries to follow their example."[110] According to US Ambassador Edward Sparks, his government was initially hesitant to aid the MNR in part because officials "did not wish to make funds available which might encourage further expropriation abroad."[111]

In relation to the oil industry, officials were also deeply concerned about precedent. In 1955 State Department official Herbert Prochnow justified his opposition to a loan to YPFB on two grounds: he feared the prospect of "government oil companies in direct competition with private American oil companies" and warned that "if the U.S. Government should show a willingness to support such government operations on a large scale, there would be greater danger of nationalization of the oil industry in various countries of the world."[112] Similar fears had shaped the US response to the Bolivian and Mexican oil nationalizations of 1937–1938 and influenced its position toward the Bolivian mining industry in the 1950s and 1960s.[113] Protecting individual corporations was less important than preserving the system of domination. US policy makers certainly acted on behalf of US corporate interests, but only rarely did particular corporations directly steer policy.

US officials understood that neither Moscow nor the MNR leadership was responsible for the problems in Bolivia. Popular nationalism and demands for socioeconomic change, products of Bolivian social conditions and political culture, were the key threats. Progressive nationalists, not Marxists, were the dominant force in the country's cities and mines. Marxists were a significant minority in many places, but the most visible ones by 1952 were Trotskyists who certainly did not take orders from Stalin's Soviet Union. In the countryside, too, the threat was not foreign subversion but rather "campesinos' present expectations and power."[114] To the extent that MNR leaders promoted any revolutionary change at all, it was largely in reaction to pressures emanating from the grassroots.

US and Bolivian officials understood that US aid was intended to help the MNR moderates bring these popular forces under control. The conditions attached to US aid were thus more than just an imperialist imposition. The agenda of the US government roughly coincided with the existing agenda of MNR core leaders, at least insofar as both sought to contain the radical impulses of the revolution's rank and file. The modest structuralist goals of the MNR moderates, such as their desire for diversification, were readily jettisoned or compromised under pressure.

After 1955 the balance of power would shift in the moderates' favor. Yet their victory would prove illusory in two ways. First, the moderates' hostility to social revolution and their commitment to retaining US favor would end up jeopardizing even their own more limited goal of economic revolution. Second, despite the rightward lurch in economic and social policies after 1955, the radical forces would not be entirely suppressed. Their displeasure with the government would reach a fever pitch by the early 1960s, spelling doom for the MNR.

The frustration of the economic and social revolutions should not obscure the very real changes in Bolivia in the early years of the revolution. The constraints on US officials are reflected in the decision to aid rather than attack the MNR and to accept the mine nationalizations, which they reluctantly admitted were almost universally supported within Bolivia.[115] Land expropriations likewise proceeded despite US reticence. These measures alongside MNR social spending produced a marked reduction in income inequality by 1956.[116] Such policy changes reflect the extent to which MNR officials, too, were subject to popular pressures. Many party moderates had envisioned a more tempered set of reforms, but in crafting the final policies they were repeatedly forced to compromise with radical elements.

CHAPTER 3

The Political Economy of Containment: Privatization, Austerity, and the MNR's Shift to the Right, 1955–1964

After 1956 the simmering tensions within the MNR erupted into a boil, as the loose spending and monetary policies that had contained them ran up against hyperinflation, economic underdevelopment, and US pressure. The mid-1950s marked the start of a clear rightward shift in the MNR's economic policy. The conservative tendencies within the party leadership gained strength, bolstered by US intervention and MNR leaders' own success in pitting the urban middle class, peasantry, and certain working-class sectors against militant workers and the left. By the time of the November 1964 military coup that overthrew President Paz, the government's economic policy had already moved decisively to the right.

Three major economic reforms were crucial to this process: a 1955 oil privatization decree, a 1956 monetary stabilization and austerity plan, and the Triangular Plan to overhaul the mining industry in the 1960s. Collectively, these three reforms sought to roll back resource nationalism in the mining and hydrocarbons sectors as well as the progressive aspects of the government's fiscal and monetary policies. The latter two plans also aimed to reduce the political power of the Bolivian labor force, particularly the miners' unions.

First, the 1955 oil code reform reopened most of Bolivia's territory to private oil companies, to whom it offered generous enticements. This reform plus the "stabilization" plan a year later further weakened the Bolivian state oil enterprise, YPFB, which since 1952 had performed quite well. The stabilization plan, crafted by US banker and corporate lawyer George Jackson Eder—thus often called the "Eder Plan"—attacked the country's hyperinflation in standard monetarist fashion by slashing government spending and establishing a single, devalued exchange rate for the currency. In so doing, Eder sought to reduce the power of the "privileged" mine workers, restore "free rein to private enterprise," and "purge" the government of elements sympathetic to resource nationalism, socialism, structuralism, and Keynesianism—what he called the "forces of darkness."[1] The Triangular Plan was a third key episode in this battle. Billed by the United States, West Germany, and the Inter-American Development Bank as a generous loan program to "rehabilitate" Bolivian tin mines, the plan gave its architects a chance to discipline Bolivian workers, further privatize the Bolivian economy, and test the usefulness of conditional economic aid in containing resource nationalism and popular militancy. Like Eder's austerity plan, the Triangular Plan accelerated the estrangement of the MNR from the miners.

These three plans had profound significance for Bolivia and the broader hemisphere. They arrested Bolivia's revolutionary momentum in two ways, by overhauling policy itself and by accelerating political cleavages. The conflict had crucial hemispheric implications from the viewpoint of US officials who considered the battle of economic ideas just as important as the specific policy changes embodied in the three plans. Looking beyond the facile US rhetoric of anticommunism to the conflicting economic ideas circulating in the country can allow for a deeper understanding of the Bolivian Revolution, postwar Latin American nationalism, and US policy in the region.

The implementation of the plans highlights the role of power relations in the shaping of economic policy. Economic ideas are inseparable from ideology and material interests, which tend to shape both the diagnosis of problems and the solutions offered. Which ideas are adopted depends on the balance of power in a society. The 1955 oil code promoted privatization despite US and Bolivian officials' own admissions that YPFB was an efficient state enterprise. The austerity plan singled out social spending as the primary cause of inflation and, by reorienting fiscal policy to prioritize payment on Bolivia's foreign debt and compensation to the deposed tin oligarchy, further damaged the country's fiscal health. Similarly, the effort to "rehabilitate the mines" targeted the mine workers themselves as the main source of COMIBOL's problems. The designers of the stabilization and Triangular plans sought to promote the reprivatization of the country's nationalized mines, arguing that private enterprise was inherently more efficient than state enterprise. In both cases the architects ignored a plethora of additional factors underlying Bolivia's fiscal and monetary troubles: its extreme dependence on mineral exports, the long-term de-capitalization of the mines, declining ore grades and world tin prices, high foreign debt and indemnification payments, the MNR's siphoning of funds from COMIBOL, Bolivia's shortage of domestic food production, and the increase in consumption as a result of the 1953 agrarian reform. For ideological and political reasons, these factors—and the critics who tried to call attention to them—received little attention. Power and ideology, far more than technical concerns about fiscal balance or economic efficiency, shaped the oil code and the stabilization and Triangular plans.[2] US power was of course fundamental to this process, but MNR leaders likewise embraced the three reforms for their own reasons.

A Most Liberal Invitation to Foreign Oil Companies

From the 1920s onward, no Latin American commodity was more important to US policy makers than oil, and none was more central in their fight against resource nationalism. Mexico's 1917 Constitution was the first major challenge to US and European control over the region's resources. Article 27 established the state's rights to the subsoil and thus posed a serious potential threat to foreign oil companies. In the 1920s the US government was able to obtain assurances from the Mexican government that protected US oil companies, but only temporarily; in 1938 the Cárdenas administration expropriated foreign oil holdings and established a state oil enterprise. In the 1920s and 1930s Argentina, Bolivia, Brazil, Chile, Colombia, and Uruguay began experimenting with economic nationalist policies that, to varying degrees, challenged foreign control over oil resources.[3]

While not as cataclysmic as the 1938 Mexican nationalization, the Bolivian government's expropriation of Standard Oil a year before was deeply vexing for US officials. The nationalization and establishment of a state oil company, YPFB, had crucial implications for Bolivia's incipient oil industry as well as US corporations' access to Bolivian—and perhaps other countries'—oil. Although the strength of Bolivian nationalism and the start of World War II prevented the Roosevelt administration from punishing Bolivia too severely, it conditioned all subsequent economic aid on compensation to Standard and Bolivian encouragement of private investment in oil exploitation.[4] This goal continued to figure centrally in the US diplomatic mission in Bolivia in the years prior to 1952, as evidenced by Ambassador Irving Florman's 1950 report on opening Bolivia's oil sector to US companies.[5] In early 1951 the Bolivian government began negotiations with US companies eager to access Bolivian oil, and officials like Florman considered themselves partners in the companies' effort.[6]

Florman's goal suffered a setback with the revolution. Although in September 1952 the new government signed a contract with Texas oil tycoon Glenn McCarthy—the first private contract since the 1937 nationalization—it signed no further contracts for four more years. Instead, it more than tripled annual investment in YPFB, notably expanding exploration, well-drilling, and the workforce.[7] The investment paid off. After just two years the enterprise was supplying nearly the entire domestic market—saving tens of millions of dollars in import costs—and exporting a modest surplus.

By 1955 production of crude oil had increased fivefold over the 1952 level, due largely to rising production at the Camiri oil field in the southern Santa Cruz department. Most of the crude was being refined at one of five Bolivian refineries into gasoline, kerosene, diesel, or fuel oil.[8] Although total production levels remained small compared to larger oil-producing nations, the industry's quick growth was impressive and boded well for Bolivia's diversification drive. CEPAL praised YPFB's increase in production and noted improvements in "refining and transport within the country" and "its organization and its technical personnel."[9] Even State Department officials privately acknowledged YPFB's "remarkable growth" after the revolution, conceding that the state enterprise had "a reputation for efficiency." YPFB's progress was particularly impressive given its amortization and interest obligations after the Standard nationalization, which limited what it could reinvest in production.[10]

Yet these favorable assessments did not make US officials reconsider their goal of promoting private oil investment. Progress toward that goal came in October 1955 when President Paz decreed a new petroleum code—rubber-stamped by Bolivia's congress a year later—that offered highly attractive opportunities for foreign oil companies. The code divided the country into four major zones, reserving three for private concessions and one for YPFB (figure 3.1). Private companies were offered low taxation rates—an 11 percent royalty and 30 percent profits tax—and concession rights for forty years.[11] Although YPFB's designated zone included key known oil reserves, it represented only

Figure 3.1. Zones created by the 1955 oil code. The reform reserved three major zones for exploitation by private companies (with zone 3 subdivided into three), plus a zone in the southeast for YPFB. Map by the author, based on one in *La Nación*, October 27, 1955.

11 percent of the national territory. One provision even allowed the Bolivian president to rent out territory in YPFB's own zone to private concessionaires.[12] James Siekmeier observes that "the new Code was one of the most generous in all of Latin America" for private oil companies.[13] Not surprisingly, US oil companies eagerly anticipated the decree and met frequently with State Department officials to discuss it.[14] Reflecting the high priority placed on passage of the new law, US officials hinted that the MNR's failure to implement the code might jeopardize future US aid.[15]

Still, MNR officials played a more important part in the oil reform than most observers have realized.[16] US corporate lawyer Wortham Davenport, a man with "very high prestige in the oil industry," according to Ambassador Edward Sparks, worked with Bolivian government personnel to design the new code. While precise authorship is unclear,[17] MNR officials' basic position was not; prior MNR documents stressed their desire for an "open-door" oil policy.[18] They did not view

YPFB as a replacement for private capital. Even many top officials in YPFB and the Ministry of Mines and Petroleum favored liberalization, arguing that the state oil company and private investment should be complementary.[19] In private discussion with US officials, President Paz approvingly characterized the code as "a most liberally contrived invitation to the foreign oil industry" and insisted "that whatever might stand in the way of such an accomplishment, provided it could be done rationally, should be swept aside."[20] The Bolivian ambassador to Washington, Víctor Andrade, courted US oil executives over lunch in New York. Before domestic audiences Paz and other MNR leaders used the advice of foreign experts to bolster their own arguments for a partial privatization of the oil industry.[21] Although the US government put heavy pressure on the Paz administration to pass the new oil code, it encountered little resistance from Bolivian leaders.

Bolivian officials handled the task of selling the new legislation to the public. Their primary justification was, in Paz's words, "the state's inability to provide [YPFB] with the necessary capital." Paz framed the reform as a concession to reality, given "that Bolivia lacks capital as a result of its long semicolonial exploitation."[22] However, his government also portrayed it as beneficial to YPFB itself. A statement from the presidential palace claimed the reform would "facilitate operations, permitting [YPFB] to extend its range of action." The official MNR paper, La Nación, called it a "legislative masterpiece" that "will safeguard Bolivian sovereignty and interests." Even Mario Torres, the left-leaning minister of mines and petroleum, claimed that the law "both contains the necessary guarantees for the investor and ensures the defense of national interests."[23]

As it turned out, the MNR faced little immediate opposition to the code. Until 1958 the law did not elicit much popular reaction, due partly to the opaque nature of the design process and scant attention from the press. The code came in the form of a presidential decree that was then approved without debate by the legislature. Nationalist politician Amado Canelas later wrote "that many [cabinet] Ministers signed the Decree without really knowing if it was good or bad, nationalist or 'entreguista' [a sell-out to foreign interests]."[24] Also perhaps significant was the MNR's relative ability to placate labor prior to the implementation of the stabilization plan. Only several years later, with workers bearing the brunt of austerity while foreign oil companies seemed poised to profit, would the code become a deeply contentious issue.

Oil investors rushed to Bolivia after 1955. Within two years nineteen foreign companies—eighteen US companies plus the British giant Shell—had obtained concessions.[25] The Bolivian Gulf Oil Company, of which Gulf owned 80 percent, received a contract for 2 million hectares in zones 1 and 2 plus another 1.5 million hectares in YPFB's designated zone. Shell got nearly 2 million hectares. Even some US officials quietly acknowledged the lopsided nature of the concessions. For example, a no-bid contract went to Tennessee Gas in 1957 for an "area [that] should have been worth much more than the Bolivian Government obtained for it, i.e., merely an advance on royalties."[26] Yet despite the generous concessions, many companies invested little money in exploration and drilling, and only a handful were producing oil or gas a decade later.[27]

The code had many detrimental effects on YPFB itself. After another impressive year in 1957, its production levels steadily declined. By 1962 YPFB was no longer able to meet domestic consumption needs.[28] The exhaustion of existing wells played some role, but the code also constrained YPFB's ability to develop new reserves. CEPAL argued that "under the 1955 Petroleum Code the areas with the highest production potential were thrown open to foreign companies, whereas YPFB was in effect restricted to working its traditional oilfields," some of which were nearing exhaustion. YPFB's designated zone was rapidly becoming "a virtually unproductive area." Moreover, some of the productive spots within the YPFB zone like the Madrejones oil field were leased to US companies, which would become a source of protest by 1958.[29] The 1956 austerity plan further hurt YPFB by reducing its budget and cutting in half its foreign exchange receipts. Average annual investment in YPFB was 50 percent less in 1962–1965 compared to the previous decade.[30] While the oil code and austerity plan were not wholly responsible for YPFB's woes, they were certainly important contributors.

The 1955 oil code was the first major attempt after 1952 to roll back resource nationalism and promote privatization in a key sector of the economy. YPFB may have been remarkably efficient from a technical perspective, but US policy makers viewed it with hostility, given their goals of promoting US companies' access to Bolivian oil and protecting the privileged US economic and geopolitical position throughout Latin America. In 1958 the US ambassador, Philip Bonsal, wrote to a superior that the "problem of maintaining the position of American oil companies in Bolivia and in other parts of South America is, as you are undoubtedly more aware than I am, one of the most important with which we are faced."[31]

Purging the Forces of Darkness

As the ink on the oil code decree was drying, Bolivian inflation was spinning out of control. Food prices in La Paz had skyrocketed, and the cost of living index was twenty-two times higher in 1956 than it had been four years earlier. Since 1952 the cost of living in urban La Paz had risen by almost 150 percent a year.[32] By the middle of the decade even most on the Bolivian left agreed on the need for some program of monetary stabilization.

The precise content and direction of that program were far more controversial, however. The controversy revolved around three issues: the question of whether to eliminate inflation or merely bring it under control; disagreements over the causes of the inflation; and the struggle over who would bear the costs of stabilization. On the first question, leftist intellectuals like Guillermo Lora argued in favor of a controlled inflation, writing that "in all revolutionary periods inflation has become a necessity" in order to achieve economic growth and redistribution.[33] This position was, and remains, popular among a broad range of Keynesian, structuralist, and socialist economists around the world.

Regarding the causes of the inflation, many Bolivian observers and CEPAL economists argued that it derived not only from MNR government spending but also from prerevolutionary government policies and structural characteristics of the economy. The inflationary trend dated back to the high deficits following the Chaco War. Heavy external debt obligations—largely composed of interest—amounted to more than half of government revenue in the years prior to 1952.[34] In a 1955 letter to the US State Department the Bolivian Foreign Ministry cited declining ore grades, lack of capital, and old equipment in the mines among its list of "internal and external" causes of inflation. CEPAL argued that inflation "was attributable in no small measure to Bolivia's economic and institutional backwardness," emphasizing the long-term decline of tin yields and world prices dating back to the 1920s, the failure of the tin barons to invest in exploration and technology, and the "under-developed state of its economy" more generally. CEPAL noted that the dismal state of Bolivian agriculture, owing primarily to the feudal legacies of the pre-1953 era, was also to blame. In 1957 Bolivia remained reliant on agricultural imports, which comprised around 45 percent of the country's total in the mid-1950s, even though Bolivian land was capable of producing most of the imported products. These factors exacerbated inflation by limiting production and the availability of foreign exchange.[35]

CEPAL and others also pointed to the more proximate causes of inflation. Some of the inflation derived from the agrarian reform, the nationalization of mines, and the MNR's accommodationist stance toward foreign interests. The Bolivian government noted that the increase in consumer demand resulting from land reform had contributed to inflation. The nationalization had led to a substantial brain drain of skilled labor and posed the daunting administrative challenge of creating a unified state mining entity out of many disparate private mines. Less inevitable, perhaps, was the loss of millions of dollars in indemnification payments to the tin barons, which would cost the country $22 million by 1961. The MNR itself bore some of the responsibility for inflation, CEPAL argued. Its loose monetary policies and dramatic increase of social spending, fueled by popular demands for employment and better wages and benefits, had contributed to the problem, and the system of multiple exchange rates had encouraged speculation that helped fuel inflation. The large expansion of the mining workforce, the decline in mining productivity since 1952, and what CEPAL deemed the often unreasonable demands of labor were also significant.[36]

While CEPAL and many Bolivian observers focused on the structural features of the economy and enumerated multiple causes for inflation, the US government and MNR conservatives focused almost exclusively on social spending and the wages and benefits of the mine workers. The latter groups' analysis carried the most weight, given the MNR's extreme reliance on the United States; in the 1950s US aid covered up to one-third of the national budget, and the United States was also the main export destination.[37] Not surprisingly, the design of the anti-inflationary program reflected the US-favored diagnosis of Bolivian inflation.

In mid-1956 President Paz asked George Jackson Eder to serve as executive director of the National Monetary Stabilization Council, "an invitation" that Eder later admitted was "extended virtually under duress and with repeated hints of the curtailment of U.S. aid."[38] These hints did not stop until after the stabilization plan had been enacted; throughout 1956 and early 1957 Eder, Assistant Secretary of State Henry Holland, and others repeatedly told MNR officials that US aid might cease if Bolivia did not carry out the program in full. At one point during the plan's implementation, when Juan Lechín questioned the haste with which Eder and the council were making decisions, Eder warned him that if Bolivia "wanted to count on the continuation of U.S. aid, it would have to take another path."[39] The $25 million stabilization fund provided by the International Monetary Fund (IMF) and the International Cooperation Administration (the predecessor of the US Agency for International Development) provided an added incentive for MNR leaders to comply. In Eder's words the fund was "the sugarplum for which they were willing to swallow the disagreeable purge prescribed as a cure."[40]

That cure involved a "Fifty-Step Plan" drafted by Eder and based loosely on US Treasury and State Department guidelines.[41] Treasury officials conveyed their desire to see four major changes in particular: a single exchange rate for the boliviano, a balanced federal budget, compensation to the former mine owners, and resumption of payment on Bolivia's foreign debt.[42] The plan was partly based on monetarist doctrine, which emphasized the need for low government spending and a fixed rate of increase in the money supply. Eder's plan sought to ensure that "the government refrains from borrowing and spending more than its income." While these objectives reflected the larger US agenda in Latin America, the goals of compensation and debt repayment were somewhat more specific to Bolivia's situation. The Fifty-Step Plan explicitly required the MNR to reach "satisfactory" agreements with the previous owners of nationalized properties and foreign creditors.[43]

The long-standing State Department goal of combating resource nationalism and state enterprise was also fundamental to Eder's plan, which was intended "to establish a favorable climate for investment."[44] In addition to mandating the "cessation of the expansion of government into fields that can be filled by private initiative," it allowed the Bolivian president "to transfer to private investors—preferably Bolivian—all government public utility (including transportation and communication), industrial, and business enterprises." Not just state ownership but indeed any state infringement on the prerogatives of capital was deemed unacceptable. In a rebuke to structuralists, Marxists, and others who asserted the need for state policies to stimulate development or redistribute wealth, Eder insisted that "poverty can only be alleviated by hard work, thrift, and investment, by greater productivity and increased abundance for all to share." Bolivia could only be saved by "a return to a free market economy."[45]

Central to Eder's cure was its rapid implementation. He insisted from the start that "whatever had to be done must be done instantly." Given the previous four years of fiscal "profligacy" and the current inflationary crisis, "there had to be a complete and instantaneous break with the past."[46] The first stabilization measures, which included the elimination of price controls, a freeze on wages after a one-time compensatory raise, and the establishment of a single exchange rate that would fluctuate with the market, took effect on December 16, 1956, after little publicity. Haste was an asset, as "a gradual approach . . . simply would not have worked"; in fact, the rapid deflationary and liberalizing measures would have "an almost anaesthetic effect" on the population.[47]

One reason for Eder's insistence on rapid implementation was that he correctly anticipated resistance to the plan. Workers' criticisms usually agreed on the need for monetary stabilization but took issue with the plan's content, pointing out that the stabilization measures consciously put most of the burden on workers and unfairly singled out social spending and wages as the main causes of inflation. At COB meetings in late December 1956, delegates complained that the compensatory wage increases in the plan "did not equal the rise in prices of [previously] subsidized goods." The factory worker delegate said, "The remedy has turned out to be worse than the sickness."[48] The plan hit the miners especially hard since it targeted the state subsidies to the *pulperías*, the company stores where miners and their families obtained most of their basic goods.[49] Popular resistance to the stabilization plan would ebb and flow throughout 1957 and intensify significantly thereafter.

Eder himself acknowledged this resistance among the general population. As a public relations move he proposed a public comment period to allow feedback on the stabilization program, but he noted that "it proved an advantage that the majority of the population in Bolivia were illiterates." Eder counseled future stabilizers to avoid paying much attention to public opinion. Instead, they must remember that "stabilization is not a popularity contest" but a prescription designed by money doctors who know what is best. The profligate must have the "moral revolution" forced upon them, since they were not going to convert on their own. He lamented that "it would be unrealistic" to expect total "immunity from public opinion" but hoped that tight control over the restructuring process coupled with skillful PR work could marginalize any resistance.[50]

Such advice reflected Eder's more general disdain for popular opinion. Since "the passions of the mob were swayed from day to day in one direction or the other," any reliance on public input would be unwise. The money doctor was an apolitical, technocratic expert whose actions should remain insulated from popular pressures.[51] Eder's rhetoric of "moral revolution" suggests that he viewed his mission in quasi-religious terms. He equated inflation-driven growth and redistribution with sin and depravity and embraced the role of the stern inquisitor who would flush out wicked impulses and prevent any relapse among the sinners.

Racism reinforced Eder's elitism and moral self-righteousness. What he described as the "Latin American psychology" was an even greater problem in Bolivia given the country's majority indigenous population. Bolivia's Indians were "inclined to loaf" and would "work only under the stress of hunger." They tended to squander their money on "*fiestas*, alcohol, and coca" or alternatively "to hoard" it and thus hurt the economy. Eder was optimistic that these traits were not "ineradicable characteristics," but he cautioned against endowing Indians or the popular sectors in general with any real power given their state at the time.[52] The contempt for common Bolivians was echoed in State Department correspondence that blamed Bolivian poverty partly on race and culture. One 1959 memo commented that underdevelopment was "understandable when it is remembered that about 70% of the Bolivian population is Indian, about 25% half-breed, and only 5% white."[53] This discourse reinforced claims that protest was irrational. US officials blamed campesino demands on "government-paid propagandists" and "leftist agitators" who riled up the peasantry with "demagogic rantings" about land reform. One official even scoffed at the idea that there was any "austerity" or "real sacrifice" in Bolivia.[54]

Eder took charge within the stabilization council itself, and with the backing of the US Embassy and the new President, Hernán Siles Zuazo, exercised almost complete control over most aspects of the stabilization process. When the council's members were being chosen in summer 1956, Eder helped prevent Communists, Trotskyists, and leaders of the COB other than Juan Lechín from being selected. He derided labor as a "factional interest." Eder and the US embassy specifically rejected at least two candidates with unsuitable "ideological backgrounds," one of whom had "an intemperate anti-American bias," according to Eder. He even sought to marginalize the UN mission that was present in Bolivia at the time. UN advisers, he claimed, were "to a large extent socialistically inclined" and were "engaged in socialist or Marxist indoctrination throughout the world."[55] Eder maintained control over all specific policy steps, writing the Fifty-Step Plan himself and overseeing its implementation. He refused all calls for amendments that would reduce the burden on workers, publicly resisting "any modification to the plan."[56]

The Eder Plan did stop inflation, but it had other goals as well. Behind the discursive veneer of medical terminology and theological metaphors lay the less-advertised objectives of rolling back resource nationalism and restoring labor discipline, especially in the tin mines where "anarchy" had erupted after the 1952 nationalization. Eder deeply resented the "privileged position" of the mine workers and blamed them for holding back the economy, suggesting that their wages be limited to $1 per day. He insisted on the need to eliminate "the current burdensome labor legislation" that the MNR and prior governments had implemented. Wage freezes were a central condition—a "solemn moral obligation"—that was required of the MNR for continued US funding.[57] More broadly the plan took aim at Bolivia's "exaggerated social security structure." Reducing employer and government contributions to the National Social Security Fund was a top priority.[58]

The stabilization plan was thus much more than a series of technical measures meant to restore monetary stability; it was an effort to restructure the country's entire social and economic agenda. And as Eder conveyed in his memoir, he saw his one-year stint in Bolivia as part of an ideological battle over the proper route that Third World countries should follow to develop their economies. He understood his work as an effort to refute Keynesians, structuralists, Marxists, and resource nationalists—in short, all who argued the need for strong state policy to combat underdevelopment and inequality.[59] Just prior to CEPAL's 1957 conference in Bolivia, Eder privately expressed his fear that CEPAL head economist Raúl Prebisch would "bring about a consensus that Bolivia's economic improvement can only be achieved by further intervention and expansion of Government activities in business, industry and every field of the economy."[60] Purging such attitudes, Eder emphasized, was just as important as changing policy.

He rebuked even the mild redistributive inclinations evident among MNR moderates as well as the notion that Bolivia's underdevelopment resulted in any way from structural obstacles. During his time working with MNR officials, Eder saw his major psychological task as being to "convince them that they alone were to blame for Bolivia's present troubles."[61] Eder's critiques of the MNR leadership were overly harsh; Presidents Paz and Siles Zuazo were sympathetic to Eder's basic objectives, and it was mutually understood that foreign advisers like Eder and the IMF would serve as domestic scapegoats in order for MNR leaders to impose unpopular policies.[62] Yet Eder demanded a full renunciation of anything resembling structuralist or Keynesian economics and so criticized even the MNR moderates.

The attitudes of the general population were even more worrisome. The famous 1946 Thesis of Pulacayo approved by the miners union was a major target of Eder's ire for its Trotskyist platform, especially its promotion of "the revolution of the workers" and its attacks on "the system of private property" and "Yankee imperialism."[63] Since then, workers and peasants had become increasingly radicalized by the promises of the revolution and had come to expect a genuine redistribution of wealth, land, and political power. Within the MNR as well as among the population, the break with the past that Eder envisioned included not just policy but also morals, attitudes, and expectations.

An extensive informational campaign was launched to accomplish this goal. Eder personally drafted a number of public statements for President Siles to help justify the economic cure to the public.[64] In this effort Eder also enjoyed the full-time support of the US Information Service (USIS), an agency charged with "promoting popular acceptance of private capital investment" in Bolivia through wide-ranging cultural and educational campaigns. For a time the agency was devoted entirely to "popularizing stabilization" through leafleting, planting stories in Bolivian news media, and using other propaganda tactics.[65] Bolivian leaders and journalists played key roles in the propaganda effort; Siles Zuazo waged a vigorous campaign of his own, resorting to a hunger strike at one point to counter worker resistance. Meanwhile, the pro-government press constantly implied that the plan enjoyed near-unanimous backing among the population. Upon leaving Bolivia Eder would publicly "thank the national press for its effective informational efforts."[66]

Changing Bolivians' minds was a difficult task, though, and the success of the propaganda effort was decidedly limited. USIS poll results, the private observations of State Department officials, and Eder's own insistence on the need to insulate policy from public pressures all attest to Bolivians' disdain for austerity. A USIS poll in late 1957 found that about half of La Paz workers felt they had been personally hurt by the Eder Plan. In mid-1958, Assistant Secretary of State Roy Rubottom noted, "It is not surprising that resistance is growing to unpopular measures which the Government has no real alternative but to impose."[67] By 1959, many of the labor unions that initially were persuaded to support the plan had withdrawn their support as the cost of living continued to increase.[68] The post-1956 trend toward remilitarization of the country suggests that the Eder Plan was not nearly as popular as US and MNR officials publicly claimed. The US "public safety" program of military and police aid in the late 1950s was largely intended "to ensure success to the economic stabilization plan." The tenfold increase in US military aid to Bolivia from 1961 to 1964 would be a further hint of the plan's unpopularity.[69]

If the Eder Plan failed to change public attitudes, it did have major impacts on policy. Its consequences for economic growth and diversification were devastating. Fiscal austerity and the end to subsidized exchange rates constrained economic growth by further limiting the MNR's ability to finance economic development projects, while the rise in interest rates deterred domestic private investment. Manufacturing production dropped 30 percent during the first year. In 1961 Bolivian Labor Minister Alfredo Franco Guachalla charged that "the stabilization plan has put Bolivian industry at serious risk of disappearing." Two years later the Labor Ministry reported that more than half of all industrial operations had gone under since the enactment of the stabilization plan. A 1967 CEPAL report noted that industrial production had grown little in the previous decade, having "suffered a severe setback" as a result of the plan, though it picked up somewhat in the early 1960s. CEPAL pointed out that the plan had reduced the budget for the state oil company, contributing to a marked decline in state oil production after 1956. After a few years even US State Department sources were privately noting that austerity had meant "the deferment of many development projects."[70]

The plan also had marked effects on income distribution. By targeting the supposed privileges of workers as the primary problem and prioritizing debt service and compensation to the tin barons, it contributed to rising inequality in the late 1950s and early 1960s.[71] In turn, austerity and regressive redistribution helped catalyze major political realignments, including the estrangement of miners from the MNR and from other popular sectors and, for several years after 1956, a growing divide within urban labor.

By the late 1950s US officials in Bolivia were congratulating themselves on the apparent success of their efforts. Following the implementation of the Eder Plan they noted with satisfaction that "Bolivian Government expenditures have been cut back sharply" and inflation halted. Just as important, "the power and influence of left wing extremists has been weakened, and a program has been embarked upon, slowly and to a large extent secretly, to redress the balance of physical force in the country in favor of the moderate elements."[72]

Restoring Discipline in the Mines

Events soon rendered these appraisals overly optimistic. By 1960 the state mining corporation, COMIBOL, faced a crisis. After turning modest profits in the middle years of the decade, it lost more than $29 million in 1958–1960, making for a net loss of $16 million since its creation in 1952.[73] The corporation's bleak outlook in turn threatened the entire economy, which, despite the early progress of YPFB, still relied on minerals for virtually all its export earnings.[74] Moreover, the Eder Plan reduced spending for economic development and disproportionately hurt the mine workers, further jeopardizing the government's legitimacy among key sectors and producing a serious political crisis in addition to the economic one. The collapse of the government of Paz Estenssoro, now in his second term (1960–1964), once again became a real possibility. US officials knew that COMIBOL's survival was crucial for Paz's political survival and feared "that a successor government would most probably be of the extreme left." Preventing Paz's overthrow therefore acquired the same urgency as in 1952–1953, even if doing so would require "extraordinary financial assistance" from the United States.[75]

Two geopolitical developments around this time heightened US officials' sense of emergency. First, the Cuban Revolution of January 1959, and its radicalization over the next two years, underscored the danger of independent revolutionary nationalism. What one Kennedy official called "the spread of the Castro idea of taking matters into one's own hand[s]" deeply worried US officials, who feared the loss of control over countries they considered to be in the United States' backyard.[76]

US officials in Bolivia, as elsewhere, noted with alarm the support for the Cuban Revolution among ordinary Bolivians and expressed concern over pro-Cuba public marches. By 1961 they routinely warned of "Castro-Communist subversion" in Bolivia, with the phrase becoming a blanket term for all sentiment to the left of MNR government policy.[77]

Second, in 1960 the possibility of Soviet economic aid to the MNR resurfaced. Soviet leader Nikita Khrushchev publicly offered to finance the construction of a tin smelter in Bolivia so that Bolivian tin could be refined domestically, and the offer received wide publicity and support in the country.[78] In response, US Assistant Secretary of State Thomas Mann wrote a series of lengthy memos in November 1960 about "the danger of losing Bolivia." The absence of US action, he said, could result in "Soviet penetration and control of Bolivia's mining industry." A literal Soviet takeover was of course highly unlikely; Mann's main fear was that Soviet aid "could conceivably . . . put COMIBOL on its feet . . . and supplant U.S. failure with Communist success," with "staggering" consequences for US control elsewhere in Latin America.[79] Since 1952 a central US goal in Bolivia had been to avoid "actions or results which would make nationalization attractive" and "tempt other countries to follow their example."[80]

These factors helped convince US planners of the need to aid COMIBOL, retreating from the long-standing policy of prohibiting the use of aid by state-owned enterprises. In March 1961 the US and West German governments joined the Inter-American Development Bank in a partnership that would end up delivering $62 million in aid to COMIBOL over the next decade.[81] The stated purpose of the Triangular Plan was the "rehabilitation and recovery" of the state-owned mines. Bolivian politicians' descriptions of the program promised "the capitalization of COMIBOL" and a range of technical improvements that would increase efficiency and enhance Bolivia's competitiveness in international minerals markets.[82]

US motives were first and foremost political, though. Simply stabilizing the Paz government and preventing leftist political elements from achieving power were the immediate goals. But the plan also provided a chance to discipline unruly mine workers and erode state control over the nationalized mining industry. Internal US discussions reveal a remarkably single-minded emphasis on the miners themselves as the source of COMIBOL's problems. One of the chief foreign advisers appointed to oversee the Triangular Plan's implementation, Victor

Bjorkman, wrote that "the whole cause of failure can be laid to failure [*sic*] of management of COMIBOL to win the right to manage. . . . The workers, through the medium of the Syndicate, refuse to allow the rational and economic use of materials and equipment." A 1960 State Department memo offered the same diagnosis, arguing that "the Bolivian Government's problem is essentially political; namely, how to force the extreme left to accept drastic cutbacks in advantages which the Bolivian laboring classes have come to enjoy at the expense of all other sectors in the economy."[83]

Bolivian officials made similar arguments. In April 1961 President Paz publicly called for "labor discipline and responsibility." COMIBOL President Guillermo Bedregal complained to Paz about "the intransigence of the union leaders," arguing that with the "unraveling of the principle of authority" in the mines, "the Administrators of the mines find themselves deprived of the right to manage." He alleged that the unionists were "under the thumb of imperialism"—presumably of the Soviet variety—and that they threatened "all which constitutes the essence of Bolivianness," including "its Christian and democratic tradition." Other officials blamed the miners' protests on "a decided minority" of "conspirators," usually communists, who fomented "red subversion" by "trick[ing] the workers" into opposing government policies. Officials' speeches often juxtaposed "the conspirators responsible" for the unrest with *los compañeros trabajadores*, thus implying that the former were totally separate from the category of workers, who were by definition loyal and compliant.[84]

MNR officials had in fact been formulating many of the outlines of the Triangular Plan since coming to power in 1952. Guevara Arze's 1955 *Plan inmediato de política económica* blamed *pulpería* subsidies and "excess" miners for many of COMIBOL's problems. Even the leader of the MNR left, Juan Lechín, argued that "the main problem lies in the absence of real work discipline." The *Plan inmediato* emphasized the MNR's desire for private US and European investment in the Bolivian mining industry, specifically to exploit recently discovered iron deposits at Mutún, near the Brazilian border. Ambassador Andrade intimated to US reporters as early as February 1956 that Bolivia's mines "one day will be returned to private ownership."[85] One of the Triangular Plan's central aspects, worker layoffs, began under the MNR three years prior to the start of the plan's implementation.[86] Thus, the Triangular Plan was not a unilateral imposition by foreigners. US intervention gave moderate and right-wing MNR leaders—sometimes with tacit support from leaders like Lechín—the leverage necessary to implement a shared agenda.

The diagnosis that identified labor as "the whole cause" of COMIBOL's ills ignored a host of other factors. The roots of the crisis extended far back in time. The 1950 UN mission headed by Hugh Keenleyside had given a pessimistic assessment of the mining industry: "No important new tin mines have been developed in Bolivia during the last 20 years, and the gradual exhaustion of the known high grade tin ore reserves can only result in increased costs of production and a steadily declining output in the near future. The average assays of ores mined have already decreased 40% within the last 5 years."[87] By the 1930s most major Bolivian mines had already begun their decline, reflected in depleted ore reserves and declining ore grades. To make things worse, the Big Three tin corporations that controlled 80 percent of Bolivian tin production had devoted little money to exploration or new machinery. The long-term trend was thus one of rising costs and declining productivity. Falling tin prices following the end of the Korean War added to COMIBOL's difficulties.[88]

The MNR inherited these problems, but from 1952 to 1960 it did relatively little to combat them. It neglected the mining sector as it prioritized road construction, education, oil, and other projects. It also steadily siphoned money out of COMIBOL through direct taxes and hidden taxation resulting from artificial exchange rates, and it failed to reinvest the money necessary to increase production and efficiency.[89] Economist Melvin Burke even contests the widely believed notion that COMIBOL was unprofitable in the late 1950s. If the claims of the COMIBOL administration are credible, the MNR government extracted at least $100 million in "hidden taxes" during the first five years; if so, COMIBOL had actually netted significant profits by 1960, and high taxation rates were largely responsible for its apparent insolvency. This evidence raises the possibility that COMIBOL "was actually a profitable public enterprise which simply never had access to the surplus it generated."[90] There are also some indications that COMIBOL was more efficient than the private mines; although the labor force in the privately owned mines was roughly equal in size to that of COMIBOL, private mines produced no more than 35 percent of total mineral sales. Burke concludes that "deceptive accounting" was part of the effort of certain government officials "to discredit labor."[91] These facts suggest that rhetoric about the inherent inefficiency of state enterprise and the culpability of the labor force derived from political motivations rather than impartial economic analysis.[92]

The official diagnosis did not go uncontested. In the late 1950s and early 1960s the miners union and sympathetic politicians in the Bolivian Congress decried government attempts to blame workers. They instead blamed the COMIBOL administration and its "parasitic bureaucracy" along with other factors beyond the workers' control. At one point in October 1957—the same month that COMIBOL announced plans to lay off 5,200 workers—miners from several of the major mines reported that they were working only half the day due to power shortages. Miners and leftist politicians noted that the US and Soviet "dumping" of mineral reserves on the world market had lowered prices and cost the country tens of millions of dollars. They condemned anticommunist rhetoric as a fig leaf for the assault by MNR moderates and rightists "against the democratic freedoms of this country."[93]

Even some observers who were sympathetic to the US-MNR agenda cast serious doubt on the official dogma that labor costs were "the whole cause of failure." In 1957 US fiscal adviser to Bolivia Roger Freeman reported that "a large part, and possibly the major part" of COMIBOL's deficit "was the result of the Government's paying the mines only a fraction of the proceeds of their ore output." President Paz, while assigning much of the blame to the lack of "labor discipline," sometimes acknowledged that "the causes of this [problem] are several," including decapitalization and "the lack of investments in recent years."[94] A 1967 CEPAL report acknowledged a range of "economic, financial and socio-political factors" behind the decline in productivity but emphasized that the crisis "was very largely due to the deterioration in technical mining conditions and the low tin content of the ore."[95] A German government consultant named J. G. A. Hertslet went even further in a letter to the State Department in 1961:

> The main problem of the Bolivian mineral industry is not so much the problem of the unrest of the workers, the fancy social privileges and benefits they have been granted after the events of the 1952 revolution, but the crucial problem is the question, whether Bolivia still has enough tin and other minerals in order to fulfil [sic] the export quotas. . . . Bolivia is not in the position presently to produce more, even if COMIBOL would work efficiently. . . .
>
> The only possibility I envisa [sic] to give Bolivia a new economical

basis is the establishment of a certain amount of semi-finished industries, based on the minerals and natural riches of Bolivia.[96]

But such views, which turned the premises of the Triangular Plan on
their head, had little impact.

Contrary to imagery of pampered miners living in luxury, wages and
working conditions in 1960 remained abysmal. By one calculation, real
wages actually fell from 1950 to 1955. The rate of accidents increased
over the same period in some of the major mines. In the mid-1950s the
government itself estimated that perhaps half of all COMIBOL miners
suffered from silicosis and other lung and cardiovascular illnesses. According to a 1956 report by the US firm Ford, Bacon & Davis, the average life expectancy of a Bolivian tin miner who worked below ground
was twenty-seven years; those miners who worked above ground averaged thirty-three years. A typical miner lasted between six and eight
years on the job, a figure comparable to the longevity of the typical
field slave in Brazil or the Caribbean during the most brutal periods of
plantation slavery.[97]

Nor were the miners as intransigent and irrational as official statements alleged. In 1958 the MNR began offering monetary compensation to all miners who voluntarily retired, and it seems that many
COMIBOL workers were willing to cooperate as long as they received
decent severance. According to a classified US report from the late
1950s, "This system has worked out rather well in the nationalized
mines but so far has had only a limited effect in reducing the number
of supernumerary employees in private establishments." In 1962, a report noted that "all workers 'dismissed' thus far have left COMIBOL
voluntarily."[98]

A systematic analysis of COMIBOL's performance has confirmed
what a range of dissident voices and even many MNR officials were
saying at the time, that many factors rather than simply labor costs
were inhibiting profitability. Drawing on COMIBOL data and a series
of contemporary studies by foreign firms, Melvin Burke concludes that
COMIBOL's dismal outlook was attributable to "a multitude of complex interrelated factors"; labor costs were not the only or even the primary source of its problems. This fact was not permitted to interfere
with the design of the Triangular Plan, though.[99]

Given the array of factors responsible for the crisis, the decision to
target the miners was not simply based on technical concerns. And even
if smashing the miners union into submission could save COMIBOL

some money, it was bound to be less effective than alternative options in promoting long-term productivity. So what explains the disproportionate focus of US and MNR officials on labor? Targeting labor was the most desirable option for at least three reasons. First, it was a way of "decreasing . . . labor's role in the economy" and, by extension, the government—a goal shared by US and MNR leaders. Many MNR officials recognized the multiple causes of COMIBOL's crisis, but they viewed the labor problem as both the easiest "to resolve by our own means" and the focus most likely to appeal to the Triangular Plan partners.[100] Second, US officials viewed the mining crisis, like the 1956 inflation crisis, as an opportunity to promote the privatization of nationalized assets.[101] The conditions attached to the Triangular Plan loans included "reduction of the mines labor force" in the state sector and the "reorganization of COMIBOL."[102] These stipulations were intended to pacify the workforce and partly reprivatize the mining industry, simultaneously taking aim at the miners, a large state-run enterprise, and the plague of resource nationalism. Finally, the plan would send a message to populations outside Bolivia that defiance of the US-led hemispheric order was futile and cooperation with that order was the only sensible choice for underdeveloped nations. Imparting that message became more urgent after the Cuban Revolution.[103]

The specifics of the plan followed from these goals. US officials proposed "to strengthen the hand of management" and government vis-à-vis the miners through a series of "internal disciplinary measures." Chief among them were massive layoffs. Reestablishing managers' right to "free hire and fire," which had been curtailed by MNR legislation, was a key priority. The first step, emphasized Thomas Mann, would be "the elimination of those union leaders who have defied the authority of the Central Government."[104] Beyond targeted firings, the Triangular Plan partners demanded the layoffs of thousands of excess miners. Various nongovernmental reports acknowledged the existence of surplus workers, so the problem was real, but US officials knew that the layoffs would also weaken the miners union by increasing the ranks of unemployed; many miners termed the layoffs a "white massacre."[105] The layoffs were consistent with the planners' efforts to rein in labor militancy; as Burke notes, to eliminate surplus workers from the COMIBOL payroll "was to simultaneously destroy their political and ideological opponents." State Department officials understood perfectly well that "these reforms tended to undercut the power base" of left-wing MNR leaders.[106] The US government could have resolved the problem of surplus workers by funding further mineral exploration, expanding COMIBOL's productive capacity, or promoting industrial diversification, but instead officials sought to boost private mining at COMIBOL's expense. Economists' recommendations that layoffs be delayed until "suitable alternate employment" was created received low priority.[107]

By reducing the size of the state-employed workforce, the layoffs also contributed to the "promotion of private enterprise." Not only would they help weaken the tin miners union as a political force and collective bargaining unit, they were also part of an assault on state-owned industries and resource nationalism more generally. The other component of this attack was the US insistence on the increased participation of private foreign business in Bolivian mining. Months before loan negotiations even began, Thomas Mann stressed that US aid "would be carefully conditioned upon the acceptance by the Bolivian Government of sound foreign management for COMIBOL." Long desired but deemed unrealistic by US planners prior to late 1960, the signing of "a private management contract" would thereafter be a firm US condition. Three years later US officials had raised their expectations even more, actively pursuing the prospects for "establishing one or more mixed companies, with COMIBOL retaining 51 percent ownership and, in each case, the private company granted complete control of operations." The goal of privatizing COMIBOL, entirely or in part, was part of a larger hemispheric campaign targeting nationalization as a concept.[108]

Finally, another condition required COMIBOL to use at least half the amount of the foreign loans to buy US imports—a requirement inconsistent with free trade but beneficial to US exporters. The US Agency for International Development (USAID), the entity in charge of disbursing the US portion of the Triangular Plan money, privately acknowledged that this stipulation "cannot but raise costs" for COMIBOL.[109] Partly as a result, by 1963 Bolivia was obtaining "almost all its manufactured imports from the US."[110] The Triangular Plan partners refused to renegotiate the loans' repayment, thus intensifying Bolivia's rising debt obligations and external dependency. James Wilkie notes a "34 per cent increase in Bolivia's external public debt between 1960 and 1965." By 1970 COMIBOL owed $40 million to its foreign creditors.[111]

What amounted to $62 million in loans during the 1960s did relatively little to improve COMIBOL's efficiency. Only $4 million went to mineral exploration and only small amounts to acquiring new technology. Government records showed a return to profitability by 1966, but factors unrelated to actual production were the primary causes of the apparent turnaround. The government provided massive tax breaks to COMIBOL, such as by cutting export taxes by over 50 percent in 1966. The Triangular Plan partners also stopped pushing for continued compensation to the tin barons, potentially saving COMIBOL millions of dollars. And perhaps most importantly, mineral prices on the global market increased substantially in the 1960s; tin prices alone rose by 66 percent over the course of the decade. Rising tin prices were the main factor in the near-doubling of the value of Bolivian exports—from $69 million to $118 million—from 1963 to 1966.[112]

Of course, improving efficiency was not the primary goal of the Triangular Plan partners, who were much more interested in privatization and labor discipline. As hoped, the plan contributed to the further denationalization of COMIBOL. Throughout the 1960s COMIBOL purchased up to 36 percent of the tin it exported from private mining companies. In 1965 it began leasing many of the smaller state mines to private firms under the military junta's new mining code. By 1970 private mining had surpassed COMIBOL, with a workforce four times larger and twice the production levels.[113] COMIBOL retained control of only the largest mines.

Efforts to "obtain discipline among labor" were also quite successful in the short term. In 1966 former US economic adviser Cornelius Zondag noted with approval "the change in the attitude of labor itself . . . as evidenced by its recent cooperation."[114] The strategy involved both economic coercion and military force. By mid-1963 the US embassy had decided "that the various aid programs (both AID and military) should be used as appropriate to help solve COMIBOL's labor problems." The US government had been supplying military aid to Bolivia since 1957, with most going toward the creation of government "internal security" forces. Consistent with the Alliance for Progress elsewhere, the Kennedy administration substantially increased military aid to Bolivia.[115] After army leaders overthrew the Paz government in November 1964, they ordered the occupation of the mines, slashed wages by 36 percent in the first year for miners but not for administrators, and laid off more than 1,300 workers. In October 1965 Bolivian Catholic Church officials sent an open letter to the junta condemning the "subhuman standard of living" of the miners. In contrast, US officials responded with enthusiasm, reassuring the new regime of the United States' "strong moral support" for the "forceful and effective measures" being taken.[116] But the key shift occurred prior to the military coup. The Paz government abolished what was left of "workers' control" in August 1963, and more workers (3,700 in 1961–1964) left the labor force before the military occupation than after. In late 1963 COMIBOL officials had already applauded "COMIBOL's victory over labor."[117]

Why did MNR leaders embrace three major reforms detrimental to their stated goals of economic development and social justice? Part of the answer lies in the stark asymmetry of power between the US government and the MNR, which was heavily dependent on US aid for its survival. MNR leaders' experiences reinforced their sense of the need to maintain US favor. Initial US hostility to the MNR's coalition government with Gualberto Villarroel in the 1940s had confirmed for Paz Estenssoro the impossibility of "being against the United States." Paz's views were also shaped by his reading of events in places like Iran and Guatemala where more assertive anti-imperialism resulted in US-backed coups.[118] Many analysts have thus emphasized imperial power and related resource constraints when explaining MNR actions. For example, accounts of the 1955 oil reform typically cite US coercion, the government's lack of capital, or both to explain the MNR's embrace of private investment.[119]

Imperialism does not fully explain MNR actions, however. The mainstream party leadership was not ideologically opposed to private capital, wage cuts, or greater restrictions on workers' power. MNR officials were not consciously seeking to undermine their state enterprises, unlike many US officials, but they had no objection to encouraging private investment alongside public, and they welcomed the chance to target workers' wages and power. Explanations that stress Bolivia's lack of capital, meanwhile, fail to account for why the MNR looked to Western oil companies for capital while ignoring European lenders and the Soviet Union, which offered Bolivia a $150 million loan in 1958, as well as other potential sources such as ending compensation payments to the former tin barons.[120] Pursuing these other options could plausibly have delivered better results for YPFB and COMIBOL. The problem was that defying the United States would have risked a cut-off in aid along with retaliation by private capital and possibly a military intervention. Doing so thus would have required a more radical social revolution and a change in Cold War foreign alignments, akin to the path pursued by Cuba after 1959, if the revolution was to have any chance of survival. Paz and company were unwilling to contemplate this path due to their own ideological predispositions. Faced with pressure from the North and threats from more radical forces below, they chose to cast their lot with the US government and private capital.

It was thus their own beliefs, goals, and fears, in combination with US pressures and a lack of resources, that led MNR leaders to embrace privatization and regressive policy reforms after 1955. In doing so they ultimately compromised even their own modest plans for economic modernization.

Resistance and the Paths Not Taken

Nonetheless, the US and Bolivian governments were always constrained by the revolutionary rhetoric of the time and, more concretely, by the threat of mobilization from tens of thousands of angry Bolivians. US officials overseeing the stabilization program often lamented the degree to which they, as well as Paz, Siles, and other MNR leaders, were handcuffed by "the Bolivian politico-social context." While they continued to push for a freeze on miners' wages and other austerity measures, they privately conceded that some "slippage in government policy" was inevitable due to "the pressure from powerful labor and political groups." George Eder bemoaned MNR "vacillation" in imposing the stabilization measures and the wage increases forced upon the government by miner resistance.[121] The Eder Plan's call to eliminate grocery subsidies at the mines triggered massive protest, with miners and their wives occupying the *pulperías* at Catavi, Huanuni, San José, Quechisla, and other mines. In June 1957 the Second Congress of the COB threatened a general strike if the government refused to modify the stabilization measures, though the strike plan failed due to the government's successful attempt to split the COB.[122]

Mine-worker resistance to the Triangular Plan was also fierce. In mid-1961 the tensions that had been brewing between the MNR and miners reached a boiling point. Just as the Triangular Plan partners were signing their memorandum of understanding to begin the plan, the miners union issued a series of economic demands and in early June began what became an eighteen-day strike. When the government jailed a number of union leaders and refused to release them, outrage spread through the mines, with threats of strikes, denunciations of the MNR leadership, and alleged acts of sabotage to impede production. At the Siglo XX mine, women formed a Housewives Committee (Comité de Amas de Casa) to help defend the miners union there. At one point during the strike the press reported that twenty thousand women from the mines were threatening to descend on La Paz. The threat posed by this resistance was obvious: while 152,075 work days were lost to strikes in 1960, the number in 1961 was 489,789.[123] The miners' estrangement from the MNR accelerated rapidly thereafter.

The strikes and protests have been well documented, but often neglected are the concrete alternative policies that the protesters advocated.[124] Delegates to the 1954 COB congress discussed the formation of "pools" of primary-commodity producers among the underdeveloped countries to prevent devastating price fluctuations and ensure fair prices for raw materials like tin.[125] In place of the Eder Plan's strict austerity and zero-inflation policies, the COB proposed higher taxes on capital and demanded wage increases and price controls to shield workers from the effects of devaluation and rising prices.[126] Intellectual allies like Trotskyist Guillermo Lora pointed out that controlled inflation could be used as a way to redistribute wealth; as long as workers' wages rose faster than the prices of goods they purchased, the result would be a downward redistribution of income.[127]

A core popular demand regarding the tin industry was a smelter that would enable Bolivia to refine its own tin, freeing it from its dependence on US and British smelters.[128] The need for a smelter had long been central to resource-nationalist thought in the country, and it was the key plank in the left's proposed alternatives to the Triangular Plan. The miners' congress in Huanuni in May 1961 passed a list of nine demands including acceptance of the Soviet aid offer to fund a smelter, an end to indemnification payments to the tin barons, more funding for mineral exploration, and state control over all mining revenue. A week later, the economic commission of the factory workers' congress echoed the call for a smelter.[129]

These demands in turn exerted pressure on politicians in the national legislature. In 1962 a group of Bolivian senators wrote to Paz Estenssoro demanding that he accept the Soviet aid offer. In response Paz promised a tin smelter at some point in the future, but in the short term he committed only to sending minerals to the USSR for "intensive metallurgical studies." Empty promises did little to placate popular demands, as revealed by incidents like the 1963 threat of the Pro-Smelters Committee in Oruro to launch "a total blockade of the communications system in this part of the country" if Paz did not accept a Czech offer to build an antimony smelter in Oruro.[130]

The arguments for smelter construction resonated widely. Although a 1961 Bolivian government report estimated the cost of a tin smelter at $20 million, this amount was less than the compensation paid to the former tin barons to that point and about one-third the amount of the Triangular Plan loans, the total cost of which ended up being far more due to interest.[131] The Soviet Union had offered to fund the construction of the smelter "with no strings attached," as even George Eder admitted. Moreover, nationalists of all political stripes insisted on smelter construction, and even right-wing military leaders after 1964 had to genuflect to this central tenet of Bolivian resource nationalism by promising them one.[132]

The MNR's failure to build a tin smelter contributed to heightened discontent by the early 1960s. Why would the MNR promote, or at least acquiesce to, a program of mass firings and privatization for the mining industry while neglecting the options that could help put the industry and the economy on a more solid long-term footing? After a decade of revolution and no smelter, many Bolivians agreed with Senator Ñuflo Chávez's allegation that "there is a real conspiracy of foreign interests to avoid smelting in the country" (figure 3.2).[133] Public opinion also indicted certain Bolivian elites. The *rosca*, it had long been believed, conspired to prevent the construction of smelters and violently resisted state attempts to assert greater control over the industry, most clearly in its alleged murder of President Busch in 1939. After 1952 the tin barons joined forces with the US government to thwart the revolution. Left-wing nationalist Sergio Almaraz Paz accused COMIBOL of cooperating with foreign smelting companies that wanted to prevent Bolivia from obtaining its own smelter.[134] Such beliefs reflected the conviction, common throughout Latin America and especially pronounced in Bolivia, that US political and economic elites opposed the industrialization of the Third World. Dependency theorists would articulate this notion more fully later in the 1960s.

The US position on Latin American industrialization was slightly more complex than such arguments suggested. Prior to World War II the US government explicitly opposed the idea of Latin American industrialization. Leading planners invoked neoclassical theories of comparative advantage and often outright racism to justify a neomercantilist world order in which the United States and Europe produced manufactured goods while the rest of the world supplied them with cheap raw materials and labor. This argument survived into the postwar era, but US officials could no longer vocalize it without drawing protest from Latin Americans.[135] In addition, not all postwar US of-

Este horno regalarà EE.UU. a Bolivia

El yanqui Strom Embajador de Estados Unidos
Dicen es técnico en hornos y panaderías
Entre muchas de sus habilidades y boberías
Busca vernos a los bolivianos bien desunidos

Tiene la misión de EE.UU. de fundir a Bolivia
En horno calentado con dólares envilecidos
No estará contento hasta no vernos hundidos
Para que el imperialismo satisfecho se ría

Figure 3.2. "The United States will donate *this* furnace to Bolivia." According to this 1960 cartoon from a Communist Party paper, the US government would not allow Bolivia a "furnace" (*horno*) for smelting tin but would give it one for melting its industries. The cartoon shows US ambassador Carl Strom roasting the state tin and oil companies, railroads, and "national industry." Source: *El Pueblo*, October 29, 1960. Archivo Hemerográfico, Biblioteca y Archivo Histórico de la Asamblea Legislativa Plurinacional, Bolivia; photo used with permission.

ficials were neoclassical ideologues like George Eder.[136] By the 1950s many had started to favor the idea of Latin American industrialization in the interest of ensuring a stable, US-friendly political order and reducing the need for US aid. Nor were foreign capitalists always opposed to the prospect of Latin American industrialization, and sometimes they favored it for their own interests.[137]

In practice, however, US support for industrialization was quite limited, especially in the Bolivian case. The charge that the US government opposed a Bolivian tin smelter was correct. The development of smelting operations in Bolivia in the 1960s occurred despite the Triangular Plan, not because of it.[138] And US policy hindered industrialization and diversification in other ways, too. The United States required Bolivia to use its aid to buy US food products, which hampered the development of Bolivian agriculture.[139] It insisted on low tariffs for industrial imports. It discouraged the rise of industries that would compete with powerful US business sectors; any Bolivian industrialization would have to complement, not threaten, US corporations. It prohibited the use of US aid to assist state enterprise (mining and oil) until 1961. The stabilization plan hindered industrial development in the name of stopping inflation.[140] Moreover, Bolivia was not Brazil or Mexico; if US officials and corporate executives sometimes favored industrialization in these countries, they tended to view Bolivia as a more classic extractive economy whose purpose was to supply the First World with cheap raw materials.[141] In short, there was much evidence to support popular suspicions that US elites opposed Bolivian industrialization. That US opposition derived not so much from any dogmatic or ideological commitment as from concrete conflicts of interest. David Green observes that even if US officials did not intentionally seek to perpetuate underdevelopment, "their relationship to private interests may have promoted it."[142]

The highly selective nature of US support for industrialization is further evidence of the importance of power in economic policy making. There were policy alternatives available, and they were widely discussed in both intellectual and popular circles. These alternatives were not guaranteed to work, of course, and certainly none of them offered a panacea for Bolivia's profound structural problems. My argument is simply that the alternatives had a reasonable likelihood of producing at least as much growth and equity as monetarism and privatization but were defeated because of asymmetrical power relations.

Yet foreign powers and their MNR allies were not the only ones who shaped economic policy. Popular demands had an effect not only on official discourse and political culture but often on economic policy as well. Although the MNR and the military regime that followed launched an all-out assault on mine workers' rights, they were compelled to take steps toward the construction of mineral concentration mills and smelters as well as oil refineries. In 1963 the Paz administration established the Corporación Nacional de Fundiciones (National Smelter Corporation) to oversee the various small smelting operations in the country and explore future smelter possibilities. The regime of General René Barrientos signed a contract in 1966 with a German firm for the construction of Bolivia's first large-scale tin smelter. By 1970 the new smelter was operating in Oruro along with another for antimony, and the government had plans for tungsten, copper, lead, zinc, and bismuth smelters as well.[143] And despite the Triangular Plan partners' hopes and threats from Bolivian officials, nothing approaching a full privatization of the mining industry would occur until 1985, largely due to the furious popular response to privatization efforts in the 1960s.[144]

Resource nationalism and redistributive demands placed powerful constraints on US and MNR power. This pattern is apparent not just in mining but also in the realms of urban industry, hydrocarbons, and agriculture. Though in many ways the revolution was defeated by the forces of reaction after 1956, popular resistance also limited the power of those forces in meaningful ways.

CHAPTER 4

The Battle for Men's Minds: Economic Paradigms, Propaganda, and the Iconography of Revolution

Of what lasting value is an agreement negotiated between the American Embassy and the host government if public opinion in the country does not support its government's position?
THOMAS SORENSEN, US INFORMATION AGENCY, 1968

Most modern counterinsurgency doctrine emphasizes the need to win over the civilian population in war zones through more than just military means. Western military invasions of Vietnam, Iraq, and Afghanistan have been accompanied by much talk of the need to conquer the hearts and minds of civilian populations in those countries. Since the end of the Cold War, US policy makers and intellectuals have increasingly advocated the use of "soft power" to win the allegiance of foreign peoples, and the US government has employed a range of cultural, ideological, and economic means alongside military violence.[1]

Half a century before, the US and Bolivian governments experimented with a similar approach. An extensive "informal diplomacy" campaign led by the US Information Agency accompanied the more overt forms of intervention. Propaganda efforts were intended, in the words of one official, "for the purpose of persuading other people to think and act in ways that will further American purposes."[2] Such candid admissions were often accompanied by highly moralistic language about the proper path that Third World societies should take. USIA crusaders tended to view the world in stark, Manichean terms. Like John Foster Dulles, Eisenhower's secretary of state, they considered ideas like resource nationalism and Third World neutralism "immoral."[3] In 1950 a Truman official coined the phrase "Campaign of

Truth" to characterize overseas propaganda efforts. This Orwellian label was an appropriate reflection of the psychology of most US policy makers in the postwar decades. Like George Eder, US propaganda agents frequently used motifs of war when describing their activities. A 1951 report seeking to justify funding for propaganda efforts asked, "Shall it be democracy or totalitarianism south of the border? Shall the battle be fought now with books and brains or later with bombs?" References to the "battle for men's minds" were common in the 1950s and 1960s.[4]

This archaic—or maybe not so archaic—rhetoric obscured the real issues at stake. The main conflict in places like Bolivia was not between democracy and totalitarianism but rather among differing ideas about the path to economic development and the meanings of democracy. Internal US reports on Bolivia often admitted as much once they moved past rhetoric and engaged in substantive analysis. US propaganda agents explicitly sought to dislodge deep-seated public beliefs about the world economy, particularly the widespread suspicion of imperialism and class exploitation, and foster trust in the mutually beneficial nature of international and domestic class relations. Resource nationalism, they hoped, would be replaced by an abiding faith in free enterprise, foreign investment, and US goodwill, while Bolivian workers would realize the folly of class struggle and join hands with their employers for their mutual advancement. This project was ambitious, for it sought to reverse some of most pervasive currents in working-class political culture.

USIS messaging dovetailed with the efforts of Bolivian government officials seeking to promote foreign investment and suppress popular militancy. Starting in the mid-1950s the MNR leadership reopened the oil sector to private investment, imposed a harsh austerity plan, and initiated a drastic downsizing of the state mining corporation. Implementing this agenda entailed the repression of labor as well as a concerted state effort to sow division among popular sectors. After 1956 MNR officials sought to foster an alternative, "restructured" COB led by moderate labor leaders and also prohibited formal labor-peasant alliances. On the level of discourse, they began subtly redefining Bolivian identity in a way that de-emphasized the miners and the working class and instead lauded the campesino, the middle class, and the army as icons of the nation. The MNR's appeal to nationalism helped it achieve a modest degree of success in its quest for legitimacy. That success proved partial and temporary, however, and neither MNR leaders nor army officials were able to make Bolivians forget their commitment to resource nationalism and other promises of the revolution.

USIS propaganda had even less success in changing Bolivians' views. Despite marked changes in economic policy after 1955, US officials would often lament that public attitudes about economic development, class conflict, and international relations remained quite consistent. The US failure to achieve ideological hegemony in Bolivia is evident in its increased reliance on military aid to the MNR starting in the late 1950s.

A Hedge against Revolution

The US government's first sustained effort at overseas propaganda was during World War II when it created the Office of War Information to promote the Allied cause.[5] That office's chief agency for Latin America was the Office of the Coordinator of Inter-American Affairs (OIAA), led by Nelson Rockefeller. The OIAA's Coordination Committee for Bolivia distributed newspaper articles, newsreels, radio programs, and films promoting Bolivian cooperation with the Allies. Though dissolved soon after the war, the OIAA laid the foundation for postwar propaganda efforts in Latin America.

Like so much else about the US government, the OIAA campaigns were fraught with contradiction. One January 1944 report describes a visit to the town of Sorata to show OIAA films. When a power outage occurred, local soldiers wielded whips to conscript Indian laborers to fix the power lines and relocate a utility pole. The report admitted that "their work was not necessarily [performed] 'voluntarily'" and the treatment of the natives was "a little bit primitive" but concluded that "the uses of Democracy were well served under methods which are by custom under a feudal set-up."[6] Although not particularly extreme—US intervention often took much more violent forms—the incident embodies the contradictions of a state that invoked democracy while behaving in antidemocratic ways around the world.

By whatever means, OIAA outreach efforts reached a large proportion of the population during the war. By late 1945 each US-supplied film was being shown about six hundred times per month in Bolivian schools. Total showings numbered around four hundred a week and took place in at least thirty-six cities and towns. According to one report, more than a half million Bolivians saw the films, and 100,000 saw US newsreels in just one four-week period; more than 150,000 attended other OIAA programs. These figures are impressive given Bolivia's population of just three million at the time.[7]

The messaging ranged from subtle to overt. Wartime film titles included *How to Swim* and *Picturesque Massachusetts* but also *Airways to Peace* and *Nazi Atrocities*. Films like *Steel, Man's Servant* and *Soldiers of the Sky* showcased US industry, technology, and weaponry. Others, like *Champions Carry On* and *Busy Little Bears* (shown to children), praised personal characteristics such as hard work and perseverance. Still others offered general praise for the United States without focusing on any one area of society or government.[8]

The number of film showings diminished after 1945, but other aspects of the informal diplomacy campaign intensified.[9] The Truman administration created a number of short-lived but laboriously named agencies like the US International Information and Educational Exchange (USIE), a program that adapted the OIAA mission to the emerging Cold War. Many of the strategies and messaging themes of anti-Nazi campaigns proved useful for the antileft campaigns of the postwar era. As the Cold War heated up and governments around the hemisphere launched a full-fledged assault on workers' rights, social democracy, and radicalism, US propaganda efforts in Bolivia likewise picked up.[10] USIE focused special attention on newspapers. By 1949 "all newspapers in Bolivia" were using USIE-provided materials, and one report boasted that "USIE can practically guarantee the publication of its material in the most influential papers." The newspaper with the largest circulation, *La Razón*, featured around five hundred column inches of USIE materials per month. Agents enjoyed a close relationship with newspaper editors, particularly at *La Razón* and the other major right-wing daily, *Los Tiempos*. A 1950 report claimed that USIE efforts had "stirred editors into writing more and more editorials which, in addition to published USIE releases, abetted in disclosing to the papers' readers the evils of Communism." The report noted that USIE was broadcasting on "over 19 radio stations" and getting hundreds of hours of "free air time" on major radio stations each month.[11]

The ideological tone of US propaganda became more pronounced by the late 1940s. In 1949 the USIE introduced a radio program called *Family Hour*, which imparted a steady stream of anticommunist lessons, plus a magazine entitled *Did You Know?*, which ran "articles explaining the destructive tactics of communism." The following year the USIE staff produced another family-oriented radio program featuring two parents and a college-age son. The Catholic parents "painstakingly explain to the son—who leans to the 'left'—the moral corruptness and abysmal life Communism will give him should he continue interested in its doctrine." Much of the program's script came directly from US congressional reports on communism and anticommunist diatribes by US authors. The program aired on at least eleven stations, with "careful and discreet steps" taken "to assure that the source of origin would not be revealed."[12]

Pro–United States messages were at least as prominent as anti-Nazi and anticommunist ones. Just as they would after 1952, US officials had to contend with widespread adverse images of the United States. They lamented how "most people south of the border" viewed the United States as "a nation of highly materialistic, pleasure-mad alcoholics."[13] But Bolivians seemed to reserve their most serious criticisms for the US government and corporations. In 1951 agents noted the widespread usage of the term "Yankee imperialism," a "catch phrase" that they attributed to a "misunderstanding and distrust of the United States, its objectives and policies." Instead of reflecting a visceral hostility to North Americans in general, the sentiment was usually rooted in a concrete sense of class, ethnic, and/or national exploitation. According to one US agent, the average Bolivian mine worker viewed all owners and supervisors with contempt, whether they were "Bolivian or foreigner." Informal diplomacy was required to combat these "misrepresentations."[14]

Agents were particularly worried about unfavorable attitudes among what they considered the leadership class in Bolivian society. The "priority target groups" for US efforts, in descending order of importance, were (1) middle-class professionals, particularly teachers, media directors, and others with substantial influence over public opinion; (2) church officials, government officials, urban workers, and young people; and (3) rural workers.[15] Cadets and officers at the Bolivian Military Academy were also crucial targets, particularly during the war. In a 1943 memo Kenneth Wasson, the head OIAA agent in Bolivia, noted that the academy's students tended to come "from the country's best families" and predicted that this population would comprise "many or most of the country's future leaders. Reaching these boys at an impressionable age and creating in their minds a favorable attitude towards the United States seems to me a very worthwhile accomplishment."[16]

The same memo mentions regular lunch-hour film showings in La Paz "in one of the poorer sections of town." Wasson's description illuminates the logic of the US outreach strategy as well as his perception of lower-class Bolivians:

> What benefit may accrue to us from the showing of films to audiences such as these, is a question which may well be asked. These people, under present circumstances, have no voice in government; they do not look promising as a source of future leadership. They are an element of the population which simply doesn't count . . . but I have the feeling that our efforts are not entirely wasted. . . . The pictures must stir some sort of emotional response; the audience is not the kind from which to expect an intellectual reaction.
>
> Furthermore, who can predict what political and social changes may take place after the war, even in a country like Bolivia? . . . These showings, then, may perhaps be justified—if on no other grounds—as a hedge against revolution.[17]

The last two sentences would prove prophetic, though the "emotional response" of the poorer elements in 1952 would not be quite the type that US agents wanted.

Chasquis for Private Capital Investment

Although the informal diplomacy of the early postwar era failed to prevent a revolution, it served as the basis for US propaganda and cultural campaigns after 1952. The media technologies, outreach strategies, and messaging pioneered during and after the war by the OIAA, USIE, and other bodies prefigured the campaigns of the USIA following the revolution. Created in August 1953, the USIA and its foreign branches, the USIS, quickly became a fixture in US foreign policy. By 1952 "foreign propaganda" had become "a permanent feature of American government," notes a former official.[18] USIS efforts in Bolivia after 1952 were still intended as a "hedge," not against revolution itself, but against a certain kind of revolution.

When US officials warned of the Bolivian tinderbox, they were referring not just to government policies but to public attitudes.[19] Defusing the situation required more than just traditional diplomacy. Consequently, the US propaganda campaign in the country expanded significantly after the revolution. According to an official evaluation of the USIS program in late 1954, "The sweeping economic and sociological changes taking place in Bolivia give the Information Program increased importance in maintaining proper attitudes toward the United States."[20] The most important "proper attitude" concerned capitalist enterprise. Throughout the 1950s, the primary "country objective" of the USIS campaign was "promoting popular acceptance of private capital investment," a goal that coincided with that of George Eder, the Triangular Plan partners, and the State and Treasury Departments.[21]

USIS agents devoted particular energy to promoting the austerity plan enacted in December 1956. They planted articles in Bolivian newspapers, published newsreels and news bulletins, and operated an extensive film and radio campaign with the cooperation of the Bolivian Film Institute.[22] An interesting tactic consisted of public opinion polls with questions "deliberately weighted so as to convert people and to keep them enthusiastic about the stabilization program." A 1958 report notes that Bolivia "is the only country so far where the public opinion survey has been used as a propaganda device" and suggests "that this device has been more successful than the press and radio effort." Like the MNR's own propaganda, USIS news implied near-unanimous support for austerity among the population. A USIS newsreel reported on President Siles' visit to the major mines, claiming that "everywhere the workers gave him their unanimous support and promised to double their efforts."[23]

As in earlier campaigns, USIS efforts in the 1950s and 1960s targeted especially the upper and middle classes in the cities—"the intellectuals, the opinion molders, and the political opportunists." University students were a particular target.[24] But in an apparent change from the pre-1952 period, the agency also produced materials in Quechua and Aymara for dissemination among the indigenous population. It printed a trilingual monthly news bulletin called *El Chasqui* (meaning "courier" in Quechua) and posted it on public walls around the country. USIS efforts extended beyond the cities "out into the Indian areas." The agency provided films dubbed in Quechua and Aymara for use in rural locales and co-sponsored "a radio teaching program in the Indian languages run by Maryknoll missionaries." Tens of thousands of pamphlets promising that "the life of the campesino will be better" under the 1956 stabilization program were distributed in the countryside.[25]

As in the World War II period, primitive methods were sometimes required. The USIS maintained close relations with a Canadian priest named Lino Grenier, who seems to have been an especially enthusiastic transmitter of the USIS message. Grenier and his order ran an educational campaign with USIS equipment, with Grenier himself operating near Siglo XX, one of the country's most militant mines. A USIS agent wrote that Grenier "may be something of a fanatic. He is also a fighter, I understand, and has been known to resort to the use of his fists to defend his views, and has personally participated in breaking up Communist rallies at Siglo XX." Grenier, who was in fact a martial arts expert, embodied the US and MNR governments' increasing resort to violence as a means of persuasion.[26]

In addition to popularizing stabilization, USIS messaging in the 1950s encompassed a broad array of propaganda themes. Agency newsreels condemned the 1956 Soviet invasion of Hungary and praised the 1954 overthrow of Guatemalan President Jacobo Arbenz. More subtle propaganda publicized the US space program, US government funding for an antimalaria program in Bolivia, and a thrilling US hockey team victory over the Russians in the 1960 Olympics, a plotline later borrowed for the film *Rocky IV*. A large proportion of newsreels focused on the training and accomplishments of the Bolivian army, a theme that became increasingly important in the late 1950s as the US and MNR governments started to rebuild the country's military. Most of this propaganda contributed to the broader objective of "explaining to Bolivians the advantages of international cooperation among democratic countries." As noted in a 1959 memo, a central geopolitical goal of US policy in Bolivia was "to demonstrate that people in social revolutions can make effective gains through cooperation with the US."[27]

A People's Capitalism

Ensuring cooperation with the United States became more urgent as a result of the triumph and radicalization of the Cuban Revolution. Although the fundamental goals of the US government remained the same, new strategies and tactics emerged to counter the threat. The Kennedy administration's approach was both more sophisticated and more brutal than Eisenhower's; the Alliance for Progress, inaugurated in March 1961, combined economic development aid and propaganda efforts with military assistance and the creation of the first modern-day death squads in Latin America.[28]

The shift in policy toward Bolivia was less marked—largely because Alliance-type relations with the US government had existed since 1953—but US intervention there did undergo some substantial changes in the early 1960s. In addition to increasing military aid, the Kennedy administration expanded the USIS campaign.[29] By June 1961 the list of USIS "country objectives" had expanded beyond just "promoting popular acceptance of private capital investment" to include several related aims:

> Country Objectives: 1) To foment among Bolivians the conviction that their best interests will be served by alignment with the United States and the democratic civilization for which it stands, and recognition of the free world leadership. 2) To show that American aid to Bolivia is materially benefitting the Bolivian people and has as its sole aim the democratic economic development of the country. 3) To combat actively growing Communist influence and the tendency to accept Marxist dogma in Bolivia.[30]

The official USIS country plan a year later also listed several cultural objectives. USIS work should promote "the creation of a Bolivian national culture" and "a sense of national pride that will over-ride class, educational, economic, and political differences." This national pride would take Bolivians' minds off trivialities like poverty and ethnic discrimination, instead "directing national attention and interest to the development of the country" and "emphasizing work and discipline" rather than class struggle.[31]

Such statements were implicit admissions of the hurdles that USIS agents faced. Far more worrisome than the five thousand or so registered Communists and Trotskyists in the country was the deep suspicion of US motives, foreign corporations, and capitalism in general that was widespread among workers and the poor. Most Bolivians had no formal affiliation to Marxist parties and at times even repudiated them, but "a leftist thought pattern" was widespread and posed a continuous dilemma for US policy makers.[32] If Soviet-style communism inspired little support among Bolivians, neither did US-style capitalism and the racism, militarism, and imperialism widely associated with it. In late 1958 Ambassador Bonsal complained "that such concepts as the role of the free world economy in helping underdeveloped countries, private enterprise as the key for better living standards, [and] the constructive role of the United States in situations such as Bolivia, are under severe attack." Conversely, loose notions of socialism and greater national independence held a strong appeal all over the continent, particularly in the wake of the Cuban Revolution. Reports from Bolivia in the 1960s noted the "widespread sympathy for the aspirations and objectives of the Cuban revolution."[33]

The solution was "people's capitalism," a messaging theme intended to put a kinder face on the capitalist system.[34] One goal of this campaign was to show the social successes of capitalism in the United States, where, Bolivians were assured, "the current picture is totally distinct from what Marx described."[35] A series of articles in the USIS-produced magazine *Foro Universitario* entitled "Socialism in the United States" were meant to counter the common Latin American perception of US-style capitalism as coldhearted and bereft of social welfare measures. In the process, they also put forth a watered-down definition of socialism stripped of any reference to nationalization, attacks on private property, or workers' control. One such article from 1967 noted that the Republican and Democratic Parties had adopted some of the Socialist Party's longtime platforms such as higher taxation on the rich, regulations on big business, and federal disaster relief, and it pointed to Lyndon Johnson's Great Society programs as further evidence of this pattern. The article even appropriated the phrase "permanent revolution," usually associated with Trotskyism, and gave it a very different meaning: "This revolution has produced a vigorous and elastic socioeconomic structure in which the ideals of human freedom and social welfare could be applied with ever-better results."[36] The USIS attempt to co-opt and redefine the concepts of socialism and revolution is a testament to those concepts' appeal among the Bolivian public.[37]

USIS messaging sought to counter a variety of other so-called misconceptions about US society, domestic policy, and role in the world. Among the most widespread misconceptions were the belief "that the US is utterly materialistic" and "that the US favors area dictatorships over the democracies." Polls conducted elsewhere in Latin America produced similar results, adding a long list of further grievances regarding US policies, ignorance, and tendency to "look upon Latin America as a colony." In a 1958 poll of residents in Buenos Aires, Lima, and Caracas, a majority in one or more of the cities, especially Buenos Aires and Lima, condemned US "interference in internal affairs of other countries," the "unfair prices" that the US government and importers paid for the country's goods, the "economic exploitation of our country by North American companies," US "support of dictators," and the "racial discrimination" in the United States.[38] White supremacy and the federal government's stoic response to the civil rights struggle of the 1950s and 1960s were particularly damning indictments in the eyes of people around the world.[39] The favorable comments about the United States that respondents deemed most justified were the "high standard of living," the "efficiency of production," and "scientific and technological progress"—characteristics that say little about justice or moral virtue.[40]

USIS officials in Bolivia tailored their messaging to combat these attitudes. In addition to publicizing social welfare measures in the United States, propaganda stressed "the peaceful, scientific, civilian nature of the US space program" and of nuclear technology, the benevolent motives of US foreign intervention, and the government's commitment to black civil rights. Photo and educational exhibits informed audiences of how the government was "Protecting Minority Rights in the USA" while "Fighting for Peace" against "Aggression from the North" in Vietnam. In 1967 Bolivian college students were treated to Secretary of State Dean Rusk's take on the Vietnam War in *Foro Universitario*. Attendees of a 1964 educational panel learned about the noble "Belgian-American humanitarian efforts to rescue victims of the Congo massacre"; discussion of Belgian-American massacres in the Congo escaped mention. Sometimes the messaging slipped in other subtle lessons, as when an exhibit on the civil rights movement told Bolivians of "Quiet Marchers toward Integration," thus counseling audiences on the proper way to go about protesting (figure 4.1).[41]

In reference to Bolivia itself, the centerpiece of the people's capitalism campaign was the Alliance for Progress. *Foro Universitario* often publicized the program and Bolivian students' praise for it.[42] Much of the publicity targeted urban workers. Public exhibits in factories and other urban places were "an important instrument" for disseminating "the Alliance story at a 'grass-root' level." One exhibit publicizing a 1962 USAID loan to the Soligno textile mill in La Paz was called "The Rehabilitation of the Soligno Factory":

> The exhibit carried the message that the Alliance for Progress, by rehabilitating and putting the plant on a profit making basis, is not only assisting managements [*sic*], but the workers at the plant and the economy of the country. In addition we wished to express that the success of the rehabilitation program is determined by the amount of cooper-

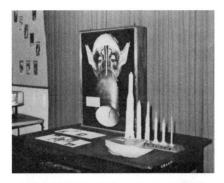

Figure 4.1. USIS public exhibits in Bolivia, 1960s. Common propaganda themes of the USIS campaign involved (top to bottom) the US space program as a symbol of capitalism's achievements, the US government's role in assisting the black civil rights struggle, and the benevolent motives of US foreign intervention. Photos included with USIS–La Paz to ICS/E Washington, May 20, 1965, in NA 306/1039/3; Schechter to USIA, December 29, 1964.

ation that the workers' union give [*sic*] to this project. With this approach it was hoped that each worker would be instilled with the feeling that he is an integral part of the Alliance and that his individual contribution would result in the success or failure of the rehabilitation program.

USIS officials and the Soligno management had the display "permanently placed at the Soligno factory, specifically in the workers' union office" (figure 4.2).[43]

Figure 4.2. "Rehabilitation of the Soligno factory." In the early 1960s the USIS devoted much effort to promoting the Alliance for Progress. Outreach campaigns like this one in the Soligno textile factory were intended to convince Bolivian workers of US goodwill and the benefits of capitalism. Photo included with USIS–La Paz (Torrey) to USIA, December 4, 1962, in NA 306/1039/3.

Outreach to Bolivian workers had two special purposes: to show that the US government looked favorably upon the idea of unions but also to delineate good from bad forms of labor activism. US-sponsored training for labor leaders and regular publications like *El Obrero*, USIS authorship of which was often not disclosed, were intended to counter the notion that the United States was inherently opposed to unions.[44] But only certain kinds of unionism were acceptable. A key goal of US policy around the hemisphere was "to promote responsible trade unionism and understanding management."[45] Good workers cooperated with their bosses and with the US-MNR agenda. Workers who resisted US-MNR policies failed to appreciate the generosity of their benefactors and therefore forfeited their rights as workers and Bolivians. The USIS message about unions thus had a public relations purpose as well as a disciplinary one.

Bolivian elites were meanwhile developing a complementary discourse about responsible workers and management. The Said textile factory in La Paz published a regular magazine that preached the virtues of "understanding between Employers and Workers" and called for the "conscious and friendly cooperation of the unions." Rather than taking "a hostile attitude" toward their employers, workers were exhorted to respect "the principle of authority and hierarchy in the factories and fields." The magazine emphasized an argument that would become a steady MNR drumbeat under the austerity plan— that increased production, not redistribution, was the key to higher living standards. Higher productivity "will result in the strengthening of the national economy and in fair rewards for all the company's workers." Each issue of the magazine showcased a handful of dedicated workers who embodied these ideals. Often the leaders of the factory's white-collar employees union would be quoted to the effect that "capital and labor . . . are not conflicting interests."[46]

Similarly, both the MNR leadership and the military regime emphasized the need for "labor responsibility and discipline." Since the early years of the revolution MNR leaders had argued that strikes were counterproductive. The official MNR paper editorialized in 1955 that "the only way to defend working-class interests in Bolivia at the current time is to support the Government" and "give it the cooperation of selfless, disciplined, and productive work."[47] The military government of René Barrientos (1964–1969) continued to insist that the government was the "servant of the working class" but more explicitly distinguished "corrupt unionism" from "responsible unionism." The "new unionism," as Barrientos explained in an October 1966 speech to factory workers, rejected "the Marxist line" and "class hatred" and instead "struggles in a civilized way" in cooperation with the government and other social classes.[48]

Accompanying the discourse of responsible labor was a message about responsible, modern enterprise. Government leaders distinguished foreign companies and the nascent Bolivian bourgeoisie from the tin oligarchy of the pre-1952 era, emphasizing their contribution to national economic development. Bolivian business owners depicted themselves as understanding, progressive, and dedicated to the revolutionary nationalist goal of industrial diversification. Antonio Said, owner of the Said textile factory, contrasted the "backward or retrograde enterprise" model of old with the new spirit of "modern enterprise" among business owners who realized "that their mission corresponds to the general economic interest." Written in 1954 amid factory workers' calls for nationalization and workers' control, Said's comments reflected a lingering wariness about the economic path of the revolution. Said defended the place of privately owned national industry by quoting Argentine populist leader Juan Perón, who had recently denounced state enterprise and defended private industry as "the most important factor in the development, wealth, and happiness of all peoples in recent times." According to Said, "These words . . . are all the more significant" given Perón's "policy of state intervention" in the Argentine economy.[49] Said appealed to Perón's reputation to prove the revolutionary nationalist credentials of the policy he himself advocated: state intervention on behalf of national industry coupled with strict respect for private property rights.

The Bolivian elites who employed this discourse were not simply parroting the US line but rather advancing their own class interests. As in postrevolutionary Mexico, the "ideological congruence" between revolutionary elites and US leaders led them to embrace similar discourses for overlapping ends.[50]

Modernization and the Mystique of Development

The psychological objective, as stated in a 1962 USIS report, was "the creation of a mystique of development" that united Bolivian workers with their bosses and the government in a spirit of cooperation. Like the Soligno factory workers, each Bolivian "would be instilled with the feeling that he is an integral part of the Alliance." A steady path to progress would follow from hard work, responsible unionism, and "alignment with the United States," where people's capitalism had allegedly delivered unprecedented economic growth and a high standard of living for everyone.[51]

The US space program was a key focus in USIS efforts to promote the "mystique of development." The program signified the supreme triumph of US technology and industry as well as the US government's peaceful application of scientific knowledge.[52] Numerous USIS public exhibits were designed to awe Bolivians with the program's accomplishments. A 1966 visit to La Paz by US astronauts Richard Gordon and Neil Armstrong was meant to drive home the message. Prior to the visit, the USIS and Bolivian Air Force organized an "Aviation Week" in La Paz high schools with forty-five showings of space films and 65,000 "pictures of the astronauts and of Bolivia viewed from space" distributed nationwide. The week of the visit itself, USIS personnel planted thirteen articles in Bolivian newspapers and produced an audio program that aired on twenty radio stations.[53]

Modernization theory provided much of the intellectual basis for US foreign policy in the 1960s.[54] Policy makers stressed the need for a "middle-class revolution" around the continent, one characterized by economic growth, moderate social reforms, and US-friendly policies, rather than a "workers-and-peasants" revolution of the Cuban variety.[55] As always, the "intellectuals and opinion molders" in Bolivia were key targets. A 1966 issue of *Foro Universitario* featured an essay by Kennedy and Johnson adviser Walt Rostow, who outlined the process of "creating modern societies" while "reducing the abyss between rich and poor sectors that exists in almost all developing nations."[56]

Rostow and other modernization theorists explained underdevelopment by pointing to the shortcomings of Latin American peoples, cultures, and values. They minimized or denied the existence of exploitation, imperialism, and structural barriers to development.[57] The incorporation of modernization theory into USIS propaganda in the 1960s was largely a continuation of George Eder's ideological battle from the previous decade but with new terminology and rhetorical bows to social justice concerns. US informal diplomacy in the 1960s ultimately reflected the same motives that had guided policy in the 1950s.

All the talk of a mystique of development and people's capitalism could not obscure the underlying conflict between fundamentally opposing ideas about the nature of capitalism and international economic relations. Most important was the conflict between the notion that international investment benefited everyone in fair proportions and the argument that such investment hurt target countries or at least disproportionately benefited foreign businesses. Proponents of the first position depicted a mutual-benefit or positive-sum relationship between foreign capital and the Bolivian population, with all parties thus sharing a common interest in the prosperity of private corporations.[58] The second view, a core tenet of resource nationalism and leftist economic thought, held that Bolivia was on the losing end of an exploitative and imperialist relation with foreign capital and the US government. Most Bolivians did not oppose all foreign investment or aid but were decidedly skeptical of its motives and opposed the undue benefits or leverage that foreigners usually enjoyed.[59] These opposing conceptions paralleled debates among economists in the United States and Latin America. While the US government line coincided with the claims of modernization theory and at times overlapped with development economics, including structuralist economics, many intellectual and grassroots voices in Bolivia echoed—and in fact prefigured—the dependency theory articulated in the 1960s.

USIS internal reports offer revealing comments on the challenges posed by public distrust of private capital and US government intervention. Commenting on US oil companies' efforts to secure contracts in the late 1950s, the US ambassador complained "that it has been a tremendous task to overcome the belief of many people here that in the exploitation of Bolivia's oil resources [by US companies], Bolivian national interest would be neglected or, at least, be placed in a subordinate position."[60] Regarding US intervention, a 1961 report noted that "the criticism is often heard that the United States aid programs are not developing the economy of the nation but merely making the rich richer" and that the US government sought to use aid as leverage to shape Bolivian policies. USIS messaging constantly stressed that "that the United States aid program has the basic purpose of helping this country achieve a sound and diversified economic development" and that US aid was "of material benefit to all of the Bolivian people." Officials visiting Bolivia publicized US aid programs like Point IV to illustrate how "free nations can work together for their mutual benefit."[61]

Part of the conflict of economic visions stemmed from starkly different visions of what constituted fairness. The authors of the 1956 study of the mining industry published by Ford, Bacon & Davis complained that foreign investors in Bolivia were deprived of "an equitable share of the proceeds from mine operations" and stressed the need for "the fair sharing of the profits and responsibilities between the essential partners of production." Yet the study proposed a maximum tax rate of only 25 percent on private business. The authors' explanation of Bolivian resentment pointed to "mistaken" popular conceptions about foreign industry and a labor force that was "not informed." But public resentment was not due to lack of information. Most Bolivian workers were unlikely to agree that foreign investors should get 75 percent of total profits or to think of those investors as genuine partners.[62]

Other fundamental disagreements involved ownership of economic resources and workplace relations. The US government remained ideologically opposed to the idea of state-operated enterprises throughout the period, although it eventually—and grudgingly—agreed to lend money to COMIBOL and YPFB in the interest of political stability. In Bolivia the existence of state-run industries was also linked to another evil—workers' control, or at least worker participation in administrative decisions. This system was anathema to the "principle of authority" and the hierarchical boss-worker relationship held so dear by US and Bolivian elites alike. George Eder had fiercely condemned public ownership and worker decision-making power. Nonetheless, these ideas remained central to Bolivian economic thought and political culture in the 1960s. As USIS officials routinely lamented, such attitudes were deeply rooted in Bolivian political culture, and even a far more extensive propaganda effort would have had difficulty eradicating them.

Complicating this battle of economic ideas were the internal contradictions of US government messaging and policy. The uneasy coexistence of monetarist and Keynesian economics that was evident in US policy in the 1950s continued in the 1960s, though the Kennedy administration was moderately more sympathetic to Keynesianism and structuralism than the Eisenhower administration had been.[63] One of the many contradictions of US policy was the disjunction between the economic policies employed at home and those promoted abroad. The US government presented the US economy as a model for Bolivia, but it was not necessarily eager for Bolivia to embrace the Keynesianism and state intervention in the economy that had allowed for US economic development, and officials certainly feared the left-leaning or redistributive variants of such policies. Publicity about the US space program sought to impress Bolivians with the accomplishments of US science and industry, but it never mentioned the state subsidies that allowed for the space program and high-tech sectors to prosper. USIS propaganda praised the social safety net in the United States, but US policy sought to whittle down the already meager Bolivian welfare state.[64] These contradictions made people's capitalism an even harder sell among Bolivians.

The MNR's Redefinition of Revolutionary Identity

Though it lacked the material resources to carry out extensive informational campaigns, the Bolivian government played a crucial role in the effort to remold Bolivian popular nationalism. Its messaging complemented that of the USIS, but was usually formulated independently.

Starting in the mid-1950s the MNR sought to redefine revolutionary nationalist priorities and iconography by shifting the emphasis from mine workers and the urban working class to three groups: the peasantry, the middle class, and the army. The militant mine worker faded or was demonized in official speeches, largely supplanted by these three new symbols of the revolution. The revolution became less about uplifting the exploited worker and more about redeeming the humble campesino and fostering the growth of the middle class in a development process aided by a purportedly revolutionary and productive army. This shift manifested in policy as well as discourse; land reform and expansion of the army accompanied the economic policy measures targeting workers.[65] These discursive and policy shifts reflected the MNR's need to cultivate alternative bases of support to counter the power of the working class, especially miners, at a time when the latter were fiercely resisting austerity and the Triangular Plan.

The exaltation of the peasantry as emblematic of the nation was particularly noticeable starting with Víctor Paz Estenssoro's second term. In an April 1961 speech calling for labor discipline in the mines, Paz simultaneously reflected on the achievements of the revolution, proclaiming that "the most notable of them is that of the campesinos who went from being servants to citizens and today enjoy full membership in the national community."[66] A 1963 government publication on agrarian reform linked "the abolition of servitude" in the countryside to the unification of the national community, proclaiming that "the spiritual strength of a people has been united on a single path: that of Bolivia, before a national goal of conquering underdevelopment."[67] Campesinos assumed an even more central place in revolutionary iconography under the Barrientos regime. Barrientos spoke Quechua and made frequent visits to the Cochabamba countryside, long a center of unrest, to speak to indigenous campesinos in their native tongue. The 1964 Military-Peasant Pact solidified this alliance and guaranteed peasant support for the military government in much of the countryside for the next decade.[68]

Concrete attempts at co-optation and control accompanied the government's rhetorical overtures. The rate of land redistribution jumped in the early 1960s and probably helped consolidate peasant allegiance to the government. After distributing only 320,502 hectares in 1959, the government handed out 852,771 hectares the next year—prior to the Alliance for Progress—and 1.2 million in 1961. Annual distribution figures continued to increase through 1963 before tapering off in 1964. The number of land titles issued followed a similar trend; it more than doubled, from 9,193 in 1958 to 18,380 in 1959, doubled again in 1960, and then averaged 44,400 per year from 1961 to 1963. In the late 1950s the MNR expanded its public health and education initiatives in the countryside, partly to promote peasant allegiance.[69]

Meanwhile, corporatist-style structures sought to impede direct collaboration between peasants and workers. In 1957 MNR moderates outlawed the worker-peasant bloc associated with the MNR left, claiming that it violated party statutes. In 1960 the Communist Party paper *El Pueblo* accused the government and some peasant leaders of "sowing divisions between countryside and city."[70] The paternalism of much of the urban left and working class would have made genuine collaboration difficult under any circumstances, but MNR policy piled more bricks onto the wall of separation between urban workers and campesinos.

Closely related to the MNR's courting of campesinos was its rehabilitation of the Bolivian military. In a 1958 speech to the Bolivian Congress, President Hernán Siles Zuazo spoke of "a new style of popular Army" that "each day seems more like an armed body of citizens." In contrast to the "Praetorian guards" of the past, the new army of the "people in arms . . . is deeply identified with their yearnings for freedom and justice" and follows a "doctrine of peace."[71] *La Nación*, the official government newspaper, carried many articles and editorials contrasting the old and new armies. If the old army had been "the docile instrument of the feudal mining oligarchy" and "an insatiable parasite in whose bosom gestated all of the torments that bloodied this country," the new army "exists through the people."[72] Siles, Paz, and even the left-leaning Juan Lechín had long been wary of the independent leftist militias that had arisen along with the revolution, and they insisted on maintaining a formal army after the MNR took power.[73] From the mid-1950s onward they placed increased emphasis on rehabilitating the army in both material and discursive terms.

This shift coincided closely with US objectives in Bolivia and around Latin America. The constructive role of the Bolivian military was a major point of overlap between USIS propaganda and MNR rhetoric. As noted above, many USIS newsreels by the mid- to late 1950s publicized the US training of Bolivian soldiers and other military activities. In the early 1960s, "civic action" programs became an important strategy for improving the public image of the Bolivian army and of other militaries throughout Latin America. In any Latin American country facing popular rebellion, "the military will be a strong bulwark on the side of democracy and freedom," according to a 1962 State Department planning document. But the USIA noted that because many Latin Americans were slow to grasp the democratic credentials of their countries' militaries, "civic action and psychological warfare" would be necessary "to improve the military image."[74]

This project was part of the MNR's outreach to campesinos in the late 1950s and early 1960s. The army's civic action program focused particularly on agricultural production and prioritized peasant recruitment. Since 1953, "middle-class elements and campesinos" had been specifically targeted for recruitment to the military academies, suggesting that MNR leaders may have seen the rebuilding of the army as part of a strategy for countering working-class power.[75] The MNR undertook a deliberate policy of strengthening peasant militias loyal to the government, despite US misgivings, and relied on them to

Figure 4.3. "1960: The Year of the Middle Class." Víctor Paz's 1960 campaign literature reflects the MNR leadership's attempts to cultivate alternative bases of support. Pages boast of the job opportunities and social security benefits the revolution delivered to the middle class (top) and emphasize the Catholic and non-Communist nature of the MNR (bottom). Source: *1960: Año de la clase media*, UMSA-B, FB 324.6 P348m/MFN 1084. Used with permission.

threaten and occasionally attack unruly workers and students.[76] The government-promoted "colonization" of the eastern lowlands by highland peasants, which was part of an attempt to foster the development of agriculture and hydrocarbons, represented a further conjoining of the military and peasant foci of the government's political project.[77]

A third shift starting in the late 1950s was the MNR's greater emphasis on the middle-class character of Bolivia. The urban middle class had grown substantially since 1952, particularly as a result of the expanded government civil service. MNR efforts to cultivate middle-class support became especially apparent as the 1956 austerity plan alienated working-class sectors. One of Víctor Paz's 1960 campaign pamphlets was entitled "1960: The Year of the Middle Class." The pamphlet reminded readers that the MNR had extended social security benefits to public employees and white-collar workers and "democratized education to open up the positions previously reserved for children of the oligarchy to the children of the middle class" (figure 4.3).[78] Though it preceded the Kennedy administration, this message coincided with the Alliance for Progress's emphasis on middle-class revolution.

Reach and Impact

The reach of USIS efforts was impressive, especially considering Bolivia's lack of communications and transportation infrastructure. By the late 1950s, all of Bolivia's major newspapers, magazines, and book publishers and all thirty-five of its radio stations were "using USIS materials with reasonable frequency." The newspaper space occupied by USIS materials was the highest in Latin America.[79] By early 1961 USIS materials were filling around two thousand column inches per week in the five major La Paz newspapers alone, with one report boasting that "USIS can place in four of them practically any article it considers of special importance."[80] Radio programs and film showings reached broad sectors of the general population. In the early 1960s USIS agents were distributing fourteen weekly radio programs, often with Quechua and Aymara translations, and holding at least ten film showings per day during the dry months. In 1962 alone USAID provided at least two million textbooks for use in schools; combined with the doubling of school enrollments in the ten years prior, they probably allowed US government messaging to reach most of Bolivia's youth. Although USIS officials often complained about the lack of infrastructure and how it hampered their outreach efforts, it seems probable that most of Bolivia's population was exposed to USIS materials.[81]

USIS campaigns are just one part of the story. I have also highlighted the collaborative relations between the USIS and a range of Bolivian elites including MNR leaders, army officials, business owners, and media directors. This collaboration was important in two ways. First, Bolivian media owners and editors were crucial in enabling the USIS to disseminate its message given ordinary Bolivians' miniscule interest in publications and radio stations from the United States and their skepticism of USIS-labeled materials.[82] Second, Bolivian elites' own discourse usually reinforced that of the United States. The coordination of messaging among these groups was sometimes formalized, but Bolivian elites ultimately did not need USIS instruction; they developed their own discourses of the good worker, the modern entrepreneur, the noble peasant, the revolutionary middle class, and the popular army. Bolivian political, economic, and military elites enjoyed a degree of legitimacy and direct access to the general population that the foreign-run USIS campaign did not.

Reach and impact are two separate questions, though. The wide dissemination of USIS and MNR propaganda says little about the effect of that propaganda on its audiences. In private correspondence, USIS officials constantly bemoaned Bolivians' hostility toward US policy and the agency's lack of success in remolding popular attitudes. Resource nationalism proved especially stubborn. In a 1958 USIS progress report on the goal of "promoting popular acceptance of private capital investment," the writer lamented that "the post is engaged in an uphill struggle with attitudes that range from hostile and suspicious to merely skeptical or apathetic." This sort of skepticism was rooted not in any formal or dogmatic identification with communism, especially of the Soviet variety, but in a pervasive "leftist thought pattern" and the belief, common in postwar Latin America, "that the first beneficiaries of the development of a country's resources should be the people of that country."[83] A 1962 report on "the battle for men's minds in Latin America" acknowledged that communism was not the main threat: "If any single current in the wide field of political thought is winning men's minds in Latin America, it is Latin America's own and indigenous nationalism."[84] Such sentiments were an endless source of frustration for the US policy makers charged with combatting them.

MNR officials had a modestly greater degree of success. By the early 1960s the MNR and army had achieved the support or at least acquiescence of most of the country's campesinos and the urban middle class in its attacks on the labor left.[85] Worker-peasant collaboration was infrequent between 1955 and the 1970s. Nonetheless, there were still formidable constraints on the Bolivian government due to popular resistance. In the 1960s the discourse of revolutionary nationalism remained hegemonic, meaning that even the most reactionary politicians had to couch their actions in the languages of resource nationalism, industrialization, national independence, and social justice.[86] Grassroots resistance partially limited the rightward lurch of economic policy as well. Although the years 1956–1969 did feature a marked policy shift to the right, they also saw a rising tide of popular combativeness that placed important limits on what the United States and the MNR moderates could do. The story of La Paz factory workers during these years illustrates this point.

CHAPTER 5

The Limits of Containment:
Anti-Austerity and Resource Nationalism
in La Paz Factories

Alfonso Cordero was among the thousands of armed workers who converged on La Paz in April 1952 to overthrow the military government and clear the way for the MNR. Exactly a decade later, Cordero stood up before ten thousand La Paz factory workers and declared, "We who made the revolution are being betrayed by it."[1] The tenth anniversary of the revolution came amid bitter conflicts between the MNR and its working-class base. The year before, in June 1961, Cordero and 120 La Paz unions filled the streets to protest the MNR government's imprisonment of two union leaders. When the MNR's minister of education vowed that they would only be released "over his dead body," the leader of the factory workers' union shot back that the workers were "used to overthrowing armies" and would continue fighting "against Yankee imperialism, which is imposing its will by means of the State Department." Several days later a protest march ended with four protesters killed, apparently by government forces.[2] The confrontation was but one example of the deepening conflict between Bolivia's increasingly combative popular sectors and a government working alongside US advisers to tame the revolution. By 1962 it was clear that the beast would not be tamed easily.

The history of La Paz factory workers highlights several key points about revolutionary Bolivia. First, it challenges the notion that either the US or MNR government controlled events on the ground. Despite formal allegiance to the MNR throughout most of the period, factory workers' obedience to the national government was highly tenuous. As early as 1952 many workers made a distinction between the revolution and the politicians in government. The factory workers' challenge to government policy became especially apparent in the late 1950s as rank-and-file workers confronted both the MNR and entrenched union executives. And the gathering unrest was not limited to the factories; by the early 1960s the factory workers were among the leaders of a newly emergent popular coalition that included miners, construction workers, teachers, university students, and some campesinos. The original revolutionary coalition had splintered on the shoals of the 1956 stabilization plan and MNR co-optation, but it began to coalesce once again around a program of resource nationalism and anti-austerity in the late 1950s and especially during Paz Estenssoro's second term in the early 1960s. This resurgent coalition challenged MNR economic policy from the left and partly constrained the Bolivian state's ability to overhaul policy.

Second, this case study shows that economic policy debates were not the exclusive domain of elites. The urban working class frequently intervened in these debates, although its interventions took the form of union resolutions and direct actions rather than academic treatises. Factory workers and their union officials were among the most prominent participants in this process of policy making from below. Their demands partially overlapped with those of La Paz's small manufacturing bourgeoisie—which likewise wanted tariffs and other protectionist measures—but the workers defied the factory owners' and MNR leaders' vision of class harmony by advocating better wages and benefits, nationalization, and even workers' control over their workplaces. Nor did they limit themselves to demands for better wages or benefits. They also articulated coherent positions on complex issues like industrialization and mineral and hydrocarbon policies, becoming leading voices of resource nationalism.

While resource nationalism was not the only important economic idea circulating among factory workers, it was a central part of their structure of feeling. Alongside anti-austerity, it was one of the two most important bases for coalitional mobilization after 1956. Anti-austerity and resource nationalism were closely linked, and not only because La Paz workers' resource nationalism included demands for increased spending; factory workers' resource nationalism also became more vociferous by the late 1950s as the effects of austerity sank in. Workers faced with economic deprivation became more inclined to tackle broad social issues rather than retreating into an insular bread-and-butter unionism. Their militancy hastened the breakdown of the MNR pact with labor and the failure of revolutionary consolidation.

This history challenges the applicability of the concept of "labor aristocracy" for the case of La Paz workers. Many observers have speculated that by virtue of its wages, job security, and work and living conditions, a large proportion of the urban proletariat will be politically cautious and focused on narrow wage issues rather than seeking control of the means of production or fomenting revolutionary political change.[3] Many scholars studying underdeveloped countries have argued that the scarcity of industrial employment means urban wage workers will be particularly resistant to revolutionary politics and easily co-opted by states and employers. In Frantz Fanon's formulation, industrial workers in such economies have "everything to lose" and "because of the privileged place which they hold in the colonial system constitute also the 'bourgeois' fraction of the colonized people."[4] In the Latin American context, the labor aristocracy concept is certainly helpful in explaining revolutionary institutionalization and the longevity of populist regimes in Mexico, Brazil, Argentina, and other countries.[5]

The argument is less convincing in the case of La Paz factory workers. Their growing confrontation of the MNR and military governments contradicts the US embassy's optimistic assessment in early 1952 that the factory workforce was "more concerned with straight trade-union questions, such as wages" than with politics and that it would form the core of the "responsible trade unions in Bolivia."[6] This history also challenges the emphasis of some left historians on the "backwardness" of the factory workforce "with reference to the miners," calling for a reappraisal of the importance of this working-class sector in the MNR era.[7] While the labor-aristocracy depiction does hold some truth—given, for instance, factory workers' disdain for rural Indians, described below—it fails to explain the workers' increasing combativeness and relatively broad social outlook.

Two factors explain the rising militancy of La Paz workers during the MNR period. First, in structural terms, the fiscal and infrastructural weakness of the Bolivian state and the persistent underdevelopment of industry meant that certain means of ensuring quiescence were less available to the MNR and factory owners than in other countries. Second, and less traceable to structural conditions, was La Paz's working-class "political culture of opposition."[8] In the case of La Paz factory workers, militancy was fueled by their sense of class, sectoral, and national identity—and perhaps to some extent ethnic identity—combined with diverse ideological currents. Long-standing ideologies and ideas like Marxism, anarchism, resource nationalism, and industrial protectionism all played a role in forging factory workers' political identity. So, too, did other factors more specific to the historical context of the 1950s, namely, the collective memory of factory workers' sacrifices in bringing the MNR to power and a notion of moral economy that held MNR leaders responsible for fulfilling revolutionary aspirations. At the same time, this collective identity was neither monolithic nor uncontested but rather the product of ongoing intraclass struggles. It was also in some respects quite reactionary.[9]

Assessing the attitudes of rank-and-file workers poses important methodological challenges, for the words of most workers never find their way into the documentary record. Here I use three types of evidence to infer rank-and-file consciousness: (1) the record of mass-based activities like marches, strikes, and union votes; (2) the appraisals of elite sources like the National Chamber of Industries (CNI) and the USIS, which were not inclined to exaggerate their own unpopularity;[10] and (3) the rhetoric of union leaders. With regard to this last source, my methodological assumption is that in a union that is at least moderately democratic—meaning that leaders feel pressure to be perceived favorably by their constituents—the leaders' rhetorical demands vis-à-vis employers and the government can be viewed as rough reflections of rank-and-file attitudes.

Factory Workers and the MNR to 1956

Manufacturing "remained in diapers" in Bolivia up to the 1930s, as a member of the Bolivian Congress put it in 1956.[11] Nonetheless, the two decades following the Chaco War witnessed the growth of a substantial urban industrial sector focused on the production of textiles, food, beverages, and other light consumer goods for the domestic population, with textiles being the most important industry by value and by number of workers. The Great Depression and Chaco War gave a boost to manufacturing, leading to significant rural-to-urban migration. By 1938 there were 332 manufacturing establishments in La Paz, which accounted for the vast majority of Bolivian factories. By the mid-1940s the city had more than 8,300 factory workers, of whom 3,400 were employed in the textile industry.[12] This growth was significant given the small population of La Paz—301,000 in 1942—and Bolivia more generally, which was slightly more than three million in 1950.[13]

The modest industrial expansion gave rise to a variety of new organizations on both sides of the labor/capital divide. In 1931 employers formed the predecessor of the CNI, in which the owners of the city's new factories played a prominent role.[14] Meanwhile, individual unions emerged in dozens of businesses around the city to confront working conditions that one historian describes as "inferior to those prevailing in the mines": long working hours, starvation wages, and employers who refused to abide by even the meager social legislation then in place.[15] There were also efforts to link workers on an industry basis. Around 1936 the city's textile workers formed a Textile Union, and in 1941 twenty-six unions joined together to form the La Paz–wide National Union of Factory Workers (USTFN).[16]

The factory workers unions were characterized by the same ideological conflicts as in the late 1930s, featuring competition between the anarchist FOL and Marxist labor bodies like the FOT and the CSTB. Anarchist influence declined in the 1940s, however, around the same time that MNR loyalists (*movimientistas*) started to gain popularity. The CSTB's decline, meanwhile, came after it supported Villarroel's 1946 overthrow and allied itself with the first of the right-wing *sexenio* (1946–1952) governments. The MNR profited at its expense. The USTFN withdrew from the CSTB soon after the 1946 coup and remained close to the MNR thereafter.[17]

Despite the USTFN leadership's generally nonconfrontational approach to politics and workplace relations, La Paz factory workers played a vital role in the urban resistance during the *sexenio*. In early 1950 they joined with print workers, bank workers, vendors, railroad workers, and miners in a Coordinating Committee to protest working conditions and political repression in the country. The government of Mamerto Urriolagoitia had just enacted a series of executive decrees devaluing the currency and severely restricting union activities, even prohibiting certain sectors like the railroad workers from unionizing altogether, and it would soon outlaw all communist parties. When the government arrested the committee's leaders, they were replaced by new faces, including glass worker Germán Butrón, who was elected general secretary. Opposition parties, meanwhile, formed a Committee of Four, composed of the Marxist parties (the POR, PIR, and PCB) and the MNR.[18]

Factory workers provided the biggest spark. In late April Butrón and his fellow glass workers went on strike, and a wave of solidarity strikes followed. The major textile and shoe factories, including Said, Forno, Soligno, and García, all shut down.[19] On April 27 the

Coordinating Committee called a general strike, citing the "reactionary, oligarchic, and pro-imperialist nature of the regime governing the country" and calling for "worker unity."[20] The strike ended only after the government sent the army into the Villa Victoria neighborhood, where many factory workers lived, killing anywhere from thirteen to one hundred factory workers and arresting hundreds more.[21] The Villa Victoria massacre and the factory workers' vital role in the three days of fighting in April 1952 would assume a central place in the workers' collective memory.

These sacrifices helped define La Paz factory workers' sense of the rights and benefits to which they were entitled and would become essential parts of their strategic-discursive tool kit after 1952. Factory workers would frequently cite their role in the armed struggles of 1950 and 1952 to justify postrevolutionary demands for better wages and benefits and greater political influence. In one typical case from early 1953, workers at the Said textile factory demanded the dismissal of an abusive factory supervisor whom they characterized as an "executioner of workers," pointing to his active collaboration with the armed forces in the violent repression of May 1950. They repeatedly threatened to go on strike and warned that "the Union will not be held responsible for the consequences" if the supervisor reappeared in the factory.[22] Union statements often referred to factory workers as "the authentic representatives of nationalist concerns" and situated the sector as the "urban vanguard" of the revolution.[23] It was factory workers who had "taken up arms to carry out the actions of April 9," a factory workers' delegate to Congress told lawmakers in 1958, and who "as men, have taken to the streets to defend the National Revolution on all occasions." The revolution was "the revolution of the factory workers," who were the country's "most combative" sector and "the sustaining force of the National Revolution."[24]

The factory workers' relations with the MNR were complex. The La Paz Factory Workers Federation had close ties to the party during the right-wing *sexenio* and declared "unconditional support" for Víctor Paz Estenssoro after he took power.[25] At first glance, much of their political rhetoric suggests a strong allegiance to MNR leaders, particularly Paz, and by extension to the cautious reformism and class collaborationism those leaders advocated. But La Paz factory workers often used revolutionary nationalism to their advantage with the government as well as their bosses in the factories. In the process they infused the concept with a radicalism seldom present in the government's own discourse and exercised a significant constraining influence on government practice as well.

Unlike the COMIBOL mine workers, factory workers were employed by private capitalists. Their relationship to the MNR regime was therefore more complicated; the state was both a target of demands and a secondary target that could be enlisted to exert pressure on their employers. The state was the target of factory workers' petitions for industrial rehabilitation loans, protective tariffs, anticontraband measures, and demands pertaining to the development of tin, oil, education, and other sectors. It was a secondary target in cases like the Said conflict in which workers appealed to the government to expel an abusive supervisor.

An April 1953 resolution from the La Paz federation offers an indication of the dynamic between the factory workers and the national government in the early MNR period. The resolution first praises Víctor Paz as "a living example of modesty, sincerity, honor, and hard work, of whom all Bolivians feel proud." But two sentences later the federation states its "DEMANDS of his immediate colleagues, those who share the reins of Government with him, that they abstain from the luxury cars, the bourgeois banquets, and worst of all the scandalous orgies of reckless and irresponsible people in taverns and night clubs, because we feel that is the worst affront, the worst insult that they can make to the working and peasant class."[26] The complaint reflects a definition of morality firmly rooted in class consciousness and the desire for accountable, representative government. The fiscal costs imposed by the indulgences of a few MNR leaders were minor in the larger scheme of things, but the transgressions had profound symbolic importance for the workers, who viewed them as violations of an implicit moral contract between the revolutionary government and the pueblo.[27] Though focused on the personal behavior of officials rather than larger policy questions, the resolution put the government on notice about the workers' expectations and implied that other "bourgeois" behavior would not be tolerated.

The resolution's praise for the person of Paz Estenssoro reflected a common element in factory worker discourse in the early years. When police raided the home of a union leader in 1953, the factory union responded with a resolution blaming the "enemies of the Revolution, encrusted in the heart of the Government."[28] Workers often depicted their own protests as a defense of the true spirit of the revolution. When the Fanase factory workers threatened to strike in October 1952 over their employer's refusal to address their grievances, union leaders claimed to be taking action "not only for ourselves but for the future of the entire working class." A 1956 factory workers' statement promised to guard against the "betrayal" of the "vacillating middle-class men who are embedded in the heart of the government."[29]

The vows of allegiance to the MNR and to Paz in particular can be read two ways: as indications of subservience or as a strategic discourse for the advancement of the workers' interests. Most often, they were probably something in between. When factory workers professed loyalty to the MNR they were generally not signaling "blind faith" in the government; they expected something in return.[30] Many appeals for government support did not exactly ring of humble supplication. When the La Paz federation's general secretary, Daniel Saravia, requested the expulsion of the Said supervisor in early 1953, he also threatened "that the workers, given that their just requests are not being addressed, will take the necessary measures to defend the National Revolution."[31] Yet most workers probably took the MNR's revolutionary nationalist rhetoric seriously and believed that the MNR leadership might fulfill its promises, though the belief diminished as time wore on.[32] Between the two poles of subservience and clever strategic manipulation lies a complex psychopolitical realm.

Early worker critiques of MNR leaders were often subtle and implicit, coming in the form of divergences between worker and government statements on various issues but without erupting into overt conflict. While MNR leaders supported the US-backed coup in Guatemala in June 1954 or at most spoke out half-heartedly against it, the factory workers' second congress the next month said the new Guatemalan regime had been "imposed by imperialism" and was filled with "enemies of the American proletariat."[33] While Juan Lechín advocated *control obrero* (workers' control) in industry as "the best way of cooperating in production" to "achieve greater output," factory workers at the 1954 congress placed more value on its inherent contribution to social justice and a more democratic workplace.[34] The first factory-worker statements on the stabilization plan in December 1956 officially supported the plan but with the crucial qualification that the plan had to "maintain the social and economic conquests of the working class" to that point.[35] Thus, the factory workers' early relationship to the MNR rarely involved overt conflict, though quiet tensions were often apparent.

Disagreements generally stayed within the bounds of revolutionary nationalism, with parties diverging over the meaning and extent of the "national revolution." Few critics outside the extreme right proposed to overthrow the MNR. Even many of the Marxists who were skeptical of nationalism and sought the overthrow of capitalism often adopted this discourse and shied away from condemning the MNR altogether. Revolutionary nationalism had achieved hegemonic status, and political contenders had to work within this "common discursive framework" to advance their claims.[36] The 1956 stabilization plan would threaten to tear apart the fragile coalitions of 1952–1956, including the factory workers' alliance with the MNR, but without altering this fundamental dynamic of contention. Even most of those who supported the 1964 overthrow of the MNR cited the party's lack of compliance with revolutionary nationalist ideals rather than repudiating those ideals.

We Who Made the Revolution Are Being Betrayed

The monetary stabilization plan hurt factory owners and their workers, especially the latter. The plan's elimination of the system of multiple exchange rates was devastating since most urban industry had depended on the importation of raw materials at subsidized rates. The shortage of raw materials had been a frequent source of worker and owner complaints even prior to 1956, but the elimination of the exchange-rate subsidy intensified the problem. By 1962 the National Chamber of Industries reported that "53 percent of factory equipment is going unused for lack of raw materials."[37]

Workers' real wages suffered, despite the compensatory one-time increases that accompanied the plan.[38] The perception of falling real incomes was widespread among urban workers. In a poll of La Paz workers in late 1957, around half of respondents "thought that their own personal situations had worsened" as a result of stabilization.[39] CEPAL reports blamed three factors in addition to the currency devaluation itself: the elimination of government price subsidies for certain consumer goods, the increase in fuel and transportation prices, and the reduction of overtime hours in industry. Reduced purchasing power led to less consumption, which amplified industry's troubles and threatened the jobs of workers.[40]

The stabilization plan thus increased the material burdens on industrial workers while eroding the capacity of factory owners to ensure worker quiescence through monetary incentives. It also limited the MNR's ability to maintain the workers' allegiance. Although factory workers were not employed by the government, they depended heavily on its subsidization of consumer goods and, indirectly, on the manipulation of exchange rates that allowed for the cheaper acquisition of raw materials. By eating away at workers' real wages and reducing the co-optative power of both employers and the state, the stabilization plan undermined the material basis for worker loyalty and destabilized the network of uneasy alliances that had been held together by high spending.

Factory workers' responses to stabilization and austerity varied significantly depending on the conditions, management style, and political culture prevailing in individual factories. Some evidence suggests that factories with greater capital, higher wages, and more paternalistic managers witnessed relatively less worker militancy than their counterparts. Contrasting developments in two otherwise similar La Paz textile factories, Said and Soligno, highlight the importance of factory-specific conditions.

Founded in 1929 by a Palestinian immigrant and his sons, the Said factory soon became one of the country's largest manufacturing establishments, employing nearly five hundred workers by 1935. Besides paying workers relatively high wages and instituting overtime pay, the Saids implemented a variety of corporate welfare programs at a time when few other owners were doing so. By the late 1930s the factory was already providing medical and dental services, "the first proletarian school in the country," and even an ophthalmology hospital for workers.[41] By the early 1950s the factory offered diverse activities for workers, including twice-weekly movie showings in Said's theater, sports leagues for soccer, boxing, and tennis, and annual *carnaval* celebrations. Along with the material benefits they offered, these programs allowed the elder Said to cultivate an image of himself as a benevolent father figure and to promote values conducive to class harmony and increased production. The factory gave out periodic awards for exemplary work, often to indigenous and female laborers, to drive home the benefits of hard work and loyalty.[42] A 1954 issue of the factory's official magazine, *Revista Said*, publicized the factory's school with a quote from the director telling workers to "feel proud of this altruistic contribution and remain grateful for its founder, who in addition to being one of the active promoters of industry is also [an active promoter] of education."[43]

Antonio Said frequently employed the language of God, country, and family to reinforce traditional values of patriarchy, hierarchy, and class harmony. He established a Female Workers Club in the late 1940s that featured classes on cooking, sewing, and other "feminine labors" for the participants, with the explicit goals of "cultivating in them love of the homeland, observance of familial norms, etc."[44] The use of religion was even less subtle. Jesus Christ was the "patron saint of the factory." Every year Said sponsored a trip for all workers to the Copacabana shrine on the shores of Lake Titicaca. On one such trip in 1955, the shrine's director preached God's word to the assembled workers: "United in our duties, in patriotism, we are constructing the national glory, because we are part of the Bolivian family without distinctions." Capitalism, country, and the Almighty melded seamlessly together in common cause. "Before the great Workshop which is the homeland, we must all work together and in harmony, for God wills it that way."[45] Such exhortations were indicative of the paternalism with which Said sought to ensure worker quiescence. Perhaps in no other Bolivian factory were the paternalistic structures and management style so highly developed.[46]

This background may help explain the differing responses of the Said and Soligno workers to the stabilization plan. Said remained a bastion of support for the Siles government during the plan's crucial first year, refraining from overt challenges to either the government or Said management. The Said union was among the unions that publicly disavowed the COB second congress's June 1957 call for a general strike in opposition to the plan. The Soligno workers, meanwhile, initially supported the plan but were conspicuously absent from several mid-year newspaper accounts intended to publicize factory workers' continued enthusiasm for stabilization.[47] In a May 1957 incident that captures this contrast, the Soligno union and twenty other factory unions on the Popular Revolutionary slate accused the Said leadership of rigging elections for the La Paz federation to favor pro-Siles candidates, saying that the elections "have been directed from the National Political Committee [of the MNR]."[48]

Soligno workers continued to be among the most unruly in the years that followed. Workers in one section of the factory went on a hunger strike in November 1958 over the poor quality of materials provided to them. When the government declared the strike illegal, meaning that workers would not receive pay for their days on strike, a group of workers apparently assaulted supervisory personnel—prompting a flurry of media commentary and accusations of "terrorism" from the National Chamber of Industries.[49] Soligno workers simultaneously pressured the government for industrial loans and enforcement of tariffs on manufactured goods. Partly as a result of their actions, including strike threats, Soligno was one of three factories targeted for major rehabilitation loans, along with USIS propaganda, under the Alliance for Progress in 1961.[50] Meanwhile, USIS propaganda often profiled Said's workforce as an exemplar of responsible unionism.[51]

The contrast between Said and Soligno notwithstanding, divisions among factory workers and within the COB more broadly faded somewhat in the years after 1957. By 1959 most factory workers were united in their condemnation of the stabilization plan. The fourth congress of the Bolivian General Confederation of Factory Workers (CGTFB) in March 1959 declared that the stabilization plan "has no other outcome but mass firings, hunger, and misery" and that the government's economic policies since 1956 "have done nothing but accentuate ever more the misery and hunger of the working family, reducing production costs through the gradual reduction of real wages and the reduction of the number of workers." The congress resolved that the plan had been "imposed by our feudal bourgeoisie and by imperialism by means of dollar loans" and accused President Siles and his administration of "a capitulating surrender [*entreguismo*] before imperialism." Perhaps most surprisingly, the delegates to the congress voted to repudiate the very idea of cogovernment with the MNR, declaring that "so-called cogovernment has never existed" and rejecting "any attempt to create a new cogovernment."[52]

Paz's second term brought renewed economic growth,[53] but by 1961 protests flared up again in the country's cities and mines. In May the La Paz Factory Workers Federation threatened to strike over the government's failure to provide rehabilitation funds to the city's factories. When the government responded by arresting two union leaders, Daniel Saravia and Max Toro, ten thousand La Paz factory workers marched to demand their release. Around this time union statements began placing greater emphasis on noneconomic demands than they had previously; while they continued to request government assistance, they insisted on the need for civil liberties. They demanded that the government respect the *fuero sindical*, meaning union independence and right to protest, as well as the factory workers' independent radio station in La Paz.[54] They deepened their ties with the national mine workers' federation, the FSTMB, and a number of other sectors such as construction workers and university students, often signing formal solidarity agreements to support each other's struggles.

Sacrifice and betrayal were key themes in these protests. Factory workers' statements presented their sector as the self-sacrificing victims of back-stabbing politicians. Alfonso Cordero told the workers' rally in April 1962 that the workers "who made the revolution" through their valiant combat were "now being betrayed by it"—or, more precisely, by the politicians at the top of the MNR.[55] The CGTFB newspaper argued in 1963 that "factory workers have been the most sacrificed in these eight years of Monetary Stabilization."[56] The factory workers' self-identification as an urban vanguard charged with ensuring that revolutionary ideals were fulfilled became more common in the aftermath of the stabilization plan.

Worker protests did not let the factory owners off the hook. Although the workers wanted many of the same things the owners wanted—government loans, cheaper raw materials, protective tariffs, and enforcement of anticontraband laws—the owner-worker relationship deteriorated rapidly after 1957. In the second half of 1958 several La Paz factories went on strike over a variety of grievances, targeting both employers and the state; while some demanded higher wages, others demanded higher-quality raw materials. In October the CGTFB announced a national strike over the failure of the CNI to respond to worker petitions, and the owners threatened a lock-out in response.[57] In November Labor Minister Aníbal Aguilar complained of a "virtual Cold War . . . between the forces of labor and capital" and organized a seminar in La Paz to try to "reconcile the interests of workers and bosses," who were "mutually attacking each other."[58]

Aguilar's efforts proved fruitless. The following February the CGTFB announced that it would hold a massive march targeting factory owners. In response the CNI accused "some union leaders" of promoting "a permanent class war with the destruction of private industrial enterprise as its predictable outcome" and expressed shock at this "act of repudiation of the businesses that provide them with paid work and opportunities for material and moral progress." The CNI leaders appealed to Aguilar, who assured them that the march would not take place.[59] Suppressing the march did little to pacify the factories, though. The first one hundred days of 1959 averaged about one strike every two days nationwide.[60]

The Scheming and Corrupt

The torrent of discontent among the factory workers after 1956 would have had far less impact had it not been for a parallel confrontation within the unions themselves. The stabilization plan turned up the heat on union leaders, who were caught between their disgruntled bases and a federal government intent on imposing austerity. As MNR economic policy drifted rightward, many workers started to blame entrenched union officers as well as MNR politicians and capitalists.

Rank-and-file displeasure with union leaders became more apparent starting in 1957. Wálter Delgadillo Terceros, himself a leader of the CGTFB in the 1980s, notes the increasingly frequent rank-and-file denunciations of the *mañudos* and *viciosos* in union leadership positions; these labels translate loosely as "scheming" and "corrupt." Both terms were "applied to leaders who are adept at exploiting [the privileges of their positions] and at not working in the factory."[61] Many workers felt betrayed not just by the MNR leadership but also by their own elected representatives. When Alfonso Cordero spoke about "being betrayed," he was reflecting a widespread sentiment—and perhaps trying to stave off any potential criticism of himself as a union official for not standing up to the government. At the same rally at least one other high-level CGTFB official was booed off the stage and prevented from speaking by the workers in the crowd.[62]

Union leaders serving in government positions were particular targets. Since 1952 various labor representatives had accepted positions under the MNR's system of cogovernment, particularly in the Ministry of Labor. In May 1957 one factory worker complained that "before stabilization the petitions [to government ministries] flew right through and were resolved quickly; now things have changed, because the ministers have pitted themselves against us."[63] That same month Félix Lara, a factory worker representative who had been appointed minister of labor, was berated by a workers' assembly and forced to resign his government position.[64]

But the most dramatic remonstrations were still to come. Delegates to the fifth conference of La Paz factory workers in January 1959 voted to prohibit worker representatives from taking government positions. The move was directed particularly at CGTFB General Secretary Abel Ayoroa, who was then doubling as minister of labor. Ayoroa's refusal to resign led to his ouster within the CGTFB at the factory workers' national congress in March—and, remarkably, to the ouster of the entire CGTFB executive committee. This rank-and-file rebuke was virtually "unprecedented" in the history of Bolivian unionism, notes Christopher Mitchell. The new group of officials had harsh critiques of MNR policy and reflected the spirit of outrage and frustration that characterized the 1959 congress.[65] In the years that followed, the new officials themselves would also be subjected to scrutiny and occasional denunciation by critics who perceived them as being too cozy with the MNR and military governments.[66]

The increased criticism of the MNR government from the factory workers unions in the late 1950s and early 1960s was not the result of a few singular leaders but of a widespread and growing rank-and-file disenchantment with government policies and employer intransigence. Indeed, it seems to have been worker pressures on union leaders that often pushed the latter to press the government and bosses. This process of internal union revitalization, however incomplete, helped pave the way for the factory workers' confrontation with the MNR.[67]

Militant voices in the CGTFB, as in most individual unions, were generally affiliated with either the MNR left or one of the Marxist parties, the Trotskyist POR or the Communist Party, the PCB. Significantly, however, most of the new elected leaders were still self-identified *movimientistas* rather than Marxists. The MNR left seems to have held a modest advantage over the Marxists within the confederation throughout this entire period.[68] At the fifth congress of the CGTFB, in May 1961, for instance, the *movimientistas'* political resolution defeated the one presented by the Trotskyists and Communists by a vote of 135–108. The theses differed primarily "in their appraisal of the current political situation," according to a newspaper report, with the winning resolution reaffirming general support for the Paz administration.[69] Although the Marxist parties enjoyed substantial support, as the May 1961 vote suggests, the majority of factory workers were not ready to renounce all support for the MNR. In 1961 most workers still held out hope that MNR leaders might be pushed to fulfill the ideals of revolutionary nationalism, particularly now that Siles had been replaced by Víctor Paz, who had presided over those hopeful years at the beginning of the revolution. Some workers may also have doubted the Marxist left's ability to govern, especially given a hostile international context, or feared that the fall of the reformist MNR could usher in a more reactionary alternative, as it eventually did.

On the other hand, workers' unwillingness to break with the MNR does not necessarily indicate approval of MNR policies, nor does it mean that workers were willing to sacrifice in the interest of boosting production while capitalists prospered. As the political activities of the CGTFB and the La Paz Factory Workers Federation suggest, continued attachment to the MNR did not preclude what was at times scathing criticism of government policy. In this sense, focusing on the intra-union conflicts between the MNR left and Marxists can obscure the substantial commonalities among the two groups.[70] The increased rank-and-file support for both factions by the late 1950s is an indication of widespread disillusionment and willingness to criticize the MNR leadership. Workers who voted for Marxist representatives and most of those who supported the MNR left were united in their repudiation of the government's economic policies, including austerity and the "pawning" of the nation's resources; they differed over the proper stance toward the government and in the extent of their critique of capitalism.[71]

Keynesians and *Dependentistas* in the Factories

Workers in La Paz came to detest the stabilization plan, but what exactly did they want in place of it? Popular demands focused heavily on wage and benefit levels, as one would expect, but many workers also insisted on the need for structural transformations in the economy. Though they rarely cited any experts, union statements on the economy embodied many of the same arguments that economists in the Keynesian, structuralist, Marxist, and dependency schools were making, or would soon make, in more academic form. The mix of policy prescriptions that emerged from these statements belies the frequent charge that critics of austerity and corporate capitalism lacked alternative proposals. Despite disagreements within the workforce—particularly over the question of capitalist ownership—La Paz workers in the 1950s and 1960s were broadly united around a progressive resource nationalism that sought state intervention to promote the capture of resource rent, industrialization, diversification, and a more egalitarian distribution of the economic surplus. This agenda reflected the influence of prerevolutionary agitation dating back to the 1920s, but it received fuller articulation in the 1950s. After 1956, as austerity wrought havoc on workers' real incomes, its tone would become more strident and its content more radical.

Factory workers' statements on the economy often emphasized the need for fundamental changes in the structure and model of development. Many workers were keenly aware of the inherent problems of Bolivia's mono-export economic structure and insisted on the need to overcome external dependency and increase the country's self-sufficiency through diversification. Factory workers often emphasized their sector's importance in the attempt to build "a prosperous and independent national economy." The manufacture of consumer goods was deemed essential to fulfilling these revolutionary mandates. Factory workers appealed to their own importance when demanding wage increases from employers as well as state policies like loans, tariffs, mandatory profit reinvestment, and the suppression of contraband.[72] Only through "the most patriotic defense of national industries" could the economy and the country be saved, argued a statement of the Cochabamba workers federation in 1954.[73]

Like many other groups, the factory workers also emphasized the importance of constructing mineral smelters.[74] The industrialization of the mining and hydrocarbons sectors was considered central to the progress and diversification of the broader economy. Many working-class voices viewed natural resources not just as a source of rent for redistribution but as potential levers for creating a more stable economy. To that end factory worker representatives frequently advocated smelter construction and, after 1960, the acceptance of the Soviet offer to fund a tin smelter.

Factory-worker unions joined the miners and other groups in calling for a different development "model," meaning the mode of administering the economy. They demanded the strengthening of the state sector and often advocated its expansion into other realms of the economy. The defense of COMIBOL and YPFB, the two biggest state companies, was a concern of many unions around the country, not simply the miners and oil workers themselves. Various factory workers' congresses during the early 1960s called upon the state to invest more capital in COMIBOL, YPFB, and other state enterprises and for workers to defend against any attempts at reprivatization. Resolutions condemned foreign financiers for seeking to "weaken and destroy state enterprises" and thereby reinforce Bolivia's subjection "to the orders of the North."[75]

A related priority for many workers was deepening economic cooperation among underdeveloped countries. A typical 1959 speech by a COB representative argued "that Bolivia's main enemy is foreign capitalism, which amounts to a few big trusts [controlling everything]."

The speaker went on to call for the formation of a "United States of the South" and proposed "a Latin American *Bandung*," referring to the 1955 conference of Third World governments in Indonesia that became known for its message of nonalignment in the Cold War. The CGTFB in 1956 had envisioned "the formation of the United States of Latin America."[76] At other times these calls explicitly advocated closer economic ties to the Soviet bloc, particularly in the interest of financing smelter construction. In the early 1960s statements of solidarity with the Cuban Revolution became common from Marxist as well as MNR-left factions.[77] Integration was deemed necessary for economic and political reasons, and the two rationales were closely linked; unity would facilitate joint economic efforts like common markets and regional planning, and economic development would in turn increase Latin America's political independence. Similar ideas would receive emphasis in structuralist and dependency writings by the 1960s.

Like the US policy makers who viewed Bolivia as a test case in the struggle to contain Third World nationalism, many Bolivians also saw their revolution as a test—for the ability of Third World peoples to cast off the shackles of imperialism and dependency. Workers' statements often ascribed a transcendent importance to their particular struggles, which they linked not only to "the future of the entire working class" in Bolivia but to the future of all oppressed peoples around the world. In their December 1956 statement the leaders of the factory workers' confederation declared that "the Bolivian Revolution constitutes the keystone in Latin America, an example for other American peoples who struggle for national liberation in their own places." In October 1956 a representative of the miners told the Congress that "workers and peasants around the world have been watching these events, because a victory of the Bolivian Revolution [will] reverberate and promote the revolutionary victory of other countries."[78] Here "victory" meant not just survival but also breaking the bonds of national dependence on foreign powers as well as traditional domestic elites. This goal was broadly shared by all major political factions within the factory workers unions, although Marxists are most often associated with it.

Even the more mundane wage demands often reflected an understanding of larger economic forces. In a public appeal to the National Chamber of Industries in 1963, CGTFB leaders justified their call for graduated wage raises of 20 to 60 percent by emphasizing the potential benefits to the economy. The "subhuman" conditions in urban industry were immoral, but they also impeded national economic development because "impoverished masses cannot constitute the Market that industry requires. The only way of invigorating and stabilizing our economy is to remunerate workers adequately, for only then can they become the main consumers of the country's industrial production. . . . We don't think it's necessary to have a profound knowledge of economics to understand such a simple truth."[79] Though their rhetoric was self-interested, the CGTFB leaders understood the potential benefits of higher wages for the entire economy and used the logic of wage-led growth to their advantage.

The CGTFB congress a month before denounced a number of common capitalist claims about the relation of wages to prices and economic growth. To the argument that higher wages automatically translated to higher prices for the consumer, the congress pointed out that wages since 1956 "have been virtually frozen, and, nonetheless, prices have risen by more than 80 percent." Both inflation and deflation were understood as means of wealth redistribution: "With inflation the exploiting classes increased their profits by taking money from workers' pockets under the pretext of capitalizing the country." The congress decried those who insisted that "industrial rehabilitation" was first necessary before wages could be increased, arguing that wage increases need not cripple factory operations if, for example, state subsidies were increased or profit levels reduced. This analysis was wrong about the forces favoring inflation—the exploiting classes staunchly opposed it—but it was otherwise accurate.[80]

The most threatening aspect of factory-worker agitation, however, was the challenge to that most cherished of capitalist principles, the freedom of the bosses to hire, fire, and otherwise organize the workplace as they pleased. Factory workers' public statements often demanded greater union supervision and control over factory operations. In November 1958 the CNI filed its own petition to the government, emphasizing the need for discipline in the factories. By "discipline" it meant specifically the "autonomy of management in order to organize and manage factories without union interference."[81] The petition's demands for tariffs, the elimination of contraband, and industrial loans coincided with workers' demands, but on the question of workplace control the two parties were firmly opposed.

Factory workers themselves were not entirely united on this question either, though. The role of the bourgeoisie, which at its root was a debate over the capitalist system itself, was a source of much disagreement within the factory workforce: Should workers control the factories, or should they simply exercise greater influence over decision making? Over which decisions should they have a say? Should the government promote the growth of a "national bourgeoisie" that would drive industrial capitalist development, as Bolivian capitalists, middle-class leaders, and Stalinists all advocated? Or should it "skip" this historical phase and create a socialist system in which workers owned the factories, as the Trotskyists argued? These debates had important implications, especially for political strategy; workers could either join in a cross-class alliance with the nationalist bourgeoisie and middle class against the forces of imperialism or reject such alliances and struggle simultaneously against imperialism and their domestic class oppressors. In practical terms, it was unclear whether opting for the latter would mean withdrawing all support from the MNR government. This debate reflected a broader ideological conflict within Bolivia's popular sectors, which pitted most of the MNR left and the Stalinists against the Trotskyists.

Many workers resented capitalists and imperialists but stopped short of advocating an end to the bourgeoisie itself. Union discussions of workers' control highlight the tension between this group and the Trotskyist left. The concept of workers' control was more complicated in revolutionary Bolivia than in the traditional socialist formulation. The system instituted in the nationalized mines provided for union input over some decisions, such as hiring and firing, but stopped far short of putting workers themselves—let alone the rest of the population—fully in charge of production, allocation, and consumption. Juan Lechín advocated workers' control "not to crush capitalism . . . but to prevent the abusive use of capital and the extraction of capital from the country." Many Bolivian workers aspired "more to share in the control of traditional managerial functions rather than to overthrow them," as historian Charles Maier says of labor unions in postwar Europe.[82] Moreover, even the MNR's limited system of workers' control was compromised by bureaucracy.[83]

Within the CGTFB, too, workers and union leaders advocated a range of workers' control arrangements that differed in their priorities and in the extent to which worker representatives would exercise real power. Many factory worker statements seemed to envision unions acting merely as auditors, for instance, overseeing loans and budgets to prevent employers from stealing funds.[84] CGTFB Executive Secretary Stanley Camberos interpreted the concept this way. Camberos was elected in 1959 due to rank-and-file discontent with the pro-Siles conservatism of his predecessors, but he was a *movimientista* who believed in working within the capitalist system to improve workers' lives—or at least he doubted the viability of worker-run enterprises. In a 1961 comment that revealed his capitalist inclinations, Camberos tried to defuse calls for wage raises by insisting that "if we ask for raises the owners are going to hand over the keys to the factories."[85] Some of the Marxist jaws in the audience must have dropped in disbelief at this warning.

On the other hand, those who supported or acquiesced to capitalist relations of production were not necessarily straightforward class collaborationists. Many factory workers were not Marxists but still advocated measures like wage raises, tax hikes, and government and employer subsidies that would result in a substantial redistribution of wealth. While some factory-worker demands coincided with the demands of the national bourgeoisie—both workers and owners favored more government aid to industry—popular demands also contained a redistributionist thrust that set them clearly apart from the owners.[86] It was not only Trotskyists who agreed with Deputy Alberto Jara, one of the miners' representatives in Congress, when in 1956 he railed against the "economic policy of forming a bourgeoisie at the expense of the workers." Jara argued that "in Bolivia the situation is such that it is not possible to expect that both the Revolution and the *rosca* can advance at the same time. If the Revolution advances, it is the reaction that will recede, or vice versa."[87] Likewise, most non-Marxist factory workers in 1961 probably agreed with the chair of the factory workers' Economic Commission, Ceferino Tórrez, when he argued for closer relations with the Soviet bloc given that "the interests of the capitalist camp are contrary to the interests of our country's economy."[88] The militant but not necessarily Marxist nature of factory-worker demands throughout this period suggests that the ideological terrain within the factory workforce was more complicated than simply liberal versus Marxist or collaboration versus confrontation.

Outside the working class the tensions within revolutionary nationalism were starker. Some were apparent at the March 1959 mass protests in response to an unnamed US official's comment to *Time* magazine that Bolivia should be dissolved and divided among its neighbors. When the article was reprinted in La Paz dailies it incited mass outrage, bringing together groups that did not often collaborate. The MNR's official organ published an uncharacteristically harsh condemnation, and President Siles made several public appearances to denounce *Time*, suggesting that the government may have been seeking to use nationalism to unify the populace at a time of acute social divisions and protest.[89] But if the protests in La Paz gave the impression of unity, the speeches, signs, and actions of the contingent groups betrayed vast differences. Orlando Capriles of the COB proclaimed that "the workers, the campesinos, and other unionized Bolivians say to the Northern colossus: you shall not pass."[90] He decried the desire to "divide up Bolivia, as the body of Túpac Amaru was divided up."[91] Capriles linked that desire to the economic exploitation of Bolivia and stressed the working class's central role in the construction of a new economic order. The working class would "defend the sovereignty of Bolivia and our right to economic independence, for which we fought on April 9." Workers were "the most profoundly Bolivian class" and were therefore "the axis and motor of national struggle" as well as class struggle. "Bolivia's main enemy is foreign capitalism," Capriles argued. Many workers' signs also linked national honor to economic justice and independence: "No More Exploitation [*saqueo*]," "Bolivia Is Not for Sale," and "Death before Slavery."

Hernán Flor Medina of the Confederation of Chaco War Veterans gave a very different speech, emphasizing the unity of all Bolivians in response to *Time*'s affront. The article had triggered "the patriotic reaction of all of the Bolivian people, who regardless of social class and political creed make known through this multitudinous protest their virile strength as a sovereign and free people." He praised the State Department's public disavowal of the comment and added, "We are sure that the unfortunate article in *Time* magazine in no way reflects the feelings of the democratic American people or their government." The stark contrast with Capriles' speech reflects the divides among revolutionary nationalists over questions of class, economic policy, and foreign relations.

The Virile Mestizo Patriot

The March 1959 protests highlight the prevalence of gender and ethnic tropes in discussions of economic dependence, natural resources, and national honor. Calls for the "virile" defense of the nation against foreign aggression might be unsurprising from a military man like Flor Medina, but gendered language was never confined to just military circles and the right. In 1966 various legislators attacked one of the Barrientos regime's generous contracts with a foreign mining company for "handing over the national wealth," calling it "a gift" from "our motherland, our poor Bolivia to the powerful Americans" that "has not sufficiently taken into account [the need for] industrialization."[92] One impugned the lack of patriotism evident in the contract, defining patriotism as "that grand trait that exists in the soul of man" that compels him to leave his wife and children "when the invader appears at the gates." The patriot, said the speaker, defends his nation "with manliness" [*hombría*] and refuses to submit.[93] Male factory workers sometimes depicted themselves as manly defenders of revolutionary ideals and national wealth, as when a representative boasted in 1958 that "as men" the factory workers had "taken to the streets to defend the National Revolution on all occasions."[94] In these debates the nationalist and the revolution were both cast as masculine, assigned the historic task of redeeming an emasculated nation by protecting its resources from exploitation by rapacious foreign capitalists.

Revolutionary nationalist discourse was often racialized as well. Workers and leftists—whites, mestizos, and Indians alike—sometimes spoke of the revolution as the struggle of an indigenous nation to defeat its North Atlantic colonizers. Some, like Orlando Capriles, evoked the memory of past indigenous rebellions against colonial oppression.[95] Other times workers resorted to thinly veiled racism in the service of class and nationalist demands, denouncing the "Jewish" and "Semitic" capitalists who exploited the country; in addition to the tin oligarch "Hochschild the Jew," this group included the "Semitic bosses" that candy-factory workers singled out for criticism in an August 1952 resolution and perhaps also the "unscrupulous foreign merchants" condemned by the Said factory union in 1959 for invading the Bolivian market with "the disloyal competition of foreign manufacturing."[96] These gendered and ethnic undertones were by no means universal, and the more chauvinistic and racist ones were less common on the left than among military nationalists or the right. But such tropes and the sexism and racism they reflected were important elements in the discourse and practice of the mostly male, mostly mestizo leadership of labor unions and the left in the 1950s and 1960s.

Urban unions were surprisingly inattentive to the needs of Bolivia's rural indigenous population. Conspicuously absent from most of their statements on the economy were the issues of agrarian reform and agricultural development. Urban workers had a pragmatic incentive to support the peasantry; given the high concentration of landownership and the vast quantities of uncultivated farmland, a radical redistribution of land, capital, and credit in the countryside stood to expand the market for Bolivian-made consumer goods and facilitate urban industry's access to raw materials. But although urban unions often spoke of "workers and campesinos" working together and occasionally made reference to agricultural policy, concerted outreach efforts were rare.

The neglect of agrarian issues was indicative of a broader disdain for peasants and the indigenous population, an attitude shared not only by MNR leaders and the right but also by most leaders in urban unions and left parties. The COB's early history illustrates this disdain. The body gave nearly three times as many votes to proletarian sectors as to peasants, and the number of votes allocated to middle-class sectors and the Executive Committee also outnumbered the peasant votes. The first COB congress in 1954 made space for 177 proletarian delegates but only 50 peasant delegates and 56 from the middle class; moreover, the peasant delegates sent by the National Peasant Confederation were summarily dismissed and replaced with government designees.[97] The COB leadership justified these skewed ratios by saying that "the proletariat is the natural leader of the Revolution" and "the motor force that will drive the transition from the Old to the New Society."[98]

However critical they were of the MNR mainstream, most Marxist organizers and left intellectuals seemed to agree with the government's disdainful assessment of rural Indians. Nor did their attitude change much in subsequent years. Writing decades later, leading Trotskyist intellectual Guillermo Lora said the subordination of the peasantry within the COB "should be considered progressive." In March 1965 the La Paz factory workers federation, obviously incensed by the recent military-peasant alliance, issued a statement saying that "the peasant masses, given the backwardness and isolation in which they live, are inimical to the Bolivian Revolution."[99] Even many Aymara and Quechua migrants to the city ended up internalizing these urban and ethnic prejudices as they sought to define themselves as part of a "middle class" separate from the "lower class" of peasants and Indians.[100]

The combination of ethnic, urban, and ideological arrogance militated against the formation of a coalition of workers and campesinos. In a parallel way, male chauvinism within the unions reproduced unequal gender relations and prevented women from becoming formal leaders. Although 35 percent of textile-factory workers in 1950 were women, nearly all factory union leaders in the 1950s and 1960s were men; women were usually confined to serving as liaisons with other women.[101] The importance of these sectoral, ethnic, and gender divisions is hard to overestimate. Similar divisions have sometimes had a decisive impact on revolutions in other countries and certainly helped facilitate the rightward policy drift in Bolivia after 1955.[102]

There is scattered evidence of minority currents that were significantly more attuned to the interests of women, rural farmers, and indigenous Bolivians. In July 1954 La Paz newspapers received a twenty-two-point petition from "some factory worker leaders" purporting to represent the demands of the factory workers' congress then in progress. After *El Diario* published the petition, CGTFB top officials wrote in to say that in fact the Executive Committee had not passed it and was only conducting a "careful study" of the document. Although the origin of the petition is unclear, the scope of its demands was impressive. It called for wage raises, higher taxation of the owners, "workers' control in the concession and use of profits," and greater political freedoms. Most striking, however, were its calls for "equal pay for equal work" for men and women, the acceleration of agrarian reform, a national literacy campaign, and bilingual education for indigenous students.[103] The petition's accidental publication allows for a glimpse into the differences within the factory workforce in the 1950s. Similar dissident thoughts were no doubt common, perhaps especially among the many women and indigenous workers who labored on the factory floors.

Most union leaders as well as the leaders of the MNR and the left parties did not embrace these dissident sentiments, or, to put it another way, the dissidents rarely attained leadership positions. By the 1950s the dominant strain of revolutionary nationalism was male-oriented, ethnocentric, and far more concerned with mineral resources, oil, and urban industrialization than with agrarian development. Like so many insurgent projects throughout history, it vehemently attacked certain hierarchies but not others.

Great Britain in the Nineteenth Century

The existence of these internal tensions and contradictions did not negate the challenge posed by popular economic ideas to the joint US-MNR agenda. Despite all its limits, popular economic thought in La

Paz reflected a fairly coherent set of ideas about economic relations and potential alternatives. Whether or not rank-and-file workers formally identified with the Marxist left (the majority did not), "revolution" meant a higher standard of living—employment, good wages, a safe workplace, education for their children, and so on—as well as a new model of economic development. Not all workers demanded the socialization of the factories, and some were more chauvinistic, racist, and insular than others, but most were united in their demands for resource nationalism, industrialization, diversification, and a more equitable distribution of wealth.

Neither the US nor the MNR government was able to dislodge these core economic beliefs. The tenuousness of the conservative triumph after 1956 is evident in the increasingly militant history of La Paz factory workers. This group, as much as any other except the mine workers, would continue to pose problems for the regimes that took power after 1964. Their actions prevented a full-scale rollback of gains at the factory level, limited the government's ability to abandon resource nationalism and slash public spending, and imbued revolutionary discourse with an emphasis on working-class rights that no regime would be able to ignore.

US and MNR problems in La Paz were not limited to the factories. From the perspective of both governments, relief over the left's exclusion from power was tempered by their own legitimacy deficit on the ground. The US embassy, the USIS libraries, and other US-affiliated offices were occasionally attacked and raided by Bolivian protesters, as happened in March 1959 after the appearance of the infamous *Time* article.[104] The US government's failure to reshape Bolivians' fundamental ideas about the economy and international relations was often acknowledged in classified USIS reports. Sacrosanct concepts like market capitalism and the goodwill of the US government remained "under severe attack" despite US efforts. US officials desperately reassured Bolivian audiences that US aid "is in support of the Bolivian effort to promote economic development." When an ambassador must state publicly, "Our purpose is not to exploit the governments and peoples of the free world," the situation is difficult indeed.[105]

One candid embassy memo from 1959 on the "possible worsening of the Bolivian situation" compared the US position in Bolivia to that of besieged imperial powers of the past: "In some respects the U.S. position in the immediate future would seem to bear a strong resemblance to that which Great Britain occupied in many areas during the 19th century: a determined force for order which [is] not and indeed cannot afford to be concerned about its rating in public opinion polls."[106] Like Britain, the United States increasingly turned to military force when its lack of legitimacy on the ground began to translate into political and economic unrest. The Eisenhower administration began sending military aid to the MNR in 1957, with one rationale being "to ensure success to the economic stabilization plan." US military aid to Bolivia rose significantly under Kennedy, funding a 45 percent increase in the size of the Bolivian military by 1965.[107] This increase was consistent with Kennedy-era policy toward Latin America but also reflected the particular failure of the soft-power approach in Bolivia. It was a tacit admission of Hannah Arendt's point: "Violence appears where power is in jeopardy."[108]

The military became important in the suppression of unrest in the mines, universities, and city streets starting in the late 1950s. Political arrests and harassment during the early 1960s gave way to more direct violence under Barrientos. Factory workers, along with miners, construction workers, teachers, and restaurant workers, were the most important early sources of opposition to the military regime. In response to wage cuts and anti-union decrees in May 1965, these five groups formed a National Strike Committee that coordinated a strike wave in the mines and cities.[109] The general strike that ensued elicited a harsh reaction from the government. Barrientos sent military forces to the mines and the factory workers' neighborhoods of Villa Victoria and Pura Pura in La Paz. Workers' barricades were little match for government firepower, which apparently included the use of machine guns, bazookas, and aerial bombings, and killed at least nineteen people. A report in the government-friendly paper *El Diario* described soldiers "firing their weapons on all moving objects. The fire spread through the whole zone and assumed spectacular proportions." Soldiers also appear to have targeted the radio stations of the factory workers and construction workers, destroying both.[110]

In a perverse way, the course of events underscores the extent to which the Bolivian government was itself a captive of popular aspirations. Factory workers expected government leaders to advance a revolutionary agenda and criticized them when they did not. Although most were hesitant to condemn the MNR altogether, they gradually asserted greater independence from the party. The "unconditional support" for Paz Estenssoro in the early years gave way by late 1957 to calls for "conditional support" and "loyal criticism," then to angry de-

Figure 5.1. La Paz workers' opposition to the Barrientos regime. The cartoon at left dramatizes the political cleavages of the 1960s, depicting the military-peasant alliance and the miner–factory worker alliance. La Paz workers march on May Day 1965 (top right), several weeks before the military entered factory workers' neighborhoods (bottom right). Source: *El Diario*, December 2, 1966; May 3 and 25, 1965. Archivo Hemerográfico, Biblioteca y Archivo Histórico de la Asamblea Legislativa Plurinacional, Bolivia. Photos used with permission.

nunciations of "cogovernment" itself by 1959. After Barrientos seized power in 1964, the Tenth Departmental Conference of La Paz factory workers denounced him by comparing him to the MNR, arguing that in fact "the MNR has not lost power" because the same "reactionary, antipopular, and antiworker" policies "continue in force . . . under the Military Junta."[111] The MNR's turn to repression of the workers, as well as the 1964 coup itself, reflected the party's inability to contain popular expectations.

State attempts at co-optation are a further reflection of the factory workers' continuing power. The military junta led by Hugo Ballivián had sponsored the founding of the CGTFB in October 1951 in the hopes of taming the worker militancy manifested the previous year.[112] The MNR government later tried to appropriate the memory of the May 1950 strike by establishing a Factory Workers Day on May 18.[113] Barrientos implicitly acknowledged the factory workers' continued importance in national politics when he visited the March 1965 La Paz factory workers' conference and promised that his government would "maintain all the social gains of the National Revolution."[114] The small bourgeoisie in Bolivia, led by the National Chamber of Industries, even developed a tamed version of revolutionary nationalist discourse that emphasized its own patriotic role in promoting "modern enterprise"—as distinct from the parasitic model of the pre-1952 era—and "national industry in the service of the country."[115]

Sources of Factory-Worker Militancy

The Bolivian manufacturing sector of the 1950s had at least some of the characteristics that might be expected to produce a tranquil labor aristocracy. A large population competed for a small number of jobs; a study in the mid-1970s found that just 3.4 percent of peasants who migrated to La Paz found stable factory work, leading the authors to conclude that "to be a factory worker continues to be a privilege."[116] The owners were mostly Bolivians, not foreigners who might have given worker resentments a nationalist edge. And manufacturing was not a strategic export sector, so the workforce lacked the leverage of the mine workers.[117]

So what explains the failure of the Bolivian government and owners to ensure quiescence in La Paz factories? Part of the answer lies in the weakness of the Bolivian state, particularly in fiscal terms. Prior to the revolution the state bureaucracy was small and the state's taxation capacity vastly deficient, forcing the government to rely on export duties and other taxes on the mining industry for almost half of all revenue.[118] Per capita gross domestic product (GDP) and government spending were much lower than in most other Latin American countries (table 5.1). Moreover, the state's physical presence—as measured by courts, schools, police, and so forth—was largely limited to the arc extending from northwestern Potosí, the site of Siglo XX and other major mines, through La Paz and eastward to Cochabamba.[119] Even within that region it often showed itself stunningly incapable of exercising its authority. Part of the explanation for Bolivia's defeat in the Chaco War lies in the state's insufficient capacity to conscript Indian soldiers and its helplessness to stem the tide of desertions from the ranks. The prerevolutionary state was plagued by military and administrative weakness and a lack of legitimacy among broad swaths of

Table 5.1. Manufacturing workforce and per capita GDP, 1950

Country	Total working population (millions)	Workforce in manufacturing (%)	Per capita GDP (1950 dollars)
Argentina	6.7	29.9	496
Bolivia	1.1	9.1	103
Brazil	17.0	17.1	195
Chile	2.2	22.7	303
Cuba	1.8	16.7	365
Haiti	1.2	5.8	74
Mexico	8.2	14.6	210
Venezuela	1.7	41.2	550
United States	60.1	28.6	1,880

Note: Sources are often inconsistent, in part because much of the manufacturing workforce was in very small-scale operations. The figure 9.1 percent for Bolivia is in fact misleadingly high: more than 80 percent of those workers were employed outside any "registered industry"; UN ECLA, *Economic Survey of Latin America: 1956*, 64, and "Economic Policy of Bolivia in 1952–64," 64.
Sources: All figures are taken or calculated from UCLA, Committee on Latin American Studies, *Statistical Abstract*, 5–6.

the population. Among the MNR's top priorities after 1952 was the construction of a modern state that could administer the nation and also garner the support of civil society.

The state's weakness was partly the result of Bolivia's historic dependence on mineral exports. Mining operations were confined to a small portion of the total territory and never led to the level of secondary industrial development that other types of primary commodity exports helped produce in countries like Argentina.[120] The tin barons sent a large portion of their profits abroad instead of reinvesting domestically. Although the mining sector was taxed at a higher rate than others, the revenue was still insufficient to spur significant government reinvestment, particularly in the absence of a conscious state commitment to do so. After 1952 mineral monoculture made the MNR heavily reliant on the United States. This dependent relationship and particularly the 1956 austerity plan further constrained the MNR's ability to devote resources to diversification and industrialization.

The state's fiscal problems affected the manufacturing sector and factory workforce in several ways. Most Bolivian factories were dependent on the import of raw materials for production, owing to the low level of Bolivian agricultural production, and at state-subsidized rates of exchange. The 1956 plan ended the system of multiple exchange rates that had subsidized urban industry since before the revolution, contributing to a wave of factory closings, layoffs, and unused capacity that persisted into the next decade. Other forms of state subsidization like industrial loans or the provision of power and other infrastructure also became more difficult under stabilization. Finally, factory workers were directly affected by the elimination of government subsidies on consumer goods and services. Rather than making factory workers more insular, economic austerity seems to have increased their propensity to identify with other workers and to confront problems of national importance, especially regarding natural resource policies.[121]

A second, related explanation for the noncompliance of La Paz factory workers is the small size and limited capital of Bolivia's industrial bourgeoisie. The growth of a sizable consumer market was unlikely in a small country whose economy was historically centered on mineral extraction for export and noncapitalist forms of agriculture. The levels of formal education and technical training were very low, and transport and electrical infrastructure were nearly nonexistent. The lack of a strong and diversified agricultural economy also contributed to manufacturers' dependence on raw material imports, while the country's landlocked position raised the cost of foreign trade. The 5.7 percent annual growth rate from 1961 to 1964 was scarcely reflected in the manufacturing sector, in which more than half of all enterprises closed from 1958 to 1963.[122]

MNR officials and factory owners alike were thus severely constrained in their capacity to buy off the factory workforce. State leaders and the captains of Bolivia's fledgling industry were increasingly unable to satisfy even the bread-and-butter demands of the workforce. Collaborationist labor leaders found themselves less and less able to deliver material benefits to their constituencies. The tacit capital-labor compromise of the post–World War II era, in which employers agreed to grant wage raises in exchange for labor's collaboration in boosting production, was not nearly as feasible in Bolivia as it was in the United States, Western Europe, and more developed Latin American countries such as Mexico.[123]

The contrast with Mexican labor is particularly illuminating given Mexico's revolutionary past. Unlike the MNR, the postrevolutionary state in Mexico was ultimately able to ensure the support of organized labor throughout the twentieth century through a combination of co-optation and repression of union dissidents. Kevin Middlebrook attributes particular importance to the early revolutionary regimes' conscious efforts "to increase state capacity" immediately after the revolution and to form hierarchical coalitions with the country's labor unions. He argues that "the long-term survival of many of Mexico's most prominent labor leaders cannot be explained without noting that, in many cases, they were able to use political connections to improve the living standards of their members."[124] These co-optative efforts were successful in part because of the relatively high level of economic development in Mexico prior to the revolution and the country's sustained economic growth throughout the middle decades of the twentieth century.[125] A similar trend was evident in much of the industrialized world. Elites in severely underdeveloped countries had more difficulty, however. Charles Maier argues in a discussion of pre–World War II Europe, "If defenders of interwar capitalism proposed a social bargain—the increasing satisfaction of material wants in return for a restoration of industrial authority—they had to be able to pay up."[126]

Structural conditions or class position do not fully explain political behavior, however. After all, austerity and deprivation often produce less militant workers, fueling a more insular and exclusionary vision of unionism. Political culture helps determine which path a workforce takes in response. Ideas, ideologies, and nonclass identities, all rooted in historical experiences, were profoundly important in shaping the consciousness and action of the La Paz working class. Working-class political culture in the city during the MNR period reflected a variety of ideological currents that had been circulating for several decades prior to 1952: Marxism, anarchism, resource nationalism, industrial protectionism, and a mix of quasi-Keynesian and quasi-*dependentista* understandings of political economy. A quarter century of organizing and propaganda efforts by anarchists and Marxists had contributed to the radicalization and the independent spirit of the labor movement, even though most labor leaders and rank-and-file workers were not formally anticapitalist. There was also significant cross-pollination among working-class sectors; factory-worker leader Germán Butrón, for one, originally came from Catavi, where he had worked in the mines.[127] By the 1950s revolutionary nationalism—encompassing resource nationalism, dependency thinking, and aspects of Marxism and anarchism—had become embedded enough in the country's political culture that it placed definite constraints on the actions and language of politicians, capitalists, and even labor leaders.

In the case of La Paz factory workers, particularly important was the collective memory of struggle and sacrifice during the *sexenio* and the April 1952 revolution. This memory increased the workers' identification with the revolution but also made them keenly sensitive to perceived betrayal by both MNR and union leaders. Alfonso Cordero's 1962 declaration, "We who made the revolution are being betrayed," resonated deeply with veterans of the 1950 strike and repression in Villa Victoria and the street fighting that helped topple the old regime in 1952. The factory workers' increasing combativeness by the late 1950s resulted partly from the widespread perception that those who claimed to represent them had violated an implicit pact.

What role did ethnic identity play in shaping the political identity of the factory workers and other working-class sectors? Anthropologists have often noted how the city of La Paz, like most of Bolivia and the Andes more generally, is marked by a profound "ethnic-social duality," shaped as much by indigenous influences as European ones.[128] The 1942 citywide census counted 23 percent of all residents as indigenous, but that percentage surely underestimates the number of people of indigenous descent and the indigenous influence on the city. At least twice as many (51 percent) spoke Aymara or Quechua alone or in addition to Spanish. Working-class neighborhoods tended to have much higher percentages of Indians and mestizos, too; in the factory-worker neighborhood of Villa Victoria, 39 percent were registered as indigenous and another 51 percent as mestizo.[129] Moreover, the post-1952 period brought successive waves of Aymara migration to the city. Many of these migrants came from communities with long histories of struggle against haciendas and the state, including in the very recent past when the younger generations were coming of age. Most continued to maintain close ties to their communities of origin after going to the city. And whatever the self-identification of residents in working-class neighborhoods, Villa Victoria and similar areas were often labeled "indigenous zones" by the city's elites. Even the alternative label "popular classes," also used by elites in reference to the same neighborhoods, tended to carry implicit ethnic connotations.[130]

The experience of ethnic and cultural discrimination helped shape the consciousness of indigenous migrants to La Paz. In polling conducted in 1976–1977, migrants who identified themselves as members of the "lower class" often cited racial and sociocultural discrimination in addition to "class" exploitation.[131] This perception may also have influenced political militancy. One of the most popular occupations for recent migrants, construction work, was composed almost entirely of Indians (61 percent) and mestizos (36 percent). It also featured one of the most militant workforces in mid-twentieth-century Bolivia.[132] Though difficult to measure, the experience of ethnic discrimination probably intensified class resentment in many cases. It also seems that indigenous residents were less than eager to cooperate with the US Information Service in La Paz. A 1962 report lamented "the difficulty in finding people who can be effectively used for voicing films" in Aymara and Quechua.[133]

The concrete impact of indigenous or mestizo or *cholo* identity is hard to discern in the case of the La Paz factory workers. Though many were of indigenous descent, prior analyses have stressed this workforce's assimilation to dominant creole culture and language. The results of the 1976–1977 polls suggest that of all Aymara migrants to La Paz, those who found work in the factories were "those who least perceived sociocultural conflict" because of their "special effort to ignore their campesino origins."[134] In the 1950s and 1960s most urban unions, like the MNR government, denigrated indigenous identity and made acculturation a prerequisite for leadership positions. Wálter Delgadillo notes that the indigenous migrant "had to first assimilate the forms of creole expression to be admitted to the union hierarchy."[135] Thus, while ethnic identity undoubtedly influenced workers' attitudes, class and national identities remained the formal bases for most political mobilization.[136] Not until the 1970s would a self-proclaimed indigenous movement again emerge in Bolivia.

The Paradoxes of Labor Militancy

The MNR could never count on a reliable labor aristocracy in La Paz. The city's factory workers became increasingly combative over the course of the 1950s and articulated a broad range of demands, with resource nationalism a primary current within their economic thought. To explain this pattern I have highlighted a combination of structural and sociocultural conditions affecting the city's factory workforce. Economic underdevelopment and state weakness were important, as were the historically constructed class, nationalist, and sectoral identities nourished by collective memories and radical traditions.

However, the evidence also suggests a more complicated and contradictory political history than the factory workers' own boastful statements implied. In some ways, La Paz factory workers were indeed a labor aristocracy. Factory-worker militancy coexisted with more conservative attitudes. Most of the leadership as well as the dominant culture within urban labor and the left remained dismissive of Indians, peasants, and women. While urban unions did take an interest in national and international affairs, they were shortsighted in other ways, such as in their neglect of agricultural development.

Social scientists often say that working-class radicalism impedes economic development and successful revolutionary consolidation because it forces states to prioritize consumption over investment. For this reason, many observers of the Bolivian Revolution have argued, as MNR moderates did in the 1950s, that any government dominated by the left would have proven unsustainable, particularly given Bolivia's poverty and underdevelopment. In another sense, however, Bolivian workers were not radical enough. While labor militancy may at times have been one of the many factors inhibiting economic development, the lacunae in urban labor's outlook also helped to preclude the broad-based, cross-sectoral alliances that could have forced a more radical anticapitalist turn in the revolution's course or at least prevented a reactionary turn. There is no way to know whether a more radical revolution could have succeeded in mid-century Bolivia, but its chances would have been better if not for the urban left's own shortcomings.

CHAPTER 6

Oil and Nation: The Crusade to Save Bolivia's Hydrocarbons

Oil and natural gas embody both the frustrations and the hopes at the heart of Bolivian history over the past century. For successive generations of Bolivians they have symbolized the tragic history of mono-export dependence, underdevelopment, and imperialism that has plagued Bolivia since the colonial period. At the same time, Bolivians have looked to hydrocarbons as the key to overcoming those problems. The struggle to achieve and maintain national control over oil and gas is a recurring theme in Bolivia's history since the 1920s. These resources came to have an even more profound symbolic importance to Bolivian nationalism than tin, partly because of the collective memory of the Chaco War.

Oil drilling in Bolivia began at the end of the nineteenth century, but it was only in the early 1950s that the Bolivian government and public began to pin their hopes for development on the country's oil; natural gas only became a major topic of debate in the mid-1960s, and its production did not occur on a large scale until the 1970s. Economic diversification was central to the MNR's promises. By 1952 the tin sector was already in clear decline, increasing the urgency of that task. YPFB's initial progress after the revolution seemed to vindicate public expectations; before 1954, Bolivia's oil production had not even been sufficient to supply the small domestic market, but a rapid increase from 1952 to 1956 seemed to bode well for the future of the state oil company.

Grand hopes were soon dashed, however, as the 1955 oil code, the 1956 austerity plan, and the MNR's own shortsightedness handcuffed YPFB. Starting in 1958 hydrocarbons policy became a central focus of political tensions in Bolivia. The questions of how, by whom, and in whose interest Bolivia's oil and gas reserves should be developed underlay much of the country's turbulent political history from then until the military regime of General Alfredo Ovando (September 1969–October 1970) abrogated the oil code and nationalized the US-owned Bolivian Gulf Oil Company in 1969. The struggle to change the MNR's oil policy reflected a broader disenchantment with the perceived betrayals of the revolution and was a key factor in the resurgence of a resource-nationalist coalition in the 1960s. As in 1936–1939 and 1952, a broad bloc of popular forces again coalesced around the desire to assert control over Bolivia's natural resources.

The campaign for a new hydrocarbons policy highlights several important facets of resource nationalism in Bolivia. First, the forces opposing the existing policy were remarkable for their diversity; they included urban workers, miners, students, middle-class professionals, war veterans, dissident military leaders, and campesinos. They included the left, much of the MNR, part of the right, and many with no political affiliation. Resource nationalism was an extremely flexible concept with the potential for mobilizing diverse sectors of society, often operating in synergy with other ideological currents such as Marxism, Catholicism, developmentalism, and patriarchy. Whatever their other differences, these disparate sectors were united by their resource nationalism and repudiation of what they perceived as the betrayal of revolutionary ideals in the oil sector.

However, unity among these groups was often fleeting. Nationalist mobilization did not paper over the differences for long. The public debate over oil policy and the string of mobilizations around it in the late 1960s showcase the conflicting economic, social, and political visions present in postrevolutionary Bolivia. Soon after the Gulf nationalization the left's demands again brought it into conflict with more conservative nationalist forces and, yet again, with the US government.

Here I focus principal attention on the proposals of the nationalist left, which spoke for a much larger proportion of the Bolivian population than party membership figures suggest. In their specific proposals for an alternative policy and their basic assumptions about how the capitalist economy worked, the MNR left and Marxist parties coincided with most of urban society and likely much of rural society as well, though the evidence is less clear. After reviewing their ideas, I argue for a reappraisal of Bolivian resource nationalism. Commentators then and since have often characterized resource nationalism as the result of irrational conspiracy theory, reflecting xenophobia toward things foreign and, in particular, toward North Americans. But these caricatures belie the rationale behind resource nationalism and ignore important nuances in the economic ideas of its adherents.

The persistence of a left-leaning oil nationalism in Bolivia is further evidence of the limits to conservative forces' power on the ground. Although the oil companies and US and MNR officials were indeed able to limit the growth of YPFB, they could not destroy it. The United States in 1961 was compelled to do something it had repeatedly sworn not to do, issuing a loan to the state enterprise. And even as Barrientos and other right-wing leaders moved away from economic nationalism and attacked workers' wages and rights, they nonetheless couched their policies in the rhetoric of resource nationalism, industrialization, and social justice. US and Bolivian leaders saw their freedom circumscribed by public demands and expectations. Although on the surface the revolution was defeated, popular resource nationalism nonetheless left a profound imprint on both policy and political culture.

Our Last Hope

By the time of the Chaco War, oil was already a central feature of the emerging nationalist consciousness in La Paz and other cities. With the expansion of oil production in the 1920s and the conspicuous entry of Standard Oil, the resource took on growing practical importance to Bolivia's economy and a symbolic importance many times greater. For urban nationalists it became intimately linked to the quest for national sovereignty and economic development.

"Bolivia's economic future is contained in its oil," wrote nationalist author Pedro López in 1929. Future prosperity as a nation required that Bolivians "learn to utilize and take advantage of the brilliant energy of liquid gold." López envisioned a grand future in which oil allowed Bolivia to overcome its "state of prostration and economic poverty" and "turn itself into a true *economic power*." Oil was the source of the nation's life and vitality, the "blood of the earth."[1] Similar body metaphors, often gendered, became more popular in nationalist discussions of oil after the war.[2]

The war against Paraguay helped solidify oil's place in the nationalist imaginary. The notion that foreign oil companies had instigated the war, or at least profited from it, was widespread in the decades that followed.[3] For nationalists it led logically to two conclusions. First, the

Chaco War became a cautionary tale about the imperialist machinations of foreign governments and capitalists. Left nationalist Sergio Almaraz Paz would later write that Bolivia and Paraguay had been "manipulated by puppet masters from New York and London."[4] Second, the belief that more than 56,000 Bolivians had died for oil made the continued defense of the country's hydrocarbons a national imperative. YPFB, established just after the war, became a symbol of national dignity and promise. By contrast, those who would expose Bolivia's virgin oil to foreign exploitation would often be cast as traitors to the nation. The MNR gained visibility in the 1940s in part by its leaders' rhetorical defense of Bolivian oil resources and calls for strengthening YPFB. Some of those same leaders, in turn, would find themselves the targets of nationalist denunciations during the MNR's time in power.

By the late 1940s oil's importance to the economy was increasing, with some politicians and experts predicting a takeoff for YPFB. At the 1945 constitutional convention one politician assigned a monumental responsibility to the state oil company, arguing that it "signifies the last hope of economic redemption for Bolivia" and would be "called upon to resolve in the near future all of the country's economic, industrial, and social problems."[5] YPFB analysts seemed to agree about the potential for dramatically increasing production. In 1947 an internal memo asserted "that Bolivia is now in a position to embark upon a new economic cycle which may be called the Petroleum Cycle."[6] Production levels remained modest but did quadruple between 1937 and 1950, to around 500,000 barrels.[7] US officials in Bolivia spoke of the "brilliant prospects" for oil production and decided to make the development of Bolivia's eastern oil fields a key focus of the 1942 Bohan plan.[8] The growth of state oil companies elsewhere gave hope to Bolivian nationalists. YPFB's creation was directly inspired by the Argentine state entity, Yacimientos Petrolíferos Fiscales, created in 1922, and Argentina provided key assistance to YPFB in the late 1930s and 1940s. Mexico's oil nationalization and state oil company were also keenly watched by Bolivian nationalists. Specialists from Argentina and Mexico helped train YPFB personnel.[9]

The early years of the revolution encouraged nationalists' hopes, but only temporarily. The MNR devoted substantial sums to YPFB between 1953 and 1956, resulting in a dramatic increase in production. YPFB drew widespread praise—even from US officials, speaking privately—as an efficient enterprise and, from Bolivian nationalists, as an embodiment of national economic aspirations. As tin production dropped in the 1950s, nationalists came to recognize "the certainty of tin's displacement by oil" and pinned even greater hopes on the development of the industry.[10] However, the 1955 oil code and 1956 austerity plan effectively brought YPFB's progress to a halt. The oil reform opened the door to private companies and confined YPFB to a small corner of land in the Bolivian southeast, while austerity led to drastic reductions in its operating budget. Private companies were even given large concessions within YPFB's designated zone. To add to YPFB's woes, MNR officials placed little priority on exploration to locate new oil reserves and continued to use YPFB to subsidize the rest of the economy through low fuel prices.[11] The grand hopes of the early 1950s gradually dissipated by the end of the decade, and the industry's frustrated potential began fueling an upsurge of protest starting in 1958.

The Crusade to Defend YPFB

From 1958 through 1969, hydrocarbons policy was a consistent focus of political conflict. In 1958 disparate sectors of Bolivian society began to coalesce around their opposition to the MNR's "open-door" oil policy and specifically the 1955 oil code. Leftist resistance to the code included, most notably, the Trotskyist and Communist parties centered in the mines and universities, the MNR left, and diverse working-class sectors, including oil workers themselves. Broad segments of the working population in and outside the cities began to criticize the government's oil policy from nationalist and progressive angles. Oil was a lightning rod for middle-class nationalists of many stripes, as well, including growing numbers of military officers, lawyers, and newspaper editors and journalists. Although the different players within this resurgent national-popular coalition disagreed on precisely what policy should look like, they were united in their condemnation of the *entreguismo* of the MNR and the ensuing Barrientos regime.

Most criticisms of the oil code revolved around its generous provisions for foreign investors and the detrimental impact on YPFB. Critics deemed the taxation rate far too low and pointed to other oil-producing countries that reaped up to six times more money per barrel than Bolivia.[12] They condemned hidden tax breaks like the infamous "depletion allowance" that compensated foreign companies for the exhaustion of reserves and effectively exempted 27.5 percent of total production from taxation.[13] And they pointed to myriad other ways in which the code and the MNR's broader oil policy seemed to privilege foreign oil companies at the nation's expense. Common complaints included the failure to compel companies to refine the oil within Bolivia or to reinvest profits in the domestic economy, the tailoring of pipeline infrastructure to the needs of companies exporting through Chile to the United States rather than to neighboring markets to the east, and the generous time window before companies had to begin drilling; this last complaint reflected the perception that foreign oil companies were less interested in production than in accumulating reserves in order to drive up global prices.[14]

Denunciations of the oil code and ensuing contracts channeled long-standing popular suspicions of foreign capital in general. Foreign companies were accused of repatriating most of their profits and contributing little to Bolivia's industrialization while draining the country of precious natural resources. The resources themselves were exported to markets in the developed world rather than benefiting Bolivian consumers. Because of their economic leverage and political alliance with the US government and Bolivian officials, foreign companies paid low tax rates and were given other public subsidies such as taxpayer-funded transport infrastructure. Their presence deformed the domestic economy while impeding the development of manufacturing industries, thus keeping countries like Bolivia dependent on low-value-added raw material exports. These quasi-*dependentista* arguments were common among mid-century Bolivian nationalists and leftists.[15]

Extractive industry was deemed particularly suspect, as it was in many other countries of Latin America.[16] For instance, a YPFB chief engineer who became a prominent critic of the government's oil policy in the 1960s differentiated "between investments dedicated to transformative industry and investments dedicated to the extraction of a national treasure." Oil extraction had a particularly low multiplier effect, meaning that its ripple effects on economic growth in the country were minimal.[17]

Many Bolivians felt that YPFB, meanwhile, was being systematically deprived of lucrative oil reserves by the code's provisions and of funding by the recent austerity plan and the US refusal to lend it money.[18] The widely accepted explanation for this pattern was an imperialist alliance between foreign oil corporations and the US government that worked to advance the companies' interests and weaken YPFB. Reporting on widespread rumors in Bolivia in 1959, embassy officials wrote that Bolivians thought "that the refusal of the US Government to help YPFB demonstrates a conspiracy between the Government and the foreign oil companies to monopolize petroleum production in Bolivia." Bolivians perceived a "desire to strangle YPFB by preventing it from obtaining needed financing abroad." In a public speech the general manager of YPFB "bitterly blamed foreign private oil interests for YPFB's inability to obtain development capital."[19]

A main source of opposition to the code was the oil workers themselves. By 1958 the Bolivian Oil Workers Union Federation (FSTPB) was calling for major modifications to the code and condemning the effort to starve YPFB of resources. In July it threatened to strike if taxes on foreign oil companies were not raised.[20] In October, just prior to the FSTPB's fifth national congress, the federation and La Paz union leaders issued a public statement arguing "that the Stabilization Council and the International Monetary Fund have refused any financial aid for the development of the only state entity which offers promise to the country in order that the entity not prosper." They warned the public to "be on the alert" to "preserve the life of the petroleum industry of Bolivia which you have defended with your blood in the Chaco war."[21]

The FSTPB congress in December 1958 typified the rhetorical balancing act of urban workers' organizations in the 1950s, simultaneously declaring its support for the Siles government and criticizing policy. It pledged support for the government "as long as it stays loyal to the principles of April and acts upon the needs and aspirations of the working class and the Bolivian people." In a jab at the Siles administration, it reiterated its support for the COB, which it called "today the only guarantee for defending the gains achieved and obtaining additional gains in the future." The oil code was the focus of attention. Its "liberal structure threatened the future of the nation," said an official resolution.[22] Although delegates emphasized their support for foreign investment in the oil industry, they demanded a number of major changes to the code and oil policy more generally. The Cochabamba refinery workers proposed a substitute code that would stop concessions within YPFB's zone, force companies to drill quickly rather than sit on their reserves, compel them to refine more of their oil in Bolivia, eliminate the "depletion allowance" and other tax loopholes, and give YPFB control over all pipelines. In addition, the delegates advocated three policy changes that would become central to left and nationalist demands: that the government expand exploration activities in order to boost YPFB's reserves; that it accept loans and investments from anywhere, a reference to the January 1958 Soviet offer of a loan to

LAS PLANTAS DE YPFB, SIMBOLO DE SOBERANIA NACIONAL

Figure 6.1. "YPFB refineries, symbol of national sovereignty." Source: *El Petrolero*, February 1959, 11. Used with permission of the Biblioteca Arturo Costa de la Torre.

YPFB worth $60–80 million; and that it expand cooperation and solidarity with other primary-commodity-exporting nations.[23] The proposal passed and marked a major turning point in the FSTPB's position toward the government's oil policy.

Much like the miners and factory workers, oil workers cast themselves as the guardians of nation and revolution. FSTPB leaders proclaimed their constituency's "most renowned patriotic zeal and love for [YPFB]."[24] The death of YPFB would mean "the defeat of the Bolivian people," argued the Cochabamba refinery workers' newspaper, since the state enterprise was "the last chance that our country has to be Great, truly Free, and genuinely Just." Protecting the country's "virgin wealth" and avoiding the "fateful cycle of tin" was a crucial national imperative.[25] In the various strikes and strike threats by oil workers that began in 1958, the tightening of the oil code's lax provisions and the patriotic defense of YPFB were often key themes alongside more traditional wage demands (figure 6.1).[26]

While state oil workers were a natural constituency for oil nationalism, they were not alone. Soon after the 1958 FSTPB congress, the US embassy reported on a "crusade to defend YPFB" involving the factory workers confederation, the national peasant confederation, and the COB. The factory workers officially condemned the "machinations of Yankee imperialism" to "destroy YPFB to benefit US firms which only seek [to] preserve concessions as reserves in order [to] control inter-

national prices." The same resolution called upon the Siles administration to accept the Soviet loan offer and modify the existing oil code
"to reflect [the] nationalist sentiment of our people."[27]

Within the legislature the representatives of the MNR left also began "raking the [government] over the coals on oil policy" in 1958,
in the words of a frustrated US official.[28] Early congressional opposition was led by Senators Oscar Donoso, Ciro Humboldt, Juan Lechín,
and Mario Torres, the latter two also top officials in the miners federation and the COB. The senators demanded that the government re-
vamp the oil code to increase taxes and ensure YPFB's access to capital reserves. Specific contracts that followed the code came under fire,
particularly in the case of the concession to the US company Fish for
exploration and drilling in the Madrejones region within YPFB's own
zone.[29] Other congressional criticisms focused on the plan to construct
a pipeline from Sicasica in La Paz department to Arica on the Chil-
ean coast; the critics questioned why the government planned to construct a pipeline that would primarily benefit Gulf and other foreign
companies. Some, like Humboldt, argued that the Siles administration
should explore the option of the Soviet loan, given the denial of loans
by the United States and Export-Import Bank.[30] Starting in 1966,
journalist-turned-legislator Marcelo Quiroga Santa Cruz would take
over as Congress's most vehement critic of the oil code at a moment
when the prosperity of Gulf and the prospect of large unexploited gas
reserves intensified opposition to official policy.[31]

Outside Congress, middle-class intellectuals played important roles
in the opposition to MNR oil policy. The "crusade to defend YPFB"
found support in the university circles of La Paz, Cochabamba, and
other cities where the Marxist parties had a firm base among students and professors. Communist and Trotskyist party leaders, some
of whom held high-ranking faculty positions, were among the first
to publicly denounce "the return of imperialist companies" and the
MNR's attack on "the foundations of oil nationalization." Their efforts included organizing public forums on campus to discuss oil.[32] A
US memo alleged that opposition to the oil code "began in the halls of
the University of Cochabamba" and spread from there to other cam-
puses and into the FSTPB and other unions.[33] Some leftist intellectuals did have close ties to the FSTPB, but the characterization over-
simplified reality by implying that the oil workers were swayed by a
handful of Marxist professors. As the congressional furor suggests,
the campaign included many non-Marxists on the MNR left, making

it more difficult for the government to ignore. Among the most prominent was Gustavo Chacón, who had helped develop oil policy for the Busch and Villarroel governments. In the 1960s Chacón criticized the MNR and Barrientos governments in nationalist terms, accusing them of betraying "the sacrifice of the 50,000 Chaco martyrs, whose blood had paid for YPFB's creation and later the expiration of Standard Oil's concessions."[34]

Three popular books were especially important in inspiring urban resistance to the oil code. The 1958 *Petróleo en Bolivia* by Sergio Almaraz included the most detailed repudiation of the MNR's oil policy to date. Almaraz condemned the historical domination of the Bolivian oil industry by foreign companies, which he characterized as an oligopoly determined to accumulate reserves while impeding industrial development in the country. MNR leaders, he said, had done a 180-degree turn from the time in the early 1940s when they defended the country's oil.[35] He detailed YPFB's success and argued that it should again be given full control over oil production. The book's popularity worried US officials in La Paz; one sent a lengthy critique of its arguments back to Washington.[36]

Amado Canelas' 1963 *Petróleo: Imperialismo y nacionalismo* built on Almaraz's arguments. Canelas was a Cochabamba newspaper editor and well-known nationalist voice within the legislature. His book was a typical statement of Bolivian *dependentista* thought, emphasizing how foreign investment had not developed the country's economy but rather kept it "dependent and backward." Canelas argued that foreign investment brought a highly distorted and inequitable form of growth characterized by "the prosperity of a few" and "an artificial civilization." He insisted that foreign investment should be limited to non-key industries and that the state had to play "the guiding role in the economic development of dependent and backward countries."[37] Canelas and Almaraz served as advisers to the Cochabamba oil workers union, one of the most ardent critics of MNR oil policy within organized labor.[38]

A third book, published in 1966 by former YPFB head engineer Enrique Mariaca Bilbao, gave a disaffected insider's perspective. Mariaca was one of a group of YPFB engineers and geologists who had watched "the gradual abandonment of the state enterprise" by the government. In 1963 they presented a series of requests to the Paz administration calling for a large increase in government funding to allow the discovery of new reserves, the return of lands in YPFB's zone, the acceptance of the Soviet loan, and assurance that YPFB would have a monopoly over the domestic market. The lack of response prompted Mariaca to resign in protest later that year. His book revealed details about the government's abandonment of YPFB and presented a damning comparative analysis of oil concessions in other oil-producing countries.[39] It quickly gained a broad audience. Like the books by Almaraz and Canelas, Mariaca's attracted many fans in university circles and even within parts of the military. His analysis reportedly had an important influence on General Ovando, who would preside over the Gulf nationalization in 1969.[40]

Very few of these critics had been formally trained as economists. Prior to the 1950s there was little opportunity for most Bolivians to acquire such training and little market for economists. Most middle-class critics were lawyers, journalists, or engineers who took an interest in economic policy for ideological, moral, or personal reasons.[41] For Mariaca, YPFB's troubles "demanded that technicians abandon" the tradition of "dedicating themselves exclusively to the technical aspects of their profession" and commit "to the struggle in defense of oil."[42] Most working-class Bolivians, meanwhile, had at most a primary school education.

But despite their lack of formal training, many of these voices advocated fairly coherent alternatives to the reigning oil policy. Sergio Almaraz, like most critics, advocated the use of oil as a lever to "develop a more solid and independent economy." The Cochabamba refinery workers' newspaper argued that "oil can and should constitute one of the firmest pillars for a new type of Bolivian economy." The Trotskyist POR likewise emphasized the need for "the recovery of our sources of raw materials" as a prerequisite for diversifying and "industrializing the country."[43] Such statements implied the need for three fundamental changes in the economic structure: diversification of exports, import substitution, and the industrialization of export sectors. Oil was not a panacea in itself but a generator of surplus that could be plowed back into industrial development. Bolivia could "sow the oil," as some other resource-rich countries sought to do.[44]

This goal was impossible to achieve, maintained most critics, without a reassertion of national control over production and export by YPFB. National control would not only return more of the surplus wealth to Bolivia but also permit a greater degree of economic planning.[45] The surplus product could be reinvested in accordance with short- and long-term national needs. Bolivia would benefit as well from the power to decide its export partners. Rather than prioritizing the far-away US market, it could build closer ties to nearby markets like Argentina and Brazil and specifically the state oil enterprises in those countries. The focus on neighboring export markets was a key part of critics' alternative proposals for regional integration and cooperation among underdeveloped nations.[46] A State Department source noted that the POR, a more radical critic, advocated "a Latin-American petroleum pool controlled by the workers" that would include state oil companies in Bolivia, Argentina, Mexico, Brazil, and Chile.[47]

Most leftist and nationalist critics agreed on the need to strengthen YPFB and its control over oil production, but there was a range of views about what "national control" meant and how far it should go. Some stopped short of advocating full nationalization, arguing that foreign investment could be harnessed to national needs, including YPFB's own development. The 1958 oil workers' congress emphasized its openness to foreign capital provided that it abide by strict limitations. It resolved that "mixed ventures" (*sociedades mixtas*) should be allowed in YPFB's zone.[48] Others condemned the very presence of foreign oil companies and insisted that all production and sale be under YPFB's control. Guillermo Limpias, a COB official, argued that YPFB could not "develop as the Bolivian people wish as long as it has by its side the treacherous and watchful monopolies with a blade hidden under their poncho, ready to plunge it into the heart of the nation—that is, into YPFB."[49] Many called for the revocation of oil concessions—in YPFB's zone in the southeast and/or the entire country—and the renationalization of all oil infrastructure. By the mid-1960s the campaign for nationalization was gaining steam.

Advocates of full nationalization pointed to YPFB's impressive growth in the early 1950s to prove that foreign investment in the oil sector was not necessary.[50] If YPFB needed extra capital, it could be obtained from the USSR in the form of a low-interest loan, as advocated by diverse critics of the MNR oil policy, or from European countries. After a substantial initial capital investment, they said, the company would be self-sustaining.[51] These more radical voices were not advocating autarky; Mariaca and Almaraz favored the judicious use of "foreign experience," and they and others suggested that foreign investment in sectors other than oil might be permissible.[52] Even POR leaders spoke of the need for foreign imports of technology and capital but insisted that any foreign investment "establish real worker control over exploitation" and be subordinated to national needs.[53] Few argued that Bolivia should entirely stop trading with foreigners, even North Americans.

Though most Bolivians did not reject all foreign investment or aid, they were decidedly skeptical of its motives and opposed the undue benefits that foreigners usually enjoyed as a result. Most probably agreed with Senator Humboldt that "foreign companies, by definition, do not work for the benefit of the Nation."[54] Amado Canelas argued that Bolivia's small domestic market made "the monopolistic consortia" especially uninterested "in promoting the development of our transformative industries."[55] Even most of those who welcomed foreign investment in oil seemed to be under no illusions about this clash of interests. The oil workers' 1958 support for foreign investment, for example, was conditioned upon a list of rules that implied deep skepticism of the companies' motives and scruples. Though such critiques were not anticapitalist, they shared a suspicion of private enterprise.

By the end of the 1950s public and congressional resistance to the oil code began to have some effect on both the MNR and US governments. In 1959 top MNR officials proposed a revised royalty structure, and in 1964 Paz Estenssoro decreed an expansion of YPFB's territory from 12 to 30 million acres.[56] At the tail end of the Eisenhower administration, the United States finally granted a $6 million loan to YPFB, ending the long-standing US policy of refusing to aid state oil enterprises.[57] Ambassador Bonsal had earlier warned that Bolivian opinion would grow even more hostile toward foreign oil companies if those companies were viewed as advancing at YPFB's expense: "If YPFB continues unable to secure financing, I am very much afraid that the attitude toward foreign oil companies may deteriorate." He predicted that "the continued existence of a moderate-sized, prosperous independent YPFB can do a great deal to ensure continued development of the bulk of Bolivian oil resources by private companies."[58] The 1961 loan, in the words of another official, reflected a tacit recognition "that the co-existence of private and public enterprise in the petroleum industry is the maximum which can be expected in Bolivia (at the present time)."[59] This and subsequent loans resulted partly from Bolivian leaders' astute leveraging of the Soviet loan offer and the Cuban Revolution to wrest money from the United States.[60] But domestic pressures were the main reason for the MNR government's more assertive posture regarding YPFB.

The Slippery Contours of Oil Nationalism

The culmination of the struggle against the oil code came in September and October 1969 when General Ovando staged a successful coup against Barrientos' successor, Luis Siles Salinas, and proceeded to abrogate the oil code and then expropriate the holdings of Gulf Oil. These acts drew celebration from diverse sectors and political tendencies, not only in the cities but also in many parts of the countryside, as well as hostility from the US government and a boycott from foreign oil companies.

Gulf had become increasingly unpopular over the previous decade as a result of the widespread perception that it was profiting at YPFB's expense. In the wake of the oil code the government signed an extremely generous contract with the company that allowed it to repatriate 79 percent of its profits. Gulf was the only foreign company to find oil and in December 1966 began exporting it to California. Thanks to its massive investment in exploration—over three times the total YPFB budget—Gulf soon accumulated six times the reserves of the state company and by 1967 was producing four times as much oil.[61] It was a logical lightning rod for disillusion with the prior regimes' economic policies.

The attacks came from two principal sources: military nationalists and a loose coalition of urban workers, students, and the left. Military nationalism, including a left-leaning variant emphasizing social justice, had a long history in Bolivia dating back to Toro, Busch, and Villarroel. By the late 1960s it was on the rise in a number of Latin American countries, among them neighboring Peru.[62] Soon after the November 1964 military coup, Ovando began clandestinely organizing nationalists opposed to Barrientos, including military men and intellectuals like Marcelo Quiroga and newspaper editor Alberto Bailey. In 1968 Ovando published an "open letter to other senior officers," arguing that

> in order that the country be ours, basic industries must belong to the state . . . National resources, and the terms of their exploitation, also constitute an inseparable part of national sovereignty. The country must move towards control of their full exploitation through its own resources and entities. . . . [W]ith reference to petroleum, the Davenport Code must be annulled as soon as possible, and a tax established that reaches 50% of gross production, special regulations for gas must

be established and control for the state obtained over its refining, transport, marketing and industrialization through YPFB.[63]

The letter thus advocated a radical change in hydrocarbons policy.[64] Military nationalists likewise denounced the regime's mineral policy, especially the perceived giveaway of the Mutún iron mine to foreign interests.[65]

Inside and outside the military command, widespread suspicions about Barrientos' close collaboration with Gulf Oil and the US government undermined his nationalist posturing. Rumors about the regime's cozy relationship with Gulf and the CIA circulated around the country. Barrientos received at least $460,000 from Gulf between 1966 and 1968, and the payments were widely suspected, though not publicly confirmed at the time. In early 1969 the newspaper *Presencia*, under the editorship of Alberto Bailey, published a wave of articles drawing attention to Barrientos' relationship with the CIA.[66] By the time Barrientos died in a helicopter crash a few months later, his legitimacy had already suffered a blow, a result of the contradiction between the nationalist rhetoric and antinationalist policy that has undermined many right-wing military regimes.[67]

The Ovando coup of September 26, 1969, toppled Siles Salinas and brought to power the military-intellectual coalition that Ovando had been cultivating since 1965. A manifesto issued the same day, written primarily by General Juan José Torres, called for a mixed economic model in which the state would reassume control over key export sectors and subsidize private national industry. Private foreign enterprise would be welcomed provided that it "truly and effectively contributes to the development of the national economy." Given the "misery and dependency" of Bolivia's economy, development "cannot be based on an exclusively capitalist system or on an exclusively socialist system, but rather on the revolutionary nationalist model, in which state ownership [and] social, cooperative, and communal ownership of the means of production coexist with private ownership."[68] Though there was some disagreement within the new government over whether Gulf should be nationalized, Torres, Marcelo Quiroga (the new minister of mines and petroleum), and other proponents won out. Gulf's properties were expropriated a few weeks later on an officially declared "Day of National Dignity"; Quiroga was the main architect behind the move (figures 6.2 and 6.3).[69]

While the Ovando regime embodied a long tradition of economic

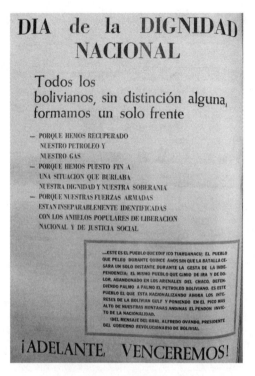

Figure 6.2. "Day of National Dignity." This full-page newspaper ad celebrating the nationalization of Gulf Oil is typical of military nationalism's corporatist discourse: "All Bolivians, without distinction, form a single front," and "Our Armed Forces are inseparably identified with the popular yearnings for national liberation and social justice." Source: *El Diario*, October 20, 1969. Archivo Hemerográfico, Biblioteca y Archivo Histórico de la Asamblea Legislativa Plurinacional, Bolivia. Used with permission.

Figure 6.3. General Ovando, flanked by General Torres (left), appears on the balcony overlooking the Plaza Murillo in La Paz on the Day of National Dignity, October 20, 1969. Source: *El Diario*, October 21, 1969. Archivo Hemerográfico, Biblioteca y Archivo Histórico de la Asamblea Legislativa Plurinacional, Bolivia. Photo used with permission.

nationalism within the Bolivian military, its rhetoric and actions also reflected mounting political pressure from diverse sectors of civilian society. The changes to hydrocarbons policy were largely intended to attract popular support for a weak regime facing a divided military and a skeptical US government.[70] For a time, Ovando's political calculation appeared to pay off. His October announcement was greeted with enthusiasm by many peasants and veterans and with cautious approval from much of urban labor and the left.[71]

Veterans of the Chaco War of the early 1930s had long been identified with the defense of Bolivian oil. Nationalists often spoke of the mutilation of veterans' bodies as a metaphor for the mutilation of the Bolivian nation. Many veterans embraced this characterization in order to justify demands for employment and pension benefits. In February 1969 a group of veterans in the Distinguished Ex-Combatants national organization referred to themselves as the "defenders of oil" and claimed that they had "protected the rich hydrocarbons that can now be industrialized." They criticized the government's delay in releasing their pension payments and contrasted their economic deprivation with Gulf Oil's massive profits.[72] In June 1969 veterans successfully pressured the government to grant them administrative control of all the country's gas stations.[73] And just as veterans' organizations had supported the resource nationalism of Toro and Busch thirty years earlier, the primary veterans' groups supported the regimes of Ovando and General Torres, who succeeded him.[74]

Most peasant unions expressed support for Ovando and the Gulf nationalization. The national peasant confederation issued a statement celebrating the nationalization and, interestingly, denouncing MNR leaders Paz, Siles Zuazo, and Lechín for having "allowed the most shameful pillaging of hydrocarbons" from the country by way of the 1955 oil code.[75] The statement suggests that the infamous military-peasant pact that helped consolidate military rule after 1964 was not based merely on campesino ignorance or the co-optation of rural leaders. Rather, continued peasant support for the military depended in part on military leaders' ability to maintain at least an outward appearance of loyalty to revolutionary nationalist ideals like agrarian reform and resource nationalism; peasant leaders probably felt similar pressure from their bases. Rural political action focused less on mineral and hydrocarbon policies than urban groups did, but campesinos were not oblivious to these issues.

As in earlier years, however, the most sustained pressure for resource-nationalist policies came from the urban working classes and student population. The nationalization was in large part an effort to shore up support among these crowds. Worker discontent with the oil code only increased during the 1960s, particularly after Gulf started exporting oil to the United States in 1966. Several local branches of the university students federation, notably those in La Paz and Cocha-

Figure 6.4. "To be Christian is to be on the left." Student demonstration in support of progressive priests. Source: *El Diario*, June 7, 1969. Archivo Hemerográfico, Biblioteca y Archivo Histórico de la Asamblea Legislativa Plurinacional, Bolivia. Photo used with permission.

bamba, remained outspoken opponents of the regimes' oil and gas policy throughout the 1960s. Their activities included a number of public forums on the economy that were covered prominently in the media and attended by high-level officials, even presidents. In early 1968 a natural gas commercialization contract with Gulf elicited harsh condemnation from Cochabamba students who harangued against the government for "submissively serving the interests of Gulf Oil" by consenting to the export of unrefined gas that would then be processed in new petrochemical plants in Chile. They also accused Barrientos of misleading the public about the proportion of hydrocarbon revenues accruing to the state through taxation and royalties.[76]

Paralleling developments elsewhere in Latin America, the late 1960s witnessed a split in the Catholic Church between the traditional hierarchy and a new crop of more progressive voices. While Bolivian leftists had long regarded Church leaders with suspicion, their attitudes soon began to change. Some priests openly allied themselves with militant mine workers, the urban student movement, and the left, prompting the Barrientos and Siles Salinas regimes to warn "political priests" against "interfering" in social conflicts.[77] In response, students at a rally in La Paz declared "solidarity with our revolutionary religious leaders" and argued that "to be Christian is to be on the left" (figure 6.4). Many urban students mourned the death in combat of Colombian priest Camilo Torres, who had joined the guerrilla struggle in his country.[78] Other Church figures avoided open involvement in activism but did start to criticize poverty, working conditions, and government repression, particularly in the mines and elsewhere. Their public critiques had an important legitimating effect for the left and helped undermine the regimes' accusations of subversion and conspiracy. Opposition leaders in Congress could proclaim that "if to criticize is to conspire, the Church too conspires."[79]

Although these progressive Catholic voices were most focused on poverty and social conditions, their message was fully compatible with resource nationalism. The connection between poverty and the draining of national resource wealth was sometimes made explicit. Anticapitalist priests who operated a radio station at the Siglo XX mine denounced the "capitalists" who "do what they want with the price of our tin," who "continue sucking out our wealth" while "90 percent of the population is tattered and starving."[80] The unfair terms of global trade were condemned even by the Church hierarchy. In 1968 hundreds of Church leaders decried how "industrialized nations sell us ever more expensive products and purchase ours at such variable, and usually cheaper and cheaper, prices." Like many other critics in Bolivia, they blamed the problem in part on US efforts to drive down prices by dumping its strategic tin reserves on the world market.[81] A variety of other self-identified Catholic voices joined the debate over natural resource policies. A new Christian Democratic Party (PDC) often spoke in defense of resource nationalism and attacked US intervention. The oil code and the government's effort "to denationalize YPFB" were particular targets of the party's criticisms.[82]

The multiple sectors, identities, and affiliations represented in the campaign for a different oil policy recall René Zavaleta's famous characterization of Bolivia as *abigarrada*—roughly, a society in which diverse identities and loyalties overlap and create a complex web of economic, social, and political relations. The class, ethnic, gender, religious, regional, and cultural identities of the population at large are obliquely related to one another, sometimes synergistic and sometimes conflicting. An individual may emphasize or identify with one category of identity at certain moments and other categories at other moments.[83]

Class and national identities were the two most prominent categories around which political mobilization occurred in mid-twentieth-century Bolivia. Very often these identities were mutually reinforcing. Anticapitalism, for instance, coexisted and overlapped with popular nationalism, as suggested by the careers of well-known resource nationalists like Sergio Almaraz, Marcelo Quiroga, René Zavaleta, and

Andrés Soliz Rada, all of whom were involved with Marxist groups at some point.[84] Though some Marxists condemned nationalism as a retrograde form of false consciousness and many left-wing MNR nationalists officially repudiated the Marxist parties, the two groups were united in their basic demands for resource nationalism, political independence, and a major redistribution of wealth and power. They differed more in their stances toward the MNR government than in their economic policy preferences. In practice, nationalist anti-imperialism and Marxism often reinforced one another. Rueful recognition of this fact sometimes came from US government and intellectual sources. In 1966 two Cold War ideologues from the United States, Arthur Whitaker and David Jordan, reflected pessimistically on the "fusion of nationalism with communism" in Latin America. Contrary to Lenin's view that "Marxism is irreconcilable with nationalism" and Cold War rhetoric that painted communism as separate from nationalism, Whitaker and Jordan lamented that nationalism and Marxism were often mutually reinforcing in Bolivia, Cuba, and other countries.[85]

Of course, nationalists were a very diverse group, and some were explicitly anti-Marxist. The neofascist FSB party was among those calling for Gulf's nationalization during the 1960s.[86] Ovando's nationalism was also quite conservative. He quickly promised compensation to Gulf, a move criticized by the oil workers federation and others.[87] His government did seek to limit the repatriation of profits by foreign companies, but it was hostile to demands for redistribution. Just a week after the nationalization Ovando announced wage freezes for workers, and major redistributive reforms were absent from the rest of his tenure.[88] He sought none of the progressive tax reforms, wage increases, or state support for small agriculture—let alone more radical measures like genuine workers' control—that were demanded by the left. "We do not want socialism," he proclaimed.[89] Ovando's overall record suggests that the Gulf nationalization, though partly a response to a popular outcry, was also intended to suppress class-based demands by rallying nationalist support for the regime.

The regime's economic policy reforms were mostly developmentalist rather than redistributionist; they were designed to foster the growth of a national bourgeoisie while also expanding the state role in strategic sectors. Echoing CEPAL structuralism, Ovando promised to "reform the structures" that impeded national development. In that spirit, he sought to limit profit repatriation, established commercial and diplomatic relations with the Soviet bloc, and pursued regional economic integration by joining the newly formed Andean Pact.[90] These moves met with ambivalence from the left throughout Ovando's year in power. A minority within the left advocated a coalition with relatively progressive elements within the military and middle classes, while an opposing minority saw the Ovando regime as reactionary and advocated active struggle—including armed struggle—against it. The major current, however, chose to express cautious and limited support for certain government actions while forcefully criticizing others and pursuing independent mobilization; the POR and most urban and miners' unions fell into this group.[91]

The massive street celebrations that followed the Gulf nationalization could not hide the mutual suspicions between these sectors and the new regime. The La Paz press reported on a heated confrontation between a government cabinet member and "a huge group" of students and workers from the Departmental Workers Central (COD) of La Paz during the local march accompanying the Day of National Dignity. The group approached a government building in the Plaza Murillo and began chanting "Workers to Power!" When the cabinet official approached they shouted insults until the police intervened. In his speech to the crowds that day, COB leader Orlando Capriles cautiously praised the nationalization but expressed skepticism about the new government, warning of state bureaucracy and the danger of a "new *rosca*" emerging. He advocated a development policy that prioritized basic needs over expensive consumer goods: "We don't need tax-free luxury cars, or Persian rugs, or fine liquors. We need tractors, machines, tools, and laboratories." He emphasized the importance of achieving national food security to overcome dependence on US wheat and flour imports. In closing he repeated that Bolivians would rather "die than live as slaves," a slogan that was common on that day of nationalist fervor but which acquired a distinctive class content in the hands of the COB, students, and the left. In other cities and towns, popular organizations combined praise for the regime's nationalization with demands for further policy changes; the COD in Sucre called for the nationalization of the Matilde mine.[92]

Ovando's successor, General Juan José Torres (October 1970–August 1971), was more progressive than Ovando in both tone and policy. He nationalized several foreign holdings including the Matilde mine. Although he was not explicitly a socialist, he sometimes used the word and did not openly disavow it. The differences between Ovando and Torres reflected not just personal ideology but also the differing political contexts in which they took power. The immediate reason for Torres' displacement of Ovando was the threat of a general strike that prevented an October 1970 right-wing military coup attempt from succeeding. In January 1971 another coup attempt was defeated for similar reasons. As a result Torres felt more beholden to labor and the left, which pulled him leftward and led him to concede more power to popular forces than he would have preferred. He was compelled to condone the 1971 Popular Assembly experiment, led by labor unions and the left, that proposed a radical democratization of society. Torres' fear of unleashing popular radicalism may have doomed him when he refused to distribute arms to urban workers and students in the face of the August 1971 right-wing military coup.[93]

Torres was the most progressive military leader in Bolivia's history, but for many on the left his regime still reflected the dangers of a cross-class nationalist coalition. Though dependency theory, resource nationalism, and a vague notion of social justice were widely endorsed, the terms themselves specified little preference about the ideal distribution of wealth and power within Bolivian society. Not all nationalists wanted redistribution, let alone socialism. For this reason Marxists often accused nationalist coalitions and dependency theorists of obscuring "the fundamental importance of class struggle" within the nation.[94]

Similar points could be raised about Bolivian nationalism's elision of other hierarchies. Most urban variants of nationalism and Marxism were ethnocentric and chauvinistic, tacitly embracing ethnic, cultural, and gender hierarchies at the same time that they attacked class and national ones. Indigenous workers typically had to adopt mestizo forms of speaking and acting in order to ascend the union or party hierarchy, while women were almost entirely excluded from formal leadership positions. Dissident currents and ideas did exist within the urban left but were much weaker in the period after 1952 than in the previous quarter century. Not until the late 1970s would less hierarchical organizing models resurface, and even those would fall short in some of the same ways.

Hydrocarbons highlight the complex, contradictory nature of Bolivian nationalism. On one hand, during the 1960s the goal of regaining national control over the country's oil and gas resources united disparate sectors of society. Marxists and military officers both came to play vital roles in the campaign for an alternative oil policy, reflecting the internal diversity of the campaign. The "Oil War," wrote Amado

Canelas in 1963, was becoming a "powerful amalgamating factor."[95] Precious natural resources do not always become "conflict goods" in the sense of dividing a society; they can also serve as unifying symbols for diverse domestic groups in opposition to foreigners, including domestic "foreigners." At the same time, conflicts almost inevitably lurk just beneath the surface, often emerging in full force after the expulsion of the foreigners, when the nation must decide with more precision what path it will follow.

Protest, Myth, and Pathology

The conflict over Bolivian hydrocarbons in the 1950s and 1960s highlights the failure of the US government and MNR mainstream leaders to achieve hegemony, particularly with regard to the urban working population. They were never able to convince most Bolivians that they shared a common interest with foreign companies or disabuse them of the notion that "Bolivian national interest would be neglected" if those companies displaced YPFB.[96]

Faced with this failure, one response from US and MNR officials was to bemoan the irrationality of popular economic attitudes. The pathologization of protest movements had a long tradition in Western intellectual thought and was on the rise in US academia in the late 1950s and 1960s, partly in response to the upsurge in US protest activity. In 1962 sociologist Neil Smelser analyzed the "generalized beliefs" that animated popular mobilization, arguing that

> collective behavior is guided by various kinds of beliefs—assessments of the situation, wishes, and expectations. These beliefs differ, however, from those which guide many other types of behavior. They involve a belief in the existence of extraordinary forces—threats, conspiracies, etc.—which are at work in the universe. They also involve an assessment of the extraordinary consequences which will follow if the collective attempt to reconstitute social action is successful. The beliefs on which collective behavior is based (we shall call them *generalized beliefs*) are thus akin to magical beliefs.[97]

Smelser and others argued, in Freudian fashion, that the participants in collective action were often unaware of the true reasons for their participation. "The striking feature of the protest movement," Smelser later wrote, "is what Freud observed: it permits the expression of impulses that are normally repressed."[98]

US officials in Bolivia similarly implied leftist and nationalist protest to be irrational. Since structural obstacles to economic development were nonexistent, George Eder contended, "they [Bolivians] alone were to blame for Bolivia's present troubles"; and since Bolivians alone were to blame, blaming others was irrational. A 1959 US memo made generous use of irony quotes when describing the campaign against the oil code: "An emotional campaign is under way by the [anti-]Siles opposition and leftists to the effect that Bolivia is being 'drained of her natural resources,' with the implication that the 'draining' is being done by the private 'capitalistic' oil companies and the 'Tin Barons' through the 'connivance' of the Department of State."[99] Other officials sympathized with the economic plight of ordinary Bolivians but claimed that poverty itself led to irrationality: "As long as the average Bolivian lives on the verge of economic disaster, we can expect emotional reactions to developments which might be passed over without notice by people in more comfortable circumstances."[100] US press commentary on Bolivia often characterized protests as "riots" and used metaphors of contagion and wildfire to describe their spread.[101]

The labeling of Bolivian protest as "anti-American" was another common rhetorical technique for discrediting it. Leftist and nationalist protesters, it was claimed, were driven by a visceral hostility toward all things North American.[102] Like the Bolivian miners who were allegedly opposed to all modern technology, resource nationalism and opposition to US intervention were supposedly animated by xenophobia rather than rational assessment of policy.

The record of Bolivian popular resistance in this era reveals a much more nuanced perspective, however—one characterized more by "conscious hostility" toward specific targets like oil companies, the State Department, or imperialism than by indiscriminate rage toward the United States as a country or all the people who lived there.[103] As noted above, most Bolivian nationalists did not seek the total exclusion of North Americans from the country or from trade partnerships, provided that the arrangements were fair and equitable. Even those who advocated barring US companies from economic activity inside Bolivia were seldom guided by blanket anti-American sentiment.

Many Bolivian resource nationalists and leftists even invoked US citizens, leaders, and history to bolster their arguments. May Day celebrations often included "workers' homage to the Chicago martyrs," a reference to the anarchists executed (and probably framed) for the deaths of several police at Haymarket Square in 1886.[104] Soon after the Cuban Revolution a group of Bolivians formed the Abraham Lincoln Committee of Friendship and Solidarity with the Cuban People, giving Lincoln a very different significance than the one intended by the US Information Service in its periodic propaganda on the former president.[105] In his 1966 critique of the oil code, former YPFB chief engineer Enrique Mariaca quoted former US Marine Smedley Butler, who participated in numerous military occupations and later declared regretfully that "war is a racket." Mariaca and other intellectual critics of the oil code made frequent use of the work of North American leftists like C. Wright Mills, Paul Baran, and especially Harvey O'Connor, whose writings on oil imperialism provided much fodder for Bolivian critiques.[106]

Bolivian critics who attack resource nationalism from the right have also accused resource nationalists of a simplistic focus on nationalization as "a panacea for the country." Economic nationalists, they claim, have naïvely believed that "all can be fixed with the discovery and exploitation of natural resources" under state control while downplaying the need for industrialization, diversification, and productivity growth.[107] Intellectual historian Guillermo Francovich, for instance, accuses the MNR of viewing the nationalization of the mines as a solution to the problems of the mining industry. He argues that this irrational faith in nationalization as a panacea constitutes one of the "deep myths" of Bolivian history.[108] But such arguments oversimplify the economic visions of mid-century leftists and nationalists. There were many Bolivians—especially on the left—who realized all along that the mine nationalization in itself was only one step toward building a stronger economy. The same was true of hydrocarbons. There were certainly some who placed too much emphasis on nationalization to the neglect of other problems or who overestimated the potential for rapid economic development in Bolivia, but they were not representative of the full spectrum of left-nationalist economic thought.

The pathologization of Bolivian "myths" also distorts the roots of those sentiments. Recent historians and anthropologists have started to take popular myths and rumors more seriously, emphasizing how they reflect collective anxieties that are often quite legitimate. Lauren Derby argues that the Dominican fear of "gringo chickens with worms" in the early 1990s was a product of neocolonial relations between the United States and Dominican Republic. The scare channeled long-standing fears about the unhealthy, mass-produced food that was widely viewed as a symbol of cultural and economic invasion, and it rekindled collective memories about the US-dominated sugar economy a century earlier. "If the portrayal of US corporate capitalism as a rapacious force quite literally devouring Dominicans and their humanity seems overblown," Derby writes, the exploitative relationship "was not entirely in their imaginations."[109]

Many homologous examples exist in the Andes, where the popular mind has often associated US imperialism with literal bodily incursions. One legend common in the rural Andes depicts foreigners trying to steal people's fat, blood, eyes, and other body parts. The *pishtaco*, as the foreign thief is often known, is usually racialized and sexualized as a white male who violates local communities and their residents and sells their products for pecuniary gain.[110] Another rumor, which led to the expulsion of the Peace Corps from Bolivia in 1971, held that the Peace Corps' birth control programs involved the sterilization of Bolivian women.[111] Bolivians' resource nationalism, too, has often employed corporeal imagery, with foreign resource exploitation understood as the theft of Bolivian blood or other bodily matter, often in sexualized terms as the nonconsensual penetration of the virgin Bolivian nation. Like *pishtaco* stories or fears of sterilization, resource nationalism has sometimes involved questionable assertions and rumors. But those who pathologize such beliefs ignore the exploitative relations that give rise to them. If resource myths and rumors were sometimes liberal with the historical facts, they gained acceptance because they resonated with deeply felt grievances and goals.

Moreover, the so-called myths animating Bolivian resource nationalism were often much more historically accurate than their critics allege. The US-MNR effort to overcome Bolivian resistance to private mining and oil investment was especially difficult because public conceptions of capitalist extraction and US foreign policy had such a strong basis in reality. Foreign investment had indeed siphoned away precious natural resources without contributing much to the development of other industries. The tin barons did make grand profits at the expense of ordinary Bolivians. In the first three decades of the century, taxes paid on mineral exports averaged single-digit percentages, while profits averaged 48 percent.[112] According to René Zavaleta, "The capital from a single mine (La Salvadora) equaled in one year (1920) 70 times the total income of the Bolivian state in twenty years."[113]

Mine workers themselves lived short, hard lives and often faced massive violence when they demanded a better living. It was not only leftists and nationalists who made such observations; foreign sources like the Magruder Commission, the 1956 Ford, Bacon & Davis report, and CEPAL economists raised many of the same points.[114] If Bolivian workers' economic discourse was sometimes overly optimistic about the possibility of breaking the country's external dependency, their basic assessment of its economic problems was substantially accurate.

Many of the supposed myths about foreign oil companies were likewise based in truth. Even if Standard Oil and Royal Dutch Shell were not simply the puppet masters behind the Chaco War, Standard did exercise a great deal of power in Bolivia, apparently defrauded the government of taxes, and had not cooperated with the Bolivian military in the war.[115] More generally, the big companies did form cartel-like arrangements, harvested Bolivian oil on terms very generous to foreign investors, and made little direct contribution to the country's industrial development. The efforts of Standard and other companies to restrict oil production around the world in the interest of maintaining price levels and profits are now well known.[116] And they did seek—and usually receive—the cooperation of the State Department and other branches of US government. University students' 1953 allegations that "Yankee imperialism" sought to maintain Bolivia as a "source of raw materials" and a "secure market for its products," and that the US government often used intervention as a means to those ends, are today hardly disputable.[117] Though frequently derided as conspiracy theories, popular perceptions were often rooted in fact.

The dogged persistence of the resource-nationalist tradition in the country's political culture is a testament to the limited success of the joint US and MNR hegemonic project in mid-century Bolivia. Despite all the internal contradictions, hierarchies, and opposing interests it incorporated, resource nationalism set the outer parameters of Bolivian political discourse and, at least until the 1980s, constrained policy makers' ability to privatize key sectors of the economy. Events in the early twenty-first century would show that resource nationalism had never fizzled out, as it once again became a point of coalescence for popular struggle and a key determinant of political outcomes.

Resource Nationalism and Popular Struggle in the Twenty-First Century

By the turn of this century the 1952 Bolivian Revolution had largely faded from memory in the country. One reason, no doubt, is that it appeared to have failed on so many levels. The MNR made only very limited progress toward the goals of diversifying and industrializing the economy; in 1970 minerals continued to constitute 91 percent of exports and in the 1980s were partly displaced by oil and gas exports.[1] Declining real wages and heightening inequality characterized the decades after 1964.[2] In the countryside, MNR policies helped create a new landholding elite in the east that would come to play a highly reactionary role in the country's politics.

In other ways, however, the revolution—or more specifically, revolutionary mobilization at the base level—had an impact far beyond 1964. Working-class power was slow to be crushed, even as the military regimes of the 1960s and 1970s deployed violence against miners and other workers.[3] The MNR's land reform, however inadequate, left enduring changes in the structure of rural property. Despite the privatization measures of the MNR and subsequent regimes, in the late 1970s as much as 70 percent of Bolivia's nonagricultural economy remained in state hands.[4] Education spending in the early 1980s was still much higher as a percentage of all federal expenditures than in most Latin American countries.

Full-scale economic restructuring would not come until after 1985, when the imposition of a "shock therapy" program once again made Bolivia a laboratory for regressive economic reform. This time the foreign doctor was Harvard economist Jeffrey Sachs, who presided over an austerity and restructuring program even more extreme than George Eder's. The program was not just imposed from outside, however. The MNR's own Víctor Paz Estenssoro—back from exile and newly reelected in 1985—helped lead the charge. Paz and other MNR leaders, not Sachs, formulated the original outlines of the 1985 Nueva Política Económica (New Economic Policy). Paz campaigned on an economic nationalist platform but once in office issued Supreme Decree 21060, which slashed social spending, devalued the currency, eliminated price controls and subsidies, and lowered tariffs on foreign imports.[5] Going far beyond what Eder and company had done, it essentially dismantled the state mining company, firing 90 percent of COMIBOL mine workers while making little to no provision for alternative employment. Over the next two decades large portions of the public sector, from utilities to the state hydrocarbons industry, were sold off to private interests despite vehement popular protests.[6] Scores of factories were closed. Peasant agriculture took a heavy blow, sending thousands of small farmers into the coca-growing business and increasing cocaine's importance to the Bolivian economy.[7] Familiar rhetoric about modernity and objective economic rationality accompanied these reforms, just as it had under the MNR in the 1950s and 1960s.[8]

Bolivia's undeniable economic problems may have lent this rhetoric an air of plausibility. As in 1956, the later program was in part an emergency response to a very real crisis of hyperinflation in the country. Many of the factories and mines that were closed were already in poor economic condition. But both the diagnosis and prescription reflected political choices by Bolivian leaders and their international backers. The diagnosis blamed inflation on workers' wages and the public sector, neglecting an array of other causes like the cost of indemnification to Gulf Oil (estimated at $58 million), the mountain of debt accrued by the corrupt dictatorship of Hugo Bánzer Suárez (1971–1978), and high interest rates charged by foreign creditors.[9] The architects of the restructuring plan made a conscious choice to place the burden on the working class. The plan's lead author, mine owner and future president Gonzalo Sánchez de Lozada, acknowledged the program's political inspiration, calling it "more than strictly an economic plan."[10]

Privatization and austerity were unable to extinguish the country's long popular traditions, however. Though greatly weakened since the mid-twentieth century, organizations like the COB, the miners federation, the oil workers federation, and the national body of Chaco War veterans, some of whom were still alive in the 1990s and early 2000s, continued to serve as organizational transmitters of resource nationalism and egalitarian, democratic ideals. YPFB workers, who had a clear material stake in resource nationalism, and Chaco veterans were among the most vocal opponents of hydrocarbons privatization in the mid-1990s.[11] Resource nationalism and egalitarianism were never limited to just these organizations, though. A variety of other grassroots groups like the El Alto Neighborhood Council Federation (FEJUVE–El Alto) would assume central roles in resource struggles despite having no direct link to the mineral or hydrocarbon industries, although some of their organizers drew upon experience in mine unions.

From 2000 through 2005 a series of massive mobilizations against government economic policies shook Bolivia. The continued centrality of resource nationalism was evident in October 2003 when protest erupted across the altiplano over the government's plan to export unrefined natural gas to the United States at cheap prices. This mobilization brought down President Sánchez de Lozada, who had responded to the protests with vicious violence, and another mass protest ousted his successor, Carlos Mesa, in June 2005.[12] The upsurge helped pave the way for the December 2005 election of Bolivia's first indigenous president, coca-growers union leader Evo Morales of the Movement toward Socialism (MAS) party.

The MNR and the MAS

The rise of the MAS and Evo Morales has elicited great interest from academics and activists. A substantial body of research and commentary has debated the successes and shortcomings of Morales' presidency, which began in January 2006 and after three terms is scheduled to end in January 2020.[13] Some observers have considered the MAS in light of the MNR experience a half century earlier.[14]

The two historical contexts are certainly different in many ways. The politicization of indigenous identity since the 1970s marks a major break with the MNR era, during which class and nationalism were the main formal bases for political mobilization. Though campesino identity remains an important signifier in Bolivian politics, it has been complemented by a new discourse and consciousness of indigenous rights that repudiate the assimilationist nationalism of the MNR and look for inspiration to the long history of pre-1952 indigenous struggles.[15] The resurgence of emphasis on indigenous rights ties in with debates over the economy, with many on the left discussing how indigenous traditions might be harnessed to facilitate economic transformations along the lines of participatory socialism. Many have offered proposals that transcend both corporate capitalism and traditional statist alternatives.[16]

Closely linked to discussion of indigenous rights is a new discourse of environmentalism, another major change from the MNR era. The Pachamama, or Mother Earth, is now widely viewed as a qualitatively different kind of resource that must be preserved rather than just exploited. Debates over natural resource extraction and use must now address a host of environmental issues, from local contamination and deforestation near extraction sites to the unprecedented global threat of climate change. Scientists recently reported that 1,600 years' worth of glacial ice in neighboring Peru had disappeared in a mere twenty-five years.[17] Closer to home, the ever-receding snowcap on the Illimani mountain overlooking La Paz provides a visible reminder of global warming. Even if Bolivia bears almost none of the historic responsibility for global warming, it has been forced to start grappling with the ecological implications of continued dependence on hydrocarbons extraction in a way that the MNR never did.

Another difference is the regional context, which was very different when the MAS came to power than in the early 1950s. By 2006 Latin American populations were rejecting the neoliberal economic model with a remarkable degree of unity and electing a new generation of left-leaning presidents. The Cold War had long since ended and along with it the distorted and tyrannical version of socialism of the Soviet Union. The decline of US power in Latin America was also evident in the increasing political independence of Latin American governments and in the rise of China, India, Brazil, and other economic powers that constituted an ever-larger share of foreign investment and trade in the region. These developments opened new space for the discussion of alternatives, with many activists debating what a new, "twenty-first-century socialism" might look like. For these reasons the context in 2006 was more complex—and in some ways more promising—than in 1952.

In many other ways, however, recent developments are eerily reminiscent of the earlier revolutionary period. There are definite parallels in the origins, discourses, and policies of the MNR and MAS and their relationships with their support bases. Both parties rose to power by drawing upon widespread disaffection with a political and economic system that effectively excluded the vast majority of Bolivians; while the oligarchic liberalism of the pre-1952 era had formally ex-

Figure 7.1. Legacies of revolution. This historical mural commissioned by the Morales government reflects the enduring anti-imperialism of Bolivian grassroots political culture. To the right a banner reads, "Gas [belongs to] the Bolivian people." A faceless clown figure with a briefcase of money stands atop the initials of the World Bank, IMF, and Inter-American Development Bank. Photo by the author, reproduced with permission of the lead artist, Gonz Jove.

cluded most of the population, the polyarchic democracy of the 1980s and 1990s did so by more subtle means.[18] Both channeled widespread demands for resource nationalization, economic development, greater equity, and more effective democratic institutions. In both cases the central unifying force for the popular coalitions that brought them to power was a popular demand for resource nationalism infused with a progressive class orientation. Debates over natural resource use, in turn, tended to reflect broader conflicts over how the economy and society should be organized. In the words of a man who helped organize the revolts of the early 2000s in El Alto, "The discussion over natural resources unleashed connections with other levels of analysis."[19]

Since taking over the reins of government in 2006 the MAS has faced a host of familiar problems. Popular expectations of industrialization and diversification have been met with some of the same disappointments as in the 1950s, as the economy has remained highly dependent on primary exports.[20] A much-anticipated boom in lithium—needed for the production of electric cars and abundant in Bolivia's Uyuni region—has been slow to materialize and in any case would not necessarily mean a break with Bolivia's historic trend of dependence on unrefined primary exports. The Morales government has repeatedly stressed the need to increase value added and has taken some steps toward industrializing the minerals sector, such as by advancing smelter operations in Potosí and Oruro. It has spelled out an ambitious vision for processing hydrocarbons and lithium that promises domestic production of polyethylene, fertilizer, and other petroleum derivatives in the near future and—perhaps a few more years down the road—the production of lithium cathodes, batteries, and even electric cars.[21] But substantial processing on Bolivian soil remains far off, and some of the government's promises seem unrealistic. The future prospects for lithium, processed or not, are subject to many unknowns beyond Bolivia's control. A further problem is that while minerals and hydrocarbons deliver resource rents that can fund important social programs and potentially alternative economic development, neither sector in itself is likely to generate significant direct employment for Bolivians, even in the event of substantial industrialization.[22]

As with the MNR, the disappointments have sprung not just from structural obstacles but also from the relatively cautious and conservative approach of the MAS itself. Like the MNR, the MAS rode to power on the heels of popular mobilization and, anti-imperialist and anticapitalist rhetoric notwithstanding, has proven more reluctant about radical change than much of its base. Its purported nationalization of natural gas in 2006 in fact kept most of the industry in private hands, increasing the royalties paid to the state rather than imposing state control.[23] Land redistribution and titling, while substantial, has been more modest than many had hoped and seems to have slowed since 2010, as critics allege government accommodation with the eastern landholding elite.[24] In this and other ways the MAS displays similarities with populist regimes of the mid-twentieth century, though there are also important differences.[25]

Fractures have appeared in the initial coalition of MAS supporters that reflect competition for scarce resources as well as differing visions of how the country should be transformed. Since 2011 important segments of that coalition have formally split off from the others, notably as a result of conflict over the government's planned highway construction project in the Isiboro Sécure Indigenous Territory and National Park in central Bolivia. In an important difference from the MNR period, here the list of popular grievances has included charges that the government has not fulfilled its promises on indigenous rights and the environment, which had not been major issues of national debate before the 1970s.[26] Ethnic and regional tensions have resurfaced within the initial coalition, sometimes encouraged by the government. The official version of resource nationalism remains laden with internal contradictions. For example, even as indigenous affirmation marks a break with the MNR era, resource nationalism is now sometimes used to deny the territorial rights of minority indigenous groups.[27] And in a pattern reminiscent of twentieth-century nationalism, the revenues resulting from the quasinationalization of gas have arguably reduced the government's incentive to pursue necessary structural changes such as progressive property redistribution.

Yet the MAS has thus far been able to maintain the support of most Bolivians, even if they disagree with certain aspects of its policies. This success signals yet another parallel with the MNR: both governments delivered enough genuine reform to stave off major challenges from the left in the realms of electoral and union politics. Whatever its shortcomings and conservatism, the Morales government has made substantial strides in reducing poverty and inequality, partly due to the 2006 reform. Having fulfilled, if only partially, the demand for gas nationalization and other aspects of the "October agenda" of the 2003 uprising, the MAS has been able to maintain considerable credibility among its base.[28]

Beyond the Cold War? Resources, Protest, and Pathology

Because of this policy record and the openly anti-imperialist rhetoric that has accompanied it, US officials have not looked kindly upon the MAS. The Bush and Obama administrations have labeled Morales' government part of Latin America's "bad left" as opposed to more "responsible" left governments in Brazil and Uruguay.[29] Intelligence reports have included Bolivia among the "radical populist governments" that "emphasize economic nationalism at the expense of market-based approaches." Such policies "directly clash with US initiatives" and jeopardize vital US "interests in the region."[30] Recent US strategy has parallels with the MNR era. The United States has combined efforts to undermine the MAS by funneling money to Bolivian opposition groups with attempts to influence MAS policies through economic means such as aid packages and trade preferences. While heavy US aid to the MNR after 1952 contrasts with more frontal attacks on the MAS, the other component of US strategy—using economic levers to encourage compliance with US policy goals—is certainly reminiscent of the Eisenhower and Kennedy administrations.[31]

If Washington's basic goals and fears in Latin America have not changed since the 1950s, the greater multipolarity of the global context does mark a significant change. In a sense US actions simply do not matter quite as much as they did in epochs past. As noted above, the rise of regional powerhouse Brazil and the increased presence of Asian, Canadian, and European capital give countries like Bolivia more options than they had during the Cold War.

On the other hand, formidable external constraints remain. The US government retains substantial economic and military power in the region. And while other foreign powers have partly displaced the United States, this greater multipolarity has not brought an end to Bolivia's dependence. Governments and investors in Spain and Canada have looked no more favorably upon resource nationalism than their US counterparts have.[32] In this new multipolar context the hostility to resource nationalism and egalitarianism comes from a wider variety of sources, perhaps, but the hostility is not unlike that faced by Bolivian activists of the 1950s.

In another parallel with the MNR era, recent critics have focused special attention on the alleged irrationality of Bolivian resource nationalism and demands for state intervention in the economy. Such demands are irrational because poverty and underdevelopment are mostly just "a state of mind." In the tradition of George Eder, Bolivian commentator Henry Oporto writes, "Our problem is the persistence of a mentality that prevents the country from transforming and developing itself."[33] In these critiques, overcoming poverty and underdevelopment requires only a mental shift—not strong state intervention, fundamental transformations in the economy, or redistributions of wealth and power.

Such commentators describe resource nationalism as the product of conspiracy theory. Guillermo Francovich includes resource nationalism among a series of popular "convictions whose correctness is such that they become held as sacred, as self-evident, located in a realm that separates them from any attempt at rational critique." These "myths influence the thought and behavior of peoples with a force that sometimes makes them more powerful than rational thought."[34] Similarly, US political scientist Kurt Weyland attributes the Morales administration's resource nationalism in part to the "deep-seated loss aversion" of a Bolivian population paranoid about "greedy foreigners," an attitude that makes neoliberal policies "economically rational but political suicidal."[35] The Bolivian journalist Fernando Molina asserts that such loss aversion has roots in a long-standing cultural pathology that has compelled successive rounds of disastrous nationalizations over the course of the twentieth and early twenty-first centuries. He argues that natural resources have long possessed a "supernatural dimension" in Bolivian society as "fetishes of a collective adoration" that give way to "conspiracy theories" about the "looting" of Bolivia's wealth. "Although it is not faithful to historical fact," Molina says, "this state of alert over an alleged conspiracy to loot the treasure" of Bolivia continues to captivate the popular imagination.[36] Bolivians might be forgiven for this perception given that, up to 2006, foreign hydrocarbons companies "anticipated making ten dollars for every dollar invested, some of the world's highest returns," as less antagonistic observers have noted.[37]

For neoliberal critics, a hallmark of nationalist irrationality is the belief that resource nationalization alone is a panacea for the country.[38] This simplistic thinking, and with it the inclination to rent-led economic development, has allegedly been ensconced in the collective pathology since the discovery of the vast Potosí silver mine in 1545. "State worship"—the notion that simply placing resources in state hands would cure all economic problems—developed later, in the republican period, complementing and ultimately reinforcing the rentier model after 1952 and again in the 2000s.[39] For Henry Oporto, the belief in panaceas and the worship of the state go hand in hand with a historical atavism that "denies the value and contributions of modernization" and specifically "the progress achieved in more than two decades of democratic life" from 1982 to 2005. "The so-called 'process of change'"—the label often applied to MAS-era reforms—is actually "the return to the past."[40]

This discourse makes sense as part of an effort to discredit resistance, but it is a poor reflection of reality. The caricatures of Bolivian consciousness belie the complexity of popular grievances and visions, just as similar caricatures did a half century before. They ignore the widespread popular demand for industrialization, not just nationalization, of the natural gas sector that was a key aspect of the October agenda of 2003. Bolivian social movements have proposed a wide range of alternative strategies for development that seek to transcend both corporate capitalism and the twentieth-century model of state-operated enterprises. Nor have popular organizations been the blind, herdlike supporters of the MAS that right-wing commentary has implied them to be. Since 2006 and especially since 2010, the Morales government has been forced to deal with ongoing protests from portions of its support base, which, while favoring the MAS over the options to its right, have insisted on holding the government to its promises of egalitarian development, participatory democracy, and ecological sustainability. Pressures from workers, farmers, indigenous communities, women, and others have had important effects on policy, pulling the government to the left and limiting its freedom to enact unpopular policies like the construction of a highway through the Isiboro Sécure territory.

The long-term implications of Bolivia's early twenty-first-century cycle of revolt are still unclear. The Morales government has broken with some aspects of neoliberalism, leading to important improvements for many Bolivians. But its policies have been contradictory, with a great deal of continuity accompanying the change. Despite more than a decade in office, it has done little to foster the alternative structures and popular leadership necessary for transcending capitalism. If history is any guide, the impetus for further radical change is unlikely to come from the MAS leadership. It is far more likely to come from Bolivian organizers and activists, continuing and improving upon the work of their predecessors.

Professional Backgrounds of Key Middle-Class Participants in Economic Debates, 1940s–1960s

Name, with birth and death years	Main party affiliation and government position, if any	Professional background, training, and other positions
Sergio Almaraz Paz (1928–1968)	PCB	Writer
Ricardo Anaya (1907–1997)	PIR	Lawyer, with degree in social and political science
Franklin Antezana Paz (1905–1980?)	MNR, president of Central Bank	Lawyer and professor of law; educated at Universidad Mayor de San Simón (UMSS) in Cochabamba and in Paris
José Antonio Arze (1904–1955)	PIR	Lawyer, sociologist; educated at UMSS
Ernesto Ayala Mercado (1919–1995?)	POR and MNR, senator	Lawyer; educated at Universidad de San Francisco Xavier (Sucre) and Escuela Normal de Sucre
Guillermo Bedregal (?–)	MNR, COMIBOL director	Lawyer; studied economics in Spain, Germany, and France
Amado Canelas (1928–1984)	MNR, congressional deputy	Lawyer, writer; educated at UMSS
Augusto Céspedes (1904–1996)	MNR	Lawyer, journalist; educated at Universidad Mayor de San Andrés (UMSA) in La Paz
Gustavo Chacón (1913–1999)	MNR	Adviser to Busch government (1937–1939); congressional deputy in early 1940s; foreign minister under Villarroel

Name, with birth and death years	Main party affiliation and government position, if any	Professional background, training, and other positions
Ñuflo Chávez Ortiz (1923–1996)	MNR, minister of peasant affairs, vice president, and minister of mines	Lawyer; educated at U. de San Francisco Xavier and UMSA
José Cuadros Quiroga (1908–1975)	MNR, executive secretary of MNR, minister of the interior	Journalist; educated in law at UMSS
José Fellman Velarde (1922–1982)	MNR, secretary to the president	Writer; may have studied at Universidad de Chile
Humberto Fossati (1901–1994)	MNR, president of Central Bank	Economist
Alfredo Franco Guachalla (?–?)	MNR, labor minister	Lawyer
Wálter Guevara Arze (1912–1996)	MNR, foreign minister	Lawyer; educated at Instituto Americano (IA, a Methodist secondary school in La Paz), UMSA, and University of Chicago
Alfonso Gumucio Reyes (1914–1981)	MNR, president of Bolivian Development Corporation (CBF)	Education unknown; one of MNR's founders
Mario Guzmán Galarza (?–?)	MNR, FUL representative, secretary to the president, minister of education	Lawyer, writer; educated at Universidad de La Paz
Juan Lechín Oquendo (1912–2001)	MNR, labor minister and vice president	Studied accounting at IA; worked at Said factory and as white-collar employee in mines
Guillermo Lora (1922?–2009)	POR	Writer, journalist
Enrique Mariaca (1916–2010)	MNR, YPFB head engineer	Geologist and engineer; educated at UNAM in Mexico
Tristán Marof (1896–1979)	POR and PSOB (Partido Socialista Obrero de Bolivia)	Lawyer, writer; educated at U. de San Francisco Xavier

Name, with birth and death years	Main party affiliation and government position, if any	Professional background, training, and other positions
Carlos Montenegro (1903–1953)	MNR	Lawyer, journalist; educated at IA and UMSA
Víctor Paz Estenssoro (1907–2001)	MNR, president	Lawyer; educated at IA and UMSA; president of Mining Bank under Busch (1937–1939); professor of economic and political sciences, U. de La Paz (1939–41); economy-finance minister under Villarroel (1943–1946)
Luis Peñaloza (1909–1990?)	MNR, Central Bank president	Economist; educated in Ayacucho, Peru, and Colegio Militar in La Paz; taught economic history at UMSA
Marcelo Quiroga Santa Cruz (1931–1980)	PS–1 (Partido Socialista–1), minister of mines and petroleum	Journalist
Hernán Siles Zuazo (1913–1996)	MNR, president	Lawyer; educated at IA and UMSA
Mario Torres Calleja (?–1974)	MNR, minister of mines and petroleum	General secretary of FSTMB
Arturo Urquidi (1905–1992)	PIR	Lawyer; taught history and sociology
René Zavaleta Mercado (1935–1984)	MNR, minister of mines and petroleum	Sociologist; educated at UMSA and Oxford

Note: Many other important figures could be listed as well, but biographical information on them is scant and scattered.
Sources: Compiled from entries in Barnadas with Calvo and Ticlla, *Diccionario histórico*; Costa de la Torre, *Catálogo*; Lora, *Diccionario político*. Additional details from Eder, *Inflation and Development*, 115n, 215n, 455; Mariaca Bilbao, *Mito y realidad*, inside cover; Weston, "Ideology of Modernization," 89–90.

Notes

For a list of archives and their abbreviations, see the bibliography. All translations from Spanish-language sources are mine.

Introduction

1. On the mobilizations of the early 2000s see especially Gutiérrez Aguilar, *Los ritmos del Pachakuti*; Hylton and Thomson, *Revolutionary Horizons*, 101–126; Mamani Ramírez, *Microgobiernos barriales* and *El rugir de las multitudes*; Webber, *Red October*.

2. Much research on "conflict goods" and "the resource curse" makes this assumption. The general argument is that abundant natural resources increase the likelihood of civil war by generating low and volatile growth rates, official corruption, and state weakness and by increasing the incentives and the funding sources for armed rebel groups. For examples see Bannon and Collier, *Natural Resources and Violent Conflict*; Collier and Hoeffler, *Greed and Grievance*.

3. The key regional elite bloc within Bolivia since the 1950s has been the large landowning class in the eastern lowlands of Santa Cruz and surrounding areas that has promoted a regional identity distinct from the indigenous populations to the west and has even sought quasi secession. A large proportion of Bolivia's hydrocarbon resources are found in these areas, making the question of separatism of crucial importance.

4. One early developmentalist treatment is Levin's 1960 *Export Economies*. More recent works about the curse and possible escape paths include Auty, *Sustaining Development* and *Resource Abundance*; Bebbington, *Social Conflict*; Bebbington and Bury, *Subterranean Struggles*; Behrends, Reyna, and Schlee, *Crude Domination*; Humphreys, Sachs, and Stiglitz, *Escaping the Resource Curse*; Lay, Thiele, and Wiebelt, "Resource Booms"; Lederman and Maloney, *Natural Resources*; Orihuela, "How Do 'Mineral-States' Learn?"; Ross, *Oil Curse*.

5. Coronil, *Magical State*; Karl, *Paradox of Plenty*; Tinker Salas, *Enduring Legacy*.

6. Rodman defines resource nationalism as "attempts to redirect the incidence of costs and benefits" in favor of the nation; *Sanctity versus Sovereignty*, 63.

7. In this sense, popular variants of resource nationalism challenge Benedict Anderson's famous notion of horizontally conceived national identities (*Imagined Communities*). This notion has been justly lambasted by Latin Americanists who point out, for example, that the region's elites have never viewed subordinate groups as equals. But the subordinates, too, have often placed their countries' elites outside the community, imbuing their own nationalist visions with progressive and even anticapitalist political agendas.

8. See, for instance, Klare, *Race for What's Left*.

9. Gledhill, "People's Oil"; Muttitt, *Fuel on the Fire*; Schiller, "'Now That the Petroleum Is Ours.'"

10. Bebbington, *Social Conflict*; Sawyer and Gómez, *Politics of Resource Extraction*. On Bolivia see Gustafson, "Flashpoints of Sovereignty"; Hindery, *From Enron to Evo*.

11. Grandin argues that Latin Americans "developed a sovereignty–social rights complex" that linked freedom from foreign intervention with socioeconomic rights—particularly the concept of "social property," which declared that states could infringe on private property rights in the interest of the national well-being; "Liberal Traditions," 72.

12. Representative works for the postcolonial era include Becker, *Indians and Leftists*; Bergquist, *Labor in Latin America*; Ciccariello-Maher, *We Created Chávez*; Gotkowitz, *Revolution for Our Rights*; Gould, *To Lead As Equals*; Grandin, *Last Colonial Massacre*; Larson, *Trials of Nation Making*; Winn, *Weavers of Revolution*.

13. Alexander, *Bolivian National Revolution*; Barcelli, *Medio siglo de luchas*, 257–292; Céspedes, *El presidente colgado*; Fellmann Velarde, *Víctor Paz*; Libermann, *Bolivia*; Peñaloza Cordero, *Historia del MNR*.

14. Almaraz Paz, *Petróleo en Bolivia*; Canelas, *Petróleo*; Justo, *Bolivia*; Lora, *La estabilización* and *La revolución boliviana*; Mariaca Bilbao, *Mito y realidad*.

15. Antezana Ergueta, *Hernán Siles Zuazo*; Dunkerley, *Rebellion*; Malloy, *Bolivia*; C. Mitchell, *Legacy of Populism*; Nash, *We Eat the Mines*; Volk, "Class, Union, Party"; Zavaleta Mercado, *50 años de historia*.

16. Platt, *Estado boliviano*, 18–21, 148–164; Rivera Cusicanqui, *Oprimidos pero no vencidos*.

17. Gordillo, *Campesinos revolucionarios*; Soliz, "Fields of Revolution"; Whitehead, "Bolivian National Revolution," 41–47; figure quoted in Dunkerley, "Bolivian Revolution," 329. On the pre-1952 era see also Gotkowitz, *Revolution for Our Rights*. For a critique of top-down narratives of the April 1952 uprising itself see Murillo, *La bala no mata*, esp. 29–49.

18. Siekmeier, *Bolivian Revolution*. A growing literature emphasizes the constraints on both imperial powers and internal colonialist projects. See, for instance, Gobat, *Confronting the American Dream*; Joseph, LeGrand, and

Salvatore, *Close Encounters of Empire*; Joseph and Nugent, *Everyday Forms of State Formation*; McCoy and Scarano, *Colonial Crucible*; Rodman, *Sanctity versus Sovereignty*.

19. In 1980 Bolivia spent 25 percent of federal expenditures on public education, which placed it near the top in Latin America; Wilkie and Perkal, *Statistical Abstract*, 160. See also Klein, "Social Change," 243–251.

20. Antezana J., "Sistema y procesos ideológicos" and "Veintisiete años después," 18–19.

21. "Political cultures," like Reed and Foran's more specific "political cultures of opposition," can be defined as "ways of understanding one's circumstances that various groups within a society sometimes articulate to make sense of the political and economic changes they are living through." They may draw upon "everything from historical memories of past conflicts to inchoate sentiments about injustice to long-standing religious idioms and practices to more formally elaborated political ideologies." "Political Cultures of Opposition," 338–339. I conceive of political culture and ideas as closely tied to, but not mere reflections of, the material conditions in society, with the potential to help shape material conditions as well as be shaped by them.

22. On the importance of MNR diplomacy see Siekmeier, *Bolivian Revolution*.

23. I deliberately leave the concepts of "popular" and "popular sectors" ambiguous. I understand them not as strict indicators of class position but as political identities that are somewhat fluid and contested, akin to the widespread political usage of the term *pueblo*. These concepts are powerful in their potential threats to elite power and perilous in their tendency to elide or justify hierarchies within the category of the "popular." With regard to ethnicity, *popular* in Bolivia has usually connoted nonwhiteness, though its precise meanings (indigenous, *cholo*, mestizo, and so forth) have rarely been fixed. On La Paz see Sierra, "Indigenous Neighborhood Residents," 32–33.

24. Zavaleta Mercado, *Lo nacional-popular*, 261. Zavaleta was adapting a concept from Italian Marxist Antonio Gramsci, who had written of the "national-popular collective will" in Italy; *Selections from the Prison Notebooks*, 133. Cf. Klein, *Orígenes de la revolución*.

25. I understand resource nationalism as the central element within the broader phenomenon of revolutionary nationalism, which also encompasses demands for things like agrarian reform, industrialization, diversification, popular democracy, progressive fiscal and monetary policy, better work conditions or even workers' control of production, and the abolition or reform of oligarchic institutions like the military. I use a third concept, economic nationalism, to denote resource nationalism plus related calls for industrialization and greater state control over economic policy, sometimes in conjunction with demands for workers' control.

26. It was not the only unifying force; see, for instance, Hines' discussion of mobilization around water rights in twentieth-century Cochabamba ("Dividing the Waters"). But at the national level it was perhaps the most important and recurring glue for political coalitions, especially in the cities and mines.

27. I use "populism" primarily in an economic sense, to identify actors who suppress interclass conflicts rather than confronting capitalists and, in their effort to appease all classes, tend to pursue unsustainable fiscal and monetary policies that compromise the prospects for long-term development.

28. For studies focused on the mine workers see Crespo Enríquez, *El rostro minero de Bolivia*; Dunkerley, *Rebellion*; Iriarte, *Los mineros*; John, *Bolivia's Radical Tradition*; Lora, *Historia del movimiento obrero boliviano, 1933–1952* and *Movimiento obrero contemporáneo*, 37–146; Nash, *We Eat the Mines*; Rodríguez Ostria, *El socavón y el sindicato*; Smale, *I Sweat the Flavor of Tin*; Volk, "Class, Union, Party."

29. Twentieth-century Mexico is perhaps the best point of contrast given the two regimes' surface similarities; the MNR and the Mexican PRI and its predecessors could be characterized as modernizing populists, and MNR leaders in the 1950s often invoked the Mexican example. See Knight, "Domestic Dynamics." Mexicans' consent was relative, of course; the state also relied on substantial coercion, as a host of recent studies has emphasized, among them Pansters, *Violence, Coercion, and State-Making.* Important contributions to the literature on revolutionary outcomes include Eckstein, "Impact of Revolution"; Foran and Goodwin, "Revolutionary Outcomes"; and Middlebrook, *Paradox of Revolution.*

30. I am assuming that when "the evidence is against the grain of the bias of the sources," it is more likely to be reliable; Mintz and Schwartz, *Power Structure*, xviii. For a similar approach, using official records from colonial India, see Guha, *Elementary Aspects.*

31. For a similar argument about other revolutionary movements see Goodwin, *No Other Way Out.*

32. Daepp, "Bolivia's Lithium Potential," 56. See also F. Molina, *El pensamiento boliviano*; Morales, "Post-Neoliberal Policies."

33. Weyland, "Rise of Latin America's Two Lefts," 156. These depictions have a long history in academic writing on populism, which—at least until the 1980s—tended to view it as involving the manipulation of irrational masses by cynical and charismatic leaders; for an example see Germani, *Política y sociedad.*

34. Several recent studies of Latin American nationalism discuss similar nuances. See Bachelor, "Miracle on Ice"; Gobat, *Confronting the American Dream.*

35. On the disadvantages of small country size see Auty, *Resource-Based Industrialization*, 49–68; Auty and Kiiski, "Natural Resources," 28–29; Kuznets, "Economic Growth of Small Nations." Being landlocked is a major disadvantage (Sachs and Warner, "Sources of Slow Growth"), but it may be greatly mitigated by resource abundance and "good neighbors"; Auty and Evia, "Growth Collapse," 190; Collier, *Bottom Billion*, 53–63.

36. Even a few countries more similar to Bolivia have achieved considerable success in terms of growth, diversification, and equity. On tin-rich Malaysia's postcolonial development, for instance, see Abidin, "Competitive Industrialization."

37. This book is not an economic history, and I will not dwell on the objec-

tive economic possibilities, such as whether Bolivia could ever have achieved export-oriented industrialization like that seen in South Korea or Taiwan since the 1960s. My point is merely that Bolivia's potential for sustainable and equitable growth was considerably greater than what was achieved.

38. For studies examining the transnational transmission of economic ideas and the role of the economics profession, see especially Babb, *Managing Mexico*; Fitzgerald and Thorp, *Economic Doctrines*; Hall, *Political Power*; Love, *Crafting the Third World*; Montecinos, *Economists, Politics, and the State*. Montecinos and Markoff argue that professional economists in Latin America played a much more powerful role in the transition to neoliberalism in the 1980s than in the earlier transition to developmentalist policies in the 1930s; "From the Power of Economic Ideas." I partly agree but would stress that economists usually only attain influence when their environments allow it; those environments are shaped largely by political struggles. Here my perspective shares much in common with Marxism and also with the embeddedness school in economic sociology associated with Polanyi (*Great Transformation*) and others.

39. First quotation from USIS La Paz to USIA, Washington, May 27, 1958, in US National Archives (hereafter NA) Record Group (RG) 306, Entry 1021, Box 2; second quotation from Sorensen, *Word War*, 5; third quotation from USIS La Paz to USIA, February 1, 1960, in NA RG 306, Entry 1047, Box 5; final quotation unsigned (USIA), "Are We Winning the Battle for Men's Minds in Latin America?" February 7, 1962, in NA RG 306, Entry 1032, Box 2. "Campaign of Truth" was a common slogan. See also Crandall to (US) Department of State (hereafter DoS), June 29, 1951, in NA RG 59, Central Decimal File 511.24/6–2951. Citations from the US National Archives hereafter follow one of three formats: for Central Decimal File (CDF) documents the date and decimal number are given; for Subject Numeric File (SNF) documents (1964–1966) the box number is given; all other documents follow the format RG/Entry/Box. Page numbers are given only in the case of especially long documents.

40. Grandin, "Off the Beach," 426. See also Grandin, *Last Colonial Massacre*; Grandin and Joseph, *Century of Revolution*; Joseph and Spenser, *In from the Cold*. Exemplary older works that integrate local, national, and transnational levels of analysis include Gleijeses, *Shattered Hope*, and Katz, *Secret War*.

41. First quotation from USIS–La Paz to USIA, May 27, 1958; second quotation from Office of Research and Intelligence, "Communist Propaganda Activities in Bolivia, 1956," February 25, 1957, in NA 306/1033/1.

1: The Road to Resource Nationalism

1. Green, *Containment*; Krenn, *U.S. Policy*; Philip, "Expropriation"; Solberg, *Oil and Nationalism*. On Mexico there is a large literature—see, for instance, Katz, *Secret War*; Knight, *Mexican Revolution* and *U.S.-Mexican Relations*; Meyer, *México y Estados Unidos*; Smith, *United States*.

2. Contreras qualifies the "enclave" picture somewhat, arguing that the government from the 1930s onward was capable of capturing a significant share of mineral income. Bolivia thus had aspects of a rentier economy even in the 1930s. However, neither government taxes nor company reserves were productively reinvested for development or diversification (or popular consumption); Contreras, "Bolivia, 1900–39," esp. 199–202, and "Debt, Taxes, and War." Still, Contreras may exaggerate state power and probably also overstates the mine owners' interest in national development. Gallo argues that Bolivia remained an enclave economy up to 1952, at least, despite the state's greater dependence on mining export taxes after 1930; *Taxes and State Power*, esp. 97–118. For additional overviews of the twentieth-century mining economy see Contreras, *Tecnología*, and Gómez d'Angelo, *La minería*.

3. Zook, *Conduct of the Chaco War*, 240–241.

4. On "structures of feeling" see various writings by Raymond Williams, such as *Marxism and Literature*, 128–135.

5. *Bandera Roja*, February 14, 1927. Discussing Latin America in the 1920s, Krenn notes that while "the radical European ideologies were ostensibly antinationalistic, both they and the Latin American version of economic nationalism rejected the liberal capitalist model of development in favor of state ownership or control of at least some portion of both the primary and secondary sectors"; *U.S. Policy*, 27.

6. Quotations are from "Introducción sociológica al Programa y al Estatuto Orgánico del P.I.R.," in Cornejo, *Programas políticos*, 211; and "Programa de principios de la F.U.B.," approved at Fourth National Student Convention, December 31, 1938, in Cornejo, *Programas políticos*, 301. According to Lora, the latter document was authored by Trotskyist Ernesto Ayala Mercado; Lora, *Historia del movimiento obrero, 1933–1952*, 151. See also Anaya, *Imperialismo*.

7. On the prewar origins of urban and labor militancy see especially Hylton, "Tierra común," and Smale, *I Sweat the Flavor of Tin*.

8. *Bandera Roja*, November 22, 1926.

9. Both are in *Bandera Roja*, December 13, 1926.

10. The second quotation is from Sucre socialist Víctor Vargas Vilaseca, quoted and criticized in Lora, *Historia del movimiento obrero, 1923–1933*, 25.

11. On anarchist women see Dibbits, Peredo Beltrán, and Volgger, *Polleras libertarias*; Lora, *Historia del movimiento obrero, 1923–1933*, 80, 88. Good general overviews of Bolivian anarchism are Lehm Ardaya and Rivera Cusicanqui, *Los artesanos libertarios*, and Rodríguez García, *La choledad antiestatal*. On indigenous networks outside the city see Gotkowitz, *Revolution for Our Rights*, 43–100.

12. Lora, *Historia del movimiento obrero, 1923–1933*, 158. The Socialist Workers Party call may have been the first popular articulation, though a few government figures had spoken of nationalization in the 1910s, among them the government finance minister Darío Gutiérrez in 1918, cited in Paz Estenssoro, "Bolivia," 61–62.

13. Marof, *La justicia del inca*, 32; Congress quotations from *El País* (La Paz [LP]), April 21, 1927; see also Lora, *Historia del movimiento obrero*,

1923–1933, 28, 31. Marof's phrase is often quoted as "Land to the Indian, mines to the state," but here I quote the original version.

14. CEUB, *Convenciones nacionales*, 46 (quotation), 48–49. These growing demands belie one foreign observer's 1928 statement that resource nationalism was confined to "an almost negligible radical element"; Marsh, *Bankers*, 128.

15. Klein, *Orígenes de la revolución*, 173–175, 202.

16. Estado Mayor General statement, January 1932, quoted in Klein, *Orígenes de la revolución*, 167; on popular support for the war, even from much of the left, see 174.

17. For early examples of this accusation see *El País* (Cochabamba [C]), June 30, 1937; Unión Boliviana de Defensa del Petróleo, *¡Defendamos el petróleo!* Standard was also accused of obstructing the war effort once it was under way, for instance by impeding production of aviation gas; Philip, *Oil and Politics*, 195–196.

18. Marof, *La tragedia del altiplano*, esp. 159–174; on the book's impact see Klein, *Orígenes de la revolución*, 216–219.

19. Klein, *Parties and Political Change*, 145–153.

20. *La Nación*, November 9, 1954. Although Standard and Shell did not incite the war, the Bolivian government's own quest for oil may have played a role; Cote, "Nature of Oil," 147–188.

21. This argument was a key theme in Carlos Montenegro's 1943 *Nacionalismo y coloniaje*. For an analysis of the book and its importance as a reflection of MNR ideology see Mayorga, *Discurso y política*, 93–105.

22. Álvarez España, *Los gráficos*, 94–100; Barcelli S., *Medio siglo de luchas*, 138–141; Lora, *Historia del movimiento obrero, 1933–1952*, 49–54.

23. There is some disagreement about whether the unions went on strike intending to overthrow the government (Lora, *Historia del movimiento obrero, 1933–1952*, 51) or unintentionally contributed to its fall through their purely economic demands (Álvarez España, *Los gráficos*, 96–97).

24. *El Diario*, June 23–24, 1936.

25. *El Diario*, June 2, 1936, and October 15, 1937; Lora, *Historia del movimiento obrero, 1933–1952*, 80–88.

26. Veterans' quotations from *El Ex-Combatiente*, February 13 (first), February 23 (second), October 9 (third, fifth), and September 13 (fourth), 1936.

27. *El Ex-Combatiente*, February 13 and June 29, 1936.

28. *El Ex-Combatiente*, September 13, 1936. On military service see Shesko, "Conscript Nation," esp. 304–353 on postwar "claims-making." Shesko notes that veterans "could claim new authority based on their wartime service without necessarily embracing the war itself" (351).

29. The PIR was not officially formed until 1940, but its major ideologues were active in the late 1930s.

30. *El Diario*, June 26 and 28, 1936. Dunkerley argues that military socialism "sapped the force" of the left; *Rebellion*, 28. For overviews of the period see Álvarez España, *Memorias*, 94–186; Antezana Ergueta, *Historia secreta del MNR*, 1:45–217.

31. Only the oil nationalization would bring lasting change to economic

policy. YPFB, the state oil company created in December 1936, would be a central economic player for decades to come. The mining revenue decree was rescinded by Busch's successor, General Carlos Quintanilla.

32. *El País* (C), May 11–12, 1937.

33. Lora, *Historia del movimiento obrero, 1933–1952*, 229; *El País* (C), March 1 and 15, 1939.

34. *Pueblo*, January 1, 1940. *Pueblo* was the paper of the Socialist Workers Party of Bolivia (PSOB, Partido Socialista Obrero de Bolivia).

35. *La Calle*, established in 1936, was closely associated with the MNR after 1941; on Montenegro's articles in the late 1930s see Knudson, *Bolivia*, 57–60.

36. Montenegro, *Frente al derecho*, 24–28, 32, 55.

37. Ibid., 96, 137, 5, 82.

38. Quoted in Lora, *Historia del movimiento obrero, 1933–1952*, 100. For the decree see *El Diario*, June 10, 1939.

39. *La Calle*, June 15, 1939. On the 1938 constitution and the unusually broad popular participation in the preceding convention see Klein, "'Social Constitutionalism'"; and Barragán, *Asambleas constituyentes*, 89–101.

40. Quoted in Lora, *Historia del movimiento obrero, 1933–1952*, 107. On the reaction from the La Paz LEC see also *La Calle*, June 11, 1939.

41. The attendance figure is in *El País* (C), June 16, 1939.

42. Lora, *Historia del movimiento obrero, 1933–1952*, 106.

43. *El Diario*, June 16, 1939.

44. Klein, *Orígenes de la revolución*, 89–90, 164.

45. Delgado González, *100 años de lucha obrera*, 106. Some called for immediate nationalization, while others did not. In February 1936 the Bolivian Socialist Confederation (Confederación Socialista Boliviana, CSB) and the Republican Socialist Party called for "revision of the contract" and "resolution of the current legal proceedings with a tendency toward nationalization"; Lora, *Historia del movimiento obrero, 1933–1952*, 43, 189 (quotation). The 1935 CSB program had also called for nationalization; Cote, "Nature of Oil," 196.

46. *El País* (LP), April 21, 1927 (first quotation); Lora, *Historia del movimiento obrero, 1933–1952*, 189, 222 (second quotation).

47. First quotation from *El Diario* editorial, May 23, 1936; second quotation from June 1939 CSTB-LEC manifesto quoted in Lora, *Historia del movimiento obrero, 1933–1952*, 107.

48. *El Diario*, June 16, 1939.

49. See, for instance, "Programa de principios de la F.U.B.," 304.

50. Quoted in Lora, *Historia del movimiento obrero, 1933–1952*, 100, 95.

51. In 1939 the campus newspaper *Crisol* identified "two types of foreign capital: Industrial and financial. This latter, also known as pirate capital, is what comes to South America. It leaves the country in ruins and does not build a single railroad, road, [or] school." Reprinted in *El País* (C), July 19, 1939.

52. Lora, *Historia del movimiento obrero, 1933–1952*, 80–88.

53. Lora claims at one point that the "support lent to Busch" by popular organizations and many leftists "was unconditional"; *Historia del movimiento obrero, 1933–1952*, 82.

54. This pact was the basis of the Frente Único Sindical, not to be confused with the later Frente Único Socialista that involved the LEC, CSTB, and other groups; Delgado González, *100 años de lucha obrera*, 119–123; Lora, *Historia del movimiento obrero, 1933–1952*, 168–171.

55. *El Diario*, October 15, 1937; *La Noche*, October 20, 1937; *El País* (C), February 3, 1939; Lora, *Historia del movimiento obrero, 1933–1952*, 193.

56. Hylton, "Tierra común," 161, 163–187.

57. Larson, "Warisata."

58. *La Calle*, July 6, 1937; August 13, 1942; *El País* (C), September 20, 1939; *Los Tiempos*, April 5, 1945. Urban-rural collaboration is also highlighted in Antezana Ergueta and Romero, *Historia de los sindicatos campesinos*, 1–202; and in Gotkowitz, *Revolution for Our Rights*, 159–162, 247–256.

59. Rodríguez García, *La choledad antiestatal*, 205–230; Young, "Making of an Interethnic Coalition."

60. Hylton and Thomson, *Revolutionary Horizons*, 78. On leftist and nationalist visions of agrarian policy in the pre-1952 decades see Soliz, "La modernidad esquiva."

61. C. Mitchell, *Legacy of Populism*, 18; Weston, "Ideology of Modernization," 89–90.

62. MNR program quoted in Malloy, *Bolivia*, 115–116. On MNR discourse see also Mayorga, *Discurso y política*, 73–117. Its ideology was clearly anti-oligarchic, but its precise class implications were deliberately vague.

63. For one example of vanguardist pretensions see Paz Estenssoro, "Programa del Movimiento Nacionalista Revolucionario" (hereafter "Programa del MNR"), 161.

64. Unión Boliviana de Defensa del Petróleo, *¡Defendamos el petróleo!*, 5–7, 9.

65. The MNR published a collection of his statements on the massacre in 1943: Paz Estenssoro, *Víctor Paz Estenssoro y la masacre de Catavi*.

66. Alexander, *Bolivian National Revolution*, 33–34; Zavaleta Mercado, *50 años de historia*, 45–47. For the Magruder report see Joint Bolivian–United States Labour Commission, *Labour Problems in Bolivia*.

67. "Principios y acción del 'Movimiento Nacionalista Revolucionario'" (April 1946), in Cornejo, *Programas políticos*, 149.

68. Peñaloza Cordero, *Historia económica*, 2:173 (quotation), 216, 222.

69. Malloy describes the MNR as representing the "bourgeois-reformist" opposition in contrast with the "revolutionary socialist" opposition and locates this divergence in the 1920s; *Bolivia*, 64. See also Volk, "Class, Union, Party," 180–198.

70. Eder, *Inflation and Development*, 44–45, 351; Soliz, "La modernidad esquiva," 32. In 1943 the CBF, created at the recommendation of a US economic mission, was already highlighting "the country's vital need to liberate itself from the outside through the diversification of its production and the development of its industries"; CBF, *La Corporación Boliviana de Fomento*, 7.

On the creation of state development agencies elsewhere starting in the late 1930s see Bulmer-Thomas, *Economic History of Latin America*, 222–223.

71. "Principios y acción del 'MNR,'" in Cornejo, *Programas políticos*, 148–149; Paz Estenssoro, "El MNR," 172.

72. "Principios y acción del 'MNR,'" 148–149; Paz Estenssoro, "El MNR," 171. The Thesis of Pulacayo argued that "Bolivia is a backward capitalist country," not a feudal one, and charged the proletariat with carrying out both the "bourgeois-democratic" revolution and, following it, the socialist one—a "permanent revolution" that would involve "ever deeper cuts in the private property regime"; "Tesis Central de la Federación Sindical de Trabajadores Mineros de Bolivia," November 8, 1946, in Cornejo, *Programas políticos*, 314, 319; the MNR counterthesis is on 151–177.

73. Gotkowitz, *Revolution for Our Rights*, 195–196, 241. Gallo suggests that the MNR maintained an almost singular focus on the tiny, regionally confined mining oligarchy because it was an easier target than the landowning elite; *Taxes and State Power*, 91, 141–142.

74. Montenegro, *Frente al derecho*, 12.

75. "Principios y acción del 'MNR,'" in Cornejo, *Programas políticos,* 148. See also Gotkowitz, *Revolution for Our Rights*, 170–174; Salmón, *El espejo indígena*, 125–137; Rivera Cusicanqui, *Oprimidos pero no vencidos*, 119–141; Ari, *Earth Politics*, 135–169.

76. "Principios y acción del 'MNR,'" 147–148. Malloy argues that MNR anti-Semitism "was mainly tactical"; *Bolivia*, 361n8. See also Knudson, *Bolivia*, 130–131. But Gotkowitz links anti-Semitism and opposition to Jewish immigration in particular to the MNR's exaltation of mestizo identity; *Revolution for Our Rights*, 173–174.

77. These labels were applied to Tristán Marof in the Chamber of Deputies in 1942; *La Calle*, October 2–3. On the anti-Semitism of *La Calle* and the MNR see Knudson, *Bolivia*, 104–132.

78. Dandler and Torrico A., "From the National Indigenous Congress." On rural activism before and after the famous 1945 Indigenous Congress see Gotkowitz, *Revolution for Our Rights*, 192–232.

79. Whitehead, "Bolivia," 134.

80. Dunkerley, *Rebellion*, 37; Whitehead, "Bolivia," 138; Zavaleta Mercado, *50 años de historia*, 45–47.

81. The FSTMB would remain a monumental political force for the next four decades, often representing the most militant sector of society and confounding MNR attempts to subordinate it to state control. On the MNR's role in its 1944 founding and its failure to control the federation see Barcelli S., *Medio siglo de luchas*, 164–166; Dunkerley, *Rebellion*, 13–18; and Lora, *Historia del movimiento obrero, 1933–1952*, 425–428.

82. On the MNR–Cause of the Homeland relationship see Antezana Ergueta, *Historia secreta del MNR*, 1:82–90; Céspedes, *El presidente colgado*, 110–114; and Zavaleta Mercado, *50 años de historia*, 51–56.

83. Klein, *Parties and Political Change*, 338, 383; Weston, "Ideology of Modernization," 94–95. Gallo points to a structural reason that the MNR's

targeting of the mining oligarchy may have appealed to urban popular sectors: conflicting interests regarding the exchange rate. Unlike the mining elite, urban consumers opposed devaluation because they favored cheaper imports; *Taxes and State Power*, 141–142.

84. Klein, *Parties and Political Change*, 384, 376.

85. Malloy, *Bolivia*, 149.

86. During Villarroel's regime Paz did innovate by raising taxes on the mine owners and increasing the proportion of government funds going to social expenditures. But he also reduced overall spending, particularly on programs devoted to economic development. See Klein, *Parties and Political Change*, 377–378; Wilkie, *Bolivian Revolution*, 22, 24.

87. Paz Estenssoro, "El MNR," 171, 173.

88. The FOL also took part in the rebellion of July 21, 1946, though it quickly turned against the new regime.

89. Lora, *Historia del movimiento obrero, 1933–1952*, 425–428.

90. Jeff Goodwin (*No Other Way Out*, esp. 72–133) argues that non-Marxist, moderate nationalist forces, in those colonial situations where they have been allowed to operate, have usually been able to prevent Marxists from achieving hegemony within nationalist resistance movements. Goodwin's argument could be applied to mid-century Bolivia: as long as there existed a non-Marxist nationalist force that retained substantial legitimacy among popular sectors, the Marxist parties would have great difficulty convincing workers and peasants—especially the latter—to side with them. If true, this insight obviously has important implications for the left. I do not think it implies that leftists must renounce their radicalism to attract mass support or exert influence. But it does suggest that they must engage with dominant ideological currents in order to understand their appeal rather than dismissing adherents as mere victims of false consciousness or co-optation.

91. Alexander, *Bolivian National Revolution*, 278–280; Eisenhower, *Wine Is Bitter*.

2: A New Type of Bolivian Economy

1. Klein, *Parties and Political Change*, 401.

2. Paz Estenssoro to Lechín, April 30, 1952, in ANB, Ministerio de la Presidencia de la República (hereafter ANB-PR), #0765, Caja 369.

3. This notion of "structure" and "model" is adapted from Gray Molina, "La economía boliviana," and Wanderley, "Beyond Gas."

4. These doctrines were not entirely new, since they built on long-standing intellectual currents; on nineteenth-century precedents see Gootenberg, *Imagining Development*.

5. Paz Estenssoro, "Programa del MNR," 164, 157–158, 168.

6. Malloy, *Bolivia*, 149, 174; Klein, *Parties and Political Change*, 387; Gotkowitz, *Revolution for Our Rights*; Kohl, "Peasant and Revolution"; Soliz, "Fields of Revolution."

7. The classic discussion of revolutionary nationalism as hegemonic framework is Antezana J., "Sistemas y procesos ideológicos"; see also Mayorga, *Discurso y política*.

8. UN ECLA, *Economic Development of Latin America*, 8–12. I use CEPAL in place of ECLA in the text. CEPAL documents are listed in the bibliography under United Nations, Economic Commission for Latin America, and cited as UN ECLA.

9. The term *structuralism* was not widely used in Latin America until the 1980s; Love, "Rise and Decline," 101.

10. See Felix, "Alternative View"; Seers, "Theory of Inflation and Growth."

11. UN ECLA, *Economic Survey: 1956*, and "Economic Development of Bolivia."

12. "Import-substitution industrialization" (ISI) actually began in the 1930s or earlier in many countries, including to a very limited extent in Bolivia, though not by design. For a general overview see Bulmer-Thomas, *Economic History of Latin America*, 232–312.

13. Hirschman, for one, challenges such views; "The Political Economy of Import-Substituting Industrialization," in his *Bias for Hope*, 88, 114, 123. See also Love, "Rise and Decline," 107.

14. Love, "Economic Ideas," 429–432; Roxborough, *Theories of Underdevelopment*, 32–35.

15. Love stresses the links between the two schools; *Crafting the Third World*, 182–186, 200–201, 288n70.

16. Baran considers terms of trade relatively insignificant; *Political Economy of Growth*, 231–234.

17. See especially Baran, *Political Economy of Growth*; Cardoso and Faletto, *Dependencia y desarrollo*.

18. Some Marxists criticized dependency theory for focusing more on global trade than production; see Chilcote and Johnson, *Theories of Development*. But these critiques often reflected differing emphases rather than fundamental disagreements. Many *dependentistas* analyzed the center-periphery system in conjunction with domestic class relations; Cardoso and Faletto, *Dependencia y desarrollo*; Marini, *Dialéctica de la dependencia*.

19. The proceedings of that meeting are summarized in various articles in *El Diario* throughout May 1957.

20. Gisbert Nogué, "Discurso," 18.

21. Ibid., 5, 7.

22. Ibid., 8, 12 (quotation).

23. Ibid., 7, 15.

24. Bolivia, Junta Nacional de Planeamiento (hereafter JNP), "Plan de desarrollo económico y social," 42–47.

25. Ibid., 37–39 (quotation, 38).

26. CEPAL did have important effects on Bolivia, though, including in the way it helped shift the terms of hemispheric debate; Latin American industrialization efforts and calls for social reform helped give the MNR some limited breathing room vis-à-vis the United States and foreign capital. At a time when US policy makers were growing increasingly concerned about the threat of so-

cial revolution in Latin America, CEPAL offered a more attractive moderate alternative; Montecinos and Markoff, "From the Power of Economic Ideas," 109–110, 119.

27. For instance, see Central Bank President Franklin Antezana Paz's position on inflation in Eder, *Inflation and Development*, 100, 215n. For a partial list of key middle-class professionals and their educational backgrounds see the appendix to this volume.

28. Until the 1980s, in fact, debates over economic policy would be shaped much more by noneconomists than in countries like Argentina or Chile. And even as economists assumed a more prominent role in the late twentieth century, popular interventions in economic debates remained constant.

29. Guevara Arze, *Plan inmediato*, 149.

30. Guevara Arze, *Plan inmediato*, 49; Legg, *Bolivia*, 9; UNTAA, *Report*, 45; US Embassy to DoS, April 2, 1952, p. 18, in NA 59, CDF 824.00/4–252.

31. UN ECLA, "Economic Policy of Bolivia," 63.

32. UN ECLA, *Economic Survey: 1956*, 22, and *Economic Survey: 1954*, 125.

33. COB, "Pronunciamiento de la COB sobre la nacionalización de las minas," quoted in Lora, *Movimiento obrero contemporáneo*, 343.

34. Deputy Oscar Barbery, speaking October 11, 1956, in Bolivia, *Redactor del H. Cámara de Diputados, octubre de 1956*, 151.

35. Soliz, "Fields of Revolution," 42–43.

36. According to the 1950 agrarian census, landlords who employed servile *colono* labor had only about 2 percent of their land in cultivation; calculated based on figures in Soliz, "Fields of Revolution," 43.

37. UN ECLA, *Economic Survey: 1956*, 28; US Embassy to DoS, April 2, 1952, p. 24. See also UN ECLA, *Economic Survey: 1954*, 125.

38. UN ECLA, "Economic Policy of Bolivia," 64.

39. Guevara Arze, *Plan inmediato*, 76–85; UN ECLA, *Economic Survey: 1956*, 63; US Embassy to DoS, April 2, 1952, p. 21.

40. Legg, *Bolivia*, 4; UN ECLA, *Economic Survey: 1956*, 22.

41. Malloy, *Bolivia*, 155. On the growth of military spending in the 1920s and 1930s see Contreras, "Debt, Taxes, and War," 279–281.

42. UN ECLA, *Economic Survey: 1956*, 54; UNTAA, *Report*, 1; US Embassy to DoS, April 2, 1952, p. 3.

43. Most accounts neglect this focus, emphasizing mine nationalization, agrarian reform, and universal suffrage as the main promises and achievements of the revolution.

44. Humboldt, September 19, 1958, in Bolivia, Legislatura Ordinaria de 1958, *Redactor*, 1:188.

45. Paz Estensorro, "Programa del MNR," 162, and "Ejecutoria de un programa," 13. See also Guevara Arze, *Plan inmediato*, 63–178, 182–184.

46. Guevara Arze, "Plan for the Diversification of Production" and *Plan inmediato*.

47. Guevara Arze, *Plan inmediato*, 27–31.

48. Ibid., 12, 100, 154–162, 153, 167. On import-substitution agriculture see Bulmer-Thomas, *Economic History of Latin America*, 205, 223. With the

exceptions of sugar and rice, in Bolivia this strategy was mostly unsuccessful; Zondag, *Bolivian Economy*, 180–181.

49. Francovich, *Mitos profundos*, 117–119; F. Molina, *El pensamiento boliviano*, 77, 117. CEPAL made a similar argument in the 1960s; UN ECLA, "Economic Policy of Bolivia," 65–66.

50. See, for instance, Guevara Arze, *Plan inmediato*, 47–50; and Paz Estenssoro, "Programa del MNR," 162. The government also created development planning agencies in 1953 (the Comisión Nacional de Coordinación y Planeamiento) and 1960 (the Junta Nacional de Planeamiento). However, it is certainly true that government policy in practice neglected the goals of industrialization and diversification.

51. Quoted in *Los Tiempos*, February 13, 1953.

52. Central Obrera Departamental, "Documento de crítica y autocrítica," February 19, 1954, excerpted in Crespo and Soto, *Historia y memoria colectiva*, 153–154. Several studies have examined attempts at "resource-based industrialization"; see especially Auty, *Resource-Based Industrialization*; Coronil, *Magical State*, 237–363.

53. Quoted in Barcelli S., *Medio siglo de luchas*, 316–317. See also the COB's *Rebelión*, May 1, 1952.

54. COB, *Programa ideológico*, 31. See also *El Diario*, November 12, 1954.

55. COB, *Programa ideológico*, 32–33.

56. Ibid., 22–23.

57. The CUB originated as the Bolivian University Federation (FUB, Federación Universitaria Boliviana).

58. CUB, "Informe de la X Convención Nacional de Estudiantes," 74–75.

59. Ibid., 75.

60. On one such conference in Potosí, on the mines and agrarian reform, see *El Pueblo* (LP), June 14, 1952, and *Los Tiempos*, July 17, 1952.

61. FUL–La Paz, "La nacionalización de las minas: Declaración resolutiva universitaria," June 19, 1952, p. 3, Archivo de La Paz, SISH (files of José Antonio Arze), Caja 1, Carpeta 5; CUB, "Informe de la X Convención Nacional de Estudiantes," 78.

62. CUB, "Informe de la X Convención Nacional de Estudiantes," 92–95, 78–79 (quotation, 79).

63. Ibid., 75, 78 (first quotation), 94 (second quotation).

64. Minister of Public Works Adrián Barrenechea, interviewed in *El Diario*, January 11, 1953; see also Víctor Paz Estenssoro's speech in *El Diario*, January 9, 1953. Not all individual leaders fell neatly into one camp or the other. Some of the MNR's economic revolutionaries favored a somewhat more progressive orientation for state policy or a more robust defense of nationalized industries than others did.

65. Malloy, *Bolivia*, 235, 283.

66. MNR, "Principios y acción del 'Movimiento Nacionalista Revolucionario'" (April 1946), in Cornejo, *Programas políticos*, 147.

67. Guevara Arze, *Plan inmediato*, 57–59, 112; Guevara Arze, "Plan for the Diversification of Production."

68. The same was true of much of the urban left, especially the Stalinist PIR; Soliz, "La modernidad esquiva." After 1953 colonization remained high on the MNR's agenda; Guevara Arze, *Plan inmediato*, 100.

69. Paz Estenssoro, "Programa del MNR," 166.

70. Among many leftist and indigenist critiques of the land reform see Rivera, *Oprimidos pero no vencidos*, 118–141. On the consolidation of the eastern landholding elite see Pruden, "Cruceños into Cambas"; Soruco Sologuren, "De la goma a la soya," 57–74. For individual versus collective land titling see Wilkie, *Measuring Land Reform*, 31, 34. Soliz notes the limits of the MNR's power to shape the reform, for instance showing that many communities did succeed in winning collective titles; "Fields of Revolution."

71. Under the new system two of the seven COMIBOL directors were chosen by the FSTMB, with one "worker controller" at the national level and one in each mine; Alexander with Parker, *A History of Organized Labor*, 91. For some critiques by workers and leftists see Crespo and Soto, *Historia y memoria colectiva*, 54; Lora, "La clase obrera después de 1952," 198–204.

72. Quoted in Alexander, *Bolivian National Revolution*, 103.

73. Quoted in *El Diario*, November 3, 1954.

74. MNR, "Principios y acción," in Cornejo, *Programas políticos*, 148.

75. First quotation from *La Nación*, October 23, 1954; second quotation from *Los Tiempos*, February 10, 1953.

76. In a discussion of pre-1952 debates on agrarian policy, Soliz notes that MNR leaders and even many leftists saw a tension between redistributing land and increasing production; "La modernidad esquiva," 43–44.

77. COB, "Pronunciamiento," in Lora, *Movimiento obrero contemporáneo*, 345.

78. CUB, "Informe de la X Convención Nacional de Estudiantes," 93.

79. Quoted in Malloy, *Bolivia*, 226.

80. Gotkowitz, *Revolution for Our Rights*; Kohl, "Peasant and Revolution"; Soliz, "Fields of Revolution."

81. Malloy, *Bolivia*, 149, 174.

82. Alexander with Parker, *History of Organized Labor*, 88; Lazarte, *Movimiento obrero*, 121–131; Lora, "La clase obrera después de 1952."

83. Lora, "La clase obrera después de 1952," 172–173, 190.

84. COB, *Programa ideológico*, 4–5, 31. Likewise, in the 1952 debate over the political program of the university students' confederation, the minority Trotskyist faction was defeated but not condemned, and the content of the final document was decidedly anticapitalist. The introduction to the program emphasized not ideological differences with the Trotskyists but rather the need to craft a document with broad appeal that would not come off as too ideologically dogmatic or sectarian; CUB, "Informe de la X Convención Nacional de Estudiantes," 73.

85. Lora, *Movimiento obrero contemporáneo*, 357, 329.

86. On this tension in the MNR period see Malloy, *Bolivia*, 243–279; C. Mitchell, *Legacy of Populism*, 38–63.

87. *El Diario*, July 12, 1963.

88. Writing in 1957, the US economist Paul Baran noted that "while it

might be thought at first that maximization of the rates of growth calls for plowing back into the economy all increments in output resulting from current investment, in actual fact some splitting of these increments so as to increase *both* investment and consumption may be a more effective, or even the only possible, method of attaining the largest possible increase in production"; *Political Economy of Growth*, 270.

89. See, for example, Memorandum of Conversation, August 24, 1950, and unsigned, March 21, 1951, both in NA 59/1130/2.

90. "Position Paper Prepared by the Acting Deputy Director of the Office of International Materials Policy (Evans)," November 2, 1951, in DoS, *Foreign Relations of the United States* (hereafter *FRUS* plus year or years), *1951*, 2:1162.

91. Florman to Miller, December 27, 1950, in NA 59/1130/2. On the interest of private US oil companies in Bolivia see also Miller to DoS, June 27, 1951, in the same location; Maleady to DoS, January 4 and 18, 1952, in NA 59, CDF 724.00(W)/1-452 and 724.00(W)/1-1852.

92. Green, *Containment*, 142–152.

93. De Lima to DoS, December 8, 1950, in NA 59, CDF 724.00(W)/12-850. On the continentwide assault on social democracy and the left after 1946 see Bethell and Roxborough, *Latin America*, especially the introduction by Bethell and Roxborough and the essay by Whitehead, "Bolivia." On US-Bolivian relations in 1946–1952 see Dorn, *Truman Administration and Bolivia*. On the domestic US context see Fones-Wolf, *Selling Free Enterprise*.

94. Duggan, *The Americas*, 147.

95. By contrast, most studies of Cold War–era US policy toward Latin America focus on anticommunism as the driving motivation. See R. Alexander, *Bolivian National Revolution*, 255–270; Park, *Latin American Underdevelopment*, 167–229; Rabe, *Eisenhower and Latin America* and *Most Dangerous Area*; Wood, *Dismantling of the Good Neighbor Policy*, 145–209. My argument overlaps with that of several studies on US-Bolivian relations, especially Dorn, *Truman Administration and Bolivia*, and Siekmeier, "Fighting Economic Nationalism." On the antinationalist and antilabor thrust of US policy in the broader hemispheric context see Young, "Purging the Forces of Darkness," 531–536, and "Restoring Discipline," 18–21. Historical studies that draw related conclusions about US policy for the Cold War and earlier eras include Barnet, *Intervention and Revolution*; Grandin, *Last Colonial Massacre*; Green, *Containment*; Kolko, *Confronting the Third World*; Krenn, *U.S. Policy*; Yaqub, *Containing Arab Nationalism*. These studies complement the earlier arguments of LaFeber, *New Empire*, and W. Williams, *Tragedy of American Diplomacy*, on the "Open Door" objectives of US policy and the Marxist argument of Baran, *Political Economy of Growth*.

96. Eder, *Inflation and Development*, 79, 122; figures for 1952–1964 come from US government sources quoted in Blasier, *Hovering Giant*, 144, and Whitehead, *United States and Bolivia*, 22. See also Wilkie, *Bolivian Revolution* and "U.S. Foreign Policy."

97. See, for instance, Rowell to DoS, September 26, 1952, in NA 59, CDF 724.00(W)/9-2652; and Maleady to DoS, May 2, 1952, in NA 59, CDF

724.00(W)/5-252. See also National Intelligence Estimate 92-54, March 19, 1954, in DoS, *FRUS, 1952–1954*, 4:547–557.

98. Lehman argues that MNR nationalism was less threatening than that of the Arbenz regime in Guatemala since Bolivia "accepted its place in the hemispheric system dominated by the United States"; *Bolivia and the United States*, 110. The importance of regime language and tone should not be underestimated—after all, Arbenz' economic measures were not more radical than the MNR's.

99. Economic collapse was a real possibility in the aftermath of April 1952. US officials feared that "economic collapse would lead to the disappearance of the government as then constituted, and the probable emergence of a regime hostile to the United States, possibly communistic in orientation"; unsigned document included with Holland to Dulles, November 18, 1954, in NA 59/1132/1.

100. First quotation from Rowell to DoS, February 20, 1953, in NA 59, CDF 724.00(W)/2-2053; second quotation from Rowell to DoS, May 22, 1953, in NA 59, CDF 724.00(W)/5-2253; Andrade quoted in *En Marcha*, August 12, 1952. See also Guevara Arze, *Plan inmediato*, and the Bolivian Ministry of Foreign Relations' manifesto in *La Nación*, August 6, 1954. Siekmeier emphasizes the personal agency of Andrade in his diplomatic role but also writes that "Andrade succeeded in acquiring U.S. aid for Bolivia in large part because of his understanding of U.S. motives for giving assistance"; *Bolivian Revolution*, 55–72 (quotation, 69).

101. Eisenhower, *Wine Is Bitter*, xi. Kennedy assistant Arthur Schlesinger Jr. would later clarify that "peaceful" meant "middle-class": "If the possessing classes of Latin America make the middle-class revolution impossible, they will make a 'workers-and-peasants' revolution inevitable"; "Report to the President on Latin American Mission, February 12–March 3, 1961," in DoS, *FRUS, 1961–1963*, 12:12.

102. US Embassy to DoS, April 30, 1953, in NA 59, CDF 611.24/4-3053.

103. Sparks to DoS, October 6, 1953, in NA 59, CDF 724.5-MSP/10-653. See also Lehman, "Revolutions and Attributions," 198–200; Wood, *Dismantling of the Good Neighbor Policy*, 147, 150.

104. First quotation from Bennett to DoS, September 2, 1953, in NA 59, CDF 724.5-MSP/9-253; second quotation from US Embassy to DoS, October 15, 1953, in NA 59, CDF 724.5-MSP/10-1553.

105. Blasier, *Hovering Giant*, 134; *El Diario*, March 9, 1953.

106. See, for example, Rowell to DoS, November 7, 1952, in NA 59, CDF 724.00[W]/11-752; Cabot to Dulles, November 19, 1953, in NA 59, CDF 724.5-MSP/11-1953; Acheson to US Embassy, January 9, 1953, in DoS, *FRUS, 1952–1954*, 4:520; Memorandum of Conversation, September 15, 1955, in NA 59/1132/1; Rubottom to Bonsal, June 6, 1957, in NA 59/1170/13; Bonsal to Rubottom, June 29, 1957, in NA 59/1135/1.

107. Holland to Hoover, June 1, 1955; Memorandum of Conversation, September 15, 1955; Holland to Sparks et al., April 4, 1955, all in NA 59/1132/1. See also "Agreement for a Joint United States-Bolivian Program," June 22, 1955, in DoS, *FRUS, 1955–1957*, 7:514–515. On the MNR's busi-

ness-friendly investment code adopted in 1960 see Zondag, *Bolivian Economy*, 234.

108. Blasier, *Hovering Giant*, 141; Wilkie, "U.S. Foreign Policy," 92.

109. On US stock in Patiño see Maleady to DoS, June 13, 1952, in NA 59, CDF 724.00(W)/6-1352; and Rowell to DoS, March 27, 1953, in NA 59, CDF 724.00(W)/3-2753. Overall US direct investments in Bolivia in 1950 totaled only $11 million; Wilkie and Reich, *Statistical Abstract*, 367.

110. Hudson to Atwood, April 30, 1953, in NA 59, CDF 824.00/4-3053.

111. Testimony of Edward Sparks, included in Bolivian Embassy to Guevara Arze, June 10, 1955, in *Embajada de Bolivia—Washington a Ministerio de Relaciones Exteriores, enero a junio de 1955*, p. 121, in Archivo del Ministerio de Relaciones Exteriores (RREE).

112. Prochnow to Hoover, November 19, 1955, in NA 59, CDF 824.2553/11-1755.

113. Rodman, *Sanctity versus Sovereignty*, 46–51, 129, 133; Young, "Purging the Forces of Darkness," 534n98.

114. Maleady to DoS, May 9, 1952, in NA 59, CDF 724.00(W)/5-952; Rowell to DoS, July 17, 1953, in NA 59, CDF 724.00(W)/7-1753.

115. Rowell to DoS, November 14, 1952, in NA 59, CDF 724.00(W)/11-1452.

116. Kelley and Klein, *Revolution*, 138–141, 230–231. Kelley and Klein estimate that income inequality by the late 1950s had declined to roughly 70 percent of its levels in 1950–1952. There was "a clear reversal" in this trend in the 1960s (p. 139).

3: The Political Economy of Containment

1. Eder, *Inflation and Development*, 133 (first quotation), 601 (second), 135 (third), 302 (fourth). On precedents see Drake, *Money Doctor*, esp. 175–211.

2. The same was true of agricultural policy, which increasingly favored less efficient large-scale producers; Eckstein, "Transformation of a Revolution." For similar approaches to the neoliberal turn in Latin American economic policy in the 1980s and 1990s see the essays in FitzGerald and Thorp, *Economic Doctrines*, esp. Gourevitch, "Economic Ideas."

3. Krenn, *U.S. Policy*, 21–48, 71–98; Philip, "Expropriation," 173–177; Solberg, *Oil and Nationalism*.

4. Green, *Containment*, 51–52, 194; Siekmeier, *Bolivian Revolution*, 17–21, 24.

5. Florman to Miller, December 27, 1950, in NA 59/1130/2.

6. Legg, *Bolivia*, 22. On oil companies' interest see Miller to DoS, June 27, 1951, in NA 59/1130/2; Maleady to DoS, January 4, 1952, in NA 59, CDF 724.00(W)/1-452; Maleady to DoS, January 18, 1952, in NA 59, CDF 724.00(W)/1-1852.

7. Calvo Mirabal, *Transnacionales petroleras*, 86–95; UN ECLA, "Economic Policy of Bolivia," 80; YPFB, *Política petrolera*, 11–19, 81.

8. YPFB, *Política petrolera*, 22, 32, 34–37, 81, and *Libro de oro*, "Anexos"; Zondag, *Bolivian Economy*, 121. Prior to 1952, more than half of Bolivia's foreign exchange went toward the purchase of oil and related products; Wálter Guevara Arze, "Plan de producción de petróleo y derivados" (draft), 15, in ANB-WGA, Caja 29, Carpeta 5.

9. UN ECLA, "Economic Development of Bolivia," 50. In 1955 total production was 2.7 million barrels, about 7,400 barrels a day; YPFB, *Política petrolera*, 22.

10. Bonsal to Rubottom, August 21, 1958, in NA 59/1170/13; Eaton, "Conclusions and Recommendations," n.d., p. 9, in NA 59/1170/13. See also US Embassy to DoS, November 17, 1955, in NA 59, CDF 824.2553/11-1755. In 1960 a US government-funded study of YPFB gave a generally favorable assessment; DeGolyer and MacNaughton, *Informe*. On the impact of "heavy amortization and interest payments" on YPFB see US Embassy to DoS, April 2, 1952, p. 20.

11. YPFB, *Código de petróleo*, 41–42, 27 (Articles 104, 106, and 67). Critics later argued that the effective tax rate was in fact much lower, amounting to less than 20 percent total; Almaraz Paz, *Petróleo en Bolivia*, 188; Quiroga Santa Cruz, *Desarrollo*, 26–28.

12. YPFB, *Código de petróleo*, 62 (Article 161).

13. Siekmeier, *Bolivian Revolution*, 51.

14. For a partial sample of meetings in 1955–1956 see Atwood to Holland, May 19, 1955, in NA 59, CDF 824.2553/5-1955; Memorandum of Conversation, September 7, 1955, in NA 59, CDF 824.2553/9-755; Memorandum of Conversation, August 8, 1956, in NA 59, CDF 824.2553/8-856. Close consultation with US oil representatives continued thereafter. When the US government was debating whether to provide loans to YPFB in the late 1950s the State Department sought oil companies' prior approval; unsigned, "Proposed Loan to YPFB," June 23, 1959, in NA 59/1170/13. Henry Holland, the assistant secretary of state for Latin American Affairs in 1955, would travel to La Paz as an oil company lawyer in 1957; J. Paz Estenssoro to Tamayo, July 1, 1957, in ANB-PR, #915, Caja 435.

15. Siekmeier, *Bolivian Revolution*, 51.

16. Writing prior to the declassification of many of the relevant documents, Laurence Whitehead characterized the code as "written by Americans and enacted without public debate or modification by the Bolivian authorities"; *United States and Bolivia*, 11. See also Almaraz Paz, *Petróleo en Bolivia*, 206–207; Lehman, *Bolivia and the United States*, 122; Mariaca Bilbao, *Mito y realidad*, 170.

17. Sparks in Bolivian embassy to Guevara Arze, June 10, 1955, in *Embajada de Bolivia—Washington a Ministerio de Relaciones Exteriores, enero a junio de 1955*, p. 132, in RREE. A State Department memo from late 1955 suggests that a YPFB attorney named Raoul Fernández "did the greater part of the drafting of the new law"; Leggett to DoS, November 7, 1955, in NA 59, CDF 824.2553/11-755.

18. Guevara Arze, "Plan for the Diversification of Production," 15, and *Plan inmediato*, 57–59, 67–88.

19. See J. Paz Estenssoro to Siles Zuazo, April 1, 1958, in ANB-PR, #1311, Caja 570; Bolivia, Ministerio de Minas y Petróleo (hereafter MMP), *Informe anual*, 152, in ANB-PR, #1822, Caja 778.

20. Paz comments reported in Merritt to DoS, May 10, 1955, in NA 59, CDF 824.2553/5-1055.

21. Memorandum of Conversation, July 8, 1955, in NA 59, CDF 824.2553/7-855; Calvo Mirabal, *Transnacionales petroleras*, 93; Philip, *Oil and Politics*, 258–259.

22. In YPFB, *Código de petróleo*, 4.

23. *El Diario*, October 12, 1955; *La Nación*, October 30 and 27, 1955; Torres quoted in Despatch No. 760, June 6, 1957, in NA 59, CDF 824.2553/6-657.

24. Canelas, *Mito y realidad*, 222; cf. Almaraz Paz, *Petróleo en Bolivia*, 205.

25. Despatch 285, October 8, 1958, in NA 59, CDF 824.2553/10-858. By early 1959 the number was up to twenty-one; Memorandum of Conversation, February 11, 1959, in NA 59, CDF 824.2553/2-1159. For US oil companies' praise for the new law see Almaraz Paz, *Petróleo en Bolivia*, 205.

26. Memorandum of Conversation, August 15, 1957, in NA 59, CDF 824.2553/8-1557 (quotation); Despatch 528, December 13, 1957, in NA 59, CDF 824.2553/12-1357; US Embassy to DoS, May 17, 1957, in NA 59, CDF 824.2553/5-2157.

27. UN ECLA, *Economic Survey: 1966*, 99.

28. YPFB, *Memoria anual 1957*, 3, 9, 26; Despatch 528, December 13, 1957, in NA 59, CDF 824.2553/12-1357; Despatch 696, February 19, 1959, in NA 59, CDF 824.2553/2-1859; UN ECLA, "Economic Policy of Bolivia," 81; DeGolyer and MacNaughton, *Informe*, 67–74; Fernández Soliz, *Tema: El petróleo*, 120.

29. UN ECLA, "Economic Policy of Bolivia," 80–81. By mid-1958 there were three private contracts in YPFB's zone, all with US companies; see Despatch 612, January 7, 1958, in NA 59, CDF 824.2553/1-758; Bonsal to Rubottom, August 21, 1958, in NA 59, CDF 824.2553/8-2158. In contrast to CEPAL, a 1960 study was more optimistic on the prospects for finding new oil in YPFB's zone; DeGolyer and MacNaughton, *Informe*, 29.

30. UN ECLA, "Economic Policy of Bolivia," 80, and *Economic Survey: 1966*, 99; Fernández Soliz, *Tema: El petróleo*, 105. See also UN ECLA, "Economic Development of Bolivia," 51–52; Siekmeier, "Fighting Economic Nationalism," 190–191.

31. Bonsal to Rubottom, May 20, 1958, in NA 59/1162/27.

32. Dunkerley, *Rebellion*, 86; UN ECLA, "Economic Development of Bolivia," 29.

33. Lora, *La estabilización*, 5.

34. Total external debt in 1949 was $142 million, 58 percent of which ($83 million) was interest. See Legg, *Bolivia*, 4; UNTAA, *Report*, 22.

35. Cancillería to Holland, November 26, 1955, in ANB-WGA, Caja 17; UN ECLA, "Economic Development of Bolivia," 21 (quotations), 22, 28, 54–59. Cf. UN ECLA, "Economic Policy of Bolivia," 66–73, and *Economic Sur-*

vey: 1956, 11–12. Most of these factors reflect demand-pull inflation, meaning that aggregate demand outstrips supply.

36. Cancillería to Holland, November 26, 1955; UN ECLA, "Economic Development of Bolivia," 28–36, 72, and "Economic Policy of Bolivia," 66–73, 85.

37. Unsigned (DoS), "Program [Eder Plan] in the Second Year and the Present Position," n.d., in NA 59/3172/1; Blasier, *Hovering Giant*, 143; Dunkerley, *Rebellion*, 85; Zondag, *Bolivian Economy*, 179.

38. Eder, *Inflation and Development*, 479.

39. Ibid., 159, 221 (quotation), 676, 678, 697. Lechín nonetheless supported most of the basic elements of the plan; see Lora, *History*, 305–306.

40. Eder, *Inflation and Development*, 135. According to Eder, the stabilization fund itself had been conditional on compensation to the tin barons: "the U.S. government had made a negotiated settlement a *sine qua non* for stabilization aid" (465).

41. Eder had in fact written the "Forty Points" on which the Fifty-Step Plan was based, but the two documents were "substantially identical," in Eder's words; *Inflation and Development*, 626. For the full text of the Fifty-Step Plan, see 626–647.

42. Burgess to Holland, August 1956, n.d., in NA 59/1132/1.

43. Eder, *Inflation and Development*, 526 (first quotation), 639 (second), 636–637. Bolivia resumed debt service payments in mid-1957; *El Pueblo* (C), June 13, 1957.

44. Eder, *Inflation and Development*, 454.

45. Ibid., 634 (first quotation), 636 (second), 510 (third), 220 (fourth).

46. Ibid., 341 (first quotation), x (second), 92n (third).

47. Ibid., 277n (quotations), 268–274, 629, 632–633, 635.

48. In *El Diario*, December 22 and 28, 1956.

49. On miner resistance to the Eder Plan see John, *Bolivia's Radical Tradition*, 169–172; Lora, *History*, 305–320; *El Pueblo* (LP), February 15, 1958.

50. Eder, *Inflation and Development*, 285n (first quotation), 267 (second), 153n (third), 332n (fourth, fifth).

51. Ibid., 511. This understanding of the technocrat was shared by many postwar economists and leaders, including Keynesians. As Timothy Mitchell argues, it was part of an intellectual movement to insulate the realm of economics from democratic debate; *Carbon Democracy*, 109–143.

52. Eder, *Inflation and Development*, 160 (first quotation), 15 (second, third), 16 (fourth), 100 (fifth), 17 (sixth).

53. Samuel D. Eaton, "Major Factors Inhibiting Economic Growth in Bolivia and Implications for U.S. Action" (draft), May 14, 1959, pp. 1–2, in NA 59/1170/13. Eaton did say, though, "that the Indians and the half-breeds have had little opportunity for the education or the training which would make them effective economic units."

54. Rowell to DoS, July 17, 1953, in NA 59, CDF 724.00(W)/7-1753, and April 2, 1953, in NA 59, CDF 724.00(W)/4-253. The "austerity" and "sacrifice" comments were handwritten in the margins of an undated (September 1958) memo from Rubottom to Dillon in NA 59/1170/13.

55. Eder, *Inflation and Development*, 96 (first quotation), 164 (second), 165 (third), 477 (fourth), 482n (fifth).

56. *El Pueblo* (C), May 30, 1957.

57. Eder, *Inflation and Development*, 53 (first quotation), 133 (second), 56 (third), 394 (fourth), 132. Eder's daily salary was $75 (703n3).

58. Eder, *Inflation and Development*, 71 (quotation), 378, 402–406, 635.

59. Ibid., 19, 87–88, 98–99, 102, 160, 469–482.

60. Eder to Hollister, included in Williams to Delaney, April 30, 1957, in NA 59/1170/13.

61. Eder, *Inflation and Development*, 102.

62. Briggs to Coerr, February 20, 1958, and Rose to Atwood, March 1958, n.d., both in NA 59/1162/27.

63. Quoted in Eder, *Inflation and Development*, 24.

64. For examples see Eder, *Inflation and Development*, 460, 465–466, 468; *El Diario*, May 26–30, 1957.

65. ICA-La Paz (to DoS?), June 15, 1957; USIS–La Paz to USIA, May 27, 1958; unsigned, "Notes on Bolivia (For IRI/R and IAL)," September 22, 1958, all in NA 306/1021/2.

66. *El Pueblo* (C), June 26, 1957; *El Diario*, June 16–29, 1957.

67. First quotation from unsigned (USIA) to Haddow and Parry, March 10, 1959, in NA 306/1021/2; second quotation from Rubottom to Dillon, n.d., in NA 59/1170/13.

68. C. Mitchell, *Legacy of Populism*, 73–74. On the cost of living see Zondag, *Bolivian Economy*, 56.

69. Hardin to Hoyt, May 29, 1958, in NA 59/1137/13 (quotation); C. Mitchell, *Legacy of Populism*, 91; Wilkie, *Bolivian Revolution*, 48.

70. *El Diario*, May 8, 1961 (first quotation), and June 10, 1963 (second quotation); UN ECLA, "Economic Policy of Bolivia," 89, 65 (CEPAL quotation), 80, "Economic Development of Bolivia," 51, and *Economic Survey: 1969*, 117–118; Rubottom to Dillon, undated (September 1958), in NA 59/1170/13 (last quotation). The impact on industry was a frequent theme in the left's criticism of the plan; see, for example, *El Pueblo* (LP), July 2, 1960.

71. By 1966–1967 income inequality had reached prerevolution levels; Kelley and Klein, *Revolution*, 138–140. Eder left Bolivia in summer 1957, though stabilization continued under the supervision of the US embassy and the IMF. On the IMF's role see Kofas, "Politics of Austerity."

72. Quotations from unsigned (DoS), "Summary of and Comments on USOM [US Operations Mission] Bolivia's Criticism of Aid Policy in Bolivia," n.d., and unsigned (DoS), "United States Policy toward Bolivia," n.d., both in NA 59/3172/1; Zunes, "United States and Bolivia," 40–47.

73. Statistics cited in Burke, *Corporación Minera*, 7, 13, 15.

74. The Triangular Plan and the MNR's 1961 economic plan were predicated on the renewed recognition "that we cannot escape, in the first stage of the Revolution, our mining destiny"; Bolivia, MMP, *Informe anual*, 2. See also Bolivia, JNP, "Plan de desarrollo económico y social," 172–180.

75. Unsigned (DoS), "Action to Meet Soviet Economic Pressures on Bolivia," November 4, 1960 (first quotation); and Lane to Woodward, July 13, 1961 (second quotation), both in NA 59/3172/1.

76. Schlesinger, "Report to the President," 13.

77. Unsigned, "Latin America: Guidelines of United States Policy and Operations" (draft), April 24, 1962, p. 14, in NA 59/3172/2 (quotation); Weise to Coerr, November 11, 1960, and Memorandum of Conversation, August 1, 1960, both in NA 59/3172/1. On Bolivian officials' skillful manipulation of these US fears see Siekmeier, *Bolivian Revolution*, 94–98.

78. See, for example, the statement from the Urban Teachers Federation in *El Pueblo* (LP), November 5, 1960, arguing that "the mining industry has been deliberately kept in its extractive stage by foreign monopolies."

79. Mann to Dillon, November 10 and 17, 1960, in NA 59/3172/1. The smelter offer was part of a $150 million Soviet aid offer; Bolivia, MMP, *Informe anual*, 71. "Penetration" was a key trope, appearing in several other documents decrying the Soviet aid offer.

80. Hudson to Atwood, April 30, 1953, in NA 59, CDF 824.00/4-3053.

81. Total US aid increased by 600 percent in the period 1960–1964; Burke, *Corporación Minera*, ii, 16; Dunkerley, *Rebellion*, 108.

82. *El Diario*, June 7 (first quotation) and April 6, 1961 (second quotation, from COMIBOL President Guillermo Bedregal).

83. Bjorkman quoted in Belcher to Martin et al., May 29, 1963, in NA 59/3172/3; second quotation in unsigned (DoS), "Action to Meet Soviet Pressures." The US press also chimed in. *Time* magazine referred to "the coddled, politically powerful miners" and asserted that "Bolivian labor toils hardly at all"; "The Fanned Spark" (March 16, 1959), 40–41, and "Chaos in the Clouds" (March 2, 1959), 27.

84. Paz quoted in *El Diario*, April 10, 1961; Bedregal quoted in Belcher to Martin et al., May 29, 1963, and in *El Diario*, June 9 and July 10, 1961; quotes in last two sentences from Ministry of Government and MNR executive secretary Federico Fortún Sanjinés, in *El Diario*, June 8, 1961.

85. Guevara Arze, *Plan inmediato*, 39, 45, 57–59; Lechín quoted in Canelas, *Mito y realidad*, 57; Andrade paraphrased in *World Telegram and Sun*, February 8, 1956, included in *Embajada de Bolivia—Washington a Ministerio de Relaciones Exteriores, enero a junio de 1956*, p. 76, in RREE.

86. Canelas, *Mito y realidad*, 99. The text of the MNR's 1961 economic plan did not evince the same singular focus on labor as the Triangular Plan but did stress the government's support for the plan; Bolivia, JNP, "Plan de desarrollo económico y social," 178.

87. UNTAA, *Report*, 49. The 1942 Bohan mission likewise was premised on the expectation that mining was "a declining source of wealth"; US Economic Mission to Bolivia, *Plan Bohan*, 8.

88. Burke, *Corporación Minera*, 3–4, 12, 15; UNTAA, *Report*, 45–46. See also UN ECLA, "Economic Development of Bolivia," 25–28, and "Economic Policy of Bolivia," 66–73; Canelas, *Mito y realidad*, 19–101.

89. Burke, *Corporación Minera*, 13; Roger Freeman, "The Revenue Problem of Bolivia," April 12, 1957, pp. 36–37, in NA 59/1170/13; UN ECLA, "Economic Development of Bolivia," 26, 32, and "Economic Policy of Bolivia," 63, 67.

90. Burke, *Corporación Minera*, 6, 16 (quotations); see also Canelas, *Mito y realidad*, 64–76.

91. Burke, *Corporación Minera*, 1, 11. Variations in mine size, ore grades, equipment, and other factors nonetheless make comparisons difficult.

92. State enterprise is not inherently less efficient than private enterprise. All large organizations, whether owned privately or by the state, face the same problems of motivation, limiting employee agency, and maximizing productivity. See Chang, *Bad Samaritans*, 103–121; Simon, "Organizations and Markets."

93. *El Diario*, April 4 and June 6, 1961; Cabrera, *La burocracia*; *El Diario*, October 19, 1957, and June 12, 1961. In 1962 Senator Arturo Crespo claimed that US dumping had cost Bolivia $90 million over the previous decade; Bolivia, H. Senado Nacional, *Hornos de fundición*, 17. An estimate by a US company calculated a $124 million loss for COMIBOL from just 1952 to 1957; quoted in Nash, *We Eat the Mines*, 247. The Soviet Union also dumped mineral reserves, though the United States agreed to buy them.

94. Freeman, "The Revenue Problem of Bolivia," 36–37; Paz quoted in *El Diario*, April 10, 1961. The 1955 *Plan inmediato* noted that a significant part of the expenditures categorized as labor costs derived not from high wages or benefits but from Bolivia's dependence on food imports for the *pulperías*, which consumed practically all of the foreign exchange spent on what was then termed "labor costs"; Guevara Arze, *Plan inmediato*, 27–31. See also Wálter Meneses R., "Análisis de la producción y exportación de minerales en el país durante los años 1950–1960," October 27, 1961, in ANB-PR, #1824, Caja 779.

95. UN ECLA, "Economic Policy of Bolivia," 70.

96. Hertslet to Berle, April 24, 1961, in NA 59/3172/1.

97. Canelas, *Mito y realidad*, 51–56; Ford, Bacon & Davis, cited in Burke, *Corporación Minera*, 11.

98. First quotation from unsigned (DoS), "Program [Eder Plan] in the Second Year"; second quotation from unsigned, "Report of the Advisory Group to Corporación Minera de Bolivia for the Period June, July and August, 1962," n.d., 33, in NA 59/3172/2. See also Burke, *Corporación Minera*, 37; Canelas, *Mito y realidad*, 99.

99. Burke, *Corporación Minera*, 15. See also Bolivia, JNP, "Plan de desarrollo económico y social," 169–172.

100. Unsigned (DoS), "Action to Meet Soviet Pressures"; Bolivia, MMP, *Informe anual*, 6. A 1962 memo stated that "it was the undertaking of the Bolivian Government to give back to management the right to manage that had the most influence on the other members of the plan to participate"; Bjorkman and Schippers to V. Paz Estenssoro, January 5, 1962, in ANB-PR, #985, Caja 457.

101. Unsigned (DoS), "Action to Meet Soviet Pressures."

102. Anderson to Barr, December 4, 1963, in NA 59/3172/3.

103. On the place of Bolivia in Kennedy's Alliance for Progress see Field, *From Development to Dictatorship*; Siekmeier, *Bolivian Revolution*, 88–98.

104. Lane to Woodward, July 13, 1961; Arnesen (to Moscoso?), July 19, 1963, in NA 59/3172/3; Mann to Dillon, November 10 and 16, 1960; unsigned (DoS), "Conclusions and Recommendations Regarding Bolivian Program," n.d. (1958?), in NA 59/3172/1.

105. A CEPAL report noted that the mining workforce had increased 50 percent from 1951 to 1956; UN ECLA, "Economic Policy of Bolivia," 68. The distribution of the labor force was also skewed, with a disproportionate number of workers employed aboveground.

106. Burke, *Corporación Minera*, 30; DoS executive secretary Benjamin Read, quoted in Siekmeier, *Bolivian Revolution*, 100. See also *El Diario*, April 7, 1961; Memorandum of Conversation, May 25, 1960, and Carr to Strom, November 6, 1960, both in NA 59/3172/1; Stephansky to May, August 16, 1962, in NA 59/3172/2.

107. Quoted in Burke, *Corporación Minera*, 39.

108. Unsigned (DoS), "Summary of and Comments on USOM Bolivia's Criticism"; Mann to Dillon, November 10, 1960; Anderson to Barr, December 4, 1963.

109. USAID memo quoted in Burke, *Corporación Minera*, 23. Similar conditions were attached to most US loans to Latin America under the Alliance for Progress; Rabe, *Most Dangerous Area*, 154.

110. Dunkerley, *Rebellion*, 111.

111. Burke, *Corporación Minera*, 23–24; Wilkie, *Bolivian Revolution*, 44. This problem contributed to the crisis that was used to justify the neoliberal program imposed in 1985.

112. Burke writes that the plan "salvaged the Corporation at the expense of true rehabilitation"; *Corporación Minera*, 18–34, 72 (p. 34 quotation); UN ECLA, *Economic Survey: 1966*, 92, and "Economic Policy of Bolivia," 71–72.

113. Burke, *Corporación Minera*, 40–42, 53–54.

114. Zondag, *Bolivian Economy*, 237.

115. Annual US military aid increased from $400,000 in 1961 to $3.2 million in 1964, or $4.1 million if grants of excess stock are counted; Wilkie, *Bolivian Revolution*, 48; C. Mitchell, *Legacy of Populism*, 90–92; Loveman, *For la Patria*, 183. On the internal security emphasis of US regional military aid by 1960 see Rabe, *Eisenhower and Latin America*, 147–148, and *Most Dangerous Area*, 125–147. Paz and Siles also sought US help in rebuilding the army; Lehman, *Bolivia and the United States*, 141, 148–149.

116. Canelas, *Mito y realidad*, 153, 158–160; Vaughn to Mann, June 4, 1965, and US Embassy to DoS, June 30, 1965, both in NA 59, SNF 535. USAID approved $1.8 million specifically for the military intervention in the mines; "Editorial Note," DoS, *FRUS, 1964–1968*, 31:349.

117. Guillermo Bedregal, cited in Memorandum of Conversation, November 14, 1963, in NA 59/3172/3; Burke, *Corporación Minera*, 36–37, 42, 52.

118. Paz, speaking in 1944; *Discursos*, 228. In 1954 Paz cited Iran to justify compliance with US demands, arguing that the MNR would have fallen due to a tin boycott "if we had closed ourselves off, like the Government of Mossadegh in Iran, by not paying any compensation"; *El pensamiento revolucionario*, 98.

119. On US coercion see Whitehead, *The United States and Bolivia*, 11; Lehman, *Bolivia and the United States*, 122. Those stressing lack of capital include Andrade, *My Missions*, 184; Klein and Peres-Cajías, "Bolivian Oil," 149; YPFB, *Libro de oro*, 75; Zondag, *Bolivian Economy*, 113.

120. On the Soviet loan offer see MMP, *Informe anual*, 71. Some officials at YPFB and the Ministry of Mines and Petroleum favored acceptance of the Soviet loan and even prepared detailed plans for using it (3, 72–75). Most of these officials supported the entry of private capital under the 1955 reform but warned against "neglecting the maintenance and progress of [YPFB] at the same time" (152). President Paz sometimes justified his rejection of other funding sources by arguing that transport costs from Europe and the Soviet bloc would have been prohibitive; *La revolución*, 34, 63.

121. Unsigned to Mann and Lane, October 28, 1960, in NA 59/3172/1; unsigned (DoS), "United States Policy toward Bolivia"; unsigned (DoS), "Summary of and Comments on USOM Bolivia's Criticism"; unsigned (DoS), "Program in the Second Year"; Eder, *Inflation and Development*, 299, 447–452.

122. John, *Bolivia's Radical Tradition*, 170–171.

123. Lagos, *Nos hemos forjado así*, 21 (housewives committee); *El Diario*, June 27, 1961 (press report); Canelas, *Mito y realidad*, 93 (strike days). For more on miner resistance and government repression see Field, *From Development to Dictatorship*, 25–38, 87–96, 109–130.

124. Here I take issue with the common argument that critics of the stabilization program lacked "an alternative program"; Alexander, *Bolivian National Revolution*, 215. The alternatives may have lacked unity and academic form, and certain aspects may have been impractical, but they were presented.

125. *El Diario*, November 12, 1954.

126. *El Diario*, June 29, 1957; Dunkerley, *Rebellion*, 89; Delgado González, *100 años de lucha obrera*, 249–277.

127. Lora, *La estabilización* and *History*, 303.

128. Bolivia in fact had several small smelters, including a tin smelter in Oruro dating from 1945. But these were small-scale operations and incapable of refining low-grade ore; Almaraz Paz, *El poder y la caída*, 212–233; Burke, *Corporación Minera*, 64n64.

129. *El Diario*, May 9 and 16, 1961.

130. "Oficio de la Presidencia de la República correspondiendo a minuta de los HH. Crespo, Chávez, Zuazo, Alvarez Plata, Fernández, Torres y Morales," September 24, 1962, in Bolivia, H. Senado Nacional, *Hornos de fundición*, 267–269; *El Diario*, June 18, 1963.

131. Bolivia, *Plan nacional de desarrollo*, 192. The need for a smelter is the key theme in Sergio Almaraz's 1966 history of the tin industry, *El poder y la caída*, esp. 127–233.

132. Eder quotation from *Inflation and Development*, 521. In 1967 General and President René Barrientos promised a smelter, "whatever it costs"; *Extra*, May 23, 1967.

133. Minister of Mines and Petroleum referring to Chávez, September 13, 1962, in Bolivia, H. Senado Nacional, *Hornos de fundición*, 42.

134. Speeches by Deputies Pórcel and Aracena in Bolivia, *Redactor del H. Cámara de Diputados, octubre de 1956*, 154–156, 194; Almaraz Paz, *El poder y la caída*, 88–89, 178–179.

135. A postwar report warned that inter-American relations had been strained at the 1945 Chapultepec conference when a top US official "strongly

insinuated that . . . Latin America should forsake its industrialization aims"; unsigned (DoS), "Special Report Prepared by the Psychological Strategy Board" (n.d.), in DoS, *FRUS, 1952–1954*, 1:1493.

136. The Eder Plan, like Eisenhower policy more generally, implicitly reflected contradictory currents; while it involved significant foreign aid, its conditions mandated fiscal austerity, reliance on private enterprise, and prioritization of debt service and compensation to the tin barons. Kennedy's economic policy involved a greater emphasis on aid to Latin America and modestly greater tolerance toward structuralist ideas. However, Siekmeier notes, "the division in U.S. policymaking circles was not over goals but over tactics"; "Fighting Economic Nationalism," 70.

137. Evans, *Dependent Development*; Siekmeier, "Fighting Economic Nationalism." The US ambassador to Bolivia in the late 1950s, Philip Bonsal, pushed for aid to YPFB as a way of promoting industrialization in order "to get Bolivia off the back of the American taxpayer"; memo to Rubottom, August 21, 1958.

138. Burke, *Corporación Minera*, 33–34. For Triangular Plan adviser Victor Bjorkman's opposition see *Extra*, July 31, 1966. US officials insisted that their opposition stemmed from neutral economic calculations—that it would be a waste of resources. On the National Smelting Company (ENAF) and smelting operations in the 1970s and early 1980s see Ayub and Hashimoto, *Economics of Tin Mining*, 55–62.

139. Burke, "Does 'Food for Peace' Assistance Damage the Bolivian Economy?"

140. Green, *Containment*, 76, 178; Siekmeier, "Fighting Economic Nationalism."

141. Even in Mexico and Brazil, US government support for industrialization was limited, especially in the early postwar era. On Brazil see Haines, *Americanization of Brazil*, 87–144. The United States also opposed CEPAL's 1948 formation; Green, *Containment*, 293.

142. Green, *Containment*, 303n9.

143. Burke, *Corporación Minera*, 34, 65n69; UN ECLA, *Economic Survey: 1969*, 115–117.

144. The case of the Matilde mine in La Paz department attracted particular condemnation from nationalists when the government leased it to a private company; *El Diario*, December 5, 1964; *Extra*, July 20, 1966; Quiroga Santa Cruz, *El saqueo de Bolivia*.

4: The Battle for Men's Minds

1. The epigraph is from Sorensen, *Word War*, 56. US liberals like Joseph Nye have been the foremost proponents of this strategy; *Soft Power*. Many postwar Republicans were initially skeptical, and some even charged that the programs were infiltrated by communists; Belmonte, *Selling the American Way*, 38–39, 51–57; Sorensen, *Word War*, 31–41.

2. Sorensen, *Word War*, 5.

3. Dulles, referring to neutralism, quoted in Sorensen, *Word War*, 54.

4. DoS, *Around the Good Neighbor Network* (May 1951), 5, in NA 306/1015/21; unsigned (USIA), "Are We Winning the Battle for Men's Minds in Latin America?" February 7, 1962, in NA 306/1032/2. On the campaign of truth see also Cull, *Cold War*, 51–67.

5. There were precursors, however, most notably Wilson's Committee on Public Information, which targeted both domestic and foreign audiences. See Cull, *Cold War*, 1–12; Henderson, *United States Information Agency*, 23–28.

6. Wasson to Rockefeller, January 10, 1944, in NA 229/1/225.

7. Wasson to Harrison, December 13, 1945, in NA 229/1/225. The population figure is from the 1950 census; Bolivia, *Censo demográfico*.

8. Wasson to Harrison, December 13, 1945; Maroney to Murillo, February 12, 1942, in NA 229/1/225.

9. Crandall to DoS, July 18, 1950, in NA 59, CDF 511.24/7-1850. Film showings declined to 104 showings of 64 films to a total audience of just 12,989 in July 1950.

10. See Bethell and Roxborough, *Latin America*.

11. Hunsaker to DoS, January 10, 1950, in NA 59, CDF 511.24/1-1050.

12. Ibid.

13. DoS, *Around the Good Neighbor Network*, 4.

14. First quotation from Crandall to DoS, June 29, 1951, in NA 59, CDF 511.24/6-2951; second quotation from DoS, *Around the Good Neighbor Network*, 4.

15. Hunsaker to DoS, April 19, 1950, in NA 59, CDF 511.24/4-1950.

16. Wasson to Rockefeller, August 24, 1943, in NA 229/1/225.

17. Ibid.

18. Sorensen, *Word War*, 4.

19. On the tinderbox analogy see US Embassy to DoS, April 30, 1953, in NA 59, CDF 611.24/4-3053.

20. Opsata, "Inspection Report of USIS BOLIVIA," November 24, 1954, in NA 306/1045/1.

21. USIS–La Paz to USIA (Washington), May 27, 1958.

22. On the Film Institute's collaboration, including production of Alliance for Progress propaganda shorts, see Albarracín Crespo to Otero Calderón, February 27, 1964, in ANB-PR, #1056, Caja 477.

23. USIS–La Paz to USIA, January 28, 1957, and unsigned, "Notes on Bolivia (For IRI/R and IAL)," September 22, 1958, both in NA 306/1021/2; Bolivian Newsreel No. 16, n.d., in NA 306/1098/51.

24. USIA, "Inspection Report: USIS/Bolivia," May 11, 1962, p. 19, in NA 306/1045/1. US and Bolivian students were viewed as a highly strategic sector; US officials hoped they would be ambassadors for capitalism. In the 1960s the US government sponsored official visits by Bolivian student leaders to the United States; *Foro Universitario* 1, no. 4 (November 1965): 6–9.

25. Unsigned, "Notes on Bolivia," September 22, 1958; Opsata, "Inspection Report"; ICA-La Paz (Ketner) to DoS, June 14, 1957, in NA 306/1021/2.

26. Grenier described in Williams to Pitts, September 30, 1959, in NA 59/1162/27; see also Field, "Ideology as Strategy," 174.

27. First quotation from "Briefing Book on Bolivia," n.d. (ca. 1956), p. 30,

in NA 59/1170/13; second quotation from Siracusa to Rubottom, June 1, 1959, in NA 59/1162/27; undated Bolivian newsreels, nos. 15, 17, 19, 24, 39, 55–56, 61, all in NA 306/1098/51.

28. Grandin, *Empire's Workshop*, 47–49, 94–99. See also McClintock, *Instruments of Statecraft*, esp. 230–257; Field, *From Development to Dictatorship*; Taffet, *Foreign Aid*.

29. The overall USIA budget increased by about 25 percent from 1961 to 1964; Henderson, *United States Information Agency*, 58.

30. USIS–La Paz to USIA, "USIS Country Plan for Bolivia in FY62," June 22, 1961, in NA 306/1047/5; cf. USIA, "Inspection Report."

31. USIS–La Paz (Bishop) to USIA, "FY1963 Country Plan for USIS-Bolivia," June 28, 1962, in NA 306/1047/5.

32. Quotation from US Office of Research and Intelligence, "Communist Propaganda Activities in Bolivia, 1956," February 25, 1957, in NA 306/1033/1. The Communist Party membership estimate of five thousand is from International Research Associates Inc., "Statistical Data on Communist Propaganda Activities in Latin America, 1957," January 15, 1958, in NA 306/1029/1. The official who lamented the "leftist thought pattern" was referring specifically to "government and intellectual circles," but numerous reports make clear that the same pattern characterized a large proportion of Bolivian society. An undated (ca. 1956) memo speaks of the need to counteract "the Marxist thought pattern historically popular in this nation"; "Briefing Book on Bolivia," 30.

33. Bonsal to Rubottom, November 29, 1958, in NA 59, CDF 824.06/1-1058; Weise to Coerr, November 11, 1960, in NA 59/3172/1.

34. The people's capitalism campaign was launched in 1956, but the slogan only became prominent in the Bolivia campaign in the early 1960s. See USIS-La Paz to USIA, February 1, 1961, in NA 306/1047/5; cf. Belmonte, *Selling the American Way*, 116–135; Cull, *Cold War*, 117–118; Fein, "New Empire into Old," 718; Sorensen, *Word War*, 83–84.

35. *El Obrero*, February 1958, 1.

36. Mittleman, "El socialismo en los Estados Unidos."

37. USIA surveys across the Third World found that when respondents were asked to evaluate the word "capitalism," "disapproval clearly predominated," while "USIA found a highly favorable reaction to the word socialism"; Sorensen, *Word War*, 80.

38. First two quotations from unsigned (USIA), "Misconceptions of American Culture," September 3, 1959, in NA 306/1032/1; other quotations from unsigned (USIA), "Unfavorable Latin American Notions about the United States and Its People," August 28, 1961, in NA 306/1032/2.

39. Repairing the US image on race relations became a major "Cold War imperative" in the late 1950s and 1960s; Dudziak, "Desegregation." On this theme in USIA campaigns see Belmonte, *Selling the American Way*, 159–177; Cull, *Cold War*, 113, 211–213, 233–236; Fein, "New Empire into Old," 739–740; Sorensen, *Word War*, 100–101, 171–179.

40. Unsigned, "USIA World Poll Rider Questions: Latin America," May 26, 1958, in NA 306/1023/5.

41. First quotation from USIS-La Paz (Fogler) to USIA, October 21, 1966,

in NA 306/1039/3. All other quotations come from USIA, "Statistical Report on Exhibits Program" (ca. January 16, 1966), in NA 306/1039/3, except for Congo quotation, USIS-La Paz (Schechter) to USIA Washington, December 29, 1964, in NA 306/1039/3. See also Johnson, "Las 5 normas básicas"; Rusk, "'Buscamos una paz duradera.'" Articles placed in Bolivian newspapers by the USIS frequently echoed these themes, with headlines like "President Kennedy continues his campaign for black civil rights"; *El Diario*, June 14, 1963. See also *Nuevo Mundo*, December 1952, 19.

42. *Foro Universitario* 2, no. 22 (May 1967): 9–13, and no. 13 (August 1966): 1–7.

43. USIS-La Paz (Torrey) to USIA, December 4, 1962, in NA 306/1039/3.

44. Although the US government does not seem to have undertaken an extensive labor training program in Bolivia as it did in other countries, US officials often simply bribed Bolivian labor leaders with cooperation from the Bolivian labor ministry; for instance, see Eder, *Inflation and Development*, 524.

45. Wiesman to French, September 29, 1960, in NA 59/3172/1. For an earlier statement of this goal on the hemispheric level see National Security Council, "United States Objectives and Courses of Action with Respect to Latin America" (NSC 144/1), March 18, 1953, in DoS, *FRUS, 1952–1954*, 4:8. On Mexico see Fein, "Everyday Forms," 411–416.

46. *Revista Said*, April–June 1954, 14–15 (first and fifth quotations), 32 (second quotation); January–March 1955, 2 (third and fourth quotations); October–December 1954, 35 (sixth quotation).

47. Víctor Paz in *El Diario*, April 10, 1961 (first quotation); *La Nación* editorial, November 30, 1955.

48. Barrientos, *Hacia un nuevo sindicalismo*, 19 (first quotation); all other quotations, 8–10.

49. *Revista Said*, July–September 1954, 13–15, 35. For a similar discourse of modern business in postwar Europe and the United States see Maier, "Politics of Productivity," 615–618.

50. Knight, *U.S.-Mexican Relations*, 20.

51. First quotation from USIS-La Paz to USIA, June 28, 1962, in NA 306/1047/5; second quotation from USIS-La Paz (Torrey) to USIA, December 4, 1962; third quotation from USIS-La Paz to USIA, "USIS Country Plan."

52. On similar messages in other USIS programs see Cull, *Cold War*, 104–106; Fein, "New Empire into Old," 738; Sorensen, *Word War*, 179–183.

53. USIS-La Paz to ICS/E Washington, May 20, 1965; USIA, "Statistical Report on Exhibits Program"; USIS-La Paz to USIA, October 21, 1966.

54. Gilman, *Mandarins of the Future*; Latham, *Modernization as Ideology*.

55. Schlesinger, "Report to the President," 12.

56. Rostow, "Problemas del desarrollo económico," 13, 21.

57. Valenzuela and Valenzuela, "Modernization and Dependency," 537–543.

58. On the mutual-benefit claim of development economics versus the dependency view see Hirschman, "The Rise and Decline of Development Economics," in his *Essays in Trespassing*, 12–19. Víctor Paz Estenssoro's particular version of this argument claimed that whereas politicians and capitalists

in the wealthy countries previously opposed Latin America's development, after World War II they realized that "it was good business to develop the backward countries" so the latter could purchase more manufactured goods; *El pensamiento revolucionario*, 99–100.

59. Interestingly, even YPFB officials who favored private oil investment contrasted YPFB's service to the public with multinational corporations' profit-seeking on behalf of shareholders; *Patria y Petróleo*, August 5, 1961.

60. Bonsal to Rubottom, May 20, 1958.

61. First quotation from USIS-La Paz to USIA, February 1, 1961; second quotation from USIA, "Inspection Report"; third quotation from Point IV director John Hollister, in *El Diario*, February 3, 1956.

62. Ford, Bacon & Davis, *Mining Industry of Bolivia*, 9:59–60, 55, 49, 32, 46.

63. On the Kennedy administration's mild critiques of Eisenhower's economic policy in Latin America see Taffet, *Foreign Aid*, 85–89.

64. Many Latin Americans were aware of these contradictions. The August 1961 USIA report "Unfavorable Latin American Notions about the United States and Its People" mentions the widespread perception that "North Americans refuse to recognize that there are socialistic aspects in the US economy, and disapprove of similar trends in other parts of the world." On state intervention in Western economies see Chang, *Bad Samaritans*.

65. The MNR and military junta might be said to have increased the symbolic rewards accruing to these groups but alongside distributive rewards as well; Lanning, "Governmental Capabilities," 20–21.

66. *El Diario*, April 10, 1961.

67. García, *Diez años de reforma agraria*, 8–9. On culture and state making see Gildner, "Indomestizo Modernism."

68. Soto, *Historia del Pacto Militar-Campesino*.

69. García, *Diez años de reforma agraria*, 43, 48; Bolivia, *El proceso de Reforma Agraria*, 13–17, 20–21. Land reform and agricultural support policies continued after 1964 but were heavily focused on large-scale owners, particularly in the eastern lowlands; Eckstein, "Transformation." On public health programs in the 1950s see Pacino, "Constructing a New Bolivian Society."

70. *El Pueblo* (LP), September 10, 1960 (quotation); *El Pueblo* (C), April 5, May 1, and June 25, 1957.

71. Siles Zuazo, *Mensaje al Honorable Congreso Nacional*, 91 (first three quotations), 92 (fifth quotation), 93 (fourth quotation). See also Knudson, *Bolivia*, 295–329.

72. *La Nación*, February 3, 1956, April 30, 1955, and August 8, 1958, quoted in Knudson, *Bolivia*, 308, 295, 306.

73. Dunkerley, *Rebellion*, 49–50, 81.

74. Unsigned (DoS), "Latin America: Guidelines of United States Policy and Operations" (draft), April 24, 1962, pp. 8, 59–60, in NA 59/3172/2; USIA, "Country Plan for Colombia," October 14, 1964, in NA 306/1039/5. On civic action in Bolivia see Field, *From Development to Dictatorship*, 79–87.

75. Cabinet decree quoted in *Los Tiempos*, July 26, 1953.

76. On US officials' fears of the peasantry see Alexander with Parker, *History of Organized Labor*, 113–114. For peasant leaders' threats against militant workers and the left see *El Diario*, June 8, 1961; *Presencia*, April 21, 1963; *El Mundo*, October 23 and 31, 1964; *Extra*, July 13, 1966, June 18 and July 9, 1967.

77. Knudson, *Bolivia*, 313.

78. "1960: Año de la clase media," in UMSA-B, FB 324.6 P348m/MFN 1084.

79. Dispatch RO/LA 1958 21–39 (ca. June 11, 1958), in NA 306/1032/1.

80. USIS–La Paz to USIA, February 1, 1961 (quotation), and February 1, 1960, both in NA 306/1047/5.

81. USIA, "Inspection Report"; USIS-La Paz to USIA, January 26, 1962, in NA 306/1047/5. On the textbooks see *El Obrero*, May 1962, 20; on school enrollment see Zondag, *Bolivian Economy*, 166.

82. A 1956 survey in Santa Cruz found that only 3 percent of people under thirty listened to US radio programs; unsigned, "Study of Radio, Films and Publications in Santa Cruz" (June 1957), in NA 306/1015/7.

83. First quotation from USIS-La Paz to USIA, May 27, 1958; second quotation from US Office of Research and Intelligence, "Communist Propaganda Activities," February 25, 1957; third quotation from Duggan, *The Americas*, 147.

84. Unsigned (USIA), "Are We Winning the Battle for Men's Minds in Latin America?" On the uphill struggle of USIS efforts in postwar Mexico see Fein, "New Empire into Old," esp. 724, 733–742. Haines implies greater success in postwar Brazil; *Americanization of Brazil*, 175, 185–193.

85. Expressions of peasant support must be interpreted cautiously due to patterns of boss rule in rural areas and newspapers' tendency to exaggerate popular support for the government, but they do tell us something about political dynamics in the countryside. For some examples of peasant support for the MNR and/or army and opposition to the left see *El Pueblo* (C), January 1, 3, and 9, 1957, and all of June 1957; *El Diario*, June 11 and 27, 1961; *El Mundo*, October 23 and December 20, 1964.

86. Antezana J., "Sistemas y procesos ideológicos"; cf. Roseberry, "Hegemony and the Language of Contention."

5: The Limits of Containment

1. In *El Diario*, April 12, 1962.

2. *El Diario*, June 8 and 16, 1961.

3. Engels and Lenin had written of an aristocracy within the working class in rich nations, by virtue of its sharing in imperialist spoils; e.g., Lenin, *Imperialism*, 99–108. See also Hobsbawm, "Labour Aristocracy."

4. Fanon, *Wretched of the Earth*, 109. For classic applications to Latin American labor from a variety of ideological angles see Alba, *Politics and the Labor Movement*; Landsberger, "Labor Elite"; Spalding, "Parameters of Labor." Erickson, Peppe, and Spalding, "Research on the Urban Working Class," provides an early overview.

5. On Mexico see Middlebrook, *Paradox of Revolution*; on Brazil see Weinstein, *For Social Peace in Brazil*, and Wolfe, *Autos and Progress*, 127–133; on Argentina see James, *Resistance and Integration*. See also Bergquist, *Labor in Latin America*, 169–176 (Argentina), 241–273 (Venezuela), 358–359 (Colombia). For a useful recent analysis of Venezuela see Ciccariello-Maher, *We Created Chávez*, 180–199.

6. US Embassy to DoS, April 2, 1952, p. 10.

7. Lora, *Movimiento obrero contemporáneo*, 167. See also Malloy, *Bolivia*, 140.

8. Reed and Foran, "Political Cultures of Opposition." Webber, in *Red October*, applies this concept to recent Bolivia.

9. Here my thinking has been informed by arguments about "the relative autonomy of politics" within classes and, by extension, other social groups. In asserting "the relative autonomy of '*the intraclass struggle within the class struggle*,'" Stepan-Norris and Zeitlin stress the importance of political identities and ideologies; *Left Out*, 18–20.

10. One could argue that propaganda agents have an incentive to stress the difficulty of their task in order to excuse their own failures or obtain more funding, but in that case USIS agents could still have argued that opposition was limited to a small, obstreperous minority, as MNR officials publicly claimed. Instead, they continually stressed the breadth of public opposition.

11. Deputy Oscar Barbery, October 11, 1956, in Bolivia, *Redactor del H. Cámara de Diputados, octubre de 1956*, 151.

12. Delgadillo Terceros, *Fabriles*, 26, 134–135; Legg, *Bolivia*, 18; Lora, *Movimiento obrero contemporáneo*, 154; UNTAA, *Report*, 84–88. In 1944 La Paz had 72 percent of all factories and 95 percent of all textile factories; Peñaloza Cordero, *La Paz*, 4:42.

13. Alcaldía Municipal de La Paz, *Censo demográfico*, 21; Bolivia, *Censo demográfico*.

14. The CNI began as the Cámara de Fomento Industrial in 1931; Lora, *Movimiento obrero contemporáneo*, 153–154.

15. Ibid., 158.

16. Delgadillo Terceros, *Fabriles*, 72.

17. Alexander with Parker, *History of Organized Labor*, 42, 53; Lora, *Movimiento obrero contemporáneo*, 159–162.

18. Barcelli S., *Medio siglo de luchas*, 220–227; Lora, *Movimiento obrero contemporáneo*, 278–285. The Coordinating Committee was preceded by an Emergency Union Committee, established in March 1950.

19. *Tribuna*, April 27, 1950; Barcelli S., *Medio siglo de luchas*, 224.

20. Quoted in *Tribuna*, April 28, 1950. Notably, the committee advocated "a pact with the campesino class, [our] partner in pain and suffering"; quoted in Barcelli S., *Medio siglo de luchas*, 226–227.

21. The Urriolagoitia government estimated 13 killed and 112 injured; Butrón later estimated that more than 100 were killed. See Lora, *Movimiento obrero contemporáneo*, 285–286; Delgadillo Terceros, *Fabriles*, 76. On arrests see *El Diario*, May 27, 1950.

22. Said Textile Union to USTFN, January 7, 1953 (quotations), and "Voto resolutivo de los trabajadores de la fábrica 'Said,'" January 5, 1953,

both in CGTFB, 1952 file; "Voto resolutivo de los trabajadores de la fábrica 'Said,'" March 22, 1953, in CGTFB, 1953 file.

23. First quotation from a Voto Resolutivo of the Federación Departamental de Trabajadores Fabriles (La Paz Factory Workers Federation), July 31, 1952, in CGTFB, 1952 file; second quotation from Delgadillo Terceros, *Fabriles*, 75.

24. Deputy Monje speaking October 20 and 29, 1958, in Bolivia, *Redactor del H. Cámara de Diputados, octubre de 1958*, 402–403, 526. See also Delgadillo Terceros, *Fabriles*, 77. On La Paz workers' role in the April revolution itself see Murillo, *La bala no mata*, 67–148.

25. Declaration referenced in Alberto Azaeda (general secretary of the Fanase factory union) et al. to the minister of education, December 2, 1953, in CGTFB, 1953 file. See also Delgadillo Terceros, *Fabriles*, 106, 140n6; USTFN Voto Resolutivo, January 27, 1953, in CGTFB, 1952 file.

26. Resolution from April 21, 1953, included in Saravia to Paz Estenssoro, April 22, 1953, in CGTFB, 1953 file.

27. On the notion of moral economy and how perceived violations of implicit elite-subaltern contracts can lead to revolt see Thompson, "Moral Economy."

28. Voto resolutivo del Sindicato de Trabajadores de "Industrias en Confección" y R.A., April 5, 1953, in CGTFB, 1953 file.

29. First quotation from Cordero (general secretary) and Pacheco (relations secretary) to USTFN Directorate, October 23, 1952, in CGTFB, 1952 file; second quotation from *El Diario*, December 25, 1956. These examples represent a modern variation on the "good king, bad government" motif common in petitions of the colonial period.

30. Lora, for one, alleges that the early MNR years were "characterized by the blind faith of the masses in everything the *movimientista* regime could have done"; *Movimiento obrero contemporáneo*, 409.

31. Saravia letter to an unidentified government ministry (Labor?), March 25, 1953, in CGTFB, 1953 file.

32. Such has often been true of popular interactions with populist regimes; see, for instance, James, *Resistance and Integration*, esp. 7–40; Gould, *To Lead as Equals*.

33. *El Diario*, July 10, 1954; see also the COB's later call for the expulsion of the Guatemalan ambassador in *El Diario*, November 14, 1954. On MNR support for the coup see Lehman, *Bolivia and the United States*, 115–117.

34. Workers at this congress published a statement calling for a variety of progressive reforms, including "workers' control in the allocation and use of profits." Two CGTFB leaders contacted the press the next day to say that the list of demands had not in fact been officially approved by the Congress, however; *El Diario*, July 14–15, 1954.

35. Resolution of the third congress quoted in Lora, *Movimiento obrero contemporáneo*, 174.

36. Roseberry, "Hegemony and the Language of Contention," 361–366.

37. *El Diario*, April 14, 1962. For one union petition see Jorge Ríos (union general secretary) et al., to Gerente de la Fábrica de Calzados García, September 3, 1953, in CGTFB, 1952 file.

38. In 1958 Robert Alexander estimated that factory workers' "monetary income increased about a third, and their cost of living about a half," signifying "a considerable decrease in their real wage"; *Bolivian National Revolution*, 211.

39. Unsigned to Haddow and Parry, March 10, 1959.

40. UN ECLA, "Economic Development of Bolivia," 35, and *Economic Survey: 1956*, 11.

41. Lora, *Movimiento obrero contemporáneo*, 158–159; *Revista Said*, October-December 1954, 30 (quotation); April–June 1954, 29.

42. *Revista Said*, April–June 1954, 21–22, 28; January–March 1955, 34; July–September 1954, 18–19.

43. *Revista Said*, October–December 1954, 30.

44. First quotation from *Revista Said*, July–September 1954, 24; second quotation from April–June 1954, 24.

45. *Revista Said*, April–June 1955, 9–10, 24.

46. The Said family had close ties to the famous Yarur textile family in Chile; Juan Yarur was also known for his paternalistic style. See Winn, *Weavers of Revolution*, 14–16, 32–42.

47. *El Diario*, December 30, 1956, and June 28–30, 1957.

48. Quotation from *El Diario*, May 25, 1957; see also C. Mitchell, *Legacy of Populism*, 74.

49. *El Diario*, November 13, 20, and 22, 1958.

50. *El Diario*, February 3 and 8, 1959; June 10, 1961; and May 6, 1962. The creation of an industrial Rehabilitation Fund dated back to 1958; *El Diario*, November 27–28, 1958.

51. *El Obrero*, February 1962, 11–14, 24.

52. Quoted in Lora, *Movimiento obrero contemporáneo*, 175–177.

53. Growth averaged 5.7 percent annually from 1961 to 1964; C. Mitchell, *Legacy of Populism*, 92.

54. *El Diario*, May 9, June 8–16, 1961.

55. *El Diario*, April 12, 1962.

56. *Eco Fabril*, July 1963, 2.

57. *El Diario*, September 3–4, October 3 and 16, 1958.

58. *El Diario*, November 13 and 19, 1958.

59. *El Diario*, February 5 and 6, 1959.

60. Across all labor sectors; *El Diario*, April 16, 1959.

61. Delgadillo Terceros, *Fabriles*, 115.

62. *El Diario*, April 12, 1962; Delgado González, *100 años de lucha obrera*, 315.

63. Quoted in Delgadillo Terceros, *Fabriles*, 111.

64. In a meeting with factory owners around the same time, Lara and other union leaders pledged to help "maintain on their end discipline in the workplace"; *El Diario*, May 9, 1957. For workers' May 1957 critique of Lara and his resignation see Alexander with Parker, *History of Organized Labor*, 104; Delgadillo Terceros, *Fabriles*, 102–103.

65. *El Diario*, January 24 and March 15, 1959; Alexander with Parker, *History of Organized Labor*, 108; Delgadillo Terceros, *Fabriles*, 124; C. Mitchell, *Legacy of Populism*, 75.

66. See, e.g., *El Diario*, June 28, 1961, and December 5, 1964.

67. COB leaders felt similar pressures. After 1956 the leadership was "frequently obliged to enter into direct confrontation with the regime by a rank and file it could not fully control"; Dunkerley, *Rebellion*, 85.

68. The CGTFB executive committees elected at the fourth (1959), fifth (1961), and sixth (1963) congresses were all dominated by candidates of the MNR left. See *El Diario*, May 19, 1961; *Presencia*, June 18, 1963; *Eco Fabril*, July 1963, 3–4; Delgadillo Terceros, *Fabriles*, 124; Lora, *Movimiento obrero contemporáneo*, 175–177.

69. *El Diario*, May 16, 1961.

70. In his description of the June 1963 congress, Lora writes of two "opposing tendencies: some who followed the official line and others inspired by Marxist sectors"; *Movimiento obrero contemporáneo*, 191. This dichotomy seems too reductive, at least if the goal is to gauge rank-and-file goals and values, which are not always apparent from formal political affiliations.

71. For instance, the factory workers' denunciation of Siles' *entreguismo* echoed the POR's statements about the "looting of raw materials at vile prices" and the MNR's "pawning" of the nation's "mineral, petroleum, and forest resources"; quotations from *Masas*, January 22, 1958.

72. Lora, *Movimiento obrero contemporáneo*, 181, 189, 197, 208. Quotation from a Cochabamba factory worker's public critique of factory owners in *El Mundo*, July 11, 1963. For similar examples of factory workers' strategic discourse see Central Obrera Departmental (COD, Cochabamba), "Documento de crítica y autocrítica," February 19, 1954, 153–154; *El Diario*, April 12, 1962; *Extra*, November 30, 1968.

73. COD, "Documento de crítica y autocrítica," 153.

74. *Eco Fabril*, July 1963, 2; Lora, *Movimiento obrero contemporáneo*, 180–181.

75. Lora, *Movimiento obrero contemporáneo*, 178–206 (conference quoted, 187). For the factory workers' defense of YPFB see also US Embassy to DoS, August 27, 1959, in NA 59, CDF 824.2553/8-2759.

76. Orlando Capriles, quoted in *El Diario*, March 4, 1959, and December 25, 1956.

77. For example, see the economic resolutions of the factory workers' fifth congress, summarized in *El Diario*, May 16, 1961, and Lora, *Movimiento obrero contemporáneo*, 180–181.

78. First quotation from Cordero and Pacheco to USTFN Directorate, October 23, 1952; second quotation from *El Diario*, December 25, 1956; third quotation from Deputy Alberto Jara, speaking on October 11, 1956, in Bolivia, *Redactor del H. Cámara de Diputados, octubre de 1956*, 159.

79. *El Diario*, July 12, 1963. For contemporary economists' elaboration of this logic for underdeveloped economies see Baldwin, "Patterns of Development," 176; Baran, *Political Economy of Growth*, 270.

80. Quoted in Lora, *Movimiento obrero contemporáneo*, 200–201.

81. *El Diario*, November 4, 1958, and March 20, 1959.

82. *El Diario*, July 6, 1954; Maier, "Two Postwar Eras," 338.

83. Lora, "La clase obrera después de 1952," 198–204.

84. *El Diario*, April 13, 1959.

85. *El Diario*, May 16, 1961.

86. Lora has implied that by demanding industrial subsidies, factory workers were essentially doing the owners' work for them; *Movimiento obrero contemporáneo*, 189, 197–198. I find this view too simplistic, for although government aid "benefited the bosses" (198), it also stood to benefit the workforce. Workers and bosses did have a shared interest in industrial expansion, even if they did not benefit equally and even if workers might have benefited more from a socialization of the factories.

87. Jara in Bolivia, *Redactor del H. Cámara de Diputados, octubre de 1956*, 166.

88. In *El Diario*, May 16, 1961.

89. See "Chaos in the Clouds," *Time*, March 2, 1959, 27, and "The Fanned Spark," *Time*, March 16, 1959, 40–41. The quotation itself appeared only in the Spanish-language version of the March 2 issue.

90. All quotations in this paragraph and the next come from *El Diario*, March 4, 1959.

91. The reference is to the May 1781 execution of the indigenous rebel leader in Cuzco, Peru, by Spanish colonial authorities. Túpac Amaru II was drawn and quartered, his body torn apart by four horses.

92. Senator Córdova speaking in Bolivia, Legislatura Ordinaria de 1966, *Redactor del H. Senado Nacional*, 2:129, 132.

93. Senator Montoya, ibid., 2:137.

94. Deputy Monje, October 20, 1958, in Bolivia, *Redactor del H. Cámara de Diputados, octubre de 1958*, 402–403.

95. This theme was not nearly as prevalent as it would become later in the century with the rise of indigenous rights movements. Notably, Capriles evoked Túpac Amaru—executed in Cuzco—rather than Túpac Katari, who led the 1781 siege on La Paz.

96. Hochschild quotation from Deputy Aracena speaking October 16, 1956, in Bolivia, *Redactor del H. Cámara de Diputados, octubre de 1956*, 194; "Semitic bosses" quotation from the vote of the Sindicato de Trabajadores de "Industrias en Confección," August 30, 1952, in CGTFB, 1952 file; final quotations from *El Diario*, January 30, 1959. For a parallel example of workers utilizing anti-"Turk" racism against Middle Eastern owners in Chile see Winn, *Weavers of Revolution*, 152.

97. *El Diario*, October 22, 1954; Lora, *Movimiento obrero contemporáneo*, 363, 369.

98. COB, *Primer Congreso Nacional*, 10.

99. Lora, *Movimiento obrero contemporáneo*, 363; *El Diario*, March 18, 1965. On urban La Paz and Cochabamba unions, respectively, see Federación Departamental de Trabajadores Fabriles de La Paz, *Los fabriles*, 100–112; and Crespo and Soto, *Historia y memoria colectiva*, 34, 42.

100. See the polls of migrants conducted in 1976–1977, reported in Albó, Greaves, and Sandoval, *Chukiyawu*, 1:71 and 3:156–161.

101. Bolivia, *Censo demográfico*, 174. On Cochabamba unions see Crespo and Soto, *Historia y memoria colectiva*, 137–139.

102. In the case of the Mexican Revolution, the decision of so many urban workers to fight for Carranza and Obregón against the more radical (and largely peasant) forces represented by Zapata and Villa was crucial to the *Carrancistas'* victory.

103. *El Diario*, July 14 and 15, 1954.

104. *El Diario*, March 3, 1959.

105. First quotation from Bonsal to Rubottom, November 29, 1958, in NA 59, CDF 824.06/1-1058; second quotation from USIA, "Inspection Report: USIS/Bolivia," May 11, 1962, p. 1; third quotation from Bonsal in *El Diario*, May 9, 1957.

106. Unsigned (USIA), "Possible Worsening of the Bolivian Situation," July 9, 1959, in NA 306/1032/1.

107. Hardin to Hoyt, May 29, 1958; C. Mitchell, *Legacy of Populism*, 90–92; Wilkie, *Bolivian Revolution*, 48.

108. Arendt, *On Violence*, 56.

109. *El Diario*, May 13 and 16, 1965.

110. *El Diario*, May 23 and 25 (quotation), 1965; Delgadillo Terceros, *Fabriles*, 146.

111. *El Diario*, March 17, 1965.

112. Delgadillo Terceros, *Fabriles*, 78–79; *El Diario*, October 7, 1951.

113. *El Diario*, May 21, 1969.

114. *El Diario*, March 31, 1965.

115. First quotation from Antonio Said, in *Revista Said*, July–September 1954, 35; second quotation from an ad for the National Match Factory in La Paz, in the factory workers' newspaper *Voz Obrera*, July 1969, 18.

116. Albó, Greaves, and Sandoval, *Chukiyawu*, 1:93 and 2:20 (quotation). In 1950 there were around fifteen thousand manufacturing jobs for three million Bolivians, and many of those jobs were in small enterprise; US Embassy to DoS, April 2, 1952, p. 22.

117. Foreign ownership has often contributed to worker militancy; see Bergquist, *Labor in Latin America*; Spalding, "Parameters of Labor," 206–207. Middlebrook's discussion of Mexico suggests that greater economic importance gives workers more independence and readiness to confront the state; *Paradox of Revolution*, 82, 108–109.

118. UNTAA, *Report*, 29, 34; Gallo, *Taxes and State Power*.

119. Barragán et al., "De los pre-supuestos"; Malloy, *Bolivia*, 243–279.

120. Gallo (*Taxes and State Power*) stresses the isolation of the tin enclave and the lack of incentive among both the mining and agricultural elite to promote a strong centralized state prior to 1952. The correlation between stunted capitalist development and state weakness is a key argument in Zavaleta Mercado's work, such as *Lo nacional-popular*; see also Tapia, *La producción del conocimiento local*, 305–325.

121. For an argument about how austerity can increase unions' sense of solidarity see I. Robinson, "Does Neoliberal Restructuring Promote Social Movement Unionism?"

122. C. Mitchell, *Legacy of Populism*, 92; *El Diario*, June 10, 1963.

123. Bergquist, *Labor in Latin America*, 4–7, 262, 272; Maier, "Two Postwar Eras," esp. 338–339, 345–347, and "Politics of Productivity." In 1972 Hobart Spalding predicted that global capitalism would increasingly prevent elites from satisfying "even the economist[ic] demands now espoused by organized labor," and that workers would therefore "become an increasingly progressive and revolutionary force"; "Parameters of Labor," 216. The failure of this prophecy suggests the importance of political culture in shaping responses to austerity.

124. Middlebrook, *Paradox of Revolution*, 15, 221.

125. Several scholars have argued a related point, that the ultimate success of a revolution—whether measured by the extent of socioeconomic change or simply the regime's ability to survive—depends to a large extent on the country's prior level of economic development. See especially Eckstein, "Impact of Revolution"; Foran and Goodwin, "Revolutionary Outcomes," 210–211, 240; Malloy, *Bolivia*, 341.

126. Maier, "Two Postwar Eras," 339.

127. Dunkerley suggests that unlike revolutionary regimes in Mexico, Cuba, and Nicaragua, the MNR "was unable to co-opt and control the labour movement largely because of the strength of its syndicalist traditions"; *Rebellion*, 85. On Butrón see Federación Departamental de Trabajadores Fabriles de La Paz, *Los fabriles*, 61–62.

128. Albó, Greaves, and Sandoval, *Chukiyawu*, 1:86. See also Barragán and Soliz, "Identidades urbanas."

129. Alcaldía Municipal de La Paz, *Censo demográfico*, 21, 100, 17. Various factors make the census figures unreliable; for example, there was a common tendency for respondents to deny that they were *indios* or *cholos*, and practices such as changing one's last name to de-"indigenize" it were common.

130. Albó, Greaves, and Sandoval, *Chukiyawu*, 1:32–57, and vol. 4. Sierra stresses the fuzziness and fluidity of class and ethnic identifiers in the decades prior to 1950. He argues that while class became the dominant language of public self-identification and political contention after the Chaco War, perceptions of indigeneity continued to shape both discourse and everyday life in many ways; "Indigenous Neighborhood Residents," esp. 32–33, 137, 192–196, 276.

131. Albó, Greaves, and Sandoval, *Chukiyawu*, 3:160–161. Many urban Aymaras in the 2000s continued to do so; Webber, *Red October*, 260–268.

132. Alcaldía Municipal de La Paz, *Censo demográfico*, 51–64; THOA and Sindicato Central de Constructores, *Los constructores*.

133. USIA, "Inspection Report: USIS/Bolivia," May 11, 1962, p. 21.

134. Albó, Greaves, and Sandoval, *Chukiyawu*, 2:85.

135. Delgadillo Terceros, *Fabriles*, 136.

136. This pattern has been true for most of Latin American history. Andrews notes that "it is not the norm for societies to develop strong, racially defined political movements, even in the face of deeply entrenched racial inequality"; "Workers, Soldiers, Activists," 25.

6: Oil and Nation

1. López, *Política petrolífera*, 349, 6, 400–401.
2. For instance, the subtitle to Carlos Montenegro's 1938 pamphlet was "Oil, the Blood of Bolivia" (*Frente al derecho*).
3. See CUB, "Informe de la X Convención Nacional de Estudiantes," 76; *La Nación*, October 24, 1954; *El Diario*, October 21, 1954; Almaraz Paz, *Petróleo en Bolivia*, 107–112; Dibbits, Peredo Beltrán, and Volgger, *Polleras libertarias*, 13–14; *El Petrolero*, February 1959, 31; Mariaca Bilbao, *Mito y realidad*, 59–65; Soliz Rada, *El gas*, 18. This interpretation remains common in Bolivia today, notes Webber; *Red October*, 287–288.
4. Almaraz Paz, *Petróleo en Bolivia*, 74.
5. Deputy Bedregal in Bolivia, *Redactor de la Convención Nacional, 1945*, 4:278.
6. Quoted in Philip, *Oil and Politics*, 454.
7. Cote, "Nature of Oil," 25.
8. US Economic Mission to Bolivia, *Plan Bohan (Bolivia)*, 1:9. See also US Embassy to DoS, April 2, 1952, pp. 3, 20–21.
9. Cote, "Nature of Oil," 200–204, 213–214; Zuleta, "Conexiones revolucionarias," esp. 120–122.
10. Almaraz Paz, *Petróleo en Bolivia*, vii.
11. The lack of exploration was the main reason for the resignation of YPFB's head engineer Enrique Mariaca in 1963 and is a recurring theme in his 1966 *Mito y realidad* (esp. 279–280, 310, 531–534); the complaint about subsidization was frequent among YPFB executives, such as in J. Paz Estenssoro to Chávez Ortiz, September 6, 1961, in ANB-PR, #996, Caja 460; Bolivia, MMP, *Informe anual*, 8, 155–156.
12. Almaraz Paz, *Petróleo en Bolivia*, 188; Mariaca Bilbao, *Mito y realidad*, 414–436.
13. Almaraz Paz, *Petróleo en Bolivia*, 191–195; Canelas O., *Petróleo*, 152–155; Mariaca Bilbao, *Mito y realidad*, 160–170.
14. Almaraz Paz, *Petróleo en Bolivia*, 213, 229, 97–98, 226, 255; Mariaca Bilbao, *Mito y realidad*, 223–236; *El Petrolero*, February 1959, 3; Senator Ciro Humboldt, September 19, 1958, in Bolivia, Legislatura Ordinaria de 1958, *Redactor del H. Senado Nacional*, 189.
15. For instance, see Almaraz Paz's critique of the Bohan Plan in *Petróleo en Bolivia*, 140–148, or Anaya's analysis of the Patiño company in *Imperialismo*, esp. 34–39, 42–45.
16. On 1950s Brazil see Wolfe, *Autos and Progress*, 115, 133, 142.
17. Mariaca Bilbao, *Mito y realidad*, 263–264; cf. Canelas O., *Petróleo*, 33, 81.
18. Almaraz Paz, *Petróleo en Bolivia*, 169–208; Mariaca Bilbao, *Mito y realidad*, 183–198, 256–257.
19. Ambassador Bonsal paraphrased in Memorandum of Conversation, February 11, 1959, in NA 59, 824.2553/2-1159, and speaking in Memorandum of Conversation, February 17, 1959, in NA 59, 824.2553/2-1759; Despatch 553, December 29, 1958, in NA 59, CDF 824.2553/12-2958.

20. Despatch 69, July 18, 1958, in NA 59, CDF 824.2553/7-1858.

21. Quoted in Despatch 288, October 15, 1958, in NA 59, CDF 824.2553/10–1558.

22. FSTPB resolution in *El Diario*, December 25, 1958.

23. Ibid.; Despatch 527, December 17, 1958, in NA 59, CDF 824.2553/12–1758; Canelas O., *Petróleo*, 212–215. On the Soviet offer see Mariaca Bilbao, *Mito y realidad*, 346–356.

24. *El Diario*, March 27, 1959.

25. *El Petrolero*, February 1959, 14, 30, 3.

26. On strikes see *El Diario*, April 11–12, 1959; *El Mundo*, April 15–16, 21, and 23, 1961; *El Diario*, March 31, 1965. Ironically, many MNR and US leaders viewed diversification into oil in part as a way to undercut the militant mine workers. According to economic adviser Cornelius Zondag, "Being much less labor intensive than mining, the petroleum industry in its early days was bound to have a relatively clear sailing as far as labor problems were concerned"; *Bolivian Economy*, 121. Cf. T. Mitchell, *Carbon Democracy*.

27. First quotation in US Embassy to Secretary of State, August 28, 1959, in NA 59, CDF 824.2553/8-2859; others in Embassy to DoS, August 27, 1959, in NA 59, CDF 824.2553/8-2759.

28. Williams to Pitts, September 24, 1959, in NA 59/1162/27.

29. *El Diario*, November 11, 1958; Despatch 1045, May 23, 1958, in NA 59, CDF 824.2553/5-2358; Almaraz Paz, *Petróleo en Bolivia*, 163–168; Canelas O., *Petróleo*, 185–204; Mariaca Bilbao, *Mito y realidad*, 210–222.

30. Torres speaking October 3, 1958, 235–238, and Humboldt on September 19, 1958, 190, both in Bolivia, Legislatura Ordinaria de 1958, *Redactor*. On the pipeline see also Quiroga Santa Cruz, *Desarrollo*, 53–72.

31. See Quiroga Santa Cruz, *Desarrollo*. From then until his 1980 murder by the military, Quiroga would be one of Bolivia's most vocal resource nationalists. See also his works *El saqueo de Bolivia* and *Oleocracia o patria*, and Rodas Morales, *Marcelo Quiroga Santa Cruz*.

32. Quotations from the POR in *Masas*, April 1956, 6. On the PCB see Mariaca Bilbao, *Mito y realidad*, 290–291, 293–294; Despatch 527, December 17, 1958.

33. Despatch 527, December 17, 1958.

34. Chacón, prologue, 7. See also Canelas O., *Petróleo*, 172, 294–310; Mariaca Bilbao, *Mito y realidad*, 205–206, 292–293; Philip, *Oil and Politics*, 264.

35. Almaraz Paz, *Petróleo en Bolivia*, 132.

36. Ortiz to Pitts, February 2, 1959, in NA 59/1162/27.

37. Canelas O., *Petróleo*, 13–17, 74, 34.

38. Mariaca Bilbao, *Mito y realidad*, 296.

39. Ibid., 305.

40. Philip, *Oil and Politics*, 260–261.

41. Canelas, like other prominent figures of the period (Víctor Paz, Hernán Siles, Wálter Guevara), was trained as a lawyer. Journalists included Almaraz, Marcelo Quiroga, and Alberto Bailey; see the appendix.

42. Mariaca Bilbao, *Mito y realidad*, 302.

43. Almaraz Paz, *Petróleo en Bolivia*, 287; *El Petrolero*, February 1959, 3; *Masas*, April 1958, 6; *Masas*, May 1956, 1. See also Canelas O., *Petróleo*, 90; Mariaca Bilbao, *Mito y realidad*, 377.

44. Auty, *Resource-Based Industrialization*; Coronil, *Magical State*, 237–363. Some development visions were of course a bit fantastical. In 1938 Carlos Montenegro argued that if the Standard nationalization had occurred fifteen years before, "Bolivia today would be industrialized in a large portion of its territory, or in all of it, thanks to the fruitful and miraculous impact of oil"; *Frente al derecho*, 72. Gootenberg suggests that export structures characterized by "stark simplicity and dependency" may be more apt to generate such utopian visions; *Imagining Development*, 207.

45. Mariaca Bilbao, *Mito y realidad*, 373–374.

46. *El Petrolero*, February 1959, 14; Torres, October 3, 1958, in Bolivia, Legislatura Ordinaria de 1958, *Redactor*, 235–238, and Humboldt, September 19, 1958, p. 243; Almaraz Paz, *Petróleo en Bolivia*, 260, 272.

47. Despatch 1009, May 13, 1958, in NA 59, CDF 824.2553/5-1358. On the need for Latin American cooperation see also the FSTPB congress resolution in *El Diario*, December 25, 1958.

48. *El Petrolero*, February 1959, 4, 22; Canelas O., *Petróleo*, 172, 215–228; Mariaca Bilbao, *Mito y realidad*, 205–206.

49. Quoted in Canelas O., *Petróleo*, 121.

50. See, for example, Almaraz Paz, *Petróleo en Bolivia*, 244–252, 269.

51. See, for example, *El Petrolero*, February 1959, 14; Almaraz Paz, *Petróleo en Bolivia*, 260; Canelas O., *Petróleo*, 104–107, 230–236.

52. Almaraz Paz, *Petróleo en Bolivia*, 261 (quotation), 257; Mariaca Bilbao, *Mito y realidad*, 263–264, 293–294; Canelas O., *Petróleo*, 34, 81.

53. Despatch 1009, May 13, 1958, in NA 59, CDF 824.2553/5-1358 (quotation); *Masas*, May 1956, 1.

54. Humboldt, September 19, 1958, p. 189.

55. Canelas O., *Petróleo*, 33–34.

56. Despatch 603, January 15, 1959, in NA 59, CDF 824.2553/1-1559; Zondag, *Bolivian Economy*, 113.

57. On this policy in a hemispheric context see Philip, *Oil and Politics*, 72–81; Rabe, *Eisenhower and Latin America*, 10, 17, 93–94. On the loan see Bolivia, MMP, *Informe anual*, 9.

58. Bonsal to Rubottom, May 20 (first quotation) and August 21 (second quotation), 1958. YPFB officials made the same argument when lobbying US officials for loans; J. Paz Estenssoro to Andrade, May 7, 1958, in ANB-PR, #1311, Caja 570.

59. Siracusa (quoting USOM) to Rubottom, May 14, 1959, in NA 59/1162/27; Bolivia, MMP, *Informe anual*, 9.

60. Mariaca Bilbao, *Mito y realidad*, 350–351; Siekmeier, *Bolivian Revolution*, 79–98.

61. Dunkerley, *Rebellion*, 128. Though evidence on taxation is incomplete, Klein and Peres-Cajías suggest that the code was followed by "the stagnation of oil taxes as opposed to higher production levels"; "Bolivian Oil," 160.

62. Ovando was inspired partly by Peru's Velasco regime, which took power in 1968; Dunkerley, *Rebellion*, 157. The tradition of oil nationalism within Latin American militaries extended back decades, however.

63. Philip, *Oil and Politics*, 264–265 (letter quoted, 265).

64. Philip dates the controversy over gas to January 1965, when the newspaper *Jornada* first raised the question of whether the 1955 reform also applied to natural gas; *Oil and Politics*, 262. See also Mariaca Bilbao, *Mito y realidad*, 437–444. In 1968 René Zavaleta Mercado wrote that the industrialization of natural gas "is the only way out for this cornered [*accoralado*] country"; "El gas," May 21, 3.

65. *Extra*, May 19, 1968.

66. Philip, *Oil and Politics*, 264–265, 268–269 (Gulf money).

67. Still, the Barrientos regime was not totally immune to popular pressure—in the regime's last two years, there was some discussion, mostly internal, of amending the 1955 oil law; unsigned (Wálter Guevara Arze?), "Con atención del Ministro de Minas y Petróleo," n.d., in ANB-WGA, Caja 29, Carpeta 5; Ingram, *Expropriation*, 163.

68. In *El Diario*, September 26, 1969. See also Dunkerley, *Rebellion*, 161–163.

69. Dunkerley, *Rebellion*, 164.

70. Ingram (*Expropriation*, 176) and Siekmeier (*Bolivian Revolution*, 127) draw similar conclusions.

71. *El Diario*, October 20, 21, and 26, 1969. On leftist debates over Ovando see Dunkerley, *Rebellion*, 167–170.

72. *Prensa Libre*, February 28, 1969.

73. *El Diario*, June 15, 1969.

74. *El Diario*, September 27, 1969; *Prensa Libre*, January 11, 1971.

75. *El Diario*, October 20, 23, and 26 (quotation), 1969. The question of local responses to the nationalization—and oil extraction in general—from indigenous communities near drilling sites remains largely unresearched. I have encountered mention of one instance, in about 1960, of indigenous residents reportedly throwing spears at a Gulf truck; *Embajada de Bolivia— Washington a Ministerio de Relaciones Exteriores, 1960*, pp. 157–158, in RREE.

76. Quotation in *Extra*, August 21, 1968. See also Mariaca Bilbao, *Mito y realidad*, 292–293; *Extra*, January 3, February 21–24, March 22, and July 25–26, 1968; *Prensa Libre*, April 4 and 13 and June 17–20, 1969.

77. *El Diario*, June 3 and 5, 1969.

78. *El Diario*, June 7, 1969; *Prensa Libre*, February 16, 1969. See also Communist (PCB) mine union leader Federico Escóbar's proud statement that he was "100 percent Catholic" and "100 percent Communist"; quoted in López Vigil, *Una mina de coraje*, 119.

79. *Extra*, March 6–8 and 12 (quotation), 1968.

80. *Extra*, September 6, 1968.

81. *Extra*, March 8, 1968.

82. On the PDC see *Extra*, February 21, May 19, November 22 (quotation) and 26, 1968.

83. Zavaleta Mercado, *50 años de historia*, 33; see also Zavaleta's *Lo nacional-popular*. Luis Tapia points out that Zavaleta was referring especially to the "non-articulation of modes of production" and "of other dimensions in social life" in underdeveloped capitalist countries; *La producción del conocimiento local*, 308. I have extrapolated somewhat from the term's original meaning.

84. Almaraz was initially a member of the Communist Party (PCB), Quiroga founded the Socialist Party-1 (Partido Socialista-1), and Zavaleta co-founded the Movement of the Revolutionary Left (MIR). Soliz Rada was involved with the PCB in the 1960s; he would later become the first minister of hydrocarbons under Evo Morales; interview with the author, La Paz, September 22, 2010. See also Soliz Rada's 1984 *El gas*.

85. Whitaker and Jordan, *Nationalism*, 160, 8 (Lenin quotation).

86. *Extra*, April 6 and June 26, 1968.

87. *El Diario*, October 23, 1969; M. Ayllón Ocampo (Executive Secretary, FSTPB) to Ovando, November 3, 1969, in Uriona Alurralde to Quiroga Santa Cruz, November 5, 1969, in ANB-PR, #1278. The United States still reduced aid to Bolivia by 63 percent the next year, while foreign companies boycotted Bolivian oil, as Ayllón predicted they would. The government later agreed to a $78 million settlement; C. Mitchell, *Legacy of Populism*, 112–113, 119n21.

88. *El Diario*, October 27, 1969; Dunkerley, *Rebellion*, 166–167. Ovando himself had presided over the antiguerrilla campaigns of the mid-1960s as well as the notorious 1967 San Juan massacre that killed scores of people at the Siglo XX mining camp.

89. Dunkerley, *Rebellion*, 163 (quotation), 166–167.

90. *El Diario*, September 27, 1969, section 2; Dunkerley, *Rebellion*, 166–167.

91. Dunkerley, *Rebellion*, 167–170. The May 1970 COB congress was divided over the proper stance toward Ovando. One important result of the congress, though, was the formation of an independent Comando Político coalition composed of the COB leadership, many big unions, and the major leftist parties.

92. *El Diario*, October 21, 1969.

93. Dunkerley, *Rebellion*, 177–200; C. Mitchell, *Legacy of Populism*, 118.

94. Zavaleta Mercado, "El proletariado minero en Bolivia" (1974), in his *Clases sociales*, 116.

95. Canelas O., *Petróleo*, 363.

96. Bonsal to Rubottom, May 20, 1958.

97. Smelser, *Theory of Collective Behavior*, 8.

98. Ibid., 18. For a critique of this tradition see McAdam, *Political Process*, 5–19.

99. Williams to Pitts, September 24, 1959.

100. Silberstein to Eaton et al., March 11, 1959, in NA 59/1170/13.

101. "The Fanned Spark," *Time*, 40–41. See also Guha, *Elementary Aspects*, 220–226.

102. Caricatures of so-called anti-Americanism remain common in the

United States; one example is Rubin and Rubin, *Hating America*. Less overtly reactionary treatments exist but still often reflect a bias in favor of US policy; an example is Brands, *Latin America's Cold War*. For a useful critical history of the concept see Friedman, *Rethinking Anti-Americanism*.

103. The phrase "conscious hostility" is from Rodney Hilton, cited in Guha, *Elementary Aspects*, 20–28. Weismantel makes a similar point about *pishtaco* myths in the Andes: "actual pishtaco stories do not make all whites or all males culpable, nor do they exculpate Indians and women. Rather, each version names a specific person as the agent of the crime"; *Cholas and Pishtacos*, 168.

104. *El País* (LP), May 1, 1927; *F.O.L.*, May 1, 1948; *Rebelión*, May 1, 1952. Since the anarchists were almost certainly framed for their role in the movement for the eight-hour day, the case became an international cause célèbre.

105. Unsigned (USIA), "Cuban Solidarity Movements in Latin America," March 15, 1961, in NA 306/1032/2. On USIS exhibits featuring Lincoln see Bolivian newsreel no. 48, n.d., in NA 306/1098/51; USIA, "Inspection Report: USIS/Bolivia," 30–31.

106. Mariaca Bilbao, *Mito y realidad*, 13, 377; Almaraz Paz, *El poder y la caída*, 60, 97. Commonly cited works include Baran, *Political Economy of Growth*; Butler, *War Is a Racket*; Mills, *Power Elite*; and O'Connor, *Empire of Oil*.

107. F. Molina, *El pensamiento boliviano*, 77, 117.

108. Francovich, *Mitos profundos*, 117–119.

109. Derby, "Gringo Chickens with Worms," 466. For myths and rumors in Africa see White, *Speaking with Vampires*; Reyna, "Constituting Domination." Cf. Scheper-Hughes, "Theft of Life."

110. Weismantel, *Cholas and Pishtacos*. The *pishtaco* is often a metaphor for economic exploitation, though the myth can derive from other anxieties too.

111. Siekmeier, *Bolivian Revolution*, 140–146.

112. Gallo, *Taxes and State Power*, 154n4; Gómez d'Angelo, "Bolivia," 462, 464.

113. Zavaleta Mercado, *Lo nacional-popular*, 233.

114. Joint Bolivian-United States Labour Commission, *Labour Problems in Bolivia*; Ford, Bacon & Davis, *Mining Industry of Bolivia*; Almaraz Paz, *El poder y la caída*, 106–107n1 (citing the Magruder report).

115. Klein, "American Oil Companies," 55–58; Philip, *Oil and Politics*, 194–196. The argument that the Chaco War involved the defense of Bolivian oil was not totally without merit, since in early 1935 Paraguay indeed seized several Bolivian oil fields; Klein, *Parties and Political Change*, 182–183, 186.

116. T. Mitchell, *Carbon Democracy*, 43–65. Discussing the early twentieth century, Mitchell notes "the extraordinary efforts of Standard Oil to prevent the development of rival oilfields in every corner of the world at that time" (56).

117. Quotations from CUB, "Informe de la X Convención Nacional de

Estudiantes," 75. For a quantitative study showing the positive correlation between US intervention in foreign countries and US exports to those countries for the period 1947–1989 see Berger et al., "Commercial Imperialism?"

Epilogue

1. UN ECLA, *Economic Survey: 1979*, 103. In 2013 primary goods comprised 96 percent of Bolivia's exports, and natural gas was 52 percent of the total; UN ECLA, *Anuario estadístico 2014*, 102, and electronic supplement.

2. Conaghan, "Reconsidering Jeffrey Sachs," 245; Kelley and Klein, *Revolution*, 140, 230–231; Wilkie and Reich, *Statistical Abstract*, 173.

3. Malloy and Gamarra, *Revolution and Reaction*, 94; Webber, *Red October*, 95–97.

4. Malloy and Gamarra, *Revolution and Reaction*, 100.

5. Conaghan, "Reconsidering Jeffrey Sachs"; Conaghan and Malloy, *Unsettling Statecraft*.

6. In a highly symbolic manifestation of enduring resource nationalism, some of the elderly Chaco War veterans who played such a powerful political role in earlier decades organized against the partial reprivatization of YPFB in 1996. They accused the government of trampling on "50,000 dead bodies of Bolivians who died in the Chaco in defense of oil wealth"; *Los Tiempos*, April 2, 1996, quoted in Guimarães, "La capitalización," 93. For details on hydrocarbons policy in the 1990s and early 2000s see Hindery, *From Enron to Evo*, 27–62; Molina, "Explotación," 73–78.

7. Cocaine became a major growth industry in the 1970s, with backing from the country's military regimes. The industry was dominated by the eastern bourgeoisie, though peasant coca growers came to play an important role. On the 1985–2005 period see Conaghan and Malloy, *Unsettling Statecraft*, esp. 185–202; Kohl and Farthing, *Impasse in Bolivia*, 65–124; Webber, *Red October*, 113–146.

8. Guimarães, "La capitalización de los hidrocarburos."

9. For indemnification, debt, and interest rate figures see Bailey and Knutsen, "Surgery without Anaesthesia," 48; Hindery, *From Enron to Evo*, 25; Molina, "Explotación," 72.

10. Quoted in Conaghan, "Reconsidering Jeffrey Sachs," 250.

11. On YPFB workers see Hindery, *From Enron to Evo*, 43.

12. Gómez, *El Alto de pie*; Gutiérrez Aguilar, *Los ritmos del Pachakuti*; Lazar, *El Alto, Rebel City*; Mamani Ramírez, *Microgobiernos barriales*; Webber, *Red October*.

13. Crabtree and Chaplin, *Bolivia*; Farthing and Kohl, *Evo's Bolivia*; Hindery, *From Enron to Evo*; Kaup, *Market Justice*; Webber, *From Rebellion to Reform*; Zegada et al., *La democracia*. Morales narrowly lost a February 2016 referendum to permit him to run again in 2019.

14. An insightful analysis from 2007 is Hylton and Thomson, *Revolutionary Horizons*.

15. Regalsky highlights indigenous identification and the rise of indepen-

dent rural governance structures when emphasizing why "2006 is not 1952"; "Political Processes," 38–40. On MAS discourse see Mayorga, "Nacionalismo e indigenismo."

16. Calderón, "Oportunidad histórica"; Huanacuni Mamani, *Vivir bien/ buen vivir*; Martí i Puig et al., *Entre el desarrollo*. It is unfortunately true, however, that the concept of "living well" in everyday discourse often remains underdeveloped, as Farthing and Kohl note in *Evo's Bolivia*, 88.

17. Gillis, "In Sign of Global Warming." On recent mobilization in defense of the environment, particularly by indigenous communities, see Hindery, *From Enron to Evo*; Perreault, "Extracting Justice."

18. "Polyarchy" refers to systems in which most citizens have little to no input over policy despite the existence of formal democratic structures. Exclusion is sustained by more subtle means, such as elite control over economic resources. See Robinson, *Promoting Polyarchy*, and on Bolivia, Webber, *Red October*, 30–33.

19. Quoted in Crabtree and Chaplin, *Bolivia*, 58–59.

20. Farthing and Kohl, *Evo's Bolivia*, 78–97; Kohl and Farthing, "Material Constraints"; Wanderley, "Beyond Gas" and "Economy of the Extractive Industries."

21. Crabtree and Chaplin, *Bolivia*, 88–90; Hindery, *From Enron to Evo*, 161.

22. Kohl and Farthing, "Material Constraints," esp. 232–233.

23. Kaup, *Market Justice*, 127–149; Mokrani, "Reformas de última década"; Webber, *From Rebellion to Reform*, 80–83. Some have argued that resource-nationalist measures can in fact stabilize foreign companies' presence, shielding them from criticism; Kaup, *Market Justice*; Rodman, *Sanctity versus Sovereignty*, 99.

24. Crabtree and Chaplin, *Bolivia*, 16–35; Farthing and Kohl, *Evo's Bolivia*, 113–127.

25. "Populism" is a much-abused term, typically employed in a pejorative and sloppy sense to attack any leader who confronts elite interests or advocates for the poor; a recent example is Morales, "Post-Neoliberal Policies." Recent governments in Venezuela, Bolivia, and Ecuador differ from classic populists in their efforts to promote discussion of socialism, respect for electoral democracy, and promotion of new forms of participatory decision making, especially in Venezuela. At the same time, there are some similarities with regard to the hierarchical tendencies within their parties and their accommodation of opposing class interests, especially in Ecuador and Bolivia.

26. Crabtree and Chaplin, *Bolivia*, 16–35; Hindery, *From Enron to Evo*, 216–231. One could argue that the MAS state's greater autonomy from the US government and foreign corporations has been partly negated by domestic resistance to extractivism; if the state is now less subject to US domination than in the 1950s, it is also forced to contend with local resistance movements near extraction sites.

27. Kohl and Farthing, "Material Constraints"; Perreault, "Extracting Justice."

28. Gustafson, "Amid Gas, Where Is the Revolution?" On social pro-

grams and poverty and inequality reductions see Farthing and Kohl, *Evo's Bolivia*, 98–112; UN ECLA, *Panorama social*, 86, 109–112.

29. Young, "The Good, the Bad."

30. First three quotations are from McConnell, "Annual Threat Assessment," 33; fourth quote is from Blair, "Annual Threat Assessment," 30.

31. Some recent US officials in Bolivia have explicitly lauded the earlier effort to tame the MNR, suggesting that economic coercion might similarly succeed in changing MAS government policies; Earle, "Bolivia," 14. See also Burron, "Unpacking U.S. Democracy Promotion."

32. Higginbottom cautions that rising European Union investment in Latin America is not fundamentally any different from US investment and "that the dependency school contention of a transfer of value out of the continent remains valid"; "Political Economy of Foreign Investment," 197.

33. Harrison, *Underdevelopment Is a State of Mind*; Oporto, "El mito del eterno retorno," 343.

34. Francovich, *Mitos profundos*, 6.

35. Weyland, "Rise of Latin America's Two Lefts," 156.

36. F. Molina, *El pensamiento boliviano*, 5, 44, 46.

37. Farthing and Kohl, *Evo's Bolivia*, 84–85. See also Kaup, *Market Justice*, 5.

38. F. Molina, *El pensamiento boliviano*, 77, 117; Francovich, *Mitos profundos*, 117–119.

39. The pejorative use of the term *estadolatría* appears frequently in Bolivian critiques of the country's leftists and nationalists; an example is found in F. Molina, *El pensamiento boliviano*, 88.

40. Oporto, "El mito del eterno retorno," 338, 341.

Bibliography

Archival Sources

Archives

Archivo de La Paz (ALP)
Archivo Nacional de Bolivia, Sucre (ANB)
  Ministerio de la Presidencia de la República (ANB-PR)
  Colección Wálter Guevara Arze (ANB-WGA)
Archivo Privado de Cecilia Salazar de la Torre, La Paz (APCS)
Archivo Privado de Luis Cusicanqui, La Paz (APLC)
Biblioteca y Archivo Histórico de la Asamblea Legislativa Plurinacional, La Paz (BAH)
Biblioteca Arturo Costa de la Torre de la Casa Municipal de la Cultura Franz Tamayo, La Paz (ACD)
Biblioteca Municipal Jesús Lara, Archivo Histórico, Cochabamba (AHC)
Centro de Derecho Laboral y Agrario, La Paz (CEDLA)
Centro de Investigación y Promoción del Campesinado, La Paz (CIPCA)
Confederación General de Trabajadores Fabriles de Bolivia, Archivo, La Paz (CGTFB)
Ministerio de Planificación del Desarrollo, Centro de Documentación e Información, La Paz (MPD)
Ministerio de Relaciones Exteriores, Archivo, La Paz (RREE)
National Archives and Records Administration II, College Park, MD (NA)
Universidad Mayor de San Andrés, Biblioteca Central, La Paz (UMSA-B)
Universidad Mayor de San Andrés, Hemeroteca, La Paz (UMSA-H)

Newspapers and Magazines (city) [archive]

Bandera Roja (La Paz) [ANB, APLC]
La Calle (La Paz) [BAH]
El Diario (La Paz) [BAH]
Eco Fabril (La Paz) [CGTFB]
El Ex-Combatiente (Sucre) [ANB]

Extra (Cochabamba) [AHC]
FOL: Órgano de la Federación Obrera Local (La Paz) [APLC]
Foro Universitario (La Paz and Washington, DC) [UMSA-H]
Life (New York)
En Marcha (La Paz) [ALP, ANB]
Masas (La Paz) [ACD]
El Mundo (La Paz) [AHC]
La Nación (La Paz) [BAH]
New York Times
La Noche (La Paz) [BAH]
Nuevo Mundo: Publicación del Servicio Informativo y Cultural de la Embajada de los Estados Unidos de Norteamérica (La Paz) [ANB]
El Obrero (La Paz) [ANB, CGTFB]
El País (Cochabamba) [AHC]
El País (La Paz) [BAH]
Patria y Petróleo: Noticiero de Yacimientos Petrolíferos Fiscales Bolivianos y la Revolución Nacional (La Paz) [ANB]
El Petrolero (Cochabamba) [ACD]
Planeamiento (La Paz) [ANB]
Prensa Libre (Cochabamba) [AHC]
Presencia (La Paz) [BAH]
Pueblo (La Paz) [APCS]
El Pueblo (Cochabamba) [AHC]
El Pueblo (La Paz) [BAH, ALP]
Pututu: Publicación Semanal de la Sub-Secretaría de Prensa, Informaciones y Cultura (La Paz) [ANB]
La Razón (La Paz) [BAH]
Rebelión: Órgano de la Central Obrera Boliviana (La Paz) [APLC]
Reforma: Órgano de la Federación Universitaria Local (La Paz) [ACD]
Revista Said (La Paz) [UMSA-H]
Los Tiempos (Cochabamba) [AHC]
Time (New York)
Tribuna (La Paz) [BAH]
Última Hora (La Paz) [BAH]
Voz Obrera (La Paz) [CGTFB]
World Telegram and Sun (New York)

Secondary Sources

Abidin, Mahani Zainal. "Competitive Industrialization with Natural Resource Abundance: Malaysia." In *Resource Abundance and Economic Development*, edited by Auty, 147–164.
Alba, Víctor. *Politics and the Labor Movement in Latin America*. Translation by Carol de Zapata. Stanford, CA: Stanford University Press, 1968.
Albó, Xavier, Tomás Greaves, and Godofredo Sandoval. *Chukiyawu: La cara aymara de La Paz*. 4 vols. La Paz: CIPCA, 1981–1987.

Alcaldía Municipal de La Paz, Dirección General de Estadística. *Censo demográfico de la ciudad de La Paz, 15 de octubre de 1942.* La Paz, 1943. MPD.

Alexander, Robert J. *The Bolivian National Revolution.* New Brunswick, NJ: Rutgers University Press, 1958.

Alexander, Robert J., with Eldon M. Parker. *A History of Organized Labor in Bolivia.* Westport, CT: Praeger, 2005.

Almaraz Paz, Sergio. *Petróleo en Bolivia.* La Paz: Juventud, 1958.

———. *El poder y la caída: El estaño en la historia de Bolivia.* La Paz: Los Amigos del Libro, 1966.

Álvarez España, Waldo. *Los gráficos en Bolivia: Historia de la organización y luchas de los trabajadores de este sector social.* La Paz: Renovación, 1977.

———. *Memorias del primer ministro obrero: Historia del movimiento sindical y político boliviano, 1916–1952.* La Paz: Renovación, 1986.

Anaya, Ricardo. *Imperialismo, rosca y miseria.* La Paz: Partido de la Izquierda Revolucionaria, 1947.

Anderson, Benedict. *Imagined Communities: Reflections on the Origin and Spread of Nationalism.* Rev. ed. London: Verso, 1991.

Andrade, Víctor. *My Missions for Revolutionary Bolivia, 1944–1962.* Pittsburgh, PA: University of Pittsburgh Press, 1976.

Andrews, George Reid. "Workers, Soldiers, Activists: Black Mobilization in Brazil and Spanish America, 1800–2000." *Estudios Interdisciplinarios de América Latina y el Caribe* 19, no. 1 (2008): 11–33.

Antezana J., Luis H. "Sistemas y procesos ideológicos en Bolivia (1935–1979)." In *Bolivia, hoy,* edited by Zavaleta, 60–84.

———. "Veintisiete años después, el NR todavía." Interview by Gustavo Soto and Sergio Villena. *Decursos* (Cochabamba) 8, nos. 15–16 (2006): 5–25.

Antezana Ergueta, Luis. *Hernán Siles Zuazo: El estratega y la contrarrevolución.* La Paz: Luz, 1979.

———. *Historia secreta del Movimiento Nacionalista Revolucionario.* 9 vols. La Paz: Juventud, 1984.

Antezana Ergueta, Luis, and Hugo Romero B. *Historia de los sindicatos campesinos: Un proceso de integración nacional en Bolivia.* La Paz: Consejo Nacional de Reforma Agraria, 1973.

Arendt, Hannah. *On Violence.* New York: Harcourt, Brace, and World, 1970.

Ari, Waskar. *Earth Politics: Religion, Decolonization, and Bolivia's Indigenous Intellectuals.* Durham, NC: Duke University Press, 2014.

Auty, Richard M., ed. *Resource Abundance and Economic Development.* Oxford: Oxford University Press, 2001.

———. *Resource-Based Industrialization: Sowing the Oil in Eight Developing Countries.* Oxford: Clarendon, 1990.

———. *Sustaining Development in Mineral Economies: The Resource Curse Thesis.* London: Routledge, 1993.

Auty, Richard M., and J. L. Evia. "A Growth Collapse with Point Resources: Bolivia." In *Resource Abundance and Economic Development,* edited by Auty, 179–192.

Auty, Richard M., and Sampsa Kiiski. "Natural Resources, Capital Accumulation, Structural Change, and Welfare." In *Resource Abundance and Economic Development*, edited by Auty, 19–35.

Ayub, Mahmood Ali, and Hideo Hashimoto. *The Economics of Tin Mining in Bolivia*. Washington, DC: World Bank, 1985.

Babb, Sarah. *Managing Mexico: Economists from Nationalism to Neoliberalism*. Princeton, NJ: Princeton University Press, 2004.

Bachelor, Steven J. "Miracle on Ice: Industrial Workers and the Promise of Americanization in Cold War Mexico." In *In from the Cold*, edited by Joseph and Spenser, 253–272.

Bailey, Jennifer L., and Torbjorn L. Knutsen. "Surgery without Anaesthesia: Bolivia's Response to Economic Chaos." *The World Today* 43, no. 3 (1987): 47–51.

Baldwin, Robert E. "Patterns of Development in Newly Settled Regions." *Manchester School of Economics and Social Studies* 24 (May 1956): 161–179.

Bannon, Ian, and Paul Collier, eds. *Natural Resources and Violent Conflict: Options and Actions*. Washington, DC: World Bank, 2003.

Baran, Paul A. *The Political Economy of Growth*. New York: Monthly Review Press, 1957.

Barcelli S., Agustín. *Medio siglo de luchas sindicales revolucionarias en Bolivia, 1905–1955*. La Paz: Editorial del Estado, 1956.

Barnadas, Josep M., with Guillermo Calvo and Juan Ticlla, eds. *Diccionario histórico de Bolivia*. 2 vols. Sucre: Grupo de Estudios Históricos, 2002.

Barnet, Richard J. *Intervention and Revolution: The United States in the Third World*. Cleveland, OH: World, 1968.

Barragán, Rossana. *Asambleas constituyentes: Ciudadanía y elecciones, convenciones y debates (1825–1971)*. La Paz: Muela del Diablo, 2006.

Barragán, Rossana, and Carmen Soliz. "Identidades urbanas: Los aymaras en las ciudades de La Paz y El Alto." In *¿Indígenas u obreros? La construcción política de identidades en el altiplano boliviano*, edited by Denise Y. Arnold, 471–509. La Paz: Fundación UNIR Bolivia, 2009.

Barragán, Rossana, José Peres, Jorge Derpic, and Carmen Soliz. "De los presupuestos a los presupuestos. Fiscalidad y construcción estatal disputada (1900–1954)." In *Informe sobre desarrollo humano en Bolivia, 2007: El estado del Estado en Bolivia*, Programa de las Naciones Unidas para el Desarrollo (PNUD), 127–218. La Paz: PNUD, 2007.

Barrientos Ortuño, René. *Hacia un nuevo sindicalismo*. La Paz: Presidencia de la República, Dirección de Prensa e Informaciones, 1966.

Bebbington, Anthony, ed. *Social Conflict, Economic Development, and Extractive Industry: Evidence from South America*. New York: Routledge, 2012.

Bebbington, Anthony, and Jeffrey Bury, eds. *Subterranean Struggles: New Dynamics of Mining, Oil, and Gas in Latin America*. Austin: University of Texas Press, 2013.

Becker, Marc. *Indians and Leftists in the Making of Ecuador's Modern Indigenous Movements*. Durham, NC: Duke University Press, 2008.

Behrends, Andrea, Stephen P. Reyna, and Günther Schlee, eds. *Crude Domination: An Anthropology of Oil.* New York: Berghahn Books, 2011.

Belmonte, Laura A. *Selling the American Way: U.S. Propaganda and the Cold War.* Philadelphia: University of Pennsylvania Press, 2008.

Berger, Daniel, William Easterly, Nathan Nunn, and Shanker Satyanath. "Commercial Imperialism? Political Influence and Trade during the Cold War." *American Economic Review* 103, no. 2 (2013): 863–896.

Bergquist, Charles W. *Labor in Latin America: Comparative Essays on Chile, Argentina, Venezuela, and Colombia.* Stanford, CA: Stanford University Press, 1986.

Bethell, Leslie, and Ian Roxborough. "Introduction: The Postwar Conjuncture in Latin America: Democracy, Labor, and the Left." In *Latin America between the Second World War and the Cold War,* edited by Bethell and Roxborough, 1–32.

———, eds. *Latin America between the Second World War and the Cold War, 1944–1948.* Cambridge, UK: Cambridge University Press, 1992.

Blair, Dennis C. "Annual Threat Assessment of the US Intelligence Community for the House Permanent Select Committee on Intelligence." February 3, 2010. http://www.dni.gov/files/documents/Newsroom/Testimonies/20100203_testimony.pdf.

Blasier, Cole. *The Hovering Giant: U.S. Responses to Revolutionary Change in Latin America, 1910–1985.* Rev. ed. Pittsburgh, PA: University of Pittsburgh Press, 1985.

Bolivia, República de. *Plan nacional de desarrollo económico y social, 1962–1971: Resumen.* La Paz, 1961.

———. *Redactor de la Convención Nacional, 1945,* vol. 4. La Paz, n.d.

———. *Redactor del H. Cámara de Diputados, octubre de 1956.* La Paz: Universo, 1957.

———. *Redactor del H. Cámara de Diputados, octubre de 1958.* La Paz, n.d.

Bolivia, República de, Consejo Nacional de Reforma Agraria (CNRA), Departamento de Estadística. *El proceso de Reforma Agraria en cifras.* La Paz: CNRA, 1975.

Bolivia, República de, H[onorable]. Senado Nacional. *Hornos de fundición en Bolivia.* La Paz: Universo, 1963.

Bolivia, República de, Junta Nacional de Planeamiento (JNP). "Plan de desarrollo económico y social de Bolivia, 1962–1971." *Planeamiento* nos. 3–5 (1961).

Bolivia, República de, Legislatura Ordinaria de 1958. *Redactor del H. Senado Nacional.* Vol. 1, *Agosto a octubre de 1958.* La Paz: Don Bosco, 1959.

Bolivia, República de, Legislatura Ordinaria de 1966. *Redactor del H. Senado Nacional.* Vol. 2, *Octubre a noviembre de 1966.* La Paz: Universo, 1966.

Bolivia, República de, Ministerio de Hacienda y Estadística, Dirección General de Estadística y Censos. *Censo demográfico de 1950.* La Paz: Argote, 1955.

Bolivia, República de, Ministerio de Minas y Petróleo (MMP). *Informe anual del Ministerio de Minas y Petróleo, 1960–1961.* #1822, Caja 778, ANB-PR.

Brands, Hal. *Latin America's Cold War.* Cambridge, MA: Harvard University Press, 2010.

Bulmer-Thomas, Victor. *The Economic History of Latin America since Independence.* 2nd ed. Cambridge, UK: Cambridge University Press, 2003.

Burke, Melvin. *The Corporación Minera de Bolivia (Comibol) and the Triangular Plan: A Case Study in Dependency.* Meadville, PA: Allegheny College, 1987.

———. "Does 'Food for Peace' Assistance Damage the Bolivian Economy?" *Inter-American Economic Affairs* 25, no. 1 (1970): 3–21.

Burron, Neil. "Unpacking U.S. Democracy Promotion in Bolivia: From Soft Tactics to Regime Change." *Latin American Perspectives* 39, no. 1 (2012): 115–132.

Butler, Smedley D. *War Is a Racket.* New York: Round Table Press, 1935.

Cabrera R., Sinforoso. *La burocracia estrangula a la COMIBOL.* La Paz, 1960.

Calderón, Fernando. "Oportunidad histórica: Cambio político y nuevo orden sociocultural." *Nueva Sociedad* 209 (2007): 32–45.

Calvo Mirabal, Tristán. *Transnacionales petroleras en Bolivia.* La Paz: Impresiones La Amistad, 1996.

Canelas O., Amado. *Mito y realidad de la Corporación Minera de Bolivia.* La Paz: Los Amigos del Libro, 1966.

———. *Petróleo: Imperialismo y nacionalismo.* La Paz: Librería Altiplano, 1963.

Cardoso, Fernando Henrique, and Enzo Faletto. *Dependencia y desarrollo en América Latina: Ensayo de interpretación sociológica.* Mexico City: Siglo XXI, 1969.

Central Obrera Boliviana (COB). *Primer Congreso Nacional de Trabajadores: Cartilla de orientación.* La Paz: Burillo, 1954.

———. *Programa ideológico y estatutos de la Central Obrera Boliviana aprobados por el Congreso Nacional de Trabajadores.* La Paz, 1954.

CEPAL. *See* United Nations Economic Commission for Latin America (UN ECLA).

Céspedes, Augusto. *El presidente colgado (historia boliviana).* Buenos Aires: Editorial Jorge Alvarez, 1966.

Chacón, Gustavo. Prologue to *Mito y realidad del petróleo boliviano,* by Enrique Mariaca Bilbao, 3–8. La Paz: Los Amigos del Libro, 1966.

Chang, Ha-Joon. *Bad Samaritans: The Myth of Free Trade and the Secret History of Capitalism.* New York: Bloomsbury, 2008.

Chilcote, Ronald H., and Dale L. Johnson, eds. *Theories of Development: Mode of Production or Dependency?* Beverly Hills, CA: Sage, 1983.

Ciccariello-Maher, George. *We Created Chávez: A People's History of the Venezuelan Revolution.* Durham, NC: Duke University Press, 2013.

Collier, Paul. *The Bottom Billion: Why the Poorest Countries Are Failing and What Can Be Done About It.* Oxford: Oxford University Press, 2007.

Collier, Paul, and Anke Hoeffler. *Greed and Grievance in Civil War.* Washington, DC: World Bank, 2001.

Collier, Paul, and Anthony J. Venables, eds. *Plundered Nations? Successes and Failures in Natural Resource Extraction*. Houndmills, UK: Palgrave Macmillan, 2011.

Comité Ejecutivo de la Universidad Boliviana (CEUB). *Convenciones nacionales universitarias, 1928–1929*. La Paz: CEUB, 1982.

Conaghan, Catherine M. "Reconsidering Jeffrey Sachs and the Bolivian Economic Experiment." In *Money Doctors, Foreign Debts, and Economic Reforms*, edited by Drake, 236–266.

Conaghan, Catherine M., and James M. Malloy. *Unsettling Statecraft: Democracy and Neoliberalism in the Central Andes*. Pittsburgh, PA: Pittsburgh University Press, 1994.

Confederación Universitaria Boliviana (CUB). "Informe de la X Convención Nacional de Estudiantes." *Reforma* 1, no. 1 (1952): 69–95.

Contreras, Manuel E. "Bolivia, 1900–39: Mining, Railways, and Education." In *An Economic History of Twentieth-Century Latin America*. Vol. 1, *The Export Age: The Latin American Economies in the Late Nineteenth and Early Twentieth Centuries*, edited by Enrique Cárdenas, José Antonio Ocampo, and Rosemary Thorp, 188–216. Basingstoke, UK: Palgrave, 2000.

———. "Debt, Taxes, and War: The Political Economy of Bolivia, c. 1920–1935." *Journal of Latin American Studies* 22, no. 2 (1990): 265–287.

———. *Tecnología moderna en los Andes: Minería e ingenería en Bolivia en el siglo XX*. La Paz: Biblioteca Minera Boliviana, 1994.

Cornejo S., Alberto, ed. *Programas políticos de Bolivia*. Cochabamba: Imprenta Universitaria, 1949.

Coronil, Fernando. *The Magical State: Nature, Money, and Modernity in Venezuela*. Chicago: University of Chicago Press, 1997.

Corporación Boliviana de Fomento (CBF). *La Corporación Boliviana de Fomento (sus orígenes, organización y actividad)*. La Paz: Universo, 1943.

———. *La marcha de la economía nacional: Resumen estadístico, 1975*. La Paz, 1975.

Costa de la Torre, Arturo. *Catálogo de la bibliografía boliviana: Libros y folletos, 1900–1963*. La Paz: Universidad Mayor de San Andrés, 1966.

Cote, Stephen Conrad. "The Nature of Oil in Bolivia, 1896–1952." PhD diss., University of California, Davis, 2011.

Crabtree, John, and Ann Chaplin. *Bolivia: Processes of Change*. London: Zed Books, 2013.

Crabtree, John, and Laurence Whitehead, eds. *Unresolved Tensions: Bolivia Past and Present*. Pittsburgh, PA: University of Pittsburgh Press, 2008.

Crespo, Carlos, and César Soto. *Historia y memoria colectiva: El movimiento obrero cochabambino (período 1952–1956)*. Cochabamba: Universidad Mayor de San Simón/Centro de Estudios Superiores Universitarios, 2002.

Crespo Enríquez, Arturo. *El rostro minero de Bolivia: Los mineros—mártires y héroes*. La Paz: n.p., 2009.

Cull, Nicholas J. *The Cold War and the United States Information Agency: American Propaganda and Public Diplomacy, 1945–1989*. Cambridge, UK: Cambridge University Press, 2008.

Cypher, James M. "Energy Privatized: The Ultimate Neoliberal Triumph." *NACLA Report on the Americas* 47, no. 1 (2014): 27–31.

Daepp, David. "Bolivia's Lithium Potential: The Opportunity Deeper beneath the Surface." *ReVista: Harvard Review of Latin America* 11, no. 1 (2011): 54–56.

Dandler H., Jorge, and Juan Torrico A. "From the National Indigenous Congress to the Ayopaya Rebellion: Bolivia, 1945–1947." In *Resistance, Rebellion, and Consciousness*, edited by Stern, 334–378.

DeGolyer and MacNaughton, Inc. *Técnicos petroleros evalúan YPFB: Informe DeGolyer and MacNaughton, Inc.* La Paz: YPFB/Talleres Gráficos Bolivianos, 1961.

Delgadillo Terceros, Wálter. *Fabriles en la historia nacional: Testimonio y sistematización de una experiencia sindical.* La Paz: Universidad Mayor de San Andrés, 1992.

Delgado González, Trifonio. *100 años de lucha obrera en Bolivia.* La Paz: Ediciones ISLA, 1984.

Derby, Lauren. "Gringo Chickens with Worms: Food and Nationalism in the Dominican Republic." In *Close Encounters of Empire*, edited by Joseph, LeGrand, and Salvatore, 451–493.

Dibbits, Ineke, Elizabeth Peredo Beltrán, and Ruth Volgger. *Polleras libertarias: Federación Obrera Femenina, 1927–1964.* La Paz: Taller de Historia y Participación de la Mujer, n.d.

Dizard, Wilson P. *The Strategy of Truth: The Story of the U.S. Information Service.* Washington, DC: Public Affairs, 1961.

Dorn, Glenn J. *The Truman Administration and Bolivia: Making the World Safe for Liberal Constitutional Oligarchy.* University Park: Pennsylvania State University Press, 2011.

Drake, Paul W. "The Hegemony of US Economic Doctrines in Latin America." In *Economic Doctrines in Latin America*, edited by FitzGerald and Thorp, 72–96.

———. "Introduction: The Political Economy of Foreign Advisers and Lenders in Latin America." In *Money Doctors, Foreign Debts, and Economic Reforms*, edited by Drake, xi–xxxiii.

———. *The Money Doctor in the Andes: The Kemmerer Missions, 1923–1933.* Durham, NC: Duke University Press, 1989.

———, ed. *Money Doctors, Foreign Debts, and Economic Reforms in Latin America from the 1890s to the Present.* Wilmington, DE: Scholarly Resources, 1994.

Dudziak, Mary L. *Cold War Civil Rights: Race and the Image of American Democracy.* Princeton, NJ: Princeton University Press, 2000.

———. "Desegregation as a Cold War Imperative." *Stanford Law Review* 41, no. 1 (1988): 61–120.

Duggan, Laurence. *The Americas: The Search for Hemisphere Security.* New York: Holt, 1949.

Dunkerley, James. "The Bolivian Revolution at 60: Politics and Historiography." *Journal of Latin American Studies* 45 (2013): 325–350.

———. "The Origins of the Bolivian Revolution in the Twentieth Century:

Some Reflections." In *Proclaiming Revolution*, edited by Grindle and Domingo, 135–163.

———. *Rebellion in the Veins: Political Struggle in Bolivia, 1952–82*. London: Verso, 1984.

Earle, Ethan. "Bolivia and the Changing Shape of U.S. Power." *NACLA Report on the Americas* 45, no. 4 (2012): 12–15.

ECLA. *See* United Nations, Economic Commission for Latin America (UN ECLA).

Eckstein, Susan. "The Impact of Revolution on Social Welfare in Latin America." *Theory and Society* 11, no. 1 (1982): 43–94.

———. "Transformation of a 'Revolution from Below': Bolivia and International Capital." *Comparative Studies in Society and History* 25, no. 1 (1983): 105–135.

Eder, George Jackson. *Inflation and Development in Latin America: A Case History of Inflation and Stabilization in Bolivia*. Ann Arbor: University of Michigan Press, 1968.

Eisenhower, Milton S. *The Wine Is Bitter: The United States and Latin America*. Garden City, NY: Doubleday, 1963.

Erickson, Kenneth Paul, Patrick V. Peppe, and Hobart A. Spalding Jr. "Research on the Urban Working Class and Organized Labor in Argentina, Brazil, and Chile: What Is Left to Be Done?" *Latin American Research Review* 9, no. 2 (1974): 115–142.

Escobar, Arturo. *Encountering Development: The Making and Unmaking of the Third World*. Princeton, NJ: Princeton University Press, 1995.

Evans, Peter B. *Dependent Development: The Alliance of Multinational, State and Local Capital in Brazil*. Princeton, NJ: Princeton University Press, 1979.

Fabricant, Nicole, and Bret Gustafson, eds. *Remapping Bolivia: Resources, Territory, and Indigeneity in a Plurinational State*. Santa Fe, NM: SAR Press, 2011.

Fanon, Frantz. *The Wretched of the Earth*. Translation by Constance Farrington. New York: Grove Press, 1963.

Farthing, Linda C., and Benjamin H. Kohl. *Evo's Bolivia: Continuity and Change*. Austin: University of Texas Press, 2014.

Federación Departamental de Trabajadores Fabriles de La Paz. *Los fabriles vistos por ellos mismos: Una investigación participativa con Trabajadores Fabriles de La Paz*. La Paz: Aguirre, 1992.

Fein, Seth. "Everyday Forms of Transnational Collaboration: U.S. Film Propaganda in Cold War Mexico." In *Close Encounters of Empire*, edited by Joseph, LeGrand, and Salvatore, 400–450.

———. "New Empire into Old: Making Mexican Newsreels the Cold War Way." *Diplomatic History* 28, no. 5 (2004): 703–748.

Felix, David. "An Alternative View of the 'Monetarist'—'Structuralist' Controversy." In *Latin American Issues: Essays and Comments*, edited by Albert O. Hirschman, 81–93. New York: Twentieth Century Fund, 1961.

Fellmann Velarde, José. *Historia de Bolivia*. 2 vols. La Paz: Los Amigos del Libro, 1968–1970.

———. *Víctor Paz Estenssoro: El hombre y la revolución.* La Paz: A. Tejerina, 1954.

Fernández Soliz, Jorge. *Tema: El petróleo.* La Paz: Los Amigos del Libro, 1976.

Field, Thomas C. Jr. *From Development to Dictatorship: Bolivia and the Alliance for Progress in the Kennedy Era.* Ithaca, NY: Cornell University Press, 2014.

———. "Ideology as Strategy: Military-Led Modernization and the Origins of the Alliance for Progress in Bolivia." *Diplomatic History* 36, no. 1 (2012): 147–183.

FitzGerald, Valpy, and Rosemary Thorp, eds. *Economic Doctrines in Latin America: Origins, Embedding, and Evolution.* Houndmills, UK: Palgrave Macmillan, 2005.

Fones-Wolf, Elizabeth A. *Selling Free Enterprise: The Business Assault on Labor and Liberalism, 1945–60.* Urbana: University of Illinois Press, 1994.

Foran, John, and Jeff Goodwin. "Revolutionary Outcomes in Iran and Nicaragua: Coalition Fragmentation, War, and the Limits of Social Transformation." *Theory and Society* 22 (1993): 209–247.

Ford, Bacon & Davis, Inc. *Mining Industry of Bolivia: A Report to the Bolivian Ministry of Mines and Petroleum.* 9 vols. Chicago: FBD, 1956.

Francovich, Guillermo. *Mitos profundos de Bolivia.* 2nd ed. La Paz: Los Amigos del Libro, 1987.

Friedman, Max Paul. *Rethinking Anti-Americanism: The History of an Exceptional Concept in American Foreign Relations.* New York: Cambridge University Press, 2012.

Gallo, Carmenza. *Taxes and State Power: Political Instability in Bolivia, 1900–1950.* Philadelphia, PA: Temple University Press, 1991.

García, Raul Alfonso. *Diez años de reforma agraria en Bolivia.* La Paz: Dirección Nacional de Informaciones, 1963.

Germani, Gino. *Política y sociedad en una época de transición: De la sociedad tradicional a la sociedad de masas.* Buenos Aires: Paidós, 1962.

Gildner, R. Matthew. "Indomestizo Modernism: National Development and Indigenous Integration in Postrevolutionary Bolivia, 1952–1964." PhD diss., University of Texas, 2012.

Gillis, Justin. "In Sign of Global Warming, 1,600 Years of Ice in Peru's Andes Melted in 25 Years." *New York Times*, April 5, 2013.

Gilman, Nils. *Mandarins of the Future: Modernization Theory in Cold War America.* Baltimore, MD: Johns Hopkins University Press, 2003.

Gisbert Nogué, Miguel. "Discurso del Ing. Miguel Gisbert Nogué." Speech delivered to Third Plenary Session of CEPAL international meeting, La Paz, May 1957. La Paz: Editorial del Estado, 1957.

Gledhill, John. "The People's Oil: Nationalism, Globalisation, and the Possibility of Another Country in Brazil, Mexico, and Venezuela." In *Crude Domination*, edited by Behrends, Reyna, and Schlee, 165–189.

Gleijeses, Piero. *Shattered Hope: The Guatemalan Revolution and the United States, 1944–1954.* Princeton, NJ: Princeton University Press, 1991.

Gobat, Michel. *Confronting the American Dream: Nicaragua under U.S. Imperial Rule*. Durham, NC: Duke University Press, 2005.

Gómez, Luis A. *El Alto de pie: Una insurrección aymara en Bolivia*. La Paz: HdP/Comuna/Indymedia, 2004.

Gómez d'Angelo, Walter. "Bolivia: Problems of a Pre- and Post-Revolutionary Export Economy." *Journal of Developing Areas* 10, no. 4 (1976): 461–484.

———. *La minería en el desarrollo económico de Bolivia, 1900–1970*. La Paz: Los Amigos del Libro, 1978.

Goodwin, Jeff. *No Other Way Out: States and Revolutionary Movements, 1945–1991*. Cambridge, UK: Cambridge University Press, 2001.

Gootenberg, Paul. *Imagining Development: Economic Ideas in Peru's "Fictitious Prosperity" of Guano, 1840–1880*. Berkeley: University of California Press, 1993.

Gordillo, José M. *Campesinos revolucionarios en Bolivia: Identidad, territorio y sexualidad en el Valle Alto de Cochabamba, 1952–1964*. La Paz: Plural, 2000.

Gotkowitz, Laura. *A Revolution for Our Rights: Indigenous Struggles for Land and Justice in Bolivia, 1880–1952*. Durham, NC: Duke University Press, 2007.

Gould, Jeffrey L. *To Lead As Equals: Rural Protest and Political Consciousness in Chinandega, Nicaragua, 1912–1979*. Chapel Hill: University of North Carolina Press, 1990.

Gourevitch, Peter A. "Economic Ideas, International Influences and Domestic Politics: A Comparative Perspective." In *Economic Doctrines in Latin America*, edited by FitzGerald and Thorp, 23–47.

Gramsci, Antonio. *Selections from the Prison Notebooks of Antonio Gramsci*. Edited and translation by Quintin Hoare and Geoffrey Nowell Smith. New York: International, 1971.

Grandin, Greg. *Empire's Workshop: Latin America, the United States, and the Rise of the New Imperialism*. New York: Metropolitan, 2006.

———. *The Last Colonial Massacre: Latin America in the Cold War*. Chicago: University of Chicago Press, 2004.

———. "The Liberal Traditions in the Americas: Rights, Sovereignty, and the Origins of Liberal Multilateralism." *American Historical Review* 117, no. 1 (2012): 68–91.

———. "Off the Beach: The United States, Latin America, and the Cold War." In *A Companion to Post-1945 America*, edited by Jean-Christophe Agnew and Roy Rosensweig, 426–445. New York: Blackwell, 2002.

Grandin, Greg, and Gilbert M. Joseph, eds. *A Century of Revolution: Insurgent and Counterinsurgent Violence during Latin America's Long Cold War*. Durham, NC: Duke University Press, 2010.

Gray Molina, George. "La economía boliviana 'más allá del gás.'" *América Latina Hoy* 43 (2006): 63–85.

Green, David. *The Containment of Latin America: A History of the Myths and Realities of the Good Neighbor Policy*. Chicago: Quadrangle Books, 1971.

Grindle, Merilee S., and Pilar Domingo, eds. *Proclaiming Revolution: Bo-

livia in Comparative Perspective. Cambridge, MA: David Rockefeller Center for Latin American Studies, Harvard University; London: Institute of Latin American Studies, 2003.

Guevara Arze, Wálter. *Plan inmediato de política económica del gobierno de la revolución nacional*. La Paz: República de Bolivia, Ministerio de Relaciones Exteriores, Departamento de Prensa y Publicaciones, 1955.

———. "Plan for the Diversification of Production: Memorándum para el Dr. Miltón Eisenhower." August 1953. ANB-WGA, Caja 28.

Guha, Ranajit. *Dominance without Hegemony: History and Power and Colonial India*. Cambridge, MA: Harvard University Press, 1998.

———. *Elementary Aspects of Peasant Insurgency in Colonial India*. Durham, NC: Duke University Press, 1999 (1983).

Guimarães, Alice Soares. "La capitalización de los hidrocarburos y la modernidad: Un análisis de las ideas subyacentes al modelo de gestión y de sus críticas." *Umbrales* (La Paz) 20 (2010): 71–104.

Gustafson, Bret. "Amid Gas, Where Is the Revolution?" *NACLA Report on the Americas* 46, no. 1 (2013): 61–66.

———. "Flashpoints of Sovereignty: Territorial Conflict and Natural Gas in Bolivia." In *Crude Domination*, edited by Behrends, Reyna, and Schlee, 220–240.

Gutiérrez Aguilar, Raquel. *Los ritmos del Pachakuti: Movilización y levantamiento indígena-popular en Bolivia (2000–2005)*. La Paz: Ediciones Yachaywasi and Textos Rebeldes, 2008.

Haines, Gerald K. *The Americanization of Brazil: A Study of U.S. Cold War Diplomacy in the Third World, 1945–1954*. Wilmington, DE: Scholarly Resources, 1989.

Hall, Peter A., ed. *The Political Power of Economic Ideas: Keynesianism across Nations*. Princeton, NJ: Princeton University Press, 1989.

Harrison, Lawrence E. *Underdevelopment Is a State of Mind: The Latin American Case*. Rev. ed. Lanham, MD: Madison Books, 2000.

Harvey, David. *The New Imperialism*. New York: Oxford University Press, 2003.

Healy, Kevin. *Llamas, Weavings, and Organic Chocolate: Multicultural Grassroots Development in the Andes and Amazon of Bolivia*. Notre Dame, IN: University of Notre Dame Press, 2001.

Henderson, John W. *The United States Information Agency*. New York: Praeger, 1969.

Higginbottom, Andy. "The Political Economy of Foreign Investment in Latin America: Dependency Revisited." *Latin American Perspectives* 40, no. 3 (2013): 184–206.

Hindery, Derrick. *From Enron to Evo: Pipeline Politics, Global Environmentalism, and Indigenous Rights in Bolivia*. Tucson: University of Arizona Press, 2013.

Hines, Sarah Thompson. "Dividing the Waters: How Power, Property, and Protest Transformed the Waterscape of Cochabamba, Bolivia, 1879–2000." PhD diss., University of California, Berkeley, 2015.

Hirschman, Albert O. *A Bias for Hope: Essays on Development and Latin America*. New Haven, CT: Yale University Press, 1971.

————. *Essays in Trespassing: Economics to Politics and Beyond*. Cambridge, UK: Cambridge University Press, 1981.

Hobsbawm, Eric J. "The Labour Aristocracy in Nineteenth-Century Britain." In *Labouring Men: Studies in the History of Labour*, 272–315. London: Weidenfeld and Nicolson, 1964.

Huanacuni Mamani, Fernando. *Vivir bien/buen vivir: Filosofía, políticas, estrategias y experiencias regionales*. La Paz: Coordinadora Andina de Organizaciones Indígenas, 2010.

Humphreys, Macartan, Jeffrey D. Sachs, and Joseph E. Stiglitz, eds. *Escaping the Resource Curse*. New York: Columbia University Press, 2007.

Humphreys Bebbington, Denise. "State-Indigenous Tensions over Hydrocarbon Expansion in the Bolivian Chaco." In *Social Conflict*, edited by Bebbington, 134–152.

Hylton, Forrest. "Tierra común: Caciques, artesanos e intelectuales radicales y la rebelión de Chayanta." In *Ya es otro tiempo el presente: Cuatro momentos de insurgencia indígena*, by Forrest Hylton, Félix Patzi, Sergio Serulnikov, and Sinclair Thomson, 127–187. La Paz: Muela del Diablo, 2003.

Hylton, Forrest, and Sinclair Thomson. *Revolutionary Horizons: Past and Present in Bolivian Politics*. London: Verso, 2007.

Ingram, George M. *Expropriation of U.S. Property in South America: Nationalization of Oil and Copper Companies in Peru, Bolivia, and Chile*. New York: Praeger, 1974.

Iriarte, Gregorio. *Los mineros: Sus luchas, frustraciones y esperanzas*. La Paz: Puerta del Sol, 1983.

James, Daniel. *Resistance and Integration: Peronism and the Argentine Working Class, 1946–1976*. Cambridge, UK: Cambridge University Press, 1988.

John, S. Sándor. *Bolivia's Radical Tradition: Permanent Revolution in the Andes*. Tucson: University of Arizona Press, 2009.

Johnson, Lyndon B. "Las 5 normas básicas de política exterior del Presidente Lyndon B. Johnson." *Foro Universitario* 1, no. 8 (March 1966): 1–2.

Joint Bolivian–United States Labour Commission. *Labour Problems in Bolivia: Report of the Joint Bolivian-United States Labour Commission*. Montreal: International Labour Office, 1943.

Joseph, Gilbert M., Catherine C. LeGrand, and Ricardo D. Salvatore, eds. *Close Encounters of Empire: Writing the Cultural History of U.S.–Latin American Relations*. Durham, NC: Duke University Press, 1998.

Joseph, Gilbert M., and Daniel Nugent, eds. *Everyday Forms of State Formation: Revolution and the Negotiation of Rule in Modern Mexico*. Durham, NC: Duke University Press, 1994.

Joseph, Gilbert M., and Daniela Spenser, eds. *In from the Cold: Latin America's New Encounter with the Cold War*. Durham, NC: Duke University Press, 2008.

Justo, Liborio. *Bolivia: La revolución derrotada*. Cochabamba: Serrano, 1967.

Karl, Terry Lynn. *The Paradox of Plenty: Oil Booms and Petro-States*. Berkeley: University of California Press, 1998.

Katz, Friedrich. *The Secret War in Mexico: Europe, the United States, and the Mexican Revolution*. Chicago: University of Chicago Press, 1981.

Kaup, Brent Z. *Market Justice: Political Economic Struggle in Bolivia*. New York: Cambridge University Press, 2013.

Kelley, Jonathan, and Herbert S. Klein. *Revolution and the Rebirth of Inequality: A Theory Applied to the National Revolution in Bolivia*. Berkeley: University of California Press, 1981.

Klare, Michael T. *The Race for What's Left: The Global Scramble for the World's Last Resources*. New York: Metropolitan, 2012.

Klein, Herbert S. "American Oil Companies in Latin America: The Bolivian Experience." *Inter-American Economic Affairs* 18, no. 2 (1964): 47–72.

———. *Bolivia: Evolution of a Multiethnic Society*. New York: Oxford University Press, 1982.

———. *Orígenes de la revolución nacional boliviana: La crisis de la generación del Chaco*. La Paz: Juventud, 1968.

———. *Parties and Political Change in Bolivia, 1880–1952*. Cambridge, UK: Cambridge University Press, 1969.

———. "Social Change in Bolivia since 1952." In *Proclaiming Revolution*, edited by Grindle and Domingo, 232–258.

———. "'Social Constitutionalism' in Latin America: The Bolivian Experience of 1938." *The Americas* 22, no. 3 (1966): 258–276.

Klein, Herbert S., and José Alejandro Peres-Cajías. "Bolivian Oil and Natural Gas under State and Private Control, 1920–2010." *Bolivian Studies Journal/Revista de Estudios Bolivianos* 20 (2014): 141–164.

Knight, Alan. "The Domestic Dynamics of the Mexican and Bolivian Revolutions Compared." In *Proclaiming Revolution*, edited by Grindle and Domingo, 54–90.

———. *The Mexican Revolution*. 2 vols. Lincoln: University of Nebraska Press, 1986.

———. *U.S.-Mexican Relations, 1910–1940: An Interpretation*. La Jolla: Center for U.S.-Mexican Studies, University of California, San Diego, 1987.

Knudson, Jerry W. *Bolivia: Press and Revolution, 1932–1964*. Lanham, MD: University Press of America, 1986.

Kofas, Jon V. "The Politics of Austerity: The IMF and U.S. Foreign Policy in Bolivia, 1956–1964." *Journal of Developing Areas* 29, no. 2 (1995): 213–236.

Kohl, Benjamin H., and Linda C. Farthing. *Impasse in Bolivia: Neoliberal Hegemony and Popular Resistance*. London: Zed Books, 2006.

———. "Material Constraints to Popular Imaginaries: The Extractive Economy and Resource Nationalism in Bolivia." *Political Geography* 31, no. 4 (2012): 225–235.

Kohl, James V. "Peasant and Revolution in Bolivia, April 9, 1952–August 2, 1953." *Hispanic American Historical Review* 58, no. 2 (1978): 238–259.

Kolko, Gabriel. *Confronting the Third World: United States Foreign Policy, 1945–1980*. New York: Pantheon, 1988.

Krenn, Michael L. *U.S. Policy toward Economic Nationalism in Latin America, 1917–1929*. Wilmington, DE: Scholarly Resources, 1990.

Kuznets, Simon. "Economic Growth of Small Nations." In *Economic Consequences of the Size of Nations*, edited by E. A. G. Robinson, 14–32. New York: St. Martin's, 1960.

LaFeber, Walter. *The New Empire: An Interpretation of American Expansion, 1860–1898*. Ithaca, NY: Cornell University Press, 1963.

Lagos, María L., ed. *Nos hemos forjado así: Al rojo vivo y a puro golpe. Historias del Comité de Amas de Casa de Siglo XX*. La Paz: Plural, 2006.

Landsberger, Henry A. "The Labor Elite: Is It Revolutionary?" In *Elites in Latin America*, edited by Seymour Martin Lipset and Aldo E. Solari, 256–300. London: Oxford University Press, 1967.

Lanning, Eldon. "Governmental Capabilities in a Revolutionary Situation: The MNR in Bolivia." *Inter-American Economic Affairs* 23, no. 2 (1969): 3–22.

Larson, Brooke. *Trials of Nation Making: Liberalism, Race, and Ethnicity in the Andes, 1810–1910*. Cambridge, UK: Cambridge University Press, 2004.

———. "Warisata: A Historical Footnote." *ReVista: Harvard Review of Latin America* 11, no. 1 (2011): 65–67.

Latham, Michael E. *Modernization as Ideology: American Social Science and "Nation Building" in the Kennedy Era*. Chapel Hill: University of North Carolina Press, 2000.

Lay, Jann, Ranier Thiele, and Manfred Wiebelt. "Resource Booms, Inequality, and Poverty: The Case of Gas in Bolivia." *Review of Income and Wealth* 54, no. 3 (2008): 407–437.

Lazar, Sian. *El Alto, Rebel City: Self and Citizenship in Andean Bolivia*. Durham, NC: Duke University Press, 2008.

Lazarte R., Jorge. *Movimiento obrero y procesos políticos en Bolivia: Historia de la C.O.B., 1952–1987*. La Paz: Edobol, 1989.

Lederman, Daniel, and William F. Maloney, eds. *Natural Resources: Neither Curse nor Destiny*. Stanford, CA: Stanford University Press; Washington, DC: World Bank, 2007.

Legg, H. J. *Bolivia: Economic and Commercial Conditions in Bolivia*. London: His Majesty's Stationery Office, 1952.

Lehm Ardaya, Zulema, and Silvia Rivera Cusicanqui, eds. *Los artesanos libertarios y la ética del trabajo*. La Paz: Gramma, 1988.

Lehman, Kenneth D. *Bolivia and the United States: A Limited Partnership*. Athens: University of Georgia Press, 1999.

———. "Braked but Not Broken: The United States and Revolutionaries in Mexico and Bolivia." In *Proclaiming Revolution*, edited by Grindle and Domingo, 91–116.

———. "Revolutions and Attributions: Making Sense of Eisenhower Administration Policies in Bolivia and Guatemala." *Diplomatic History* 22, no. 2 (1997): 185–213.

Lenin, V. I. *Imperialism, the Highest Stage of Capitalism: A Popular Outline*. New York: International, 1939.

Leonard, Olen E. "La Paz, Bolivia: Its Population and Growth." *American Sociological Review* 13, no. 4 (1948): 448–454.

Levin, Jonathan V. *The Export Economies: Their Pattern of Development in Historical Perspective.* Cambridge, MA: Harvard University Press, 1960.

Libermann Z., Jacobo. *Bolivia: 10 años de la revolución (1952–1962).* La Paz: República de Bolivia, Dirección Nacional de Informaciones, 1962.

López, Pedro N. *Política petrolífera.* La Paz: Boliviana, 1929.

López Vigil, José Ignacio. *Una mina de coraje.* Quito: Asociación Latinoamericana de Educación Radiofónica, 1984.

Lora, Guillermo. "La clase obrera después de 1952." In *Bolivia, hoy,* edited by Zavaleta, 169–218.

———. *Diccionario político histórico cultural.* 2nd ed. La Paz: Masas, 1986.

———, ed. *Documentos políticos de Bolivia.* La Paz: Los Amigos del Libro, 1970.

———. *La estabilización, una impostura.* La Paz: Masas, 1960.

———. *Historia del movimiento obrero boliviano, 1923–1933.* La Paz: Los Amigos del Libro, 1970.

———. *Historia del movimiento obrero boliviano, 1933–1952.* La Paz: Los Amigos del Libro, 1980.

———. *A History of the Bolivian Labour Movement, 1848–1971.* Edited and abridged by Laurence Whitehead. Translation by Christine Whitehead. Cambridge, UK: Cambridge University Press, 1977.

———. *Movimiento obrero contemporáneo.* La Paz: Masas, 1979.

———. *La revolución boliviana.* La Paz: Difusión SRL, 1963.

Love, Joseph L. *Crafting the Third World: Theorizing Underdevelopment in Rumania and Brazil.* Stanford, CA: Stanford University Press, 1996.

———. "Economic Ideas and Ideologies in Latin America since 1930." In *The Cambridge History of Latin America,* edited by Leslie Bethell, vol. 6, part 1, 393–460. Cambridge, UK: Cambridge University Press, 1994.

———. "The Rise and Decline of Economic Structuralism in Latin America: New Dimensions." *Latin American Research Review* 40, no. 3 (2005): 100–125.

Loveman, Brian. *For la Patria: Politics and the Armed Forces in Latin America.* Wilmington, DE: Scholarly Resources, 1999.

McAdam, Doug. *Political Process and the Development of Black Insurgency, 1930–1970.* Chicago: University of Chicago Press, 1982.

McClintock, Michael. *Instruments of Statecraft: U.S. Guerilla Warfare, Counterinsurgency, and Counterterrorism, 1940–1990.* New York: Pantheon, 1992.

McConnell, J. Michael. "Annual Threat Assessment of the Intelligence Community for the House Permanent Select Committee on Intelligence." February 7, 2008. Washington, DC, Office of the Director of National Intelligence. http://www.dni.gov/files/documents/Newsroom/Testimonies/2008 0207_testimony.pdf.

McCoy, Alfred W., and Francisco A. Scarano, eds. *Colonial Crucible: Empire in the Making of the Modern American State.* Madison: University of Wisconsin Press, 2009.

Maier, Charles S. "The Politics of Productivity: Foundations of American International Economic Policy after World War II." *International Organization* 31, no. 4 (1977): 607–633.

———. "The Two Postwar Eras and the Conditions for Stability in Twentieth-Century Western Europe." *American Historical Review* 86, no. 2 (1981): 327–352.

Malloy, James M. *Bolivia: The Unfinished Revolution.* Pittsburgh, PA: University of Pittsburgh Press, 1970.

Malloy, James M., and Eduardo A. Gamarra. *Revolution and Reaction: Bolivia, 1964–1984.* New Brunswick, NJ: Transaction, 1988.

Mamani Ramírez, Pablo. *Microgobiernos barriales: Levantamiento de la ciudad de El Alto (octubre 2003).* El Alto, Bolivia: Centro de Asesoramiento para el Desarrollo Social/Instituto de Investigaciones Sociológicas, Universidad Mayor de San Andrés, 2005.

———. *El rugir de las multitudes: La fuerza de los levantamientos indígenas en Bolivia/Qullasuyu.* La Paz: Aruwiyiri, 2004.

Mariaca Bilbao, Enrique. *Mito y realidad del petróleo boliviano.* La Paz: Los Amigos del Libro, 1966.

Marini, Ruy Mauro. *Dialéctica de la dependencia.* Mexico City: Era, 1973.

Marof, Tristán [Gustavo Navarro]. *La justicia del inca.* Brussels: Edición Latino Americana, 1926.

———. *La tragedia del altiplano.* Buenos Aires: Claridad, 1935.

Marsh, Margaret Alexander. *The Bankers in Bolivia: A Study in American Foreign Investment.* New York: Vanguard, 1928.

Martí i Puig, Salvador, Claire Wright, José Aylwin, and Nancy Yáñez, eds. *Entre el desarrollo y el buen vivir: Recursos naturales y conflictos en los territorios indígenas.* Madrid: Libros de la Catarata, 2013.

Mayorga, Fernando. *Discurso y política en Bolivia.* La Paz: Centro de Estudios de la Realidad Económica y Social/ Instituto Latinoamericano de Investigaciones Sociales, 1993.

———. "Nacionalismo e indigenismo en el MAS: Los desafíos de la articulación hegemónica." *Decursos* (Cochabamba) 8, nos. 15–16 (2006): 135–164.

Meyer, Lorenzo. *México y Estados Unidos en el conflicto petrolero, 1917–1942.* Mexico City: El Colegio de México, 1968.

Middlebrook, Kevin J. *The Paradox of Revolution: Labor, the State, and Authoritarianism in Mexico.* Baltimore, MD: Johns Hopkins University Press, 1995.

Mills, C. Wright. *The Power Elite.* New York: Oxford University Press, 1956.

Mintz, Beth, and Michael Schwartz. *The Power Structure of American Business.* Chicago: University of Chicago Press, 1985.

Mitchell, Christopher. *The Legacy of Populism in Bolivia: From the MNR to Military Rule.* New York: Praeger, 1977.

Mitchell, Timothy. *Carbon Democracy: Political Power in the Age of Oil.* London: Verso, 2011.

Mittleman, Earl N. "El socialismo en los Estados Unidos: La revolución permanente." *Foro Universitario* 2, no. 18 (January 1967): 1–4.

Mokrani, Leila. "Reformas de última década en el sector de hidrocarburos en Bolivia: Esquemas de apropiación y reproducción de la renta." *Umbrales* (La Paz) 20 (2010): 23–70.

Molina, Fernando. *El pensamiento boliviano sobre los recursos naturales.* La Paz: Pulso, 2009.

Molina, Patricia. "Explotación de hidrocarburos y conflictos ambientales en Bolivia." In *Miradas, voces y sonidos: Conflictos ambientales en Bolivia*, edited by Jenny Gruenberger, 71–78. La Paz: Foro Boliviano sobre Medio Ambiente y Desarrollo/Observatorio Latinoamericano de Conflictos Ambientales, 1999.

Montecinos, Verónica. *Economists, Politics, and the State: Chile, 1958–1994.* Amsterdam: Center for Latin American Research and Documentation, 1998.

Montecinos, Verónica, and John Markoff. "From the Power of Economic Ideas to the Power of Economists." In *The Other Mirror: Grand Theory through the Lens of Latin America*, edited by Miguel Angel Centeno and Fernando López-Alves, 105–150. Princeton, NJ: Princeton University Press, 2001.

Montenegro, Carlos. *Frente al derecho del estado: El oro de la Standard Oil (El petróleo, sangre de Bolivia).* La Paz: Trabajo, 1938.

———. *Nacionalismo y coloniaje: Su expresión histórica en la prensa de Bolivia.* La Paz: Ediciones Autonomía, 1943.

Morales, Juan Antonio. "Post-Neoliberal Policies and the Populist Tradition." *ReVista: Harvard Review of Latin America* 11, no. 1 (2011): 34–36.

Murillo, Mario. *La bala no mata sino el destino: Una crónica de la insurrección popular de 1952 en Bolivia.* La Paz: Plural, 2012.

Muttitt, Greg. *Fuel on the Fire: Oil and Politics in Occupied Iraq.* New York: New Press, 2012.

Nash, June. *We Eat the Mines and the Mines Eat Us: Dependency and Exploitation in Bolivian Tin Mines.* New York: Columbia University Press, 1993.

Nye, Joseph S. Jr. *Soft Power: The Means to Success in World Politics.* New York: Public Affairs, 2004.

O'Connor, Harvey. *The Empire of Oil.* New York: Monthly Review, 1955.

Oporto, Henry. "El mito del eterno retorno." Review of *El pensamiento boliviano sobre los recursos naturales*, by Fernando Molina. *Umbrales* (La Paz) 20 (2010): 337–343.

Orihuela, José Carlos. "How Do 'Mineral-States' Learn? Path-Dependence, Networks, and Policy Change in the Development of Economic Institutions." *World Development* 43 (2013): 138–148.

Pacino, Nicole. "Constructing a New Bolivian Society: Public Health Reforms and the Consolidation of the Bolivian National Revolution." *Latin Americanist* 57, no. 4 (2013): 25–55.

Pansters, Wil, ed. *Violence, Coercion, and State-Making in Twentieth-Century Mexico: The Other Half of the Centaur.* Stanford, CA: Stanford University Press, 2012.

Park, James William. *Latin American Underdevelopment: A History of Per-*

spectives in the United States, 1870–1965. Baton Rouge: Louisiana State University Press, 1995.

Paz Estenssoro, Víctor. "Bolivia." In *El pensamiento económico latino-americano*, edited by Fondo de Cultura Económica (FCE), 36–69. Mexico City: FCE, 1945.

———. *Discursos parlamentarios.* La Paz: Canata, 1955.

———. "Ejecutoria de un programa de gobierno." *Pututu*, August 22, 1953, 12–18.

———. "El MNR, réplica de la historia" (October 1948). Reprinted in *Documentos políticos*, edited by Lora, 169–179.

———. *El pensamiento revolucionario de Víctor Paz Estenssoro.* La Paz: Burillo, 1954.

———. "Programa del Movimiento Nacionalista Revolucionario" (February 1953). Speech to Sixth Convention of the MNR, La Paz, February 13, 1953. Reprinted in *Documentos políticos*, edited by Lora, 157–168.

———. *La revolución boliviana.* La Paz: República de Bolivia, Dirección Nacional de Informaciones, 1964.

———. *Víctor Paz Estenssoro y la masacre de Catavi.* La Paz: Movimiento Nacionalista Revolucionario, 1943.

Peñaloza Cordero, Luis. *Historia del Movimiento Nacionalista Revolucionario, 1941–1952.* La Paz: Juventud, 1963.

———. *Historia económica de Bolivia.* Vol. 2. La Paz: Artística, 1947.

———. *La Paz en su IV centenario, 1548–1948.* Vol. 4, *Monografía económica.* La Paz: Comité Pro IV Centenario de la Fundación de La Paz, 1948.

Perreault, Thomas. "Extracting Justice: Natural Gas, Indigenous Mobilization, and the Bolivian State." In *The Politics of Resource Extraction*, edited by Sawyer and Gómez, 75–102.

Philip, George. "The Expropriation in Comparative Perspective." In *The Mexican Petroleum Industry in the Twentieth Century*, edited by Jonathan C. Brown and Alan Knight, 173–188. Austin: University of Texas Press, 1992.

———. *Oil and Politics in Latin America: Nationalist Movements and State Companies.* Cambridge, UK: Cambridge University Press, 1982.

Platt, Tristan. *Estado boliviano y ayllu andino: Tierra y tributo en el norte de Potosí.* Lima: Instituto de Estudios Peruanos, 1982.

Polanyi, Karl. *The Great Transformation: The Political and Economic Origins of Our Time.* Boston: Beacon, 1957.

Pruden, Hernán. "Cruceños into Cambas: Regionalism and Revolutionary Nationalism in Santa Cruz de la Sierra, Bolivia (1935–1959)." PhD diss., State University of New York, Stony Brook, 2012.

Quiroga Santa Cruz, Marcelo. *Desarrollo con soberanía: La desnacionalización del petróleo.* Cochabamba: Universitaria, 1967.

———. *Oleocracia o patria.* Mexico City: Siglo XXI, 1982.

———. *El saqueo de Bolivia.* La Paz: Puerta del Sol, 1973.

Rabe, Stephen G. *Eisenhower and Latin America: The Foreign Policy of Anticommunism.* Chapel Hill: University of North Carolina Press, 1988.

———. *The Most Dangerous Area in the World: John F. Kennedy Confronts*

Communist Revolution in Latin America. Chapel Hill: University of North Carolina Press, 1999.

Reed, Jean-Pierre, and John Foran. "Political Cultures of Opposition: Exploring Idioms, Ideologies, and Revolutionary Agency in the Case of Nicaragua." *Critical Sociology* 28, no. 3 (2002): 335–370.

Regalsky, Pablo. "Political Processes and the Reconfiguration of the State in Bolivia." Translation by Mariana Ortega Breña. *Latin American Perspectives* 37, no. 3 (2010): 35–50.

República de Bolivia. *See* Bolivia, República de.

Reyna, Stephen P. "Constituting Domination/Constructing Monsters: Imperialism, Cultural Desire and Anti-Beowulfs in the Chadian Petro-State." In *Crude Domination*, edited by Behrends, Reyna, and Schlee, 132–162.

Rivera Cusicanqui, Silvia. *Oprimidos pero no vencidos: Luchas del campesinado aymara y qhechwa, 1900–1980.* 4th ed. La Paz: Aruwiyiri/Yachaywasi, 2003.

Robinson, Ian. "Does Neoliberal Restructuring Promote Social Movement Unionism? U.S. Developments in Comparative Perspective." In *Unions in a Globalized Environment: Changing Borders, Organizational Boundaries, and Social Roles*, edited by Bruce Nissen, 189–235. Armonk, NY: M. E. Sharpe, 2002.

Robinson, William I. *Promoting Polyarchy: Globalization, US Intervention, and Hegemony.* Cambridge, UK: Cambridge University Press, 1996.

Rodas Morales, Hugo. *Marcelo Quiroga Santa Cruz: El socialismo vivido.* 3 vols. La Paz: Plural, 2008–2010.

Rodman, Kenneth A. *Sanctity versus Sovereignty: The United States and the Nationalization of Natural Resource Investments.* New York: Columbia University Press, 1988.

Rodríguez García, Huascar. *La choledad antiestatal: El anarcosindicalismo en el movimiento obrero boliviano (1912–1965).* La Paz: Muela del Diablo, 2012.

Rodríguez Ostria, Gustavo. *El socavón y el sindicato: Ensayos históricos sobre los trabajadores mineros, siglos XIX–XX.* La Paz: Instituto de Investigaciones Sociológicas, 1991.

Roseberry, William. "Hegemony and the Language of Contention." In *Everyday Forms of State Formation*, edited by Joseph and Nugent, 355–364.

Ross, Michael L. *The Oil Curse: How Petroleum Wealth Shapes the Development of Nations.* Princeton, NJ: Princeton University Press, 2012.

Rostow, W. W. "Problemas del desarrollo económico." *Foro Universitario* 1, no. 6 (January 1966): 9–13, 21.

Roxborough, Ian. "The Analysis of Labour Movements in Latin America: Typologies and Theories." *Bulletin of Latin American Research* 1, no. 1 (1981): 81–95.

———. "Mexico." In *Latin America*, edited by Bethell and Roxborough, 190–216.

———. *Theories of Underdevelopment.* Houndmills, UK: Macmillan Education, 1979.

Rubin, Barry, and Judith Colp Rubin. *Hating America: A History.* New York: Oxford University Press, 2004.

Rusk, Dean. "'Buscamos una paz duradera . . . .'" *Foro Universitario* 2, no. 18 (January 1967): 5–10.

Sachs, Jeffrey D., and Andrew M. Warner. 1997. "Sources of Slow Growth in African Economies." *Journal of African Economies* 6, no. 3 (1997): 335–376.

Salmón, Josefa. *El espejo indígena: El discurso indigenista en Bolivia, 1900–1956.* La Paz: Plural, 1997.

Sawyer, Suzana, and Edmund Terence Gómez, eds. *The Politics of Resource Extraction: Indigenous Peoples, Multinational Corporations, and the State.* Houndmills, UK: Palgrave Macmillan, 2012.

Scheper-Hughes, Nancy. "Theft of Life: The Globalization of Organ Stealing Rumors." *Anthropology Today* 12, no. 3 (1996): 3–11.

Schiller, Naomi. "'Now That the Petroleum Is Ours': Community Media, State Spectacle, and Oil Nationalism in Venezuela." In *Crude Domination*, edited by Behrends, Reyna, and Schlee, 190–219.

Seers, Dudley. "A Theory of Inflation and Growth in Under-Developed Economies Based on the Experience of Latin America." *Oxford Economic Papers* 14, no. 2 (1962): 173–195.

Shesko, Elizabeth. "Conscript Nation: Negotiating Authority and Belonging in the Bolivian Barracks, 1900–1950." PhD diss., Duke University, 2012.

Siekmeier, James F. *The Bolivian Revolution and the United States, 1952 to the Present.* University Park: Pennsylvania State University Press, 2011.

———. "Fighting Economic Nationalism: U.S. Economic Aid and Development Policy toward Latin America, 1953–1961." PhD diss., Cornell University, 1993.

Sierra, Luis Manuel. "Indigenous Neighborhood Residents in the Urbanization of La Paz, Bolivia, 1910–1950." PhD diss., State University of New York, Binghamton, 2013.

Siles Zuazo, Hernán. *Mensaje al Honorable Congreso Nacional.* Speech delivered August 6, 1958. La Paz: Editorial del Estado, 1958.

Simon, Herbert A. "Organizations and Markets." *Journal of Economic Perspectives* 5, no. 2 (1991): 25–44.

Smale, Robert L. *I Sweat the Flavor of Tin: Labor Activism in Early Twentieth-Century Bolivia.* Pittsburgh, PA: University of Pittsburgh Press, 2010.

Smelser, Neil J. *Theory of Collective Behavior.* New York: Free Press of Glencoe, 1963.

Smith, Robert Freeman. *The United States and Revolutionary Nationalism in Mexico, 1916–1932.* Chicago: University of Chicago Press, 1972.

Solberg, Carl E. *Oil and Nationalism in Argentina: A History.* Stanford, CA: Stanford University Press, 1979.

Soliz, Carmen. "Fields of Revolution: The Politics of Agrarian Reform in Bolivia, 1935–1971." PhD diss., New York University, 2014.

———. "La modernidad esquiva: Debates políticos e intelectuales sobre la reforma agraria en Bolivia (1935–1952)." *Ciencia y Cultura* 29 (2012): 23–49.

Soliz Rada, Andrés. *El gas en el destino nacional.* La Paz: Los Amigos del Libro, 1984.

Sorensen, Thomas C. *The Word War: The Story of American Propaganda.* New York: Harper and Row, 1968.

Soruco Sologuren, Ximena. "De la goma a la soya: El proyecto histórico de la élite cruceña." In *Los barones del oriente: El poder en Santa Cruz ayer y hoy,* by Ximena Soruco, Wilfredo Plata, and Gustavo Medeiros, 1–100. Santa Cruz, Bolivia: Fundación Tierra, 2008.

Soto, César. *Historia del Pacto Militar-Campesino.* Cochabamba: Centro de Estudios de la Realidad Económica y Social, 1994.

Spalding, Hobart A. Jr. "The Parameters of Labor in Hispanic America." *Science and Society* 36, no. 2 (1972): 202–216.

Stepan-Norris, Judith, and Maurice Zeitlin. *Left Out: Reds and America's Industrial Unions.* Cambridge, UK: Cambridge University Press, 2003.

Stern, Steve J., ed. *Resistance, Rebellion, and Consciousness in the Andean Peasant World, 18th to 20th Centuries.* Madison: University of Wisconsin Press, 1987.

Taffet, Jeffrey F. *Foreign Aid as Foreign Policy: The Alliance for Progress in Latin America.* New York: Routledge, 2007.

Taller de Historia Oral Andina (THOA) and Sindicato Central de Constructores y Albañiles de La Paz. *Los constructores de la ciudad: Tradiciones de lucha y de trabajo del Sindicato Central de Constructores y Albañiles de La Paz (1908–1980).* La Paz: THOA, 1986.

Tapia, Luis. *La producción del conocimiento local: Historia y política en la obra de René Zavaleta.* La Paz: Muela del Diablo, 2002.

Thompson, E. P. "The Moral Economy of the English Crowd in the Eighteenth Century." *Past and Present* 50 (1971): 76–136.

Tinker Salas, Miguel. *The Enduring Legacy: Oil, Culture, and Society in Venezuela.* Durham, NC: Duke University Press, 2009.

Unión Boliviana de Defensa del Petróleo. *¡Defendamos el petróleo! Manifiesto de la Unión Boliviana de Defensa el Petróleo.* 1941. Reprint, La Paz: Universidad Mayor de San Andrés, 1996.

United Nations, Economic Commission for Latin America (UN ECLA [CEPAL]). *Análisis y proyecciones del desarrollo económico.* Vol. 4, *El desarrollo económico de Bolivia.* Mexico City: UN Departamento de Asuntos Económicos y Sociales, 1958.

———. *Anuario estadístico de América Latina y el Caribe 2014.* Santiago: United Nations, 2014.

———. "The Economic Development of Bolivia." *Economic Bulletin for Latin America* 2, no. 2 (1957): 19–72.

———. *The Economic Development of Latin America and Its Principal Problems.* Lake Success, NY: UN Department of Economic Affairs, 1950.

———. "The Economic Policy of Bolivia in 1952–64." *Economic Bulletin for Latin America* 12, no. 2 (1967): 61–89.

———. *Economic Survey of Latin America: 1951–1952.* New York: UN Department of Economic Affairs, 1954.

———. *Economic Survey of Latin America: 1954.* New York: ECLA, 1955.

———. *Economic Survey of Latin America: 1956.* New York: ECLA, 1957.

———. *Economic Survey of Latin America: 1966.* New York: ECLA, 1968.

————. *Economic Survey of Latin America: 1969*. New York: ECLA, 1970.

————. *Economic Survey of Latin America: 1979*. Santiago: United Nations, 1981.

————. "Investment in the Petroleum Industry in Latin America." *Economic Bulletin for Latin America* 13, no. 2 (1968): 3–30.

————. *Panorama social de América Latina: 2012*. Santiago: United Nations, 2013.

United Nations, Technical Assistance Administration (UNTAA). *Report of the United Nations Mission of Technical Assistance to Bolivia*. New York: United Nations, 1951.

United States, Department of State (DoS). *Foreign Relations of the United States, 1942*. Vol. 5, *The American Republics*. Washington, DC: Government Printing Office (GPO), 1962.

————. *Foreign Relations of the United States, 1951*. Vol. 2, *The United Nations; The Western Hemisphere*. Washington, DC: GPO, 1951.

————. *Foreign Relations of the United States, 1952–1954*. Vol. 1, *General: Economic and Political Matters*; vol. 4, *The American Republics*. Washington, DC: GPO, 1983.

————. *Foreign Relations of the United States, 1955–1957*. Vol. 7, *The American Republics: Central and South America*. Washington, DC: GPO, 1987.

————. *Foreign Relations of the United States, 1958–1960*. Vol. 5, *The American Republics*; vol. 6, *Cuba*. Washington, DC: GPO, 1996.

————. *Foreign Relations of the United States, 1961–1963*. Vol. 12, *The American Republics*. Washington, DC: GPO, 1996.

————. *Foreign Relations of the United States, 1964–1968*. Vol. 31, *South and Central America; Mexico*. Washington, DC: GPO, 2004.

United States Economic Mission to Bolivia. *Plan Bohan (Bolivia)*. Vol. 1 [1942]. Translation by G. V. Bilbao la Vieja. La Paz: Carmach, 1988.

University of California, Los Angeles (UCLA), Committee on Latin American Studies. *Statistical Abstract of Latin America for 1955*. Los Angeles: Regents of the University of California, 1956.

Valenzuela, J. Samuel, and Arturo Valenzuela. "Modernization and Dependency: Alternative Perspectives in the Study of Latin American Underdevelopment." *Comparative Politics* 10, no. 4 (1978): 535–557.

Volk, Steven S. "Class, Union, Party: The Development of a Revolutionary Union Movement in Bolivia (1905–1952)." *Science and Society* 39, nos. 1 and 2 (1975): 26–43, 180–198.

Wanderley, Fernanda. "Beyond Gas: Between the Narrow-Based and the Broad-Based Economy." In *Unresolved Tensions*, edited by Crabtree and Whitehead, 194–216.

————. "The Economy of the Extractive Industries: Poverty and Social Equality." *ReVista: Harvard Review of Latin America* 11, no. 1 (2011): 51–53.

Webber, Jeffery R. *From Rebellion to Reform in Bolivia: Class Struggle, Indigenous Liberation, and the Politics of Evo Morales*. Chicago: Haymarket, 2011.

————. *Red October: Left-Indigenous Struggles in Modern Bolivia*. Chicago: Haymarket, 2012.

Weinstein, Barbara. *For Social Peace in Brazil: Industrialists and the Remaking of the Working Class in São Paulo, 1920–1964.* Chapel Hill: University of North Carolina Press, 1996.

Weismantel, Mary. *Cholas and Pishtacos: Stories of Race and Sex in the Andes.* Chicago: University of Chicago Press, 2001.

Weston, Charles H. Jr. "An Ideology of Modernization: The Case of the Bolivian MNR." *Journal of Inter-American Studies* 10, no. 1 (1968): 85–101.

Weyland, Kurt. "The Rise of Latin America's Two Lefts: Insights from Rentier State Theory." *Comparative Politics* 41, no. 2 (2009): 145–164.

Whitaker, Arthur P., and David C. Jordan. *Nationalism in Contemporary Latin America.* New York: Free Press, 1966.

White, Luise. *Speaking with Vampires: Rumor and History in Colonial Africa.* Berkeley: University of California Press, 2000.

Whitehead, Laurence. "Bolivia." In *Latin America*, edited by Bethell and Roxborough, 120–146.

———. "The Bolivian National Revolution: A Twenty-First Century Perspective." In *Proclaiming Revolution*, edited by Grindle and Domingo, 25–53.

———. *The United States and Bolivia: A Case of Neo-Colonialism.* London: Haslemere Group, 1969.

Wilkie, James W. *The Bolivian Revolution and U.S. Aid since 1952: Financial Background and Context of Political Decisions.* Los Angeles: UCLA Latin American Center, 1969.

———. *Measuring Land Reform: Supplement to the Statistical Abstract of Latin America.* Los Angeles: UCLA Latin American Center, 1974.

———. "U.S. Foreign Policy and Economic Assistance in Bolivia, 1948–1976." In *Modern-Day Bolivia: Legacy of a Revolution and Prospects for the Future*, edited by Jerry R. Ladman, 83–121. Tempe: Center for Latin American Studies, Arizona State University, 1982.

Wilkie, James W., and Adam Perkal, eds. *Statistical Abstract of Latin America.* Vol. 24. Los Angeles: UCLA Latin American Center, 1985.

Wilkie, James W., and Peter Reich, eds. *Statistical Abstract of Latin America.* Vol. 19. Los Angeles: UCLA Latin American Center, 1978.

Williams, Raymond. *Marxism and Literature.* Oxford: Oxford University Press, 1977.

Williams, William Appleman. *The Tragedy of American Diplomacy.* Cleveland, OH: World, 1959.

Winn, Peter. *Weavers of Revolution: The Yarur Workers and Chile's Road to Socialism.* New York: Oxford University Press, 1986.

Wolfe, Joel. *Autos and Progress: The Brazilian Search for Modernity.* New York: Oxford University Press, 2010.

Wood, Bryce. *The Dismantling of the Good Neighbor Policy.* Austin: University of Texas Press, 1985.

Yacimientos Petrolíferos Fiscales Bolivianos (YPFB). *Código del petróleo: Edición oficial.* La Paz: YPFB, 1955.

———. *Libro de oro.* La Paz: YPFB, 1996.

———. *Memoria anual 1957.* La Paz: E. Burillo, 1958.

———. *Política petrolera, 1952–1956.* La Paz: E. Burillo, 1956.

Yaqub, Salim. *Containing Arab Nationalism: The Eisenhower Doctrine and the Middle East.* Chapel Hill: University of North Carolina Press, 2004.

Young, Kevin A. "The Good, the Bad, and the Benevolent Interventionist: U.S. Press and Intellectual Distortions of the Latin American Left." In *Latin America's Radical Left: Challenges and Complexities of Political Power in the Twenty-First Century,* edited by Steve Ellner, 249–269. Lanham, MD: Rowman and Littlefield, 2014.

———. "The Making of an Interethnic Coalition: Urban and Rural Anarchists in La Paz, Bolivia, 1946–1947." *Latin American and Caribbean Ethnic Studies* 11, no. 2 (2016): 163–188.

———. "Purging the Forces of Darkness: The United States, Monetary Stabilization, and the Containment of the Bolivian Revolution." *Diplomatic History* 37, no. 3 (2013): 509–537.

———. "Restoring Discipline in the Ranks: The United States and the Restructuring of the Bolivian Mining Industry, 1960–1970." *Latin American Perspectives* 38, no. 6 (2011): 6–24.

Zavaleta Mercado, René, ed. *Bolivia, hoy.* Mexico City: Siglo Veintiuno, 1983.

———. *50 años de historia.* Cochabamba: Los Amigos del Libro, 1998.

———. *Clases sociales y conocimiento.* Cochabamba: Los Amigos del Libro, 1988.

———. *El estado en América Latina.* Cochabamba: Los Amigos del Libro, 1989.

———. "El gas: Promesa económica o riesgo para la independencia." *Extra,* serial, May 21–June 15, 1968.

———. "Las masas en noviembre." In *Bolivia, hoy,* edited by Zavaleta, 11–59.

———. *Lo nacional-popular en Bolivia.* Mexico City: Siglo Veintiuno, 1986.

Zegada, María Teresa, Claudia Arce, Gabriela Canedo, and Alber Quispe. *La democracia desde los márgenes: Transformaciones en el campo político boliviano.* La Paz: Muela del Diablo/Consejo Latinoamericano de Ciencias Sociales, 2011.

Zondag, Cornelius H. *The Bolivian Economy, 1952–1965: The Revolution and Its Aftermath.* New York: Praeger, 1966.

Zook, David H. Jr. *The Conduct of the Chaco War.* New Haven, CT: Bookman Associates, 1960.

Zuleta, María Cecilia. "Conexiones revolucionarias: Repercusiones de la expropiación petrolera mexicana en Bolivia, 1938." *Revista de Estudios Bolivianos* 20 (2014): 110–140.

Zunes, Stephen. "The United States and Bolivia: The Taming of a Revolution, 1952–1957." *Latin American Perspectives* 28, no. 5 (2001): 33–49.

Index

Names of all Bolivian groups and institutions (but not publications) are listed by their English translations.

agrarian reform, 5–6, 42, 165; and 1952 revolution, 5–6, 38, 41, 45, 47–51, 67, 70, 107–108, 176, 205n70, 221n69; urbanites' views of, 20, 33, 47–50, 136–138, 199n60, 205n76

agriculture, 43–45, 50, 67, 87, 110, 177, 203n36, 203n48

Alliance for Progress, 82, 97, 100–102, 108, 111, 125, 215n109, 218n22

Almaraz Paz, Sergio, 5, 86, 152, 158–160, 167, 187, 216n131, 234n84

Amaru II, Túpac, 135, 227n91, 227n95

anarchism, 9, 17–20, 22, 24, 34, 118, 145, 173; and popular coalitions, 28–29; and resource nationalism, 17, 196n5

Andean Pact, 169

Andrade, Víctor, 49, 55, 64, 76, 207n100

Antezana Paz, Franklin, 187, 203n27

"anti-Americanism," 10, 172, 234–n102

anti-Semitism, 32, 136, 200n76

Aramayo, Carlos, 16, 30, 49, 55

Arbenz, Jacobo, 55, 97, 207n98

Arendt, Hannah, 140

Argentina, 61, 103, 116, 143, 152, 160

Armstrong, Neil, 104

austerity. *See* stabilization plan of 1956

Ayala Mercado, Ernesto, 187, 196n6

Ayoroa, Abel, 127

Bailey, Alberto, 162–163

Ballivián, Hugo, 141

Bandera Roja, 19

Bandung conference, 131

Baran, Paul, 173, 205n88

Barrientos Ortuño, René, 88, 103, 108, 136, 140–142, 151, 153, 158, 163, 166, 216n132

Bedregal, Guillermo, 75–76, 83, 187

Bjorkman, Victor, 75–76, 217n138

Bohan mission, 44–45, 152, 213n87

Bolivian armed forces, 5, 22, 24, 30, 33, 44, 55, 82–83, 97, 107–109, 119, 137, 140–141, 159, 162–165, 176, 215n115, 236n7

Bolivian Communist Party (PCB), 87, 108, 118, 128

Bolivian Development Corporation (CBF), 31, 45, 199n70

Bolivian Film Institute, 96
Bolivian Gulf Oil Company, 65, 233;
  as nationalist target, 15, 157,
  162–163, 165–166, 168; and 1969
  nationalization, 150, 159, 162–
  165, 168–169, 177, 234n87
Bolivian Mineworkers Union Federation (FSTMB), 33, 126, 157, 177,
  200n81. *See also* mine workers
Bolivian Mining Corporation
  (COMIBOL), 49, 61, 86, 106,
  130, 177, 205n71; debates over,
  74–79; and Triangular Plan, 60,
  74–83
Bolivian Oil Workers Union Federation (FSTPB), 155–157, 168, 177,
  234n87. *See also* oil workers
Bolivian Socialist Confederation
  (CSB), 198n45
Bolivian Socialist Phalange (FSB),
  24, 168
Bolivian State Oil Fields Company
  (YPFB), 15, 17, 30, 61, 149, 152,
  177–178, 197n31, 236n6; MNR
  views of, 62–64; officials' views,
  64, 216n120, 221n59; problems
  of, 65, 153–155, 209n10; protests
  over, 130, 153–161, 171; US policy toward, 56–57, 59–66, 106,
  151, 161, 209n14, 217n137
Bolivian University Confederation (CUB), 47–48, 51, 204n57,
  205n84
Bolivian University Federation
  (FUB), 28, 204n57
Bolivian Workers Central (COB),
  38, 43, 46–47, 50–52, 69, 84–
  85, 91, 124–125, 130–131, 135,
  137, 155–157, 160, 169, 226n67,
  234n91
Bolivian Workers Union Confederation (CSTB), 25–28, 34, 118
Bonsal, Philip, 65–66, 98–99, 161,
  217n137
Brazil, 4, 42, 61, 88, 116, 160, 179,
  182–183, 217n141, 222n84
Burke, Melvin, 77, 79–80

Busch, Germán, 17, 23–28, 32, 42,
  86, 158, 162, 199n53
Butler, Smedley, 173
Butrón, Germán, 118, 145, 223n21

Calle, La, 25, 32, 198n35, 200n77
Camberos, Stanley, 133–134
Camiri oil field, 62
"Campaign of Truth," 11, 195n39
campesinos. *See* peasants
Canada, 183
Canelas, Amado, 5, 64, 158, 161,
  170–171, 231n41
capitalism, 2, 9, 20, 33, 42–43, 47,
  124, 130, 132, 135, 167, 174,
  179, 185; debates over, 19, 23–26,
  36, 40–41, 105, 129, 132–134,
  205n84; MNR preference for,
  7–8, 13, 31, 37, 41, 48–50, 102–
  104, 220n58; and public opinion, 14, 20, 105–106, 139, 150,
  219n37; US promotion of, 11, 37–
  38, 96–102, 104–107, 139–140,
  218n24
Capriles, Orlando, 130–131, 135–
  136, 169
Castro, Fidel, 74–75
Catavi mine, 16, 30, 84, 145
Catholic Church, 18, 82, 94, 96,
  110, 166–167
Cause of the Homeland (RADEPA),
  33
Centellas, Jacinto, 19
Central Bank, 17, 24, 31–32, 45
Central Intelligence Agency (CIA),
  163
CEPAL. *See* Economic Commission
  for Latin America (CEPAL)
Chacón, Gustavo, 158, 187
Chaco War, 7, 16–17, 19, 29, 42, 66,
  117, 142, 151, 175; causes of, 21,
  197n20, 235n115; and resource
  nationalism, 7, 17, 21–22, 26, 30,
  149, 151–152, 155, 158
Chaco War veterans, 22–24, 33,
  135, 165, 197n28; alliances of,
  22–23, 26, 28; and resource na-

tionalism, 1–2, 17, 23–24, 26, 150, 165, 177–178, 236n6

Chávez Ortiz, Ñuflo, 50, 86, 188

Chayanta revolt of 1927, 28

Chile, 54, 61, 154, 160, 166, 225n46, 227n96

China, 4, 8, 179

Christian Democratic Party (PDC), 167

civil rights movement (US), 100–101, 219n41

climate change, 179

coca, 70, 177

cocaine, 177, 236n7

Cochabamba, 25, 46, 108, 130, 142, 155–159, 166, 193n26

Cold War, 37, 90, 93, 131, 168, 179, 183; in Bolivia, 11–12, 37–38, 83; historiography of, 12, 206n95

COMIBOL. *See* Bolivian Mining Corporation (COMIBOL)

Confederation of Chaco War Veterans, 135, 177

Congo, Republic of, 100

conspiracy theories, 9–10, 150–151, 171–175, 183–184

construction workers, 8, 46, 115, 126, 140, 147

consumption, 10, 25, 35–37, 52, 61, 65, 67, 117, 122, 132, 137, 144, 148, 169, 196n2, 205n88

cooperatives, 46, 163

Copacabana, 124

Cordero, Alfonso, 114, 126–127, 146

Cuba, 54, 168. *See also* Cuban Revolution

Cuban Revolution, 74–75, 104, 161; contrasted with MNR, 8, 54, 83–84, 229n127; influence of, on US policy, 80, 97; public sympathy for, 75, 99, 131, 173

Davenport, Wortham, 63, 162

Departmental Agrarian Federation (FAD), 28

Departmental Workers Central (COD), 46, 169

dependency theory, 36, 39–40, 170, 202n18, 238n32; in Bolivia, 13, 42, 86, 105, 129–131

Derby, Lauren, 173–174

developmentalism, 26, 49, 150, 168

Diario, El, 138, 140

Distinguished Ex-Combatants, 165

diversification, 2–4, 10, 13, 31, 35–36, 38–39, 42, 44–48, 57, 62, 73, 81, 87, 103, 106, 129–130, 139, 149, 159, 173, 176, 180, 193n25, 194n36, 196n2, 199n70, 204n50, 231n26

Donoso, Oscar, 157

Duggan, Laurence, 54

Dulles, John Foster, 90

Economic Commission for Latin America (CEPAL), 39, 43–44, 62, 65–67, 71, 73, 78, 122, 168, 175, 204n49; influence in Bolivia of, 40–42, 202n26; US position toward, 202n26, 217n141

economic nationalism, 12, 18, 54, 182, 193n25, 196n5. *See also* resource nationalism

Ecuador, 237n25

Eder, George Jackson, 86–87, 91, 105–106, 172, 176–177, 183, 212n57, 212n71; goals of, 60, 68–69, 71–72, 96; and 1956 austerity plan, 59–60, 67–74, 84–85, 211nn40–41, 217n136; racism of, 70

education, 6, 11, 18, 26–28, 46, 52, 72, 77, 97, 100–103, 111, 120, 138–139, 144, 159, 176, 193n19, 211n53. *See also* schools

Eisenhower, Dwight, 107, 140, 161, 183, 217n136

Eisenhower, Milton, 55

El Alto Neighborhood Council Federation (FEJUVE–El Alto), 178

employers, 91, 94, 102–103, 111–112, 115–116, 118, 120–123,

employers (*continued*)
123–126, 130, 133–134, 138,
142, 144, 225n64, 227n86,
228n117. *See also* National
Chamber of Industries (CNI)
Escóbar, Federico, 233n78

factory workers, 2, 8, 14–15, 35, 52,
69, 100–103, 117–118, 122–124,
137–138, 156, 225n38, 227n86;
alliances of, 115, 118–119, 126,
140–141, 156; internal conflicts
among, 127–129, 131, 132–134,
137–138, 148, 224n34, 226n68,
226n70; militancy of, 114–117,
118–120, 124–126, 140–148; resource nationalism of, 17, 85,
115–116, 129–131, 136, 156–157,
226n71
Factory Workers' Confederation
(CGTFB), 125–129, 131–134,
138, 141, 156, 224n34. *See also*
factory workers
Fanase factory, 120–121
Fanon, Frantz, 116
film, 123; US use of, 92–93, 96,
218n9
fiscal policy, 3, 31, 55, 60, 62, 73,
77, 82, 85, 106, 134, 138, 142–
143, 153–155, 157, 161–163,
166, 168, 174, 193n25, 194n27,
196n2, 201n86, 209n11, 232n61
Fish oil company, 157
Florman, Irving, 53, 62
Flor Medina, Hernán, 135
Ford, Bacon & Davis, 79, 106, 175
foreign debt, 27, 44, 52, 60–61, 66,
68, 73, 81, 177, 210n34, 211n43,
217n136
foreign investment, 36, 41, 48, 56,
61, 64, 68, 83, 91, 105–106, 153,
155, 158, 160–161, 174, 179
Forno factory, 118
Foro Universitario, 99–100, 104
Franco Guachalla, Alfredo, 73
Francovich, Guillermo, 173, 183
Freeman, Roger, 78

García factory, 118
gender/sexuality, 2, 13, 21, 26, 30,
135–136, 137–138, 151, 170, 174,
213n79, 235n103
Gisbert Nogué, Manuel, 40–41
Gordon, Richard, 104
Gramsci, Antonio, 193n24
Green, David, 88
Guatemala, 54–55, 83, 97, 121,
207n98
Guevara Arze, Wálter, 45, 48, 54,
76, 231n41, 233n67
Gulf Oil. *See* Bolivian Gulf Oil
Company
Gutiérrez, Darío, 196n12

Haymarket martyrs, 173, 235n104
Hertslet, J. G. A., 78–79
Hochschild, Mauricio, 16, 32, 49,
55, 136
Holland, Henry, 56, 68, 209n14
Housewives Committee of Siglo XX,
84–85
Huanuni mine, 84–85
Humanidad, 20
Humboldt, Ciro, 44, 157
hunger strikes, 72, 124
hydrocarbons. *See* natural gas; oil

India, 4, 179
indigenous people/identity, 4, 12,
29, 49, 92, 96, 108, 123, 136,
142, 146, 178–179, 182, 211n53,
227n91, 229n130, 233n75,
235n103; denigration of, 2, 31–
32, 50, 70, 116, 136–137, 146–
148, 170, 191n3; and the left,
18–20, 28–29, 136–138, 147–
148; movements related to, 5,
18, 21, 28, 32, 147, 178, 227n95,
236n15, 237n17
industrialization, 35–36, 38, 39–40,
45, 173, 176, 202n12, 202n26,
204n50; demands for, 2, 4, 20–
21, 27, 31, 46, 112, 115, 129–
130, 136, 138–139, 151, 154,
159, 163, 165, 180, 184, 193n25,

232n44, 233n64; prospects for, in Bolivia, 10, 40, 42–43, 143, 180–181, 194n37; US position on, 86–88, 216n135, 217n137, 217n141

inequality, 2–4, 18–19, 23, 37, 39–40, 43, 58, 71, 73, 176, 182, 208n116, 212n71

inflation, 59, 71, 74, 85; causes, 66–67, 69, 132; solutions, 59–60, 69, 177

Inter-American Development Bank (IDB), 60, 75, 180

International Cooperation Administration (ICA), 68. *See also* US Agency for International Development (USAID)

International Monetary Fund (IMF), 68, 72, 155, 180, 212n71

Iran, 55, 83, 215n118

Isiboro Sécure Indigenous Territory and National Park (TIPNIS), 181–182, 185

Jara, Alberto, 134

Johnson, Lyndon, 99, 104

Jordan, David, 168

Katari, Túpac, 227n95

Keenleyside mission, 45, 77

Kennedy, John F., 74, 82, 97–98, 104, 107, 111, 140, 183, 207n101, 217n136, 220n41

Keynesianism, 37, 60, 66, 71–72, 106–107, 129, 145, 211n51

Khrushchev, Nikita, 75

Klein, Herbert, 33

labor, 14, 18, 24, 27–28, 33, 38–39, 44, 49, 52, 64, 67, 73–74, 106, 170, 214n94, 229n123, 234n91; in COMIBOL, 71, 75–85, 177, 215n105; in factories, 100–103, 115–148; US and MNR concern over, 11, 14, 31, 48–49, 54, 59–60, 67, 70–71, 74–78, 80–84, 88, 91, 100–103, 107–108,

126, 213n83, 213n86, 220n44, 231n26; in YPFB, 153, 155–158, 168, 231n26. *See also* factory workers; mine workers; oil workers; *and individual unions*

Lake Titicaca, 12, 124

land ownership, 5, 39, 43, 49–50, 137, 176, 181, 203n36, 205n70. *See also* agrarian reform

La Paz, 12–14, 18–20, 22–29, 33, 35–36, 40, 47, 66, 73, 85, 95, 100, 102, 104, 111, 114–127, 129, 134–135, 137–142, 144–148, 151, 155, 157, 164–166, 169, 179, 209n14, 217n144, 223n12, 227n95

Lara, Félix, 127, 225n64

La Salvadora mine, 174

Lechín Oquendo, Juan, 33, 49, 68, 70, 76–77, 109, 121, 133, 157, 165, 188, 211n39

Legion of Ex-Combatants (LEC), 22–24, 26, 28, 199n54. *See also* Chaco War veterans

Lenin, Vladimir, 168, 222n3

liberalism, 19, 25, 36, 39, 179

Limpias, Guillermo, 160

Lincoln, Abraham, 173

lithium, 180–181

Local University Federation (FUL), 47–48, 165–166

Local Workers Federation (FOL), 22, 28, 31, 34, 118, 201n88

Lora, Guillermo, 5, 51–52, 66, 85, 137, 188, 199n53, 224n30, 226n70, 227n86

Madrejones oil field, 65, 157

Magruder report, 30, 175

Maier, Charles, 133, 145

Malaysia, 194n36

Malloy, James, 199n69, 200n76

Mann, Thomas, 75, 80–81

manufacturing, 42, 44, 73, 115, 117, 123, 142–144, 228n116; popular demand for, 4, 46, 125, 130. *See also* industrialization

Mariaca Bilbao, Enrique, 158–160, 173, 188, 230n11

Marof, Tristán, 20–21, 188, 197n13, 200n77

Marxism, 7, 9, 18–20, 22, 24, 36, 40, 42, 68, 71, 98, 103, 116, 129, 131, 137, 170, 195n38, 202n18, 219n32; and anarchism, 18–19, 34, 118; extent of appeal of, 9, 14, 20, 52, 57, 98, 128–129, 139, 145, 150, 157, 201n90; and MNR, 5, 14, 18, 29, 31–32, 51, 118, 122, 128–129, 133–134; and resource nationalism, 9, 17, 25, 42, 129, 150, 157, 159–161, 167–168, 196n5, 226n71. *See also specific parties*

Matilde mine, 169, 217n144

Mexican Revolution, 4, 8, 16, 21, 57, 61, 104, 116, 144–145, 152, 228n102; and MNR, 48, 194n29

Mexico, 10, 42, 44, 88, 144, 160, 217n141, 228n117, 229n127

Middlebrook, Kevin, 145, 228n117

military. *See* Bolivian armed forces

Military-Peasant Pact, 108, 137, 141, 165

military socialism, 23–28, 197n30

Mills, C. Wright, 173

mine workers, 1, 8–9, 14, 23, 31, 33, 59, 71, 75–83, 126, 139, 141, 166, 169, 172, 175–177, 231n26; massacres of, 16, 30, 33, 42, 234n88; resistance to government by, 84–85, 88–89; and resource nationalism, 85, 150, 157, 177. *See also* Bolivian Mineworkers Union Federation (FSTMB)

mining, 6, 16, 23, 53, 55, 57, 89, 106, 142–143, 177, 196n2, 213n78, 228n120; Bolivia's dependence on, 16, 43, 74, 143, 212n74; crisis of, 43, 45, 60–61, 66, 74, 77, 218n87; and development visions, 1–2, 20–21, 23, 27, 46, 85–88, 130; nationalization of 1952, 5, 38, 47, 49–51, 53, 67, 173; pre-1952 calls for nation-

alization of, 20–21, 23, 27; and revenue decree of 1939, 13, 17, 24–28, 32, 42, 198n31; and Triangular Plan, 14, 59–61, 75–85, 91, 212n74.

Ministry of Foreign Relations, 66

Ministry of Labor, 73, 126–127, 220n44

Ministry of Mines and Petroleum, 45, 64, 163, 216n120

modernization theory, 104–105

Molina, Fernando, 184

monetarism, 59–60, 68, 88, 106–107

monetary policy, 67, 77, 123, 193n25, 194n27, 200n83; and 1956 stabilization plan, 59–60, 68–69, 73, 122, 144

Montenegro, Carlos, 21, 25, 32, 189, 197n21, 230n2, 232n44

Morales, Evo, 1, 15, 178, 234n84

Mossadegh, Mohammad, 55, 215n118

Movement of the Revolutionary Left (MIR), 234n84

Movement toward Socialism (MAS), 178–185, 237nn25–26, 238n31

Mutún mine, 76, 163

Nación, La, 64, 109

National Chamber of Industries (CNI), 117–118, 122, 125–126, 131–132, 142. *See also* employers

Nationalist Revolutionary Movement (MNR), 2, 5–7, 53–56, 58, 61, 67–68, 72–75, 77, 79–80, 83–84, 88–89, 107, 114–117, 139–140, 143–148, 150–154, 161, 165, 168, 171, 173–183, 202n26, 205n68, 215n118, 224n30, 226n71, 238n31; anti-Semitism of, 32, 200nn76–77; appeal of, 7, 9, 13, 30, 32, 34, 37, 91, 112, 201n90, 221n65; conflicts within, 13, 35–36, 48–53, 129, 157–158, 204n64; conservatism of, 2, 7–8, 11, 13–14, 18–19, 31, 35–38, 57, 59, 63–64, 67, 76–77, 83–84, 86,

91–92, 96–97, 102–103, 110–111, 137–138, 146, 194n29, 199n62, 199n69, 200nn72–73, 207n98, 231n26; economic thought of, 18, 31, 36, 40–41, 44–45, 48–50, 149, 204n50, 213n86; and labor, 33, 38, 47, 51–52, 119–129, 133–134, 140–141, 200n81, 229n127; and peasants, 38, 49, 51, 108–110, 205n70, 205n76; and resource nationalism, 13, 18, 21, 25, 29–31

nationalization. *See* mining; natural gas; oil

National Match Factory (La Paz), 228n115

National Monetary Stabilization Council, 67, 70, 155

National Peasant Confederation, 137, 156, 165. *See also* peasants

National Smelting Company (ENAF), 217n138

National Social Security Fund, 71

National Union of Factory Workers (USTFN), 118–119. *See also* factory workers

natural gas, 1–2, 4, 15, 23, 149, 166, 178, 181, 184

neoliberalism, 6, 176–179, 184–185, 195n38, 215n111

New Economic Policy, 177

newspapers, 8, 17, 26, 128, 138, 153, 158, 162, 222n85; political role of, 19–21, 23, 25, 32, 50, 109, 124, 126, 156, 164, 198n51; US use of, 92–93, 96, 104, 111, 220n41

Nicaragua, 54, 229n127

Obrero, El, 102

O'Connor, Harvey, 173

oil, 3, 6, 48, 73, 77, 88, 149, 176, 209n8, 210n29, 233n75; and Chaco War, 21–22, 30, 151–152, 155, 158, 197n20, 235n115, 236n6; and development visions, 27, 35, 44, 151, 159–161, 172–173, 232n44; and foreign compa-

nies, 15, 17, 26–27, 56–57, 61–65, 83, 105, 154–158, 160–161, 163, 165–166, 168, 172, 174–175, 177, 197n17, 206n91, 209n14, 234n87, 235n116; MNR leaders' views on, 63–64, 83–84, 152–153, 161; and nationalism, 1–2, 15, 21–23, 26–27, 30, 120, 130, 138, 149–175, 198n45, 233n62; nationalization of 1937, 13, 17, 24–26, 28, 42, 197n31; nationalization of 1969, 150, 159, 162–165, 168–169; reform of 1955, 14, 59–66, 83, 91, 149–150, 153, 155–165, 232n61, 233n67; and US government, 14, 53, 56–57, 61–66, 87–88, 105, 154–158, 164, 167, 172, 174–175, 209n14, 231n26, 234n87. *See also* Bolivian State Oil Fields Company (YPFB); oil workers

oil workers, 153, 155–158, 160–161, 177–178, 231n26. *See also* Bolivian Oil Workers Union Federation (FSTPB)

Oporto, Henry, 183–184

Oruro, 20, 23, 85, 88, 181, 216n128

Ovando Candía, Alfredo, 233n62, 234n91; conservatism of, 168–170, 234n88; and 1969 nationalization, 150, 159, 162–165

Paraguay, 7, 16–17, 21–22, 151–152, 235n115

Party of the Revolutionary Left (PIR), 24, 34, 118, 197n29, 205n68

Patiño, Simón, 16, 30, 49, 55–56

Paz Estenssoro, Víctor, 59, 62, 74, 78, 84–85, 88, 108–111, 115, 119–121, 125, 128, 140, 158, 161, 165, 189, 201n86, 215n115, 216n120, 231n41; attacks on labor by, 76, 83, 108, 177; early career of, 30, 33; economic thought of, 33, 37, 44, 49, 64, 220n58; and the United States, 55, 83, 215n118; views of revolution of, 35

peasants, 9, 11, 43, 46–48, 57, 59, 70, 72, 104, 120, 131, 135, 142, 150, 177–178, 207n101, 228n102, 236n7; and military, 108, 137, 141, 161, 165; and MNR, 5–6, 31, 38, 49–51, 91, 107–110, 112, 137, 222n85; and urban labor/left, 18–20, 91, 108, 112, 115, 136–137, 147–148, 156, 201n90, 223n20; and US propaganda, 96, 109. *See also* agrarian reform
Peñaloza, Luis, 30–31, 189
"people's capitalism," 97–104, 105, 107, 219n34
Perón, Juan, 103
Peru, 162, 179, 227n91, 233n62
petroleum. *See* natural gas; oil
pishtacos, 174, 235n103, 235n110
Plaza Murillo (La Paz), 33, 164, 169
political parties. *See specific parties*
polyarchy, 180, 237n18
Popular Assembly (1971), 170
populism, 33, 103, 116, 181–182, 224n32; abuse of term, 237n25; definition, 194n27; of MNR, 8, 13, 18, 29, 36, 50, 194n29
Potosí, 16, 142, 181, 184
Prebisch, Raúl, 39, 71
Presencia, 163
privatization, 1, 84, 88, 130, 175–178; of mining, 6, 60, 80–82, 86, 88–89; of petroleum, 6, 14, 56, 59–60, 64–65, 236n6
Prochnow, Herbert, 56–57
Pueblo, El (PCB newspaper), 87, 108
Pulacayo, Thesis of, 31, 48, 54, 72, 200n72
pulperías, 69, 76, 84, 214n94
Pura Pura (neighborhood), 140

Quechisla mine, 84
Quintanilla, Carlos, 198n31
Quiroga Santa Cruz, Marcelo, 157, 162–163, 167, 189, 231n31, 231n41, 234n34

racism, 7, 41, 50, 70, 86, 98, 136–137. *See also* indigenous people/identity: denigration of
radio, 125–126, 140, 167, 222n82; US use of, 92–94, 96, 104, 111–112
Razón, La, 93
redistribution, 2, 31, 45, 47–49, 52, 66, 69–70, 72, 85, 102, 107, 130, 132, 137, 170, 181–183, 205n76; under MNR, 48–49, 73–74, 108, 208n116; popular demand for, 2, 5, 10–13, 16, 19, 36, 47–48, 52–54, 72, 89, 134, 168. *See also* inequality
religion, 124, 166–167. *See also* Catholic Church
Republican Socialist Party, 24, 198n45
"resource curse," 3, 191n2
resource nationalism, 1–18, 23, 36, 42–43, 54, 85–86, 89, 92, 105, 112, 116, 145, 147, 165–167, 172–173, 177–178, 192nn6–7, 193n25, 236n6; ambiguities of, 2–3, 18–19, 29, 31–32, 135–138, 170, 182, 237n23; and anticapitalism, 9, 17–18, 20, 25, 42, 129, 150, 157, 159–161, 167–168, 196n5, 226n71; and capitalism, 20, 25–26; emergence of, 7, 13, 16–18, 20–22, 27, 197n14; and MNR, 18–19, 29–34, 38, 53, 55, 63–64; portrayed as conspiracy theory, 9–10, 150–151, 171–175, 183–184; as unifier, 1, 15, 18, 20, 24–27, 86, 115, 129, 139, 150, 178, 180; US hostility to, 11–12, 37, 54, 59–63, 65–66, 68, 71, 80–81, 90–91, 112, 183. *See also* economic nationalism; mining; oil: nationalism; revolutionary nationalism
revolutionary nationalism, 7–8, 11, 16–18, 38, 54, 74, 112–113, 119, 122, 128, 134, 138, 145–146; and MNR, 29, 32, 36; relation to

resource nationalism of, 7, 11, 16, 193n25

Revolutionary Workers Party (POR), 24, 51–52, 118, 128, 159–161, 169, 226n71

Ricardo, David, 39

Rivera Cusicanqui, Silvia, 5

Rockefeller, Nelson, 92

Roosevelt, Franklin, 61

Rostow, Walt Whitman, 104–105

Royal Dutch Shell, 17, 21, 65, 175, 197n20

Rusk, Dean, 100

Russia, 4

Sachs, Jeffrey, 176–177

Said, Antonio, 103, 123–124

Said factory, 102–103, 118–121, 123–125, 136, 225n46

Salamanca, Daniel, 21–22

Salvadora mine, La. *See* La Salvadora mine

Sánchez de Lozada, Gonzalo, 1, 177–178

San José mine, 84

San Juan massacre, 234n88

Santa Cruz, 45, 62, 191n3, 222n82

Saravia, Daniel, 121, 125

Schlesinger, Arthur, Jr., 74, 207n101

schools, 11, 28, 46, 92, 104, 11, 123, 142. *See also* education

Siekmeier, James, 63, 207n100

Siglo XX mine, 84–85, 97, 142, 167, 234n88

Siles Salinas, Luis, 162–163, 166

Siles Zuazo, Hernán, 32, 40, 54, 109, 128, 134–135, 155, 157, 165, 172, 189, 215n115, 226n71, 231n41; and 1956 austerity plan, 70, 72, 84, 96, 124–125

Smelser, Neil, 171–172

smelting, 35, 56, 75, 88, 181, 213n79, 216n128, 216nn131–132; MNR positions on, 45, 85–86, 88; popular demand for, 47, 85–87, 130–131; US positions on, 87, 217n138

socialism, 2, 19, 23, 28, 31, 34, 36–37, 48–49, 60, 71, 133, 163, 168–170, 179, 199n69, 200n72, 237n25; appeal of, 23–24, 99, 219n37; and resource nationalism, 9, 17–18, 20, 25, 42, 129, 150, 157, 159–161, 167–168, 196n5, 226n71. *See also* anarchism; Marxism; *and specific parties*

Socialist Party (Bolivia), 24

Socialist Party (US), 99

Socialist Party-1 (PS-1), 234n84

Socialist Workers Party (POS), 20, 196n12

Socialist Workers Party of Bolivia (PSOB), 198n34

soft power, 90, 140

Soligno factory, 100–102, 104, 118, 123–125

Soliz Rada, Andrés, 168, 234n84

South Africa, 4

South Korea, 195n37

Soviet Union, 76, 78, 97, 131, 134, 179, 214n93; limited influence in Bolivia of, 11, 54, 57, 98, 112; loan offers from, 75, 83, 85–86, 130, 155–159, 161, 213n79, 216n120

Spain, 183

Sparks, Edward, 56, 63

stabilization plan of 1956, 14–15, 59–61, 64–74, 84–85, 88, 91, 96–97, 102, 107, 111, 115, 121–126, 129, 140, 143–144, 149, 153–154, 176, 211n40, 212n71, 216n124, 217n136. *See also* Eder, George Jackson

Standard Oil, 26–27, 151, 175, 235n116; and Chaco War, 17, 21, 30, 158, 175, 197n17, 197n20; and 1937 nationalization of, 13, 17, 24–25, 61–62, 232n44

state enterprise, 83, 103, 130, 214n92; US opposition to, 56, 60, 68, 78, 88. *See also specific state enterprises*

strikes, 22–23, 28, 84–85, 103, 117–121, 124–126, 140–141, 146, 155–156, 170, 197n23
Strom, Carl, 87
structuralism, 13, 36–37, 39–40, 42, 60, 66, 68, 71–72, 105, 107, 129, 131, 168, 202n9, 217n136; relation to MNR thought of, 36, 40–41, 45, 48, 55, 57. *See also* Economic Commission for Latin America (CEPAL)
students. *See* university students
Sucre, 23, 169, 196n10
suffrage, 5, 203n43
Supreme Court (Bolivian), 24–25

Taiwan, 195n37
taxation. *See* fiscal policy
teachers, 8, 22, 28, 94, 115, 140, 213n78
Tejada Sórzano, José Luis, 22
Tennessee Gas Company, 65
Tiempos, Los, 93
Time magazine, 134–135, 139, 213n83
tin, 1–2, 11, 15–16, 20, 27, 30, 43, 45–46, 53, 55–56, 60–61, 66, 71, 75, 77–79, 82, 85–88, 120, 130, 152–153, 156, 167, 194n36, 215n118, 216n128, 228n120. *See also* mining; smelting; tin barons
tin barons, 16, 50, 60, 66–67, 73, 82–83, 85–86, 103, 143, 149, 174, 200n73, 200–201n83, 211n40, 217n136. *See also specific tin barons*
TIPNIS. *See* Isiboro Sécure Indigenous Territory and National Park (TIPNIS)
Toro, David, 17, 23–25, 162, 165
Toro, Max, 125
Torres, Camilo, 166
Torres, Juan José, 163–165, 169–170
Torres, Mario, 45–46, 64, 157, 189
Tórrez, Ceferino, 134
Triangular Plan, 14, 59–61, 75–85,

91, 212n74; and mine workers, 84–85, 88–89
Trotskyism, 5, 9, 17, 24, 31, 38, 51–52, 57, 70, 72, 98–99, 128, 133–134, 137, 153, 157, 159, 205n84. *See also* Lora, Guillermo; Pulacayo, Thesis of; Revolutionary Workers Party (POR)
Truman, Harry, 54, 90, 93

unemployment, 19, 39–40, 80–81, 144
unions, 8, 14–15, 19, 22, 24, 28, 46, 59, 72–73, 76, 78–81, 84–85, 100–103, 114–121, 124–133, 136–138, 145–148, 155, 157–158, 165, 169–170, 178, 197n23, 225n64, 228n121, 234n91. *See also specific unions*
United Kingdom, 43, 46, 56, 85, 139–140
United States, 1, 6, 8–9, 43, 49, 152, 154, 158, 161, 164, 168, 172–173, 178, 202n26, 207nn98–99, 214n93, 215n115, 217n141, 218n24, 221n64, 234n102, 237n26; Bolivian views of, 10, 172–174; impacts of intervention by, 6–7, 73–74, 81–82, 92, 112–113, 138–140, 151, 161, 171, 175; intervention in Bolivia by, 2, 11–14, 37–38, 53–63, 67–84, 86–107, 109, 111–114, 131, 134–135, 154–157, 161–163, 172, 174–175, 182–183, 209n14, 209n16, 220n44, 234n87; military aid from, 2, 73, 82, 92, 97–98, 140, 215nn115–116; motives of, 11–14, 37–38, 53–57, 59–63, 65–66, 68–69, 71–76, 79–83, 90–107, 109, 112, 183; propaganda of, 11, 72–73, 90–107, 109. *See also specific US agencies*
University of San Andrés (UMSA), 29
University of San Simón (UMSS), 157

university students, 21, 28, 47–48, 51, 96, 115, 126, 157, 159, 175
Urriolagoitia, Mamerto, 118, 223n21
Uruguay, 61, 182
US Agency for International Development (USAID), 68, 81, 100, 111, 215n116
US Department of State (DoS), 53–56, 62–63, 66, 68, 70, 73, 76, 78, 80, 109, 114, 135, 160, 172, 175, 209n14, 209n17
US Department of the Treasury, 68, 96
US Embassy, 44, 70, 82, 90, 116, 139, 154, 156
US Information Agency (USIA), 11, 14, 90–107, 109, 111–112, 117, 125, 139, 219n29, 219n37, 220n41, 223n10; and economic paradigms, 105–107; goals of, 11, 72–73, 90–107, 109; limited success of, 72–73, 92, 106–107, 112, 138–140, 147, 174–175
US Information Service (USIS). See US Information Agency
US International Information and Educational Exchange (USIE), 93–95
US Office of the Coordinator of Inter-American Affairs (OIAA), 92–95
US Office of War Information, 92

Vargas Vilaseca, Víctor, 20
Velasco Alvarado, Juan, 233n62
Venezuela, 3, 237n25
veterans. See Chaco War veterans

Villa, Francisco, 228n102
Villarroel, Gualberto, 32–34, 53, 83, 118, 158, 162, 201n86; in popular memory, 32–33
Villa Victoria (neighborhood), 119, 140, 146

water, 1, 193n26
West Germany, 60, 75
Whitaker, Arthur, 168
Wilkie, James, 81
Wilson, Woodrow, 218n5
women, 2, 148, 170, 174, 185, 235n103; as anarchists, 18–20, 22; in factories, 137–138; in miners movement, 84–85
Women Workers Federation (FOF), 18, 20, 22
workers' control, 33, 47, 49, 51, 83, 99, 103, 106, 115, 121, 132–134, 138, 168, 193n25, 205n71, 224n34
Workers Labor Federation (FOT), 20, 22–23, 27–28, 118
World Bank, 180
World War II, 42, 46, 54, 61, 86, 92–93, 96, 221n58

Yarur, Juan, 225n46
YPFB. See Bolivian State Oil Fields Company (YPFB)

Zapata, Emiliano, 228n102
Zavaleta Mercado, René, 7, 9, 17, 167, 174, 189, 193n24, 228n120, 233n64, 234nn83–84
Zondag, Cornelius, 82, 231n26